Feminists Read Habermas

Thinking Gender
Edited by Linda Nicholson

Feminists Read Habermas:
Gendering the Subject of Discourse

Edited and with an introduction by Johanna Meehan

ROUTLEDGE

New York and London

Published in 1995 by

Routledge
29 West 35TH Street
New York, NY 10001

Published in Great Britain in 1995 by

Routledge
11 New Fetter Lane
London EC4P 4EE

Copyright © 1995 by Routledge

Printed in the United States of America

Library of Congress Cataloging-in-Publications Data

Feminists Read Habermas : gendering the subject of discourse / edited and with an introduction by
    Johanna Meehan.
        p.   cm. — (Thinking gender)
    Includes bibliographical references and index.
    ISBN 0–415–90713–6   ISBN 0–415–90714–4 (pbk.)
    1. Feminist theory. 2. Critical theory. 3. Habermas, Jürgen.
    I. Meehan, Johanna. II. Series
    HQ1190.F464   1995
    305.42'01—dc20   94–20585
                                                                                                    CIP

This book is dedicated

to my mother,

Ring Kelleher,

the origin of all my aspirations

and the model of so many.

Contents

viii / Contents

Acknowledgments

Over the years I have accumulated many intellectual debts, some general and some specific to this project.

To Thomas McCarthy, my mentor and friend, I am especially indebted. As a mentor he offered lessons in intellectual and personal integrity, and as a friend he lent them a special humor and grace. I am deeply grateful.

Seyla Benhabib endorsed this project and has been an exciting and important influence. I thank her.

In the last few years Alan Schrift and Ciaran Cronin have afforded me an intellectual camaraderie I treasure, as I do that of my sisters which extends back to our childhoods together.

Assembling and editing this collection demanded a lot more work than seems explicable; and without the help of the following people the volume would not have been produced. Editor Maureen MacGrogan believed that this anthology was a good idea and was forgiving of my tardiness. She was infallibly kind, as was editorial assistant Alison Shonkwiler. I appreciate their trust in me and this project. Gayle Salamon (student, friend, and research-assistant extraordinare) must be thanked for transforming hard work into an occasion for camaraderie and laughter. Lisa Mulholland offered support and encouragement from the inception to the printing of this project and with Jeanette Copeman lent impressive professional competence to the editing, wordprocessing, and delivery of this manuscript. I am thankful for their skills and for their kindness and affection.

And to Maura Strassberg, my staunchest ally and most critical critic, to whom I owe everything, my thanks, while woefully inadequate, are heartily offered.

A Note on the Text

I would like to express appreciation for permission to reprint the following:

Seyla Benhabib, "Women and Moral Theory, Revisited," *Situating the Self: Gender, Community and Postmodernism in Contemporary Ethics* (Polity Press, Oxford, 1992).

Jean Cohen, "The Historicist Critique," *Civil Society and Political Theory*, eds. Jean Cohen and Andrew Arato (MIT Press, 1992), pp. 201–254.

Marie Fleming, "Women and the 'Public Use of Reason,'" *Social Theory and Practice*, Vol. 19, No. 1 (Spring 1993), pp. 27–50.

Nancy Fraser, "What's So Critical About Critical Theory? The Case of Habermas and Gender," *Unruly Practices: Power, Discourse, and Gender in Contemporary Social Theory* (Minneapolis: University of Minnesota Press, 1989).

Joan Landes, "The Public and Private Sphere: A Feminist Reconsideration," new title, appeared in an earlier version as "Rethinking Habermas's Public Sphere," *Political Theory Newsletter*, 4:1 (April 1992), pp. 51–69. An earlier version of this essay, "Jurgen Habermas's 'The Structural Transformation of the Public Sphere,'" appeared in *Praxis International*, 12:1 (1992), pp. 106–127.

Introduction

Perhaps the first question this introduction should answer is why feminists *should* read Habermas at all. Habermasian theory stands squarely in a tradition of Enlightenment-inspired political theory and deontological ethics which many feminists have thoroughly rejected, and the authors anthologized here are to some extent rowing against the feminist mainstream. What these essays have in common is a shared conviction that while Habermas's discussion of gender is limited, his discourse theory is one of the most persuasive current reflections on politics and moral and social norms, and thus of great interest to feminists theorists despite its failure to specifically theorize gender. Because feminist scholarship problematizes gender relationships that are politically constructed and reinforced, regardless of often significant differences, it is essentially politically driven. Thus much feminist theory is devoted to clarifying the structure of the social and political world and the way in which gender functions to produce and reproduce male domination and female subordination. Habermas's work can be of varied use to feminists engaged in this clarification as it offers a framework for analyzing the structure of modern life, its potential for both emancipatory forms of life and forms of life issuing in political repression, market manipulation, and domination. Habermas's discourse theory is not merely useful for political diagnoses, in radically reconceptualizing the subject and underscoring the intersubjective formation of self-identity, he offers a normative ideal of self/other relationships and the discursive contexts in which they are negotiated, usefully traversing the road between public and private, personal, and political. He provides a model of subjectivity and an account of the pragmatic presuppositions of discursive validity, against which actual political and personal relations and discourses can be measured.

Although the scope of Habermas's philosophical project defies easy summary, I will offer a sketch of the central elements of his theory, followed by a brief description of the articles collected in this volume.

Habermas's Argument

Recognizing the shortcomings of Kant's monological subject and incorporating both Hegel's critique of Kant and Marx's critique of modernity, Habermas offers a discursive theory of ethics predicated upon the intersubjective constitution of identity, originating in and mediated by communication. It includes a developmental account of rationality and a critical assessment of its institutionalization in modernity's social and political institutions.

Modernity, Habermas argues, brings with it the increased rationalization of social life, or of what Habermas calls the life-world; multiple spheres of discourse, previously unified in mythological world views, are separated and made the subject of reflective elaboration. For Max Weber and the earlier members of the Frankfurt School, this disenchantment of the world was an unmitigated disaster marked by the stealthy encroachments of strategic rationality. This identification of rationality with means-end rationality undercuts normative claims by making strategic success the only appropriate criteria for the assessment of choices. Habermas counters this view and argues that in restricting their account to purposive rationality they defined rationality too narrowly. And thus, though they accurately described the progressive disenchantment of the lifeworld, they are unable to recognize or explain either the normative character of modern institutions and behaviors, or gains in the spheres of theoretical, practical, and aesthetic rationality.

Habermas replaces their account with a theoretical framework that integrates Jean Piaget's genetic structuralism with a communicative model of action. From this perspective, the differentiation of the world into the multiple spheres of the scientific, the aesthetic, and the moral, can be viewed in a positive light, making possible the increased reflexivity of social and political norms and a decentered and reflective moral point of view, expressed and embodied in a communicative form of reason.

Only a subject that has acquired the specific cognitive and communicative skills needed to recognize and redeem normative claims can take up this point of view. Habermas's account of the structure and genesis of this moral identity is, in part, the result of his critical appropriation of George Herbert Mead's account of the intersubjective constitution of self-identity and of Lawrence Kohlberg's moral stage theory. Like Mead, Habermas contends that we are not first individuals and then social agents; personal identity is essentially socially mediated, and the constitution of the self is concomitant with the establishment of relationships. Language functions as the medium in which identity is constituted, in which we understand and define ourselves, and for the coordination of social activity. Identities are formed in webs of social relationships through the taking up of myriad social roles, but most especially by taking up the role of the generalized other. This can be accomplished only when subjects can distance themselves from particular roles and recognize that all roles are structured by shared social norms. Thus the vantage of the generalized other is the vantage of a neutral observer, who can objectively survey the reciprocal expectations and interactions constitutive of these roles. Only then can the intersubjectively grounded character of norms which shape expectations and actions be grasped. For it is only when the force of the group and tradition loosens its grip, that individuals can reflectively question the legitimacy of norms and move beyond merely conventionally justified beliefs and values.

In formulating the cognitive stages of a post-conventional moral identity, Habermas turns from Mead to Kohlberg, arguing that one of the most compelling features of Kohlberg's moral stage theory derives from the cross-cultural analyses that led to his conclusion that while the content of moral problems varies from culture to culture, the forms of moral judgment are universal and can be described by analyzing the logical structure of moral thinking at different stages of development. Habermas marshalls Kohlberg's empirical studies in support of an ethical universalism that can challenge the claims of cultural and moral relativism prevalent in contemporary ethics. Habermas's relationship to Kohlberg's work is not limited to his drawing upon the latter's empirical data; his theoretical project resembles Kohlberg's insofar as the ethical universalism they defend arises from the Kantian character they share. Like Kant's, both Habermas's and Kohlberg's accounts share three philosophical features of cognitivism, universalism, and formalism, which make it possible to identify the structure of moral thought in abstraction from any particular aim or conception of the good life. This kind of moral thinking is *formal* because it shifts the burden of the moral from the content of judgment to the form of judgment (the cognitive structures involved in the process of reasoning). It is *cognitivist* because it holds that moral conflicts can be resolved through argument, which is viewed as a cognitive and interactive skill acquired through a developmental process marked by successive levels of competence. It is *universalistic* insofar as it claims that the form of moral reasoning at the same stage in any culture is identical, that there are criteria for moral reasoning which hold universally. Like Kohlberg, Habermas argues that the achievement of principled morality entails recognizing that normative claims must be supported by reasons and principles, but unlike Kohlberg, he insists that having recognized the essentially social and linguistic constitution of the subject, monological reflection must be rejected as inadequate for the identification and justification of norms. Instead, the universalizability of normative claims and the interpretations and legitimacy of needs must be taken up in public discourses where interests and need-interpretations are debated, identities defined, and their legitimacy contested.

While rejecting the Kantian view of moral subjects as those who through reflection give the moral law to themselves, Habermas is not proposing a neo-Aristotelian or communitarian ethics. Though he argues that even the very possibility of social action rests on the intersubjectively constituted and recognized norms which originate in communication, the rationalization of the modern lifeworld entails the demand that all claims be justified by an appeal for valid criteria when challenged, and the validity of the criteria does not derive in any simple way from the shared values of the community.

In fact, Habermas argues, claims raised in the context of modernity arise in three differentiated spheres of values: the cognitive, the normative, and the expressive. These parallel the formal conceptual distinctions between the objective, the social, and the subjective world. Successful communication requires that we associate the appropriate claim with each sphere: we must distinguish objective claims about the natural world from normative claims about the intersubjectively constituted social world, and both from expressive claims about inner nature. When any claim is challenged it must be defended appropriately; claims about the external world on the basis of their truth, paradigmatically achieved in scientific discourse; claims about social norms on the basis of their rightness, the validity of which are negotiated in social and moral discourse; and claims about the inner self on the basis of their sincerity, as demonstrated in narratives of character and self-reflection.

Habermas is most interested in normative, social, and moral claims and argues that while they are not identical to the claims of science, they are nonetheless analogous to them, insofar as they are defensible only by appeals to reasons accepted as legitimate by the community of modern subjects. Thus at the heart of his project is the clarification of the reasons and procedures employed in producing justifications for normative claims.

Engaging in what he calls reconstructive theory, a theorizing that makes explicit the intuitive knowledge of a socially and linguistically competent subject, Habermas elaborates what is entailed in raising and redeeming different kinds of claims and develops a framework for understanding the normative structures of communication and the competencies it involves. Among the skills he identifies as necessary to successful communication are the abilities to assimilate norms that regulate behavior, delineate the obligations of social roles, and stipulate what can be legitimately expected and demanded. Language not only serves as the medium through which these normative obligations are conveyed and justified, but it is in learning how to exchange speaker and hearer perspectives in order to justify claims of truth, truthfulness, or authenticity, raised in the context of social interaction, that we learn what norms are and what makes them valid. It is possible, Habermas claims, to reconstruct the norms embedded in and regulative of all social interaction and thus to ground a universalist ethical theory. Raising and redeeming validity claims, he argues, involves competencies that can be measured and cognitive achievements that can be ranked regardless of particular cultural values. Thus the focus of his theory is on the formal elements of normative discourse, and it rests on a firm distinction between norms that can be rationally adjudicated and justified, and values, which in his view, are too integral to our identities to permit the distancing necessary for their moral justification. In drawing this distinction Habermas seeks to preserve the deontological character of his discourse ethic, and insure that it retains its universalism and its impartiality vis-à-vis any particular version of the good life. Such a move is necessary he claims, since any truly post-conventional morality must ground the legitimacy of norms in justifiable, universalizable principles, and not in claims that they bring about a desired way of life. Taking up a post-conventional perspective makes hypothetical the taken-for-granted assumptions of the lifeworld, dissolving them into so many conventions, all in need of justification. It is in ideally constructed discourses where only the unforced force of the better argument is decisive, that Habermas believes such justifications can be provided.

Because discourse ethics excludes recognizing any specific version of the good life as normative, it sets up a purely formal testing procedure that cannot produce norms but can only test the validity of hypothetically proposed ones. While Habermas holds that the ideal criteria which structure discourses are universally valid, actual discourses themselves are always historically located, and it is this feature that distinguishes discourse ethics from other cognitivist, universalist, and formalist ethical theories and lends it its distinctive political twist. Because discourses are actual, historical, and particular, norms justified in an initial round of discursive consideration are not thereby inviolate from reconsideration, for their validation is always contingent upon the outcome of the next round of arguments.

Habermas locates the emancipatory moment of modernity, which Weber and the earlier members of the Frankfurt School missed, in the increasing reflexivity made possible by advances in communicative rationality and in its institutionalization in law and in political and moral discourses. Arguing against their reductivism, Habermas answers Hegel's question of how reason can be made practical, locating in social and political institutions the actualization of the rationality which is the intrinsic telos of communicative interaction. In distinguishing strategic rationality from communicative rationality, he distinguishes the increased rationalization of the sphere of production from the increased rationalization of other aspects of the lifeworld, arguing that while the former issues in increased repression, the increasing rationalization of communicative action makes possible, "a decreasing degree of repressiveness and rigidity, increasing role distance and the flexible application of norms—socialization without repression."[1] Habermas is not however wholly sanguine about the emancipatory potential the differentiation of these sphere makes possible. For while he argues that the media-steered mechanisms of money and power can be distinguished from communicative action, he also recognizes that in actuality they are closely linked and believes that realizing the emancipatory potential of rationalized forms of communicative interaction depends on effective resistance to the colonization of the lifeworld by these systems. Habermas is also well aware that the potency of political resistance is undermined by the imperatives of the very systems it seeks to check. And although Habermas distances himself from Weber and the early Frankfurt School in embracing the Enlightenment conviction that rationality is potentially liberatory, his is an optimism born not from naïveté, but from an ideal of decency that forecloses an adolescent retreat into cynicism.

Synopses of the Articles

The Public and the Private
The first four articles of this anthology problematize Habermas's analysis of the public and the private spheres, whose differentiation and structure he argues, are essential to the character of modernity. This distinction between public and private parallels, but is not identical to, the distinction he draws between system and lifeworld. On the one hand, action in the modern world is coordinated by systems which function according to an internal logic of means-end rationality; the market is a paradigmatic example of such a system. Choices and outcomes of action are primarily dictated by market imperatives, and only secondarily by the desires and intentions of social actors. The administrative-juridical institutions of the state functions as another system determining social action and structuring choices and

modes of interaction. On the other hand, actions are coordinated primarily by communicatively mediated norms and values, and by the socially defined ends and meanings which constitute the fabric of the lifeworld. It is from an analysis of this kind of socially coordinated action that a normative model of undistorted communication, which achieves its telic end in understanding, can be derived. The public form of such communicative action occurs and is made possible by the public spheres of participatory democracy which Habermas calls "public space."

Fraser, Cohen, Fleming, and Landes make it clear that they are persuaded of the importance of the theoretical framework Habermas develops, and they acknowledge the usefulness of his distinctions between system and lifeworld, public and private. While their criticisms and the directions of their arguments differ, all agree that inasmuch as Habermas's account suffers from a gender blindness that occludes the differential social and political status of men and women, his model of modernity falls short and needs revision and reconceptualization.

Nancy Fraser argues that while Habermas's model of classical capitalism clarifies the inter-institutional relations among various spheres of public and private life, in failing to thematize gender issues his model fails to realize its full explanatory power. While linking the relations between the economic sphere and the family, for example, he does not recognize that this relationship is affected as much by gender as it is by money, for the capitalist role of the worker is a masculine one reflected in the identification of the male as breadwinner and in the historic workers' struggle for a "family wage." If capitalism has assigned the role of the "worker" to men, it has assigned the role of consumer, which links economy and family, to women.

In addition to the role of consumer, capitalism has assigned women the tasks of child rearing and household maintenance, as well as other repetitive and unpaid tasks involved in the reproduction of daily life. Because Habermas's analysis does not consider the gendering of these role assignments, he fails to recognize and explore gender as an "exchange medium" and thus misses this gendered division of roles, in addition to failing to recognize the extent to which the role of the citizen, figuring in his scheme as the participant in political debate and in the forming of public opinion, is configured as male. Consent and public speech, prerequisite for the exercise of citizenship, are historically the prerogatives of men and have often been viewed as at odds with femininity. Thus, Fraser argues, the gender-blindness of Habermas's model occludes the subtext of masculine and feminine identity in the arenas of paid work, state administration, and citizenship as well as in the domain of familial and sexual relations. Fraser concludes her essay with the insistence that since gender cannot be assumed to be incidental to politics and political economy, the practice of good critical theory requires an integrated analysis of gender, politics, and political economy if critical theory truly is to be "the self-clarification of the struggles and wishes of the age."

Jean Cohen finds Habermas's political theory enormously important as well, and is particularly interested in his analysis of contemporary social movements, though like Fraser, she argues that Habermas's analysis suffers from a gender blindness that fails to differentiate the social and political status of men and women. This leads to a failure to appreciate a certain fluidity between the public and the private spheres, which in turn leads to his dismissal of many contemporary social movements as particularistic.

Cohen argues that Habermas's characterization of most contemporary social movements (including feminism in some of its moments) as purely defensive and particularistic responses to the encroachments of the market, media and power, and thus as not furthering the universalistic emancipatory goals of modernity, fails to recognize that these movements also generate new relations of solidarity, alter the nature and structure of civil society, and revitalize old public spaces and create new ones.

While Habermas views the feminist demands for rights, equality and participation as emancipatory, he holds other demands on the feminist agenda while important for social learning and for identity formation, to be particularistic and thus not "emancipatory" in the fullest sense. Cohen insists that the particularism Habermas identifies in the feminist movement is, like that of other contemporary movements, part and parcel of the universalistic demand for institutional change. The feminist struggle to reconfigure identities and gender relationships is an essential moment in the reconstruction of the institutions of civil and political society. Such institutional reconfigurations arise from these changes in concrete forms of life that derive from the particularistic politics Habermas dismisses as unemancipatory. Indeed, conventional gender roles are so deeply entrenched in our identities that they blind us to political injustices which are only graspable with shifts in these roles. Before one can join the struggle, one has to be able to see that there is one. Thus "consciousness-raising" becomes a crucial strategy which precedes and makes possible the universalist demands for equal rights.

Joan Landes also finds Habermas's discussion of the public sphere rich and interesting, but she argues his estimation of the liberatory potential of the public sphere is too sanguine and his description of its emancipatory mechanisms too narrow. Describing the public sphere as one in which private people come together as a public in and through the use of reason, Habermas locates its obstacles in the slippage between the actual and the ideal, and not in the notion of the public sphere itself. But Landes argues, the parameters of this public sphere include only the disembodied subjects of discursive reason and the texts which embody that reason. The exclusion of the private sphere of emotions and of the personal relations in which they are initiated and sustained constituted the de facto exclusion of women as well as a privileging of the literary institutions of the press and literature. In identifying "publicity" with universality, truth, and reason, Habermas fails to address discourses and interests associated with women. Echoing the positions of Cohen, Fleming, and Fraser, Landes argues that Habermas ". . . misses the masquerade through which the (male) particular was able to posture behind the veil of the universal." The Habermasian public sphere, identified with equality and reason, favors certain abilities and interests over others and in effect, if not in intention, excludes the problematization of the gender-determined power differential in the intimate sphere, insuring that male subjects would be its dominant inhabitants. Landes argues that Habermas's idealization of the public sphere conceals the extent to which the exclusion of women is constitutive of it and undercuts the legitimacy of particularity in which concrete differences between citizens are lodged and actual life forms are realized. Landes concludes her discussion with a series of reflections on action, the spectacle, the body, and style. Arguing that there are compelling reasons to accept Habermas's claim that textuality is modernity's dominant form of representation, she points to empirical evidence that textuality is not the only form of representation possible in the modern public sphere, and argues that attention to other forms of representation reveal inadequately reflected upon avenues for non-discursive forms of critique and subversion. Landes concludes that in the contemporary world where politics and style are inextricably tied, there is play in politics, and in play there lies a potential for political performance and gesture.

Like Fraser, Cohen, and Landes, Marie Fleming assesses Habermas's account of the structure of the private and the political, specifically focusing on Habermas's account of the emergence of the public, private, and intimate sphere as he elaborates it in *The Structural Transformation of the Public Sphere: An Inquiry Into a Category of Bourgeois Society*. She argues that Habermas is wrong to see the exclusion of women from the bourgeois public sphere as simply the failure of the bourgeoisie to realize its own normative ideals. For in fact, this exclusion was actually constitutive of the institutionalization of that sphere.

Fleming notes that, according to Habermas, deep structural changes taking place at the level of gender relations were essential to the development of the bourgeois public sphere. As the patriarchal conjugal family became the normatively dominant type, a space for "intimate," non-economically ruled relationships was carved out in the private sphere. This experience of intimacy was essential to the construction of the bourgeois concept of "humanity" which served as an ideological norm in the expansion of rights of citizenship, for it was in the sphere of the intimate that the individual knew himself as bourgeois—i.e. as property-owner—but also as a man like any other. Fleming argues that while Habermas thematizes the false universality of a citizenship which in actuality was and is structured by property ownership, the gross inequities constitutive of gender relationships in the patriarchal conjugal family remain invisible in his account and the false universality of the rubric "humanity," which in essence and in actuality was and is male, remains unchallenged.

Fleming examines Habermas's failure to consider the extent to which the protection of the basic rights and personal freedom of the intimate sphere of the patriarchal conjugal family from legal and political intrusion functioned to reinforce the rights of the male head of household, leaving women and children vulnerable, their lives invisible, and their rights unrecognized. The thrust of her argument, however, is directed at revealing the extent to which the patriarchal conjugal family is essentially tied to the institutionally separate public sphere, insofar as the bourgeois family is at the core not only of notions of citizenship defined in terms of rights to property, but also of the political ideal of autonomy itself.

While Habermas clarifies the extent to which the private is political and the political is private, Fleming urges us to consider the gendered structure of the sphere of intimacy which would reveal the extent to which the personal is political and the political is personal. She believes that despite limitations in Habermas's work, feminists can use his distinctions between the public, the private, and the intimate since distinguishing between the private and the public allows us to theorize a wide range of issues and would be especially helpful in examining modernity's social-sexual gender arrangements. Recognizing a distinction between the private and the intimate does not, she assures us, deny a connection between the family and the state and the economy, but allows us to assess that connection. If Habermas is right, as Fleming believes, to locate the genuine site of humanity in the intimate sphere, and if the intimate sphere can only be fully articulated when it is conceptualized in terms of gender, then the category of gender must become central to the philosophical discourses of modernity.

Theory and Practice

The essays by Jane Braaten and Simone Chambers reflect on Habermas's discourse ethics from the perspective of political praxis, assessing its importance and limitations in light of women's lives, and with respect to feminist goals and practices.

Jane Braaten argues that to a significant extent, Habermas's theory of communicative rationality converges with the ideals of feminism and can be put to good use by that community as it formulates its political critiques and projects. She criticizes Habermas's understanding of communicative rationality as non-substantive, and develops the thesis that feminists in the pursuit of solidarity, in effect, reverse the order of the development of Habermas's argument, deriving criteria of rationality and knowledge from substantive ideals of solidarity and community, rather than deriving ideals of solidarity from notions of rationality and abstract ideals of equality. Braaten contends that what makes an engagement with discourse ethics so promising is that it emerges from a critique of the Cartesian philosophy of the subject important for feminist theory. Habermas recognizes that fully human social relationships require a mutuality of understanding; this mutuality is achieved when a justified consensus is reached. It is in this reliance on "a procedure for epistemic justification as the guarantor of autonomy, community, and knowledge," that Braaten locates the legacy of the epistemological scepticism of the early moderns.

In Habermas's account of communication and the competencies that make it possible, it is the mutual recognition of and compliance with the rules constitutive of communicative action which make non-coercive communicative relationships possible. Braaten argues that this identification of the norms of communication clarifies the grounds for epistemic justification, but does not provide an adequate account of the ideals of social association. While recognizing and acknowledging that discourse theory was never intended to offer a substantive vision of societal institutions and associations, she contests the notion that these shared epistemological norms are "the sole fundamental constitutive activities of community, solidarity and society." One can recognize with Habermas the emerging of a distinctly modern rationality employed in the settling of normative disputes without conceding "that it constitutes the basis for the entire edifice of socialization, social integration and enculturation." Sympathy, affection, and other emotions, as well as mimetic relations, are equally important for the achievement and maintenance of social relationships.

While justice and truth can function as constitutive values of a political community, Braaten claims that substantive ideals of solidarity and community are also important. Indeed, Braaten argues that in the burgeoning feminist community it is commonly the experience of solidarity in a community, which is often defined by its oppression, that clarifies the norms of the community and clarifies the nature and possibility of this solidarity. As we experience ourselves as parts of a community of women we "learn to cultivate the norms that make that experience possible." It is in this sense, Braaten claims, that "feminist knowledge is the creation of solidarity-building." Though the ideals of this community may, as Habermas argues, converge with modernity's ideals of reason and knowledge, they are not identical to them. Braaten concludes her paper by introducing a model of feminist thought she calls "communicative thinking." While "communicative thinking reflects Habermas's notion of communicative rationality it rejects a "univocal axiomatic structure, or a regimented semantics." Braaten suggests that communicative thinking must be evaluated, not in terms of an internal structure, but "in the worth of its ideals of solidarity and community." These ideals should function as both the end and the constitutive ideals of that community.

Simone Chambers juxtaposes an analysis of Habermas's discourse theory with her reflections on the feminist anti-nuclear encampment at Greenham Common, England. While Habermas lays out the procedural conditions necessary for engaging in consensual decision making, Chambers argues that he does not consider what it would take to be able to institute those conditions. Taking the Greenham Common women as an instance of consensual community, Chambers details the commitment of these women to fully consensual decision making, and exploring the complex demands created by such a commitment, Chambers considers some of the conditions constitutive for instantiating a discourse community that Habermas does not consider. For instance, while Habermas argues that fully consensual discourse requires that all those affected by the discourse be able to speak, he does not explore what would make exercising this right either possible or meaningful. Consensual discourse requires not only the right and wherewithal to speak, but in addition, the possibility that speech will be listened to and heard in the fullest sense possible. It requires that participants adopt attitudes and responses towards one another that create a positive environment in which the procedural norms of discourse become more than abstract and significantly unexercised rights. Chambers uses the discursive practices of the Greenham Common women as an illustration of the arduous process of creating a truly consensual discourse community and argues that such a goal is not a realistic one for the day-to-day decision making in complex contemporary societies. This does not lead her to reject Habermas's discourse ethics as impossibly utopian and impractical however. Chambers argues that a distinction should be drawn between the processes of discursive decision making and discursive will-formation. While discursive decision making is impossibly clumsy from all perspectives, including that of administrative bureaucracy, Chambers accepts as a normative ideal that public opinion should be constructed and reconstructed discursively.

Discourse Theory and Ethics

The next three essays in the collection, Seyla Benhabib's, Jodi Dean's, and mine, reflect attempts to use Habermas's discourse theory to bridge the gap that arises from significant feminist critiques of deontological ethics, ranging from the issues of the universal and the particular, to criticisms of

Habermas's account of the generalized other, and to discussions of autonomy and of social and moral recognition.

Seyla Benhabib lays out the challenges that Carol Gilligan's work poses for deontological theories of the sort offered by Rawls, Kohlberg, and Habermas. She argues that while there are conflicting interpretations of exactly what Gilligan's claims are, it is most fruitful to read her work as a correction of universalistic moral theories rather than as a rejection of them, as a "contribution to the development of a non-formalist, contextually sensitive, and post-conventional understanding of ethical life." If one pursues this reading of Gilligan, Benhabib argues, her work cannot be dismissed as irrelevant to the universalist project as Habermas did at one point in the Kohlberg/Gilligan debate, claiming that Gilligan had merely confused issues of moral motivation with cognitive problems of the application of norms. While Gilligan had identified an interesting set of questions about applying abstract principles in concrete situations, from the deontologist's perspective, these problems had little bearing on the nature of those principles in the first place. Habermas, like Kohlberg, claimed that Gilligan confused issues of justice with evaluative issues of the good life, and issues of self-determination with issues of self-realization. In defending Gilligan, Benhabib counters Habermas's easy distinction between evaluative concerns and issues of justice, arguing that a consideration of concrete moral actions and choices quickly reveal the degree to which these issues are unalterably entwined. Gilligan is right, she contends, to see issues of relational obligation and care as genuinely moral ones, "belonging to the center and not at the margins of morality," and claims that her reading of Habermas's discourse ethics is a call, not just for a formal proceduralism, but for "a conversational model of a kind of enlarged mentality," that makes it possible for a universalist ethical perspective to incorporate Gilligan's insight, while retaining its desirable universalism. In this account the domain of the moral is extended to include the domain of care, but considerations of universalist morality set parameters within which an ethic of care can function, and in situations of conflict, universalist norms "trump" other moral considerations. As a discourse theorist Benhabib is committed to the values of justice and impartiality; as a feminist she is committed to recognizing the needs and well-being of the concrete other. In her view, modern moral philosophy has too often recognized only the dignity and worth of an abstract moral subject while failing to recognize our vulnerabilities and dependencies as bodily selves. While acknowledging the importance of postmodernist critiques of both metaphysically grounded accounts of a unitary subject and of post-Enlightenment morality, she defends a notion of the subject as a unitary narrative perspective, and of ethical norms as discursively negotiable and universalistic.

Jodi Dean's essay, "Discourse in Different Voices," argues that Gilligan's work on the moral development of girls, and Jessica Benjamin's work on autonomy and domination, provide necessary feminist correctives to Habermas's discourse ethics. In Habermas's account of the formation of social and moral identity, the subject's ability to take up the "objective" stance of the generalized other is crucial, and in Dean's view, involves the conflation of two notions eliding a crucial distinction between the perspective of the third person observer and the structuring of the generalized other.

The significance of this elision becomes apparent when viewed from the perspective of sexual difference. While a child's ability to adopt the observer perspective is essential to achieving a post-conventional moral consciousness and entails generalizing from particular interactions to larger, normatively defined social roles, Dean argues, the neutrality that Habermas ascribes to this observer perspective fails to take into account the content entrenched in social positionality. Insofar as identity is negotiated in a world of differently valenced gender relations, the perspective of the subject, of the third person, and the structuring content of the generalized other, cannot be conceived apart from those hierarchically ordered gender relations.

Dean turns to Jessica Benjamin's analysis of an identity formation thoroughly structured by gender, to underscore her claim that Habermas fails to recognize that the child's awareness of authority-governed complementarity is fundamentally gendered. This involves not only an awareness of male and female parent and child roles and expectations, but also of the differentiated construction of the authority of men and women. In a culture which values men and male roles and devalues women and female roles, a boy's self-identity is reinforced while a girl's sense of self is diminished. Using the work of Gilligan and Lyn Mikel Brown on adolescent girls, Dean identifies the fragility, the tenuousness, and the contradictions that accompany negotiations of female identity and lead it towards a telos generally different from that of male identity.

Dean concludes her paper with the argument that if we are to recognize and struggle beyond socially restrictive interpretations of the generalized other, Habermas's concept of the generalized other must be reconciled with a notion of a mutual recognition, necessary for both the possibility and the realization of moral subjectivity.

It is precisely with this notion of mutual recognition that I am concerned in my essay on Habermas, Benjamin, and Honneth. I argue that Habermas's sharp distinction between ego-identity and moral identity cannot be sustained. Because identity is intersubjectively constituted, the nature of these constitutive social relationships is taken up in identity and in our projected construction of the other. The disparate power relationships of one's social world inscribe themselves in these constructed identities and skew disputes about social norm in ways that remain opaque in discussion about universal rights and equality. I do not claim that we are so embedded in our identities or lifeworld that Habermas's discourse ethic is irrelevant. Habermas is right to define a certain aspect of morality in these terms, but I suggest that ideal discourse must be seen as an even more elusive goal when the full extent of the social constitution of identity is recognized. This recognition is also important insofar as it makes clear the significance of relationships between caregivers and children, and raises questions about the nature of mutual recognition which I argue is crucial for normative social relationships. I open my essay with a discussion of Jessica Benjamin's critique of traditional notions of autonomy which she argues associates maleness with autonomy and difference, and femaleness with dependence and sameness. While Benjamin dismisses Habermas's moral theory *tout court,* as reproducing a typical gendered account of morality, I argue that in fact, Habermas's redefinition of morality in terms of communicative rationality, leads him to a conception of autonomy much closer to Benjamin's own than to the more traditional psychoanalytic model she rejects. I see Benjamin's and Habermas's analyses as complementing each other and suggest that Axel Honneth's notion of respect which is articulated in terms of an account of mutual recognition, is an interesting starting place for reflections on the normatively structured psychological relationships which make this recognition possible. Honneth's clarification of the structure and preconditions for realizing non-coercive relationships of mutual recognition in the inter-psychic, intersubjective, and social/political world provides a corrective to and bridge between Benjamin's and Habermas's accounts of autonomy.

Identity and Difference
The last two essays in the anthology focus on the provocative issues of identity and difference which have recently been hotly contested by feminist theorists. As feminists grapple with political and theoretical challenges to any easy understanding of the category "women," questions of what an identity is and how it is constituted have led to theoretical responses which run the gamut from essentialism, to relational feminism, to postmodern feminism. Georgia Warnke and Allison Weir sort out these issues and what is at stake in them, arguing that Habermas's discourse ethic can be useful in thinking through them.

Warnke argues that the "dilemmas of difference" which have of late beset the academic and political practices of feminism need not be seen as a fatal blow to feminist politics, or to its potential for developing relations of solidarity, which bridge women's differing identities by recognizing and legitimating them. Warnke argues that Habermas's discourse ethics, which offers a procedure for arriving at a universal and rationally motivated consensus despite identity differences, can be useful to feminist theorists thinking through issues of identity politics, though she rejects his firm distinction between normative and evaluative issues. She explores the promise and the shortcomings of discourse ethics, using the moral and political issues raised by contract pregnancy to frame the argument that "normative questions cannot be settled independently of evaluative ones and that normative justification must include an exploration and articulation of our possibly differing values."

In order to allow for pluralistic and yet still critical feminism, we must take our interpretive and evaluative differences seriously, she argues, and suggests that perhaps reaching resolutions about these issues might resemble not philosophical or legal arguments, but interpretive discussions of art and literature. Success might then be measured in terms of the insights achieved, rather than in terms of the force of the better argument rendered. People's beliefs about the rights and or wrongs problematized by contract pregnancy stem from differences in sensibilities and associations, ideas of how to live one's life, and convictions about motherhood and parenting. These seem, Warnke suggests, to have more to do with differences in cultural heritage, family, individual experience, and values, than with the force of the better argument. The possibility of persuading us of the legitimacy of certain practices lies only in part with arguments, for accepting them is not done independently of our values, traditions, and conceptions of the good. If we were to take our interpretive and evaluative differences seriously, and evaluate our different beliefs the way we would a text, no one interpretation would be assumed to be right. This does not pitch us into value relativism, Warnke insists, for though more than one interpretation of a text can be defended, not all interpretations can be sustained. We also believe that differences in interpretations must be explained and justified and made to cohere with each other, and with any new interpretations which are proffered. If, for example, beliefs about surrogacy were not seen as distillable into competing arguments, but were seen to be the complex outcome of different understandings of ways of life and notions of individuality and rights, then we might be able to acknowledge that our moral and political disagreements do not stem from the rightness or wrongness of one party's position in relation to the other, but from different and equally valid understandings of the good. Warnke labels this recognition of different perspectives, "interpretive pluralism," and argues that adopting it forces us to recognize that moral and political arguments do not derive from some neutral positions but are always rooted in a way of life and in pre-existing values and beliefs.

Warnke is proposing not just any pluralism, but rather a "normative pluralism," which would allow us to develop our own interpretations through an engagement with those that differ. The very possibility of recognizing the plurality and a multiplicity of perspectives requires the kind of ideal discourse conditions which Habermas specifies. The norms of communicative rationality provide a way to evaluate perspectives, so that those which would limit the recognition or equal legitimacy of difference, racist or sexist interpretations for instance, could be excluded because by restricting some voices they prevent the plurality of interpretive possibilities necessary to the formulation of our individual interpretations of the good. Having protected discussion from distorting ideologies of force or intimidation, does not, however, mean that a normative consensus will be reached, for the very plurality of our evaluative beliefs would mean that there might remain different and even competing beliefs.

Warnke concludes her article arguing that the differences problematized in feminist postmodernism are only problematic for feminist politics if one accepts consensus as one's political goal, and the point of recognizing and articulating differences is thought to be the sublation of them. A feminism that is truly committed to difference, is a feminism truly committed to a plurality of perspectives arising from those differences. To this end, discourse within the parameters of Habermas's ideal speech situation functions as an arena for exploring, comparing, and working not towards consensus, but towards building a community in which we work together to develop solutions to concrete problems which will allow the diversity of our beliefs and values to be served. The agreements about problems and solutions that shape our political goals should arise from our recognitions of our differences, not from calculations of our sameness. Even in situations where differences threaten to thwart any political strategy, as members of a feminist community, we can struggle to at least keep open the possibility of shifts in perspective by continuing the discussions of these conflicts.

Allison Weir also takes up the problems that differences in identity pose for feminist theorists and activists. Weir argues that seemingly intractable discussions about difference, as well as feminist's critiques of notions of individuation, of agency, and autonomy, point to a critical need to reconceptualize our notions of selfhood. Weir argues that a useful account of identity must recognize that individual identity is embedded, embodied, localized, constituted, fragmented, fragile, and vulnerable to social, political, and linguistic forces while at the same time retaining a vision of humans as actors who learn, change, interpret, and reinterpret the world. In the essay in this collection, she works towards developing a theory of identity that bridges the gap between two feminist models of identity. The first, relational feminism, argues that most views of self-identity are premised on normative models of autonomy that too often conceal, deny, or deprecate relations of connection, attachment, and dependence. The second theory of identity she considers, which she loosely dubs "postmodern and post-Structuralist," (often referred to as difference feminism) views identity as produced by exclusions of difference by systems of power. Moving between and drawing from both these accounts, Weir proposes a model of self that defines identity in terms of the ability to participate in a social world through interactions with others; these interactions are in turn constitutive of the formation of self-identity. Contradicting the views of many feminists who hold identity and difference to be exclusive, Weir contends that the most central feature of modern self-identity is the capacity to reconcile often conflictual multiple identities and to understand, criticize, and to live with conflicting interpretations of identity. Though conceiving self-identity as entailing the capacity to resolve differences has not been popular, Weir argues that the ability to reconcile conflicts without excluding or repressing difference and non-identity, requires an ego with the ability to deal with difference reflexively, not through a denial of its connection with others, but through its recognition of itself as both intersubjectively constituted and autonomously capable, both dependent upon, and independent of others. Self-identity then, is tied up with identifications and relationships with others that are always interpreted and negotiated in terms of shared, though often conflictual meanings. Weir argues that while relational feminists have done important work clarifying the role of intersubjective relationships in the formation of self-identity, they lack an account of the role meaning and interpretation play in the process, over-emphasizing identity formation as the direct effect of relationships. On the other hand, post-Structuralists's accounts of identity focus on the mediation of identity-formation by language without adequately recognizing the significance of affective social relations with others.

Rejecting both the relational feminist accounts of a subjectivity unmediated by the realm of the symbolic, and the post-Structuralist account of a symbolically but not intersubjectively produced subject, Weir formulates a theory of identity which draws from Habermas's account of communicative rationality and from Julia Kristeva's account of identity as formed through the child's identification with the meaning of the social/linguistic/symbolic realm for the mother's subjectivity. At the crux of her argument is the claim that identity formation is always both a socially and symbolically mediated process of negotiating and interpreting fundamentally socially given and socially redeemed meanings.

Arguing that a meaningful interaction of self and other requires reflexivity and capacities for abstraction and critique, Weir takes from Habermas the account of the intersubjective constitution of individual identity through communication, which holds that one becomes a part of a social world through making and redeeming claims negotiated through intersubjectively recognized and maintained standards of normative validity. Identity is formed as a subject takes up communicative positions that require every full participant to assume speaker and hearer perspectives and offer and defend criticizable yes/no claims. Thus the full exercise of a subject's communicative agency requires that a subject be able to sort through incoherence, conflict, and ambiguity in their own claims as well as those of others, and demands the ability to criticize, assess, and redeem meanings with others, it also inevitably opens the possibility of difference, confusion, ambiguity, and even conflict but communicative competence makes it possible to translate difference, clarify confusion, disambiguate ambiguity, and illuminate conflict. In Habermas's account, identity is achieved in the development of the ability to recognize, understand, and negotiate difference, discursively.

Habermas makes it clear that the self-identity of the adult involves becoming a communicative agent, but he does not explain how it is that we come to commit ourselves to the *particular* socially produced meanings, choices, or goals which guide our practices and justify our claims. To fill in these gaps, Weir turns to Kristeva's claim that subjectivity is constituted by taking up positions and identities in a social world. According to Kristeva, socially and symbolically mediated meanings do not directly construct identity, but are interpreted through a psyche formed in the context of our symbolically mediated affective relationships with others. It is in the play between those affective bonds and their individually and socially interpreted meanings that our identities are formed and our desires are structured. Individuation is produced in the nexus of unconscious drives, affective connections, and the socio-linguistic order. Kristeva, unlike Habermas, ties individuation to a psyche formed not just in the nexus of the symbolic integration of linguistically mediated norms, but to affective responses and to the unconscious. She offers (at least in some of her writings) the view that entry into the symbolic enables the development of identity; it cannot be understood as merely repressive for it allows expression and the realization of one's specificity. As the child masters the symbolic, it escapes utter dependence as it becomes a fuller participant in the social world. She takes as a normative developmental ideal, an integrated self, which unifies the disunified and conflicting aspects of a self into a coherent identity which "is based on a reflexive and affective recognition and acceptance of the difference and nonidentity within the self." It is only when a child moves from the prelinguistic stage of affective attachment that he or she can come to recognize the complexity, the difference, and the otherness of the caregiver, and thus establish his or her own separateness and internal differentiation. The child moves from a relationship with the primary caregiver, which is driven by needs and need-satisfaction or need-denial, to a relationship based on a shared orientation to meaning; the child is driven not just by frustration and threats of punishment as Lacan proposed, but by the enticement of more complete and satisfying relationships with others, and entry into a larger social world where more and different desires can be satisfied. Weir argues that it is this affective investment in the social world of meaning that underlies differentiation within oneself, and individuation from others. For Kristeva, affective relationships are not an end in themselves, a point which Weir argues, many relational feminists miss. Affective relationships do not end only in affect, but serve as conduits for producing meaning in the linguistic and social order; it is through these meanings, and through their renegotiation, and reinterpretation that identity is constituted.

If Habermas could not provide an account of how affective relationships are constitutive of the identity of the communicative agent, and to the meanings in which it is invested, and to the norms it takes up, Kristeva lacks any account of a post-conventional psyche able to detach itself from its beliefs and desires, and subject them to reflexive scrutiny from a normative perspective. It is Weir's contention that an adequate theory of identity must include an account of both our cognitive capacity to relate to norms critically, as well as an account of the affective relationships which influence both the norms we choose and the way we relate to them.

NOTES
1.   See J. Habermas, *Communication and the Evolution of Society* (Boston: Beacon Press, 1979).

1

What's Critical about Critical Theory?

Nancy Fraser

To my mind, no one has yet improved on Marx's 1843 definition of critical theory as "the self-clarification of the struggles and wishes of the age."[1] What is so appealing about this definition is its straightforwardly political character. It makes no claim to any special epistemological status, rather it supposes that with respect to justification there is no philosophically interesting difference between a critical theory of society and an uncritical one. However, there is, according to this definition, an important political difference. A critical social theory frames its research program and its conceptual framework with an eye to the aims and activities of those oppositional social movements with which it has a partisan, though not uncritical, identification. The questions it asks and the models it designs are informed by that identification and interest. Thus, for example, if struggles contesting the subordination of women figured among the most significant of a given age, then a critical social theory for that time would aim, among other things, to shed light on the character and bases of such subordination. It would employ categories and explanatory models that revealed rather than occluded relations of male dominance and female subordination. And it would demystify as ideological any rival approaches that obfuscated or rationalized those relations. In this situation, then, one of the standards for assessing a critical theory, once it had been subjected to all the usual tests of empirical adequacy, would be: How well does it theorize the situation and prospects of the feminist movement? To what extent does it serve the self-clarification of the struggles and wishes of contemporary women?

In what follows, I am going to presuppose the conception of critical theory which I have just outlined. In addition, I am going to take as the actual situation of our age the scenario I just sketched as hypothetical. On the basis of these presuppositions, I want to examine the critical social theory of Jürgen Habermas as elaborated in *The Theory of Communicative Action* and related recent writings.[2] I want to read this work from the standpoint of the following questions: In what proportions and in what respects does Habermas's critical theory clarify and/or mystify the bases of male dominance and female subordination in modern societies? In what proportions and in what respects does it challenge and/or replicate prevalent ideological rationalizations of such dominance and subordination? To what extent does it or can it be made to serve the self-clarification of the struggles and wishes of the contemporary women's movement? In short, with respect to gender, what is critical and what is not in Habermas's social theory?

This would be a fairly straightforward enterprise were it not for one thing: apart from a brief discussion of feminism as a "new social movement" (a discussion I shall consider anon), Habermas says virtually nothing about gender in *The Theory of Communicative Action*. Now, according to my view of critical theory, this is a serious deficiency, but it need not stand in the way of the sort of inquiry I am proposing. It only necessitates that one read the work in question from the standpoint of an absence; that one extrapolate from things Habermas does say to things he does not, that one reconstruct how various matters of concern to feminists would appear from his perspective had they been thematized.

Thus, in the first section, I examine some elements of Habermas's social-theoretical framework in order to see how it tends to cast childrearing and the male-headed, modern, restricted, nuclear family. In the second section, I look at his account of the relations between the public and private spheres of life in classical capitalist societies and try to reconstruct the unthematized gender subtext. And finally, in the third section, I consider Habermas's account of the dynamics, crisis tendencies, and conflict potentials specific to contemporary, Western, welfare state capitalism, so as to see in what light it casts contemporary feminist struggles.[3]

The Social-Theoretical Framework: A Feminist Interrogation

Let me begin by considering two distinctions central to Habermas's social-theoretical categorial framework. The first of these is the distinction between the symbolic and the material reproduction of societies. On the one hand, claims Habermas, societies must reproduce themselves materially; they must successfully regulate the metabolic exchange of groups of biological individuals with a nonhuman, physical environment and with other social systems. On the other hand, societies must reproduce themselves symbolically; they must maintain and transmit to new members the linguistically elaborated norms and patterns of interpretation which are constitutive of social identities. Habermas claims that material reproduction comprises what he calls "social labor." Symbolic reproduction, on the other hand, comprises the socialization of the young, the cementing of group solidarity, and the transmission and extension of cultural traditions.[4]

This distinction between symbolic and material reproduction is in the first instance a functional one: it distinguishes two different functions which must be fulfilled more or less successfully if a society is to survive. At the same time, however, the distinction is used by Habermas to classify actual social practices and activities. These are distinguished according to which one of the two functions they are held to serve exclusively or primarily. Thus, according to Habermas, in capitalist societies, the activities and practices which make up the sphere of paid work count as material reproduction activities since, in his view, they are "social labor" and serve the function of material reproduction. On the other hand, the childrearing activities and practices that in our society are performed without pay by women in the domestic sphere—let us call them "women's unpaid childrearing work"—count as symbolic reproduction activities since, in Habermas's view, they serve socialization and the function of symbolic reproduction.[5]

It is worth noting, I think, that Habermas's distinction between symbolic and material reproduction is susceptible to two different interpretations. The first of these takes the two functions as two objectively distinct "natural kinds" to which both actual social practices and the actual organization of activities in any given society may correspond more or less faithfully. Thus, childrearing practices would in themselves be symbolic reproduction practices, while the practices which produce food and objects would in themselves be material reproduction practices. And modern capitalist social organization, unlike, say, that of archaic societies, would be a faithful mirror of the distinction between the two natural kinds, since it separates these practices institutionally. This "natural kinds" interpretation is at odds with another possible interpretation, which I shall call the "pragmatic-contextual" interpretation. It would not take childrearing practices to be in themselves symbolic reproduction practices but would allow for the possibility that, under certain circumstances and given certain purposes, it could be useful to consider them from the standpoint of symbolic reproduction—for example, if one wished to contest the dominant view, in a sexist political culture, according to which this traditionally female occupation is merely instinctual, natural, and ahistorical.

Now I want to argue that the natural kinds interpretation is conceptually inadequate and potentially ideological. I claim that it is not the case that childrearing practices serve symbolic as opposed to material reproduction. Granted, they comprise language-teaching and initiation into social mores—but they also include feeding, bathing, and protection from physical harm. Granted, they regulate children's interactions with other people, but also their interactions with physical nature (in the form, for example, of milk, germs, dirt, excrement, weather, and animals). In short, not just the construction of children's social identities but also their biological survival is at stake. And so, therefore, is the biological survival of the societies they belong to. Thus, childrearing is not per se symbolic reproduction activity; it is equally and at the same time material reproduction activity. It is what we might call a "dual-aspect" activity.[6]

But the same is true of the activities institutionalized in modern capital-ist paid work. Granted, the production of food and objects contributes to the biological survival of members of society. But it also, and at the same time, reproduces social identities. Not just nourishment and shelter *simpliciter* are produced, but culturally elaborated forms of nourishment and shelter that have symbolically mediated social meanings. Moreover, such production occurs via culturally elaborated social relations and symbolically mediated, norm-governed social practices. The contents of these practices as well as the results serve to form, maintain, and modify the social identities of persons directly involved and indirectly affected. One need only think of an activity like computer programming for a wage in the U.S. pharmaceutical industry to appreciate the thoroughly symbolic character of "social labor." Thus, such labor, like unpaid childrearing work, is a "dual-aspect" activity.[7]

Thus, the distinction between women's unpaid childrearing work and other forms of work from the standpoint of reproduction functions cannot be a distinction of natural kinds. If it is to be drawn at all, it must be drawn as a pragmatic-contextual distinction for the sake of focalizing what is in each case actually only one aspect of a dual-aspect phenomenon. And this, in turn, must find its warrant in relation to specific purposes of analysis and description, purposes which are themselves susceptible to analysis and evaluation and which need, therefore, to be justified through argument.

But if this is so, then the natural kinds classification of childrearing as symbolic reproduction and of other work as material reproduction is poten-tially ideological. It could be used, for example, to legitimize the institu-tional separation of childrearing from paid work, a separation which many feminists, myself including, consider a linchpin of modern forms of women's subordination. It could be used, in combination with other assumptions, to legitimate the confinement of women to a "separate sphere." Whether Habermas so uses it will be considered shortly.

The second component of Habermas's categorical framework that I want to examine is his distinction between "socially integrated action contexts" and "system-integrated action contexts." Socially integrated action contexts are those in which different agents coordinate their actions with one another by reference to some form of explicit or implicit intersubjective consensus about norms, values, and ends, consensus predicated on linguistic speech and interpretation. System-integrated action contexts, on the other hand, are those in which the actions of different agents are coordinated with one another by the functional interlacing of unintended consequences, while each individual action is determined by self-interested, utility-maximizing calculations typically entertained in the idioms—or, as Habermas says, in the "media"—of money and power.[8] Habermas considers the capitalist economic system to be the paradigm case of a system-integrated action context. By contrast, he takes the modern, restricted, nuclear family to be a case of a socially integrated action context.[9]

Now this distinction is a rather complex one. As I understand it, it contains six analytically distinct conceptual elements: functionality, intentionality, linguisticality, consensuality, normativity, and strategicality. However, I am going to set aside the elements of functionality, intentionality, and linguisticality. Following some arguments developed by Thomas McCarthy in another context, I assume that in both the capitalist workplace and the modern, restricted, nuclear family, the consequences of actions may be functionally interlaced in ways unintended by agents; that, at the same time, in both contexts agents coordinate their actions with one another consciously and intentionally; and that, in both contexts, agents coordinate their actions with one another in and through language.[10] I assume, therefore, that Habermas's distinction effectively turns on the elements of consensuality, normativity, and strategicality.

Once again, I think it useful to distinguish two possible interpretations of Habermas's position. The first takes the contrast between the two kinds of action contexts as registering an absolute difference. Thus, system-integrated contexts would involve absolutely no consensuality or reference to moral norms and values, whereas socially integrated contexts would involve absolutely no strategic calculations in the media of money and power. This "absolute differences" interpretation is at odds with a second possibility which takes the contrast rather as registering a difference in degree. According to this second interpretation, system-integrated contexts would involve some consensuality and reference to moral norms and values, but less than socially integrated contexts. In the same way, socially integrated contexts would involve some strategic calculations in the media of money and power, but less than system-integrated contexts.

Now I want to argue that the absolute differences interpretation is too extreme to be useful for social theory and that, in addition, it is potentially ideological. In few, if any, human action contexts are actions coordinated absolutely nonconsensually and absolutely nonnormatively. However morally dubious the consensus, and however problematic the content and status of the norms, virtually every human action context involves some form of both. In the capitalist marketplace, for example, strategic, utility-maximizing exchanges occur against a horizon of intersubjectively shared meanings and norms; agents normally subscribe at least tacitly to some commonly held notions of reciprocity and to some shared conceptions about the social meanings of objects, including about what sorts of things are exchangeable. Similarly, in the capitalist workplace, managers and subordinates, as well as coworkers, normally coordinate their actions to some extent consensually and with some explicit or implicit reference to normative assumptions, though the consensus be arrived at unfairly and the norms be incapable of withstanding critical scrutiny.[11] Thus, the capitalist economic system has a moral-cultural dimension.

Likewise, few if any human action contexts are wholly devoid of strategic calculation. Gift rituals in noncapitalist societies, for example, previously taken as veritable crucibles of solidarity, are now widely understood to have a significant strategic, calculative dimension, one enacted in the medium of power, if not in that of money.[12] And, as I shall argue in more detail later, the modern, restricted, nuclear family is not devoid of individual, self-interested, strategic calculations in either medium. These action contexts, then, while not officially counted as economic, have a strategic, economic dimension.

Thus, the absolute differences interpretation is not of much use in social theory. It fails to distinguish, for example, the capitalist economy—let us call it "the official economy"[13]—from the modern restricted nuclear family for both of these institutions are mélanges of consensuality, normativity and strategicality. If they are to be distinguished with respect to mode of action-integration, the distinction must be drawn as a difference of degree. It must turn on the place, proportions, and interactions of the three elements within each.

But if this is so, then the absolute differences classification of the official economy as a system-integrated action context and of the modern family as a socially integrated action context is potentially ideological. It could be used, for example, to exaggerate the differences and occlude the similarities between the two institutions. It could be used to construct an ideological opposition that posits the family as the "negative," the complementary other of the (official) economic sphere, a "haven in a heartless world."

Now which of these possible interpretations of the two distinctions are the operative ones in Habermas's social theory? He asserts that he understands the reproduction distinction according to the pragmatic-contextual interpretation and not the natural kinds one.[14] Likewise, he asserts that he takes the action-context distinction to mark a difference in degree, not an absolute difference.[15] However, I propose to bracket these assertions and to examine what Habermas actually does with these distinctions.

Habermas maps the distinction between action contexts onto the distinction between reproduction functions in order to arrive at a definition of societal modernization and at a picture of the institutional structure of modern societies. He holds that modern societies, unlike premodern societies, split off some material reproduction functions from symbolic ones and hand over the former to two specialized institutions—the (official) economy and state—which are system-integrated. At the same time, modern societies situate these institutions in the larger social environment by developing two other institutions which specialize in symbolic reproduction and are socially-integrated. These are the modern, restricted, nuclear family or "private sphere" and the space of political participation, debate, and opinion formation or "public sphere"; and together, they constitute what Habermas calls the two "institutional orders of the modern lifeworld." Thus, modern societies "uncouple" or separate what Habermas takes to be two distinct but previously undifferentiated aspects of society: "system" and "lifeworld." Hence, in his view, the institutional structure of modern societies is dualistic. On the one side stand the institutional orders of the modern lifeworld, the socially-integrated domains specializing in symbolic reproduction, that is, in socialization, solidarity formation, and cultural transmission. On the other side stand the systems, the system-integrated domains specializing in material reproduction. On the one side is the nuclear family and the public sphere. On the other side is the (official) capitalist economy and the modern administrative state.[16]

Now what are the critical insights and blind spots of this model? Let us attend first to the question of its empirical adequacy. And let us focus, for the time being, on the contrast between "the private sphere of the lifeworld" and the (official) economic system. Consider that this aspect of Habermas's categorical divide between system and lifeworld institutions faithfully mirrors the institutional separation in male-dominated, capitalist societies of family and official economy, household and paid workplace. It thus has some prima facie purchase on empirical social reality. But consider, too, that the characterization of the family as a socially integrated, symbolic reproduction domain and the characterization of the paid workplace, on the other hand, as a system-integrated material reproduction domain tends to exaggerate the differences and occlude the similarities between them. For example, it directs attention away from the fact that the household, like the paid workplace, is a site of labor, albeit of unremunerated and often unrecognized labor. Likewise, it does not make visible the fact that in the paid workplace, as in the household, women are assigned to, indeed ghettoized in, distinctively feminine, service-oriented and often sexualized occupations. Finally, it fails to focalize the fact that in both spheres women are subordinated to men.

Moreover, this characterization presents the male-headed, nuclear family, qua socially integrated institutional order of the modern lifeworld, as having only an extrinsic and incidental relation to money and power. These "media" are taken as definitive of interactions in the official economy and state administration but as only incidental to intrafamilial ones. But this assumption is counterfactual. Feminists have shown through empirical analyses of contemporary familial decision making, handling of finances, and wife-battering that families are thoroughly permeated with, in Habermas's terms, the media of money and power. They are sites of egocentric, strategic, and instrumental calculation as well as sites of usually exploitative exchanges of services, labor, cash, and sex—and frequently, of coercion and violence.[17] But Habermas's way of contrasting the modern family with the official capitalist economy tends to occlude all this. He overstates the differences between these institutions and blocks the possibility of analyzing families as economic systems, that is, as sites of labor, exchange, calculation, distribution, and exploitation. Or, to the degree that Habermas would acknowledge that they can be seen that way too, his framework would suggest that this is due to the intrusion or invasion of alien forces; to the "colonization" of the family by the (official) economy and the state. This, however, is a dubious proposition. I shall discuss it in detail in the third section below.

Thus, Habermas's model has some empirical deficiencies: it is not easily able to focalize some dimensions of male dominance in modern societies. Yet it does offer a conceptual resource suitable for understanding other aspects of modern male dominance. Consider that Habermas subdivides the category of socially integrated action contexts into two subcategories. On the one hand, there are "normatively secured" forms of socially integrated action. These are actions coordinated on the basis of a conventional, prereflective, taken-for-granted consensus about values and ends, consensus rooted in the precritical internalization of socialization and cultural tradition. On the other hand, there are "communicatively achieved" forms of socially integrated action. These involve actions coordinated on the basis of explicit, reflectively achieved consensus, consensus reached by unconstrained discussion under conditions of freedom, equality, and fairness.[18] This distinction, which is a subdistinction within the category of socially integrated action, provides Habermas with some critical resources for analyzing the modern, restricted, male-headed, nuclear family. Such families can be understood as normatively secured rather than communicatively achieved action contexts, that is, as contexts where actions are (sometimes) mediated by consensus and shared values, but where such consensus is suspect because it is prereflective or because achieved through dialogue vitiated by unfairness, coercion, or inequality.

To what extent does the distinction between normatively secured and communicatively achieved action contexts succeed in overcoming the problems discussed earlier? Only partially, I think. On the one hand, this distinction is a morally significant and empirically useful one. The notion of a normatively secured action context fits nicely with recent research on patterns of communication between husbands and wives. This research shows that men tend to control conversations, determining what topics are pursued, whereas women do more "interaction work" like asking questions and providing verbal support.[19] Research also reveals differences in men's and women's uses of the bodily and gestural dimensions of speech, differences that confirm men's dominance and women's subordination.[20] Thus, Habermas's distinction enables us to capture something important about intrafamilial dynamics. What is insufficiently stressed, however, is that actions coordinated by normatively secured consensus in the male-headed, nuclear family are actions regulated by power. It seems to me a grave mistake to restrict the use of the term "power" to bureaucratic contexts. Habermas would do better to distinguish different kinds of power; for example, domestic-patriarchal power on the one hand, and bureaucratic-patriarchal power, on the other, not to mention various other kinds and combinations in-between.

But even that distinction does not by itself suffice to make Habermas's framework fully adequate to all the empirical forms of male dominance in modern societies, for normative-domestic-patriarchal power is only one of the elements that enforce women's subordination in the domestic sphere. To capture the others would require a social-theoretical framework capable of analyzing families also as economic systems involving the appropriation of women's unpaid labor and interlocking in complex ways with other economic systems involving paid work. Because Habermas's framework draws the major categorical divide between system and lifeworld institutions, and hence between (among other things) the official economy and family, it is not very well suited to that task.

Let me turn now from the question of the empirical adequacy of Habermas's model to the question of its normative political implications. What sorts of social arrangements and transformations does his modernization conception tend to legitimate? And what sorts does it tend to rule out? Here it will be necessary to reconstruct some implications of the model which are not explicitly thematized by Habermas.

Consider that the conception of modernization as the uncoupling of system and lifeworld institutions tends to legitimate the modern institutional separation of family and official economy, childrearing and paid work. For Habermas argues that with respect to system integration, symbolic and material reproduction are asymmetrical. Symbolic reproduction activities, he claims, are unlike material reproduction activities in that they cannot be turned over to specialized, system-integrated institutions set apart from the lifeworld; their inherently symbolic character requires that they be socially integrated.[21] It follows that women's unpaid childrearing work could not be incorporated into the (official) economic system without "pathological" results. On the other hand, Habermas holds that it is a mark of societal rationalization that system-integrated institutions be differentiated to handle material reproduction functions. The separation of a specialized (official) economic system enhances a society's capacity to deal with its natural and social environment. "System complexity," then, constitutes a "developmental advance."[22] It follows that the (official) economic system of paid work could not be dedifferentiated with respect to, say, childrearing, without societal "regression." But if childrearing could only be pathologically incorporated into the (official) economic system, and if the (official) economic system could only be regressively dedifferentiated, then the continued separation of childrearing from paid work would be required.

This amounts to a defense of one aspect of what feminists call "the separation of public and private," namely, the separation of the official economic sphere from the domestic sphere and the enclaving of childrearing from the rest of social labor. It amounts, that is, to a defense of an institutional arrangement widely held to be one—if not the—linchpin of modern women's subordination. And it should be noted that the fact that Habermas is a socialist does not alter the matter, because the (undeniably desirable) elimination of private ownership, profit-orientation and hierarchical command in paid work would not of itself affect the official-economic/domestic separation.

Now I want to challenge several premises of the reasoning I have just reconstructed. First, this reasoning assumes the natural kinds interpretation of the symbolic vs. material reproduction distinction. But since, as I have argued, childrearing is a dual-aspect activity, and since it is not categorically different in this respect from other work, there is no warrant for the claim of an asymmetry vis-à-vis system integration. That is, there is no warrant for assuming that the system-integrated organization of childrearing would be any more (or less) pathological than that of other work. Second, this reasoning assumes the absolute differences interpretation of the social vs. system integration distinction. But since, as I have argued, the modern, male-headed, nuclear family is a mélange of (normatively secured) consensuality, normativity, and strategicality, and since it is in this respect not categorically different from the paid workplace, then privatized childrearing is already, to a significant extent, permeated by the media of money and power. Moreover, there is no empirical evidence to suggest that children raised in commercial day-care centers (even profit-based or corporate ones) turn out any more pathological than those raised, say, in suburban homes by full-time mothers. Third, the reasoning just sketched elevates system complexity to the status of an overriding consideration with effective veto power over proposed social transformations aimed at overcoming women's subordination. But this is at odds with Habermas's profession that system complexity is only one measure of "progress" among others.[23] More importantly, it is at odds with any reasonable standard of justice.

What, then, should we conclude about the normative, political implications of Habermas's model? If the conception of modernization as the uncoupling of system and lifeworld institutions does indeed have the implications I have just drawn from it, then it is in important respects androcentric and ideological.

Public and Private in Classical Capitalism: Thematizing the Gender Subtext

The foregoing difficulties notwithstanding, Habermas offers an account of the interinstitutional relations among various spheres of public and private life in classical capitalism which has some genuine critical potential. But in order to realize this potential fully, we need to reconstruct the unthematized gender subtext of his material.

Let me return to his conception of the way in which the (official) economic and state systems are situated with respect to the lifeworld. Habermas holds that, with modernization, the (official) economic and state systems are not simply disengaged or detached from the lifeworld; they must also be related to and embedded in it. Concomitant with the beginnings of classical capitalism, then, is the development *within* the lifeworld of "institutional orders" that situate the systems in a context of everyday meanings and norms. The lifeworld, as we saw, gets differentiated into two spheres that provide appropriate complementary environments for the two systems. The "private sphere"—modern, restricted, nuclear family—is linked to the (official) economic system. The "public sphere"—or space of political participation, debate, and opinion formation—is linked to the state-administrative system. The family is linked to the (official) economy by means of a series of exchanges conducted in the medium of money. It supplies the (official) economy with appropriately socialized labor power in exchange for wages, and it provides appropriate, monetarily measured demand for commodified goods and services. Exchanges between family and (official) economy, then, are channeled through the "roles" of worker and consumer. Parallel exchange processes link the public sphere and the state system. These, however, are conducted chiefly in the medium of power: loyalty, obedience, and tax revenues are exchanged for "organizational results" and "political decisions." Exchanges between public sphere and state, then, are channeled through the "role" of citizen and, in late welfare-state capitalism, that of client.[24]

This account of interinstitutional relations in classical capitalism offers a number of important advantages. First, it treats the modern restricted nuclear family as a historically emergent institution with its own positive, determinate features. And it specifies that this type of family emerges concomitantly with, and in relation to, the emerging capitalist economy, administrative state and (eventually) the political public sphere. Moreover, it charts some of the dynamics of exchange among these institutions and indicates some ways in which they are fitted to the needs of one another so as to accommodate the exchanges among them.

Finally, Habermas's account offers an important corrective to the standard dualistic approaches to the separation of public and private in capitalist societies. He conceptualizes the problem as a relation among four terms: family, (official) economy, state, and public sphere. His view suggests that in classical capitalism there are actually two distinct but interrelated public private separations. One public-private separation operates at the level of "systems," namely, the separation of the state or public system from the (official) capitalist economy or private system. There is another public-private separation at the level of the "lifeworld," namely, the separation of the family or private lifeworld sphere from the space of political opinion formation and participation of public lifeworld sphere. Moreover, each of these public-private separations is coordinated with the other. One axis of exchange runs between private system and private lifeworld sphere, that is, between (official) capitalist economy and modern, restricted, nuclear family. Another axis of exchange runs between public system and public lifeworld sphere, or between state administration and the organs of public opinion and will formation. In both cases, the exchanges can occur because of the institutionalization of specific roles that connect the domains in question. Hence, the roles of worker and consumer link the (official) private economy and the private family, while the roles of citizen and (later) client link the public state and the public opinion institutions.

Thus, Habermas provides an extremely sophisticated account of the relations between public and private institutions in classical capitalist societies. At the same time, however, his account has weaknesses. Many of these stem from his failure to thematize the gender subtext of the relations and arrangements he describes.[25] Consider first, the relations between (official) private economy and private family as mediated by the roles of worker and consumer. These roles, I submit, are gendered roles. And the links they forge between family and (official) economy are effected as much in the medium of gender identity as in the medium of money.

Take the role of the worker.[26] In male-dominated, classical capitalist societies, this role is a masculine one and not just in the relatively superficial statistical sense. There is, rather, a very deep sense in which masculine identity in these societies is bound up with the breadwinner role. Masculinity is in large part a matter of leaving home each day for a place of paid work and returning with a wage that provides for one's dependents. It is this internal relation between being a man and being a provider which explains why in capitalist societies unemployment is often not just economically but also psychologically devastating for men. It also sheds light on the centrality of the struggle for a "family wage" in the history of the workers' and trade union movements of the nineteenth and twentieth centuries. This was a struggle for a wage conceived not as a payment to a genderless individual for the use of labor power, but rather as a payment to a man for the support of his economically dependent wife and children—a conception, of course, that legitimized the practice of paying women less for equal or comparable work.

The masculine subtext of the worker role is confirmed by the vexed and strained character of women's relation to paid work in male-dominated classical capitalism. As Carole Pateman puts it, it is not that women are absent from the paid workplace; it's rather that they are present differently[27]—for example, as feminized and sometimes sexualized "service" workers (secretaries, domestic workers, salespersons, prostitutes, and, more recently, flight attendants); as members of the "helping professions" utilizing mothering skills (nurses, social workers, childcare workers, primary school teachers); as targets of sexual harassment; as low-waged, low-skilled, low-status workers in sex-segregated occupations; as part-time workers; as workers who work a double shift (both unpaid domestic labor and paid labor); as "working wives" and "working mothers," that is as primarily wives and mothers who happen, secondarily, also to "go out to work"; as "supplemental earners." These differences in the quality of women's presence in the paid workplace testify to the conceptual dissonance between femininity and the worker role in classical capitalism. And this in turn confirms the masculine subtext of that role. It confirms that the role of the worker, which links the private (official) economy and the private family in male-dominated, capitalist societies, is a masculine role, and that, *pace* Habermas, the link it forges is elaborated as much in the medium of masculine gender identity as in the medium of gender-neutral money.

Conversely, the other role linking (official) economy and family in Habermas's scheme has a feminine subtext. The consumer, after all, is the worker's companion and helpmate in classical capitalism. The sexual division of domestic labor assigns to women the work—and it is indeed work, though unpaid and usually unrecognized work—of purchasing and preparing goods and services for domestic consumption. One may confirm this even today by visiting any supermarket or department store or by looking at the history of consumer-goods advertising. Such advertising has nearly always interpellated its subject, the consumer, as feminine.[28] In fact, it has elaborated an entire phantasmatics of desire premised on the femininity of the subject of consumption. It is only relatively recently, and with some difficulty, that advertisers have devised ways of interpellating a masculine subject of consumption. The trick was to find means of positioning a male consumer which did not feminize, emasculate, or sissify him. In *The Hearts of Men*, Barbara Ehrenreich—quite shrewdly, I think—credits *Playboy* magazine with pioneering such means.[29] But the difficulty and lateness of the project confirm the gendered character of the consumer role in classical capitalism. Men occupy it with conceptual strain and cognitive dissonance, much as women occupy the role of worker. Thus, the role of consumer linking official economy and family is a feminine role. *Pace* Habermas, it forges the link in the medium of feminine gender identity as much as in the apparently gender-neutral medium of money.

Moreover, Habermas's account of the roles linking family and (official) economy contains a significant omission: there is no mention in his schema of any childrearer role, although the material clearly requires one. For who other than the childrearer is performing the unpaid work of overseeing the production of the "appropriately socialized labor power" that the family exchanges for wages? Of course, the childrearer role in classical capitalism (as elsewhere) is patently a feminine role. Its omission here is a mark of androcentrism, and it has some significant consequences. A consideration of the childrearer role in this context might well have pointed to the central relevance of gender to the institutional structure of classical capitalism. And this in turn could have led to the disclosure of the gender subtext of the other roles and of the importance of gender identity as an "exchange medium."

What, then, of the other set of roles and linkages identified by Habermas? What of the citizen role which he claims connects the public system of the administrative state with the public lifeworld sphere of political opinion and will formation? This role, too, is a gendered role in classical capitalism, indeed, a masculine role[30]—and not simply in the sense that women did not win the vote in the United States (for example) and Britain until the twentieth century. Rather, the lateness and difficulty of that victory are symptomatic of deeper strains. As Habermas understands it, the citizen is centrally a participant in political debate and public opinion formation. This means that citizenship, in his view, depends crucially on the capacities for consent and speech, the ability to participate on a par with others in dialogue. But these are capacities connected with masculinity in male-dominated, classical capitalism; they are capacities that are in myriad ways denied to women and deemed at odds with femininity. I have already cited studies about the effects of male dominance and female subordination on the dynamics of dialogue. Now consider that even today in most jurisdictions there is no such thing as marital rape. That is, a wife is legally subject to her husband; she is not an individual who can give or withhold consent to his demands for sexual access. Consider also that even outside of marriage the legal test of rape often boils down to whether a "reasonable man" would have assumed that the woman had consented. Consider what that means when both popular and legal opinion widely holds that when a woman says "no" she means "yes." It means, says Carole Pateman, that "women find their speech . . . persistently and systematically invalidated in the crucial matter of consent, a matter that is fundamental to democracy. [But] if women's words about consent are consistently reinterpreted, how can they participate in the debate among citizens?"[31]

Thus, there is conceptual dissonance between femininity and the dialogical capacities central to Habermas's conception of citizenship. And another aspect of citizenship not discussed by him that is even more obviously bound up with masculinity. I mean the soldiering aspect of citizenship, the conception of the citizen as the defender of the polity and protector of those—women, children, the elderly—who allegedly cannot protect themselves. As Judith Stiehm has argued, this division between male protectors and female protected introduces further dissonance into women's relation to citizenship.[32] It confirms the gender subtext of the citizen role. The view of women as in need of men's protection "underlies access not just to the means of destruction, but also [to] the means of production—witness all the 'protective' legislation that has surrounded women's access to the workplace—and [to] the means of reproduction, [—witness] women's status as wives and sexual partners."[33]

The citizen role in male-dominated classical capitalism is a masculine role. It links the state and the public sphere, as Habermas claims. But it also links these to the official economy and the family. And in every case the links are forged in the medium of masculine gender identity rather than, as Habermas has it, in the medium of a gender-neutral power. Or, if the medium of exchange here is power, then the power in question is masculine power. It is power as the expression of masculinity.

Thus, there are some major lacunae in Habermas's otherwise powerful and sophisticated model of the relations between public and private institutions in classical capitalism. Because his model is blind to the significance and operation of gender, it is bound to miss important features of the arrangements he wants to understand. By omitting any mention of the childrearer role, and by failing to thematize the gender subtext underlying the roles of worker and consumer, Habermas fails to understand precisely how the capitalist workplace is linked to the modern, restricted male-headed nuclear family. Similarly, by failing to thematize the masculine subtext of the citizen role, he misses the full meaning of the way the state is linked to the public sphere of political speech. Moreover, Habermas misses important cross-connections among the four elements of his two public private schemata. He misses, for example, the way the masculine citizen-soldier-protector role links the state and public sphere not only to one another but also to the family and to the paid workplace—that is, the way the assumptions of man's capacity to protect and woman's need of man's protection run through all of them. He misses, too, the way the masculine citizen-speaker role links the state and public sphere not only to each other but also to the family and official economy—that is, the way the assumptions of man's capacity to speak and consent and woman's incapacity therein run through all of them. He misses, also, the way the masculine worker-breadwinner role links the family and official economy not only to one another but also to the state and the political public sphere—that is, the way the assumptions of man's provider status and of woman's dependent status run through all of them, so that even the coin in which classical capitalist wages and taxes are paid is not gender-neutral. And he misses, finally, the way the feminine childrearer role links all four institutions to one another by overseeing the construction of the masculine and feminine gendered subjects needed to fill *every* role in classical capitalism.

Once the gender-blindness of Habermas's model is overcome, however, all these connections come into view. It then becomes clear that feminine and masculine gender identity run like pink and blue threads through the areas of paid work, state administration, and citizenship as well as through the domain of familial and sexual relations. This is to say that gender identity is lived out in all arenas of life. It is one (if not *the*) "medium of exchange" among them, a basic element of the social glue that binds them to one another.

Moreover, a gender-sensitive reading of these connections has some important theoretical and conceptual implications. It reveals that male dominance is intrinsic rather than accidental to classical capitalism, for the institutional structure of this social formation is actualized by means of gendered roles. It follows that the forms of male dominance at issue here are not properly understood as lingering forms of premodern status inequality. They are, rather, intrinsically modern in Habermas's sense, since they are premised on the separation of waged labor and the state from childrearing and the household. It also follows that a critical social theory of capitalist societies needs gender-sensitive categories. The preceding analysis shows that, contrary to the usual androcentric understanding, the relevant concepts of worker, consumer, and wage are not, in fact, strictly economic concepts. Rather, they have an implicit gender subtext and thus are "gender-economic" concepts. Likewise, the relevant concept of citizenship is not strictly a political concept; it has an implicit gender subtext and so, rather, is a "gender-political" concept. Thus, this analysis reveals the inadequacy of those critical theories that treat gender as incidental to politics, and political-economy. It highlights the need for a critical theory with a categorical framework in which gender, politics, and political-economy are internally integrated.[34]

In addition, a gender-sensitive reading of these arrangements reveals the thoroughly multidirectional character of social motion and causal influence in classical capitalism. It reveals, that is, the inadequacy of the orthodox Marxist assumption that all or most significant causal influence runs from the (official) economy to the family and not vice versa. It shows that gender identity structures paid work, state administration, and political participation. Thus, it vindicates Habermas's claim that in classical capitalism the (official) economy is not all-powerful but is, rather, in some significant measure inscribed within and subject to the norms and meanings of everyday life. Of course, Habermas assumed that in making this claim he was saying something more or less positive. The norms and meanings he had in mind were not the ones I have been discussing. Still, the point is a valid one. It remains to be seen, though, whether it holds also for late, welfare state capitalism, as I believe, or whether it ceases to hold, as Habermas claims.

Finally, this reconstruction of the gender subtext of Habermas's model has normative political implications. It suggests that an emancipatory transformation of male-dominated, capitalist societies, early and late, requires a transformation of these gendered roles and of the institutions they mediate. As long as the worker and childrearer roles are such as fundamentally incompatible with one another, it will not be possible to universalize either of them to include both genders. Thus, some form of dedifferentiation of unpaid childrearing and other work is required. Similarly, as long as the citizen role is defined to encompass death-dealing soldiering but not life-fostering childrearing, as long as it is tied to male-dominated modes of dialogue, then it, too, will remain incapable of including women fully. Thus, changes in the very concepts of citizenship, childrearing, and paid work are necessary, as are changes in the relationships among the domestic, official economic, state, and political public spheres.

The Dynamics of Welfare-State Capitalism: A Feminist Critique

Let me turn, then, to Habermas's account of late welfare state capitalism. I must acknowledge at the outset that its critical potential, unlike the critical potential of his account of classical capitalism, cannot be released simply by reconstructing the unthematized gender subtext. Here, the problematical features of his social-theoretical framework tend to inflect the analysis as a whole and diminish its capacity to illuminate the struggles and wishes of contemporary women. In order to show how this is the case, I shall present Habermas's view in the form of six theses.

First, welfare state capitalism emerges as a result of, and in response to, instabilities or crisis tendencies inherent in classical capitalism. It realigns the relations between the (official) economy and the state; that is, between the private and public systems. These become more deeply intertwined with one another as the state actively assumes the task of "crisis management." It tries to avert or manage economic crises by Keynesian "market-replacing" strategies which create a "public sector." And it tries to avert or manage social and political crises by "market-compensating" measures, including welfare concessions to trade unions and social movements. Thus, welfare state capitalism partially overcomes the separation of public and private at the level of systems.[35]

Second, the realignment of (official) economy state relations is accompanied by a change in the relations of those systems to the private and public spheres of the lifeworld. With respect to the private sphere, there is a major increase in the importance of the consumer role as dissatisfactions related to paid work are compensated by enhanced commodity consumption. With respect to the public sphere, there is a major decline in the importance of the citizen role as journalism becomes mass media, political parties are bureaucratized, and participation is reduced to occasional voting. Instead, the relation to the state is increasingly channeled through a new role, the social-welfare client.[36]

Third, these developments are "ambivalent." On the one hand, there are gains in freedom with the institution of new social rights limiting the heretofore unrestrained power of capital in the (paid) workplace and of the paterfamilias in the bourgeois family, and social insurance programs represent a clear advance over the paternalism of poor relief. On the other hand, the means employed to realize these new social rights tend perversely to endanger freedom. These means—bureaucratic procedure and the money form—structure the entitlements, benefits, and social services of the welfare system, and in so doing, they disempower clients, rendering them dependent on bureaucracies and therapeutocracies and preempting their capacities to interpret their own needs, experiences, and life-problems.[37]

Fourth, the most ambivalent welfare measures are those concerned with things like health care, care of the elderly, education, and family law, for when bureaucratic and monetary media structure these things, they intrude upon "core domains" of the lifeworld. They turn over symbolic reproduction functions like socialization and solidarity formation to system-integration mechanisms that position people as strategically-acting, self-interested monads. But given the inherently symbolic character of these functions and given their internal relation to social integration, the results, necessarily, are "pathological." Thus, these measures are more ambivalent than, say, reforms of the paid workplace. The latter bear on a domain that is already system integrated via money and power and which serves material, as opposed to symbolic, reproduction functions. So paid workplace reforms—unlike, say, family law reforms—do not necessarily generate "pathological" side-effects.[38]

Fifth, welfare state capitalism gives rise to an "inner colonization of the lifeworld." Money and power cease to be mere media of exchange *between* system and lifeworld. Instead, they tend increasingly to penetrate the lifeworld's *internal* dynamics. The private and public spheres cease to subordinate (official) economic and administrative systems to the norms, values, and interpretations of everyday life. Rather, the latter are increasingly subordinated to the imperatives of the (official) economy and administration. The roles of worker and citizen cease to channel the influence of the lifeworld to the systems. Instead, the newly inflated roles of consumer and client channel the influence of the system to the lifeworld. Moreover, the intrusion of system-integration mechanisms into domains inherently requiring social integration gives rise to "reification phenomena." The affected domains are detached not merely from traditional, normatively-secured consensus, but from "value-orientations per se." The result is the "desiccation of communicative contexts" and the "depletion of the nonrenewable cultural resources" needed to maintain personal and collective identity. Thus, symbolic reproduction is destabilized, identities are threatened, and social crisis tendencies develop.[39]

Sixth, the colonization of the lifeworld sparks new forms of social conflict specific to welfare state capitalism. "New social movements" emerge in a "new conflict zone" at the "seam of system and lifeworld." They respond to system-induced identity threats by contesting the roles that transmit these. They contest the instrumentalization of professional labor and of education transmitted via the worker role, the monetarization of relations and lifestyles transmitted via by the inflated consumer role, the bureaucratization of services and life-problems transmitted via the client role, and the rules and routines of interest politics transmitted via the impoverished citizen role. Thus, the conflicts at the cutting edge of developments in welfare capitalism differ both from class struggles and from bourgeois liberation struggles. They respond to crisis tendencies in symbolic as opposed to material reproduction, and they contest reification and "the grammar of forms of life" as opposed to distribution or status inequality.[40]

The various new social movements can be classified with respect to their emancipatory potential. The criterion is the extent to which they advance a genuinely emancipatory resolution of welfare capitalist crisis, namely, the "decolonization of the lifeworld." Decolonization encompasses three things: (1) the removal of system-integration mechanisms from symbolic reproduction spheres, (2) the replacement of (some) normatively secured contexts by communicatively achieved ones, and (3) the development of new, democratic institutions capable of asserting lifeworld control over state and (official) economic systems. Thus, those movements like religious fundamentalism, which seek to defend traditional lifeworld norms against system intrusions, are not genuinely emancipatory; they actively oppose the second element of decolonization and do not take up the third. Movements like peace and ecology are better; they aim both to resist system intrusions and also to instate new, reformed, communicatively achieved zones of inter-action. But even these are "ambiguous" inasmuch as they tend to "retreat" into alternative communities and "particularistic" identities, thereby effec-tively renouncing the third element of decolonization and leaving the (offi-cial) economic and state systems unchecked. In this respect, they are more symptomatic than emancipatory; they express the identity disturbances caused by colonization. The feminist movement, on the other hand, repre-sents something of an anomaly. It alone is "offensive," aiming to "conquer new territory," and it alone retains links to historic liberation movements. In principle, then, feminism remains rooted in "universalist morality." Yet it is linked to resistance movements by an element of "particularism." And it tends, at times, to "retreat" into identities and communities organized around the natural category of biological sex.[41]

Now what are the critical insights and blind spots of this account of the dynamics of welfare state capitalism? To what extent does it serve the self-clarification of the struggles and wishes of the contemporary women? I shall take up the six theses one by one.

Habermas's first thesis is straightforward and unobjectionable. Clearly, the welfare state does engage in crisis management and does partially over-come the separation of public and private at the level of systems.

Habermas's second thesis contains some important insights. Clearly, welfare state capitalism does inflate the consumer role and deflate the citizen role, reducing the latter essentially to voting—and, I should add, also to soldiering. Moreover, the welfare state does indeed increasingly position its subjects as clients. On the other hand, Habermas again fails to see the gender subtext of these developments. He fails to see that the new client role has a gender, that it is a paradigmatically feminine role. He overlooks that it is overwhelmingly women who are the clients of the welfare state, especially older women, poor women, and single women with children. Nor does he notice that many welfare systems are internally dualized and gendered, that they include two basic kinds of programs—"masculine" social insurance programs tied to primary labor-force participation and designed to benefit principal breadwinners, and "feminine" relief programs oriented to what are understood as domestic "failures," that is, to families without a male breadwinner. Not surprisingly, these two welfare subsystems are separate and unequal. Clients of feminine programs, virtually exclusively women and their children, are positioned in a distinctive, feminizing fashion as the "negatives of possessive individuals"; they are largely excluded from the market both as workers and as consumers and are familialized, that is, made to claim benefits not as individuals but as members of "defective" households. They are also stigmatized, denied rights, subjected to surveillance and administrative harassment, and generally made into abject dependents of state bureaucracies.[42] But this means that the rise of the client role in welfare state capitalism has a more complex meaning than Habermas allows. It is not only a change in the link between system and lifeworld institutions, it is also a change in the character of male dominance, a shift, in Carol Brown's phrase, "from private patriarchy to public patriarchy."[43]

This gives a rather different twist to the meaning of Habermas's third thesis. It suggests that he is right about the "ambivalence" of welfare state capitalism—but not quite and not only in the way he thought. It suggests that welfare measures do have a positive side insofar as they reduce women's dependence on an individual male breadwinner. But they also have a negative side insofar as they substitute dependence on a patriarchal and androcentric state bureaucracy. The benefits provided are, as Habermas says, "system-conforming" ones. But the system they conform to is not adequately characterized as the system of the official, state-regulated capitalist economy. It is also the system of male dominance, which extends even to the sociocultural lifeworld. In other words, the ambivalence here does not only stem, as Habermas implies, from the fact that the role of client carries effects of "reification." It stems also from the fact that this role, qua feminine role, perpetuates in a new, let us say "modernized" and "rationalized" form, women's subordination. Or so Habermas's third thesis might be rewritten in a feminist critical theory—without, of course, abandoning his insights into the ways in which welfare bureaucracies and therapeutocracies disempower clients by preempting their capacities to interpret their own needs, experiences, and life-problems.

Habermas's fourth thesis, by contrast, is not so easily rewritten. This thesis states that welfare reforms of, for example, the domestic sphere are more ambivalent than reforms of the paid workplace. This is true empirically in the sense I have just described—but it is due to the patriarchal character of welfare systems, not to the inherently symbolic character of lifeworld institutions, as Habermas claims. His claim depends on two assumptions I have already challenged. First, it depends on the natural kinds interpretation of the distinction between symbolic and material reproduction activities; that is, on the false assumption that childrearing is inherently more symbolic and less material than other work. And second, it depends upon the absolute differences interpretation of the system—integrated versus socially integrated contexts distinction, that is, on the false assumption that money and power are not already entrenched in the internal dynamics of the family. Once we repudiate these assumptions, then there is no categorical, as opposed to empirical, basis for differentially evaluating the two kinds of reforms. If it is basically progressive that paid workers acquire the means to confront their employers strategically and match power against power, right against right, then it must be just as basically progressive *in principle* that women acquire similar means to similar ends in the politics of familial and personal life. And if it is "pathological" that, in the course of achieving a better balance of power in familial and personal life, women become clients of state bureaucracies, then it must be just as "pathological" *in principle* that, in the course of achieving a similar end at paid work, paid workers, too, become clients—which does not alter the fact that *in actuality* they become two different sorts of clients. But of course the real point is that the term "pathological" is misused here insofar as it supposes the untenable assumption that childrearing and other work are asymmetrical with respect to system integration.

This sheds new light as well on Habermas's fifth thesis. This thesis states that welfare state capitalism inaugurates an inner colonization of the lifeworld by systems. It depends on three assumptions. The first two of these are the two just rejected, namely, the natural kinds interpretation of the distinction between symbolic and material reproduction activities and the assumed virginity of the domestic sphere with respect to money and power. The third assumption is that the basic vector of motion in late capitalist society is from state-regulated economy to lifeworld and not vice versa. But the feminine gender subtext of the client role contradicts this assumption: it suggests that even in late capitalism the norms and meanings of gender identity continue to channel the influence of the lifeworld onto systems. These norms continue to structure the state-regulated economy as the persistence, indeed exacerbation, of labor-force segmentation according to sex shows.[44] And these norms also structure state administration, as the gender segmentation of U.S. and European social welfare systems shows.[45] Thus, it is not the case that in late capitalism "system intrusions" detach life contexts from "value-orientations per se." On the contrary, welfare capitalism simply uses other means to uphold the familiar "normatively secured consensus" concerning male dominance and female subordination. But Habermas's theory overlooks this countermotion from lifeworld to system. Thus, it posits the evil of welfare state capitalism as the evil of a general and indiscriminate reification. It fails, in consequence, to account for that fact that it is disproportionately women who suffer the effects of bureaucratization and monetarization and for the fact that, viewed structurally, bureaucratization and monetarization are, among other things, instruments of women's subordination.

This entails the revision, as well, of Habermas's sixth thesis. This thesis concerns the causes, character, and emancipatory potential of social movements, including feminism, in late capitalist societies. Since these issues are so central to the concerns of this paper, they warrant a more extended discussion.

Habermas explains the existence and character of new social movements, including feminism, in terms of colonization, that is, in terms of the intrusion of system-integration mechanisms into symbolic reproduction spheres and the consequent erosion and desiccation of contexts of interpretation and communication. But given the multidirectionality of causal influence in welfare capitalism, the terms "colonization," "intrusion," "erosion," and "desiccation" are too negative and one-sided to account for the identity shifts manifested in social movements. Let me attempt an alternative explanation, at least for women, by returning to Habermas's important insight that much contemporary contestation surrounds the institution-mediating roles of worker, consumer, citizen, and client. Let me add to these the childrearer role and the fact that all of them are gendered roles. Now, consider in this light the meaning of the experience of millions of women, especially married women and women with children, who have in the postwar period become paid workers and/or social welfare clients. I have already indicated that this has been an experience of new, acute forms of domination; it has also, however, been an experience in which women could, often for the first time, taste the possibilities of a measure of relative economic independence, an identity outside the domestic sphere and expanded political participation. Above all, it has been an experience of conflict and contradiction as women try to do the impossible: to juggle simultaneously the existing roles of childrearer and worker, client, and citizen. The cross-pulls of these mutually incompatible roles have been painful and identity-threatening, but not simply negative.[46] Interpellated simultaneously in contradictory ways, women have become split subjects; and, as a result, the roles themselves, previously shielded in their separate spheres, have suddenly been opened to contestation. Should we, like Habermas, speak here of a "crisis in symbolic reproduction?" Surely not, if this means the desiccation of meaning and values wrought by the intrusion of money and organizational power into women's lives. Emphatically yes, if it means, rather, the emergence into visibility and contestability of problems and possibilities that cannot be solved or realized within the established frame-work of gendered roles and institutions.

If colonization is not an adequate explanation of contemporary feminism (and other new social movements), then decolonization cannot be an adequate conception of an emancipatory solution. From the perspective I have been sketching, the first element of decolonization, namely, the removal of system-integration mechanisms from symbolic reproduction spheres—is conceptually and empirically askew of the real issues. If the real point is the moral superiority of cooperative and egalitarian interactions over strategic and hierarchical ones, then it mystifies matters to single out lifeworld institutions—the point should hold for paid work and political administration as well as for domestic life. Similarly, the third element of decolonization—namely, the reversal of the direction of influence and control from system to lifeworld—needs modification. Since the social meanings of gender still structure late-capitalist official economic and state systems, the question is not *whether* lifeworld norms will be decisive but, rather, *which* lifeworld norms will.

This implies that the key to an emancipatory outcome lies in the second element of Habermas's conception of decolonization—namely, the replace-ment of normatively secured contexts of interaction by communicatively achieved ones. The centrality of this element is evident when we consider that this process occurs simultaneously on two fronts. First, in the struggles of social movements with the state and official economic system institu-tions; these struggles are not waged over systems media alone—they are also waged over the meanings and norms embedded and enacted in govern-ment and corporate policy. Second, this process occurs in a phenomenon not thematized by Habermas: in the struggles between opposing social movements with conflicting interpretations of social needs. Both kinds of struggles involve confrontations between normatively secured and commu-nicatively achieved action. Both involve contestation for hegemony over the sociocultural "means of interpretation and communication." For example, in many late capitalist societies, women's contradictory, self-dividing experience of trying to be both workers and mothers, clients and citizens, has given rise to not one but two women's movements, a feminist one and an antifeminist one. These movements, along with their respective allies, are engaged in struggles with one another and with state and corpo-rate institutions over the social meanings of "woman" and "man," "femi-ninity" and "masculinity"; over the interpretation of women's needs; over the interpretation and social construction of women's bodies; and over the gender norms that shape the major institution-mediating social roles. Of course, the means of interpretation and communication in terms of which the social meanings of these things are elaborated have always been controlled by men. Thus, feminist women are struggling in effect to redistribute and democratize access to, and control over, discursive resources. We are, therefore, struggling for women's autonomy in the following special sense: a measure of collective control over the means of interpretation and communication sufficient to permit us to participate on a par with men in all types of social interaction, including political deliberation and decision-making.[47]

The foregoing suggests that a caution is in order concerning the use of the terms "particularism" and "universalism." Recall that Habermas's sixth thesis emphasized feminism's links to historic liberation movements and its roots in universalist morality. Recall that he was critical of those tendencies within feminism, and in resistance movements in general, which try to resolve the identity problematic by recourse to particularism, that is, by retreating from arenas of political struggle into alternative communities delimited on the basis of natural categories like biological sex. I want to suggest that there are really three issues here and that they need to be disengaged from one another. One is the issue of political engagement versus apolitical countercultural activity. Insofar as Habermas's point is a criticism of cultural feminism, it is well-taken in principle, but it needs to be qualified by two perceptions: cultural separatism, although inadequate as longterm political strategy, is in many cases a shorter-term necessity for women's physical, psychological, and moral survival; and separatist communities have, in fact, been the source of numerous reinterpretations of women's experience which have proved politically fruitful in contestation over the means of interpretation and communication. The second issue is the status of women's biology in the elaboration of new social identities. Insofar as Habermas's point is a criticism of reductive biologism, it is well-taken. But this does not mean that one can ignore the fact that women's biology has nearly always been interpreted by men; nor that women's struggle for autonomy necessarily and properly involves, among other things, the reinterpretation of the social meanings of our bodies. The third issue is the difficult and complex one of universalism versus particularism. Insofar as Habermas's endorsement of universalism pertains to the metalevel of access to, and control over, the means of interpretation and communication, it is well-taken. At this level, women's struggle for autonomy can be understood in terms of a universalist conception of distributive justice. But it does not follow that the substantive content which is the fruit of this struggle—namely, the new social meanings we give our needs and our bodies, our new social identities and conceptions of femininity—can be dismissed as particularistic lapses from universalism. For these are no more particular than the sexist and androcentric meanings and norms they are meant to replace. More generally, at the level of substantive content, as opposed to dialogical form, the contrast between universalism and particularism is out of place. Substantive social meanings and norms are always necessarily culturally and historically specific; they always express distinctive shared but nonuniversal forms of life. Feminist meanings and norms will be no exception—but they will not, on that account, be particularistic in any pejorative sense. Let us simply say that they will be different.

I have been arguing that struggles of social movements over the means of interpretation and communication are central to an emancipatory resolution of crisis tendencies in welfare state capitalism. Let me now clarify their relation to institutional change. Such struggles, I claim, are implicitly and explicitly raising a number of important of questions: Should the roles of worker, childrearer, citizen, and client be fully degendered? Can they be? Or do we, rather, require arrangements that permit women to be workers and citizens *as women*, just as men have always been workers and citizens *as men*? And what might that mean? In any case, does not an emancipatory outcome require a profound transformation of the current gender roles at the base of contemporary social organization? And does not this, in turn, require a fundamental transformation of the content, character, boundaries, and relations of the spheres of life which these roles mediate? How should the character and position of paid work, childrearing, and citizenship be defined vis-à-vis one another? Should democratic-socialist-feminist, self-managed, paid work encompass childrearing? Or should childrearing replace soldiering as a component of transformed, democratic-socialist-feminist, participatory citizenship? What other possibilities are conceivable?

Let me conclude this discussion of the six theses by restating the most important critical points. First, Habermas's account fails to theorize the patriarchal, norm-mediated character of late-capitalist official-economic and administrative systems. Likewise, it fails to theorize the systemic, money- and power-mediated character of male dominance in the domestic sphere of the late-capitalist lifeworld. Consequently, his colonization thesis fails to grasp that the channels of influence between system and lifeworld institutions are multidirectional. And it tends to replicate, rather than to problematize, a major institutional support of women's subordination in late capitalism—namely the gender-based separation of both the masculine public sphere and the state-regulated economy of sex-segmented paid work and social-welfare, from privatized female childrearing. Thus, although Habermas wants to be critical of male dominance, his diagnostic categories deflect attention elsewhere, to the allegedly overriding problem of gender-neutral reification. Consequently, his programmatic conception of decolonization bypasses key feminist questions; it fails to address the issue of how to restructure the relation of childrearing to paid work and citizenship. Finally, Habermas's categories tend to misrepresent the causes and underestimate the scope of the feminist challenge to welfare state capitalism. In short, the struggles and wishes of contemporary women are not adequately clarified by a theory that draws the basic battle line between system and lifeworld institutions. From a feminist perspective, there is a more basic battle line between the forms of male dominance linking "system" to "lifeworld" and us.

Concluding Remarks

In general, then, the principal blindspots of Habermas's theory with respect to gender are traceable to his categorical opposition between system and lifeworld institutions and to the two more elementary oppositions from which it is compounded, the reproduction one and the action-contexts one. Rather, the blindspots are traceable to the way in which these oppositions, ideologically and androcentrically interpreted, tend to override and eclipse other, potentially more critical elements of Habermas's framework—elements like the distinction between normatively-secured and communicatively-achieved action contexts and like the four-term model of public-private relations.

Habermas's blindspots are instructive, I think. They permit us to conclude something about what the categorical framework of a socialist-feminist critical theory of welfare state capitalism should look like. One crucial requirement is that this framework not be such as to put the male-headed, nuclear family and the state-regulated official economy on two opposite sides of the major categorical divide. We require, rather, a framework sensitive to the similarities between them, one which puts them on the same side of the line as institutions which, albeit in different ways, enforce women's subordination, since both family and official economy appropriate our labor, short-circuit our participation in the interpretation of our needs, and shield normatively secured need interpretations from political contestation. A second crucial requirement is that this framework contain no a priori assumptions about the unidirectionality of social motion and causal influence, that it be sensitive to the ways in which allegedly disappearing institutions and norms persist in structuring social reality. A third crucial requirement, and the last I shall mention here, is that this framework not be such as to posit the evil of welfare state capitalism exclusively or primarily as the evil of reification. What we need instead is a framework capable of foregrounding the evil of dominance and subordination.[48]

NOTES

1. I am grateful to John Brenkman, Thomas McCarthy, Carole Pateman and Martin Schwab for helpful comments and criticism; to Dee Marquez and Marina Rosiene for crackerjack word processing; and to the Stanford Humanities Center for financial support.

2. Karl Marx, "Letter to A. Ruge, September 1843," in *Karl Marx: Early Writings*, Rodney Livingstone and Gregor Benton, trans., (New York: Vintage Books, 1975), p. 209.

3. Jürgen Habermas, *The Theory of Communicative Action, Vol. I: Reason and the Rationalization of Society*, Thomas McCarthy, trans., (Boston: Beacon Press, 1984). Jürgen Habermas, *Theorie des kommunikativen Handelns*, Vol. II: *Zur Kritik der funktionalistischen Vernunft*, (Frankfurt am Main: Surhkamp Verlag, 1981).

    I have consulted the following English translations of portions of *Theorie des kommunikativen Handelns*, Vol. II: Habermas, "New Social Movements," (excerpt from Ch. VIII, Section 3) *Telos*, 49 (1981), pp. 33–37; "Marx and the Thesis of Inner Colonization," (excerpt from Ch. VIII, Section 2, pp. 522–47), Christa Hildebrand and Barbara Correll, trans., unpublished typescript; "Tendencies of Juridification," (excerpt from Ch. VIII, Section 2, p. 522 ff), unpublished typescript.

    Other texts by Habermas: *Legitimation Crisis*, Thomas McCarthy, trans., (Boston: Beacon Press, 1975). "Introduction," in *Observations on "The Spiritual Situation of the Age": Contemporary German Perspectives*, Jürgen Habermas, ed., Andrew Buchwalter, trans., (Cambridge, MA: MIT Press, 1984). "A Reply to my Critics," in David Held and John B. Thompson, eds., *Habermas: Critical Debates*, (Cambridge, MA: MIT Press, 1982).

    I have also consulted two helpful overviews of this material in English: Thomas McCarthy, "Translator's Introduction," in Habermas, *Theory of Communicative Action*, Vol. I, pp. v–xxxvii.; John B. Thompson, "Rationality and Social Rationalisation: An Assessment of Habermas's Theory of Communicative Action," *Sociology*, 17, 2 (1983), pp. 278–94.

4. I shall not take up such widely debated issues as Habermas's theories of universal pragmatics and social evolution. For helpful discussions of these issues, see the essays in Held and Thompson, eds., *Habermas: Critical Debates*.

5. Habermas, *Theorie des kommunikativen Handelns,* Vol. II, pp. 214, 217, 348–49; *Legitimation Crisis*, pp. 8–9; "A Reply to my Critics," pp. 268, 278–79. McCarthy, "Translator's Introduction," pp. xxv–xxvii; Thompson, "Rationality," p. 285.

6. Habermas, *Theorie des kommunikativen Handelns*, Vol. II, p. 208; "A Reply to my Critics," pp. 223–25; McCarthy, "Translator's Introduction," pp. xxiv–xxv.

7. I am indebted to Martin Schwab for the expression "dual-aspect activity."

8. It might be argued that Habermas's categorial distinction between "social

labor" and "socialization" helps overcome the androcentrism of orthodox Marxism. Orthodox Marxism allowed for only one kind of historically significant activity, namely, "production" or "social labor." Moreover, it understood that category androcentrically and thereby excluded women's unpaid childrearing activity from history. By contrast, Habermas allows for two kinds of historically significant activity, "social labor" and the "symbolic" activities which include, among other things, childrearing. Thus, he manages to include women's unpaid activity in history. While this is an improvement, it does not suffice to remedy matters. At best, it leads to what has come to be known as "dual systems theory," an approach which posits two distinct "systems" of human activity and, correspondingly, two distinct "systems" of oppression: capitalism and male dominance. But this is misleading. These are not, in fact, two distinct systems but, rather, two thoroughly interfused dimensions of a single social formation. In order to understand that social formation, a critical theory requires a single set of categories and concepts which integrate *internally* both gender and political economy (perhaps also race). For a classic statement of dual systems theory, see Heidi Hartmann, "The Unhappy Marriage of Marxism and Feminism: Toward a More Progressive Union," Lydia Sargent, ed., *Women and Revolution*, (Boston: South End Press, 1981). For a critique of dual systems theory, see Iris Young, "Beyond the Unhappy Marriage: A Critique of Dual Systems Theory," Sargent, ed., *Women and Revolution*; and "Socialist Feminism and the Limits of Dual Systems Theory," *Socialist Review*, 50–51 (1980), pp. 169–80.

In Sections II and III of this essay, I am developing arguments and lines of analysis which rely on concepts and categories that internally integrate gender and political economy (see note 34 below.) This might be considered a "single system" approach, by contrast to dual systems theory. However, I find that label misleading because I do not consider my approach primarily or exclusively a "systems" approach in the first place. Rather, like Habermas, I am trying to link structural (in the sense of objectivating) and interpretive approaches to the study of societies. Unlike him, however, I do not do this by dividing society into two components, "system" and "lifeworld." See this section below and especially note 16.

9.   Habermas, *Theory of Communicative Action*, Vol. I, pp. 85, 87–88, 101, 342, 357–60; *Theorie des kommunikativen Handelns*, Vol. II, p. 179; *Legitimation Crisis*, pp. 4–5; "A Reply to my Critics", pp. 234, 237, 264–65; McCarthy, "Translator's Introduction", pp. ix, xvix–xxx. In presenting the distinction between system-integrated and socially-integrated action contexts, I am relying on the terminology of *Legitimation Crisis* and modifying the terminology of *Theory of Communicative Action*. Or, rather, I am selecting one of the several various usages deployed in the latter work. There, Habermas often speaks of what I have called "socially integrated action" as "communicative action." But this gives rise to confusion. For Habermas also uses this latter expression in another, stronger sense, namely, for actions in which coordination occurs by explicit, dialogically achieved consensus only (see below, this section). In order to avoid repeating Habermas's equivocation on "communicative action," I adopt the following terminology: I reserve the term "communicatively achieved

action" for actions coordinated by explicit, reflective, dialogically achieved consensus. I contrast such action, in the first instance, with "normatively secured action" or actions coordinated by tacit, prereflective, pregiven consensus (see below, this section). I take "communicatively achieved" and "normatively secured" actions, so defined, to be subspecies of what I here call "socially integrated action" or actions coordinated by any form of normed consensus whatever. This last category, in turn, contrasts with "system integrated action" or actions coordinated by the functional interlacing of unintended consequences, determined by egocentric calculations in the media of money and power, and involving little or no normed consensus of any sort. These terminological commitments do not so much represent a departure from Habermas's usage—he does in fact frequently use these terms in the senses I have specified. They represent, rather, a stabilization or rendering consistent of his usage.

10. Habermas, *Theory of Communicative Action*, Vol. I, pp. 341, 357–59; *Theorie des kommunikativen Handelns*, Vol. II, pp. 256, 266; McCarthy, "Translator's Introduction", p. xxx.

11. In "Complexity and Democracy, or the Seducements of Systems Theory," *New German Critique*, 35 (Spring/Summer 1985), pp. 27–55, McCarthy argues that state administrative bureaucracies cannot be distinguished from participatory democratic political associations on the basis of functionality, intentionality, and linguisticality since all three of these features are found in both contexts. Thus, McCarthy argues that functionality, intentionality, and linguisticality are not mutually exclusive. I find these arguments persuasive. I see no reason why they do not hold also for the capitalist workplace and the modern, restricted, nuclear family.

12. Here, again, I follow McCarthy in "Complexity and Democracy." He argues that in modern, state administrative bureaucracies, managers must often deal consensually with their subordinates. This seems to be equally the case for corporate organizations.

13. I have in mind especially the brilliant and influential discussion of gifting by Pierre Bourdieu in *Outline of a Theory of Practice*, Richard Nice, trans., (New York: Cambridge University Press, 1977). By recovering the dimension of time, Bourdieu substantially revises the classical account by Marcel Mauss in *The Gift: Forms and Functions of Exchange in Archaic Societies*, Ian Cunnison, trans., (New York: W.W. Norton, 1967). For a discussion of some recent revisionist work in cultural economic anthropology, see Arjun Appadurai, "Commodities and the Politics of Value," in Arjun Appadurai, ed., *The Social Life of Things: Commodities in Cultural Perspective* (New York: Cambridge University Press, 1986).

14. Habermas, *Theorie des kommunikativen Handelns*, Vol. II, pp. 348–49; McCarthy, "Translator's Introduction," pp. xxvi–xxvii. The terms "pragmatic-contextual" and "natural kinds" are mine, not Habermas's.

15. Habermas, *Theory of Communicative Action*, Vol. I, pp. 94–95, 101; *Theorie des kommunikativen Handelns*, Vol. II, pp. 348–49; "A Reply to My Critics," pp. 227, 237, 266–68; *Legitimation Crisis*, p. 10; McCarthy, "Translator's

Introduction," pp. xxvi–xxvii. The terms "absolute differences" and "difference of degree" are mine, not Habermas's.

16. Habermas, *Theory of Communicative Action*, Vol. I, pp. 72, 341–42, 359–60; *Theorie des kommunikativen Handelns*, Vol. II, p. 179; "A Reply to my Critics," pp. 268, 279–80; *Legitimation Crisis*, pp. 20–21; McCarthy, "Translator's Introduction," pp. xxviii–xxix. Thompson, "Rationality," pp. 285, 287. It should be noted that in *Theory of Communicative Action* Habermas draws the contrast between system and lifeworld in two distinct senses. On the one hand, he contrasts them as two different methodological perspectives on the study of societies. The system perspective is objectivating and "externalist," while the lifeworld perspective is hermeneutical and "internalist." In principle, either can be applied to the study of any given set of societal phenomena. Habermas argues that neither alone is adequate. So he seeks to develop a methodology that combines both. On the other hand, Habermas also contrasts system and lifeworld in another way, namely, as two different kinds of institutions. It is this second system lifeworld contrast that I am concerned with here. I do not explicitly treat the first one in this essay. I am sympathetic to Habermas's general methodological intention of combining or linking structural (in the sense of objectivating) and interpretive approaches to the study of societies. I do not, however, believe that this can be done by assigning structural properties to one set of institutions (the official economy and the state) and interpretive ones to another set (the family and the "public sphere"). I maintain, rather, that all of these institutions have both structural and interpretive dimensions and that all should be studied both structurally and hermeneutically. I have tried to develop an approach that meets these desiderata in "Women, Welfare and the Politics of Need Interpretation" and "Talking about Needs: Interpretive Contests as Political Conflicts in Welfare-State Societies" in my *Unruly Practices: Power, Discourse and Gender in Contemporary Social Theory,* (Minneapolis, MN: University of Minnesota Press, 1989, Chs. 7 and 8). I have discussed the general methodological problem in "On the Political and the Symbolic: Against the Metaphysics of Textuality," *Enclitic* , Vol. 9, Nos. 1 and 2 (1987), pp. 100–14.

17. See, for example, the essays in Barrie Thorne and Marilyn Yalom, eds., *Rethinking the Family: Some Feminist Questions* (New York and London: Longman, 1982). Also, Michele Barrett and Mary McIntosh, *The Anti-Social Family* (London: Verso, 1982).

18. Habermas, *Theory of Communicative Action*, Vol. I, pp. 85–86, 88–90, 101, 104–105; *Theorie des kommunikativen Handelns*, Vol. II, p. 179; McCarthy, "Translator's Introduction," pp. ix, xxx. In presenting the distinction between normatively-secured and comunicatively-achieved action, I am again modifying, or rather stabilizing, the variable usage of *Theory of Communicative Action*. See note 8 above.

19. Pamela Fishman, "Interaction: The Work Women Do," *Social Problems* 25:4 (1978), pp. 397–406.

20. Nancy Henley, *Body Politics,* (Englewood Cliffs, NJ: Prentice-Hall, 1977).

21. Habermas, *Theorie des kommunikativen Handelns*, Vol. II, pp. 523–24, 547; "Tendencies of Juridification," p. 3; "A Reply to my Critics," p. 237; Thompson, "Rationality," pp. 288, 292.

22. McCarthy pursues some of the normative implications of this for the differentiation of the administrative state system from the public sphere in "Complexity and Democracy."

23. McCarthy makes this point with respect to the dedifferention of the state administrative system and the public sphere. Ibid.

24. Habermas, *Theory of Communicative Action*, Vol. I, pp. 341–42, 359–60; *Theorie des kommunikativen Handelns*, Vol. II, pp. 256, 473; "A Reply to my Critics," p. 280; McCarthy, "Translator's Introduction," p. xxxii; Thompson, "Rationality," pp. 286–88.

25. I borrow the phrase "gender subtext" from Dorothy Smith, "The Gender Subtext of Power," unpublished typescript.

26. The following account of the masculine gender subtext of the worker role draws heavily on Carole Pateman, "The Personal and the Political: Can Citizenship be Democratic?" Lecture III of her "Women and Democratic Citizenship," The Jefferson Memorial Lectures, delivered at the University of California, Berkeley, February 1985, unpublished typescript.

27. Pateman, ibid., p. 5.

28. I am here adapting Althusser's notion of the interpellation of a subject to a context in which he, of course, never used it. For the general notion, see Louis Althusser, "Ideology and Ideological State Apparatuses (Notes toward an Investigation)," in *Lenin and Philosophy and Other Essays*, Ben Brewster, trans., (New York: Monthly Review Press, 1971).

29. Barbara Ehrenreich, *The Hearts of Men: American Dreams and the Flight from Commitment* (Garden City, NY: Anchor Books, 1984).

30. The following discussion of the masculine gender subtext of the citizen role draws heavily on Carole Pateman, "The Personal and the Political."

31. Pateman, "The Personal and the Political," p. 8.

32. Judith Hicks Stiehm, "The Protected, the Protector, the Defender," in Judith Hicks Stiehm, ed., *Women and Men's Wars*, (New York: Pergamon Press, 1983) and "Myths Necessary to the Pursuit of War," unpublished typescript. This is not to say, however, that I accept Stiehm's conclusions about the desirability of integrating women fully into the U.S. military as presently structured and deployed.

33. Pateman, "The Personal and the Political," p. 10.

34. Insofar as the foregoing analysis of the gender subtext of Habermas's role theory deploys categories in which gender and political economy are internally integrated, it represents a contribution to the overcoming of "dual systems theory" (see note 8 above). It is also a contribution to the development of a more satisfactory way of linking structural (in the sense of objectivating) and interpretive approaches to the study of societies than that proposed by

Habermas. For I am suggesting here that the domestic sphere has a structural as well as an interpretive dimension and that the official economic and state spheres have an interpretive as well as a structural dimension.

35. Habermas, *Theorie des kommunikativen Handelns*, Vol. II, p. 505 ff; *Legitimation Crisis*, pp. 33–36, 53–55; McCarthy, "Translator's Introduction," p. xxxiii.

36. Habermas, *Theorie des kommunikativen Handelns*, Vol. II, pp. 522–24; "Marx and the Thesis of Inner Colonization," pp. 1–2; "Tendencies of Juridification," pp. 1–2; *Legitimation Crisis*, pp. 36–37, McCarthy, "Translator's Introduction," p. xxxiii.

37. Habermas, *Theorie des kommunikativen Handelns*, Vol. II, pp. 530–40; "Marx and the Thesis of Inner Colonization," pp. 9–20; "Tendencies of Juridification," pp. 12–14, McCarthy, "Translator's Introduction," pp. xxxiii–xxxiv.

38. Habermas, *Theorie des kommunikativen Handelns*, Vol. II, pp. 540–47; "Marx and the Thesis of Inner Colonization," pp. 20–27; "Tendencies of Juridification," pp. 15–25, McCarthy, "Translator's Introduction," p. xxxi.

39. Habermas, *Theorie des kommunikativen Handelns*, Vol. II, pp. 275–77, 452, 480, 522–24; "Marx and the Thesis of Inner Colonization," p. 2; "Tendencies of Juridification," pp. 1–3; "A Reply to my Critics," pp. 226, 280–81; *Observations*, pp. 11–12, 16–20, McCarthy, "Translator's Introduction," pp. xxxi–xxxii, Thompson, "Rationality," pp. 286, 288.

40. Habermas, *Theorie des kommunikativen Handelns*, Vol. II, pp. 581–83, "New Social Movements," pp. 33–37; *Observations*, pp. 18–19, 27–28.

41. Habermas, *Theorie des kommunikativen Handelns*, Vol. II, pp. 581–83; "New Social Movements," pp. 34–37; *Observations*, pp. 16–17, 27–28.

42. For the U.S. social–welfare system, see the analysis of male versus female participation rates, and the account of the gendered character of the two subsystems in Fraser, "Women, Welfare and the Politics of Need Interpretation" in *Unruly Practices: Power, Discourse and Gender in Contemporary Social Theory*, (Minneapolis, MN: University of Minnesota Press, 1989, Ch. 7). Also, Barbara J. Nelson, "Women's Poverty and Women's Citizenship: Some Political Consequences of Economic Marginality," *Signs: Journal of Women in Culture and Society*, 10, 2 (1985); Steven P. Erie, Martin Rein, and Barbara Wiget, "Women and the Reagan Revolution: Thermidor for the Social Welfare Economy," in Irene Diamond, ed., *Families, Politics and Public Policies: A Feminist Dialogue on Women and the State*. (New York: Longman, 1983); Diana Pearce, "Women, Work and Welfare: The Feminization of Poverty," in Karen Wolk Feinstein, ed., *Working Women and Families*. (Beverly Hills, CA: Sage Publications, 1979) and "Toil and Trouble: Women Workers and Unemployment Compensation," *Signs: Journal of Women in Culture and Society*, 10, 3 (1985), pp. 439–59; Barbara Ehrenreich and Frances Fox Piven, "The Feminization of Poverty," *Dissent*, Spring 1984, pp. 162–70. For an analysis of the gendered character of the British social-welfare system, see Hilary Land, "Who Cares for the Family?" *Journal of Social Policy*, 7, 3 (1978), pp. 257–84. For Norway, see the essays in Harriet Holter, ed.,

Patriarchy in a Welfare Society. (Oslo: Universitetsforlaget, 1984). See also two comparative studies: Mary Ruggie, *The State and Working Women: A Comparative Study of Britain and Sweden* (Princeton, NJ: Princeton University Press, 1984); and Birte Siim "Women and the Welfare State: Between Private and Public Dependence," unpublished typescript.

43. Carol Brown, "Mothers, Fathers and Children: From Private to Public Patriarchy," in Sargent, ed., *Women and Revolution.* Actually, I believe Brown's formulation is theoretically inadequate, since it presupposes a simple, dualistic conception of public and private. Nonetheless, the phrase "from private to public patriarchy" evokes in a rough but suggestive way the phenomena a socialist-feminist critical theory of the welfare state would need to account for.

44. The most recent available data for the U.S. indicate that sex segmentation in paid work is increasing, not decreasing. And this is so in spite of the entry of small but significant numbers of women into professions like law and medicine. Even when the gains won by those women are taken into account, there is no overall improvement in the aggregated comparative economic position of paid women workers vis-à-vis male workers. Women's wages remain less than sixty percent of men's wages. Which means, of course, that the mass of women are losing ground. Nor is there any overall improvement in occupational distribution by sex. The ghettoization of women in low-paying, low-status "pink collar" occupations is increasing. For example, in the U.S. in 1973, women held 96% of all paid childcare jobs, 81% of all primary school teaching jobs, 72% of all health technician jobs, 98% of all Registered Nurse jobs, 83% of all librarian jobs, 99% of all secretarial jobs and 92% of all waitperson jobs. The figures for 1983 were, respectively, 97%, 83%, 84%, 96%, 87%, 99% and 88%, (Bureau of Labor Statistics figures cited by Drew Christie, "Comparable Worth and Distributive Justice," paper read at meetings of the American Philosophical Association, Western Division, April 1985.) The U.S. data are consistent with data for the Scandinavian countries and Britain. See Siim, "Women and the Welfare State."

45. See note 42.

46. This account draws on some elements of the analysis of Zillah Eisenstein in *The Radical Future of Liberal Feminism*, (Boston: Northeastern University Press, 1981), Ch. 9. What follows has some affinities with the perspective of Ernesto Laclau and Chantal Mouffe in *Hegemony and Socialist Strategy*, (New York: Verso, 1985).

47. I develop this notion of the "socio-cultural means of interpretation and communication" and the associated conception of autonomy in "Toward a Discourse Ethic of Solidarity," *Praxis International*, 5, No. 4 (January 1986), pp. 425–29. Both notions are extensions and modifications of Habermas's conception of "communicative ethics."

48. My own recent work attempts to construct a conceptual framework for a socialist-feminist critical theory of the welfare state which meets these requirements. See my "Women, Welfare and the Politics of Need Interpretation," "Toward a Discourse Ethic of Solidarity" and "Talking about Needs" in

Unruly Practices: Power, Discourse and Gender in Contemporary Socaial Theory, (Minneapolis, MN: University of Minnesota, 1989), pp. 144–60, 161–87. Each of these essays draws heavily on those aspects of Habermas's thought which I take to be unambiguously positive and useful, especially his conception of the irreducibly sociocultural, interpretive character of human needs, and his contrast between dialogical and monological processes of need interpretation. The present paper, on the other hand, focuses mainly on those aspects of Habermas's thought which I find problematical or unhelpful, and so does not convey the full range either of his work or of my views about it. Readers are warned, therefore, against drawing the conclusion that Habermas has little or nothing positive to contribute to a socialist-feminist critical theory of the welfare state. They are urged, rather, to consult the essays cited above for the other side of the story.

2

Critical Social Theory
and Feminist Critiques:
The Debate with Jürgen Habermas

Jean L. Cohen

The relation between feminism and the critical theory of Jürgen Habermas is characterized by ambivalence, as the essays collected in this volume witness. On the one hand feminists are critical of Habermas's peculiar blindness to gender issues, of his one-sided interpretation and assessment of the contemporary feminist movement, and of the ways in which his categorial framework is androcentric. On the other hand, even Habermas's most determined feminist critics are unwilling to dispense with the key categories of his thought: they make use of the concepts of communicative action, public space, democratic legitimacy, dialogic ethics, discourse, and critical social theory.

This essay takes up the relationship between Habermas and feminism, focusing on his most important work in social theory, *The Theory of Communicative Action*. Considering Habermas's social theory from two perspectives, I try to show what his categorial framework has to offer to the analysis of social movements in general, and the feminist movement in particular. But I also take seriously the critique of this framework generated from the standpoint of feminist theory and practice. My thesis is that while many of the criticisms hit the mark, the problem lies more in Habermas's prejudices regarding feminism,[1] and in his interpretation and application of his categorial framework than in the framework itself. Thus where there are problems with the theory, I try to revise rather than jettison it. I hope thereby to generate a fruitful dialogue between feminist critics and the most important living practitioner of critical social theory.

Habermas's most significant contributions to the understanding of these contemporary movements involves three theses that, taken together, offer insight into the stakes of contemporary collective action.[2] The first states that the emergence of cultural modernity—of differentiated spheres of science, art, and morality, organized around their own internal validity claims—carries with it a potential for increased self-reflection (and decentered subjectivity) regarding all dimensions of action and world relations. This opens up the possibility of a post-traditional, postconventional relation to key dimensions of social, political, and cultural life and of their coordination through autonomous processes of communicative interaction. This would form a basis for further modernization of the lifeworld through an incorporation of the achieved potentials of cultural modernity into everyday life, involving the replacement of *gemeinschaftliche* coordination by potentially self-reflective forms.

The second thesis involves the "selective institutionalization" of the potentials of modernity (self-reflection, autonomy, freedom, equality, meaning). A dualistic model of society, one that distinguishes between system and lifeworld, lies at the heart of the thesis. In this model, the processes involved in the modernization of the economy and the state are distinct from those involved in the "rationalization" of the lifeworld. On the one hand, I have the development of media-steered structures in which strategic and instrumental rationality are unleashed and expanded; on the other, the development of communicatively coordinated and egalitarian cultural, social, and socializing institutions appropriate to the new forms of decentered subjectivity made possible by cultural modernization. Societal rationalization has been dominated, however, by the imperatives of the subsystems; that is, the requirements of capitalist growth and administrative steering have predominated over lifeworld concerns. The "selective institutionalization" of the potentials of modernity has thus produced overcomplexity and new forms of power on the system side and the impoverishment and underdevelopment of the institutional promise of the lifeworld. The "colonization of the lifeworld" related to capitalist development and to technocratic projects of administrative elites has blocked and continues to block these potentials.

The third thesis insists on the two-sided character of the institutions of our contemporary lifeworld—that is, the idea that societal rationalization has entailed institutional developments in civil society involving not only domination but also the basis for emancipation. The dualistic theory of society thus places the core elements of civil society—legality, publicity, civil associations, mass culture, the family—at the heart of the discussion. The important point for us is that Habermas's sketch of developments within an already (albeit incompletely) modern civil society provides a way to understand the double character of contemporary movements and also their continuities or discontinuities with the past. The idea of the double character of the institutional makeup of civil society is a real gain because it goes beyond a one-sided stress on alienation or domination (Marx, Foucault) and an equally one-sided focus on integration (Durkheim, Parsons). We are thereby afforded a theoretical means of avoiding the stark alternative between apologetics and total revolution. If modern civil societies are not entirely reified, if our institutions are not thoroughly pervaded by inegalitarian power relations, then it becomes possible to think in terms of the positive potentials of modernity that are worth defending and expanding through a radical but self-limiting politics. Considered together with the colonization thesis, this allows us to explain why civil society is the target as well as the terrain of contemporary collective action.

Taken together, these theses reveal the stakes of contemporary movements in the struggle over the detraditionalization and democratization of social relations in civil society. The redefining of cultural norms, individual and collective identities, appropriate social roles, modes of interpretation, and the form and content of discourses (which I have called the "politics of identity") is part of this project. However, since authoritarian institutions are often reinforced by unequal control of money and power, and since the colonization of the institutions of civil society by these media prevents their further modernization, contemporary collective actors must also address political society. A "politics of inclusion" targets political institutions to gain recognition for new political actors as members of political society and to achieve benefits for those whom they "represent." A "politics of influence," aimed at altering the universe of political discourse to accommodate new need-interpretations, new identities, and new norms, is also indispensable. Only with such a combination of efforts can the administrative and economic colonization of civil society, which tends to freeze social relations of domination and create new dependencies, be restricted and controlled. Finally, the further democratization of political and economic institutions (a "politics of reform") is also central to this project. Without this effort, any gains within civil society would be tenuous indeed. While the democratization of civil society and the defense of its autonomy from economic or administrative "colonization" can be seen as the goal of the new movements, the creation of "sensors" within political and economic institutions (institutional reform) and the democratization of political society (the politics of influence and inclusion), which would open these institutions to the new identities and egalitarian norms articulated on the terrain of civil society, are the means to securing this goal.[3]

I am not arguing that Habermas himself has provided the synthetic theoretical paradigm of social movements that his framework makes possible. While available movement theories have much to learn from that framework, Habermas's own social theory could also benefit from integrating the results of other contemporary analyses. Indeed, his most recent discussion of the new social movements is misleading because it is based on a one-sided interpretation of the dualistic conception of society that he himself introduced.

Habermas's approach to social movements has evolved over time. His earlier analysis was close to that of Alain Touraine.[4] Like Touraine, he saw the New Left and especially the student movement as potential agents of societal democratization opposing technocratic projects to functionalize social institutions and the existing public sphere. These movements seemed to hold a promise of new, rational social identities and a revived democratic political culture to the extent that they sought to expand and democratize public spaces from the university to the polity.

In more theoretical terms, Habermas ascribed two interrelated roles to social movements. First, movements were the dynamic element in social learning processes and identity formation. Drawing on potentials embedded in cultural traditions and new forms of socialization, social movements transposed latently available structures of rationality into social practice so that they find embodiments in new identities and norms. Second, movements with democratic projects had the potential to initiate processes by which the public sphere might be revived and discourses institutionalized, within a wide range of social institutions. These roles were only very abstractly situated in contemporary institutional developments, however, because the old Frankfurt School thesis of "one-dimensionality" still haunted Habermas's assessment of existing social, economic, and political institutions. Thus, while he (like Touraine) criticized the revolutionary rhetoric of the sixties movements for diverting attention from the project of democratizing political and social institutions in favor of their total overthrow, he could provide no alternative to their totalizing critique of modern society.[5] I have criticized the earlier version of Habermas's theory for its "institutional deficit," that is for locating emancipatory potentials on the abstract level of cultural modernity and in socialization processes and not in the institutional articulation of civil society.[6]

Habermas resolved this difficulty by introducing the dualistic conception of society as a basis for analyzing the two-sided character of contemporary institutions.[7] He interpreted the ambivalent potentials of our social institutions in terms of a clash among system imperatives with independent communication structures. By implication, these institutions are open to both defensive struggles to protect and to democratize the communicative infrastructure of everyday life and offensive projects of radical institutional reform. It is all the more ironic that this recent work has also yielded what I consider to be an extremely one-sided interpretation of the new social movements, for in this conception, these movements appear primarily as defensive reactions against the colonization of the lifeworld.[8]

Habermas maintains that what is at stake in the new forms of resistance and conflict is the defense not of a traditional (communal, ascriptive, diffuse) sociocultural lifeworld but of one that is partially modernized. He also distinguishes between defenses of property and status acquired on the terrain of a modernized lifeworld and "defensive" action involving experiments in new forms of cooperation and community. The latter form the core of the new conflict potential. Nevertheless, the new movements are seen only as forms of resistance and retreat, seeking to stem the tide of the formally organized systems of action in favor of communicative structures. Although they signify the continued capacity of the lifeworld to resist reification, and thus take on positive meaning, Habermas is sceptical of their "emancipatory potential" and suspicious of their apparently anti-institutional, defensive, antireformist nature. In short, he does not see the new movements as carriers of new (rational) social identities but as mired in particularism. Nor does he see them as oriented toward or capable of fostering the institutionalization of the positive potentials of modernity or of transcending an expressive politics of withdrawal.

Nevertheless, Habermas is on to something when he argues that the new conflicts arise at the "seam between system and lifeworld"—over precisely those roles that institutionalize the media of money and power and mediate between the public and private spheres and the economic and administrative subsystems. Resistance to the functionalized roles of employee and consumer, citizen and client, surely characterizes much of contemporary collective action:

> It is just these roles that are the targets of protest. Alternative practice is directed against the . . . market-dependent mobilization of labor power, against the extension of pressures of competition and performance all the way down into elementary school. It also takes aim at the monetarization of services, relationships, and time, at the consumerist redefinition of private spheres of life and personal life-styles. Furthermore the relation of clients to public service agencies is to be opened up and reorganized in a participatory mode. . . . Finally, certain forms of protest negate the definitions of the role of citizen.[9]

In Habermas's view, however, the movement challenges to these roles are purely defensive. He construes the attempts of collective actors to come up with counterinstitutions within the lifeworld to limit the inner dynamics of the economic and political-administrative systems not only as "reactive," but also as tendentially antimodern communalist projects of dedifferentiation and withdrawal.[10] The only exception he sees is the feminist movement. It alone has a dual logic and a clear emancipatory potential: an offensive universalist side concerned with political inclusion and equal rights, along with a defensive particularist side focusing on identity, alternative values, and the overturning of concrete forms of life marked by male monopolies and a one-sidedly rationalized everyday practice.[11] The first dimension links feminism to the tradition of bourgeois-socialist liberation movements and the universalist moral principles. The second links it to the new social movements. As indicated above, however, the new resistance movements, including the second dimension of feminism, involve exclusively defensive reactions to colonization. Hence the label "particularist" for the concern with identities, norms, and alternative values, and hence the charge of a "retreat" into ascriptive or biologistic categories of gender. According to Habermas, the emancipatory dimension of feminism therefore involves nothing new, while the new dimension of feminism suffers from the same drawbacks as the other new movements.

I believe that this analysis of the new movements in general and of feminism in particular is misleading. Indeed, Habermas's interpretation of what is new in these movements as particularist and defensive reactions to the penetration of social life by the media of money and power involves a revival of the classical breakdown thesis.[12] This, in turn, derives from a one-sided interpretation of his own dualistic social theory. Thus, Habermas's analysis of movements does not do justice to the potential of his theory, for two reasons. The first has to do with the failure to translate the categories of the lifeworld in to a full-fledged conceptualization of civil and political society. The suggestive passages on the public and private institutions of the lifeworld neglect the one key dimension that would have enabled him to avoid the breakdown thesis—namely, that of associations. Despite his acknowledgment that contemporary struggles are situated around the dimensions of cultural reproduction, social integration, and socialization, he fails to link these to the positive side of the institutions within civil and political society.[13] Instead of recognizing that the new movements have a role to play in the further modernization of these spheres, he perceives only their defensiveness vis-à-vis the expansion of steering mechanisms. At best, he sees the new movements as having the potential to contribute to learning along the dimensions of cultural transmission and socialization, but not to institutional change within civil society.

Habermas is wrong to conclude from their focus on reinterpreting traditions and identities that what is involved in the new movements is only an anti-institutional, cultural politics. The movements also generate new solidarities, alter the associational structure of civil society, and create a plurality of new public spaces while expanding and revitalizing spaces that are already institutionalized. This involves challenging the roles that mediate between system and lifeworld. The other side of contemporary collective action, however, entails institutional change along the dimension of social integration. It involves conflict over social relations in civil institutions ranging from the family to the public spheres.

Habermas's tendency to view the subsystems as "self-referentially closed" screens out from view the possibility of institutional reform in these domains, as well. His overly rigid separation of the domains of system and lifeworld blinds him to the offensive strategies of contemporary movements aimed at creating or democratizing receptors within the subsystems, for it makes success tautologically impossible. Consequently, his account of movements does not do justice to the thesis of institutional doubleness to which the dual logic of the movements is addressed. He is thus led to a reductive analysis of the ecology, citizen initiative, green, and youth movements and to misconstrue the dual logic when he does perceive it, as in the case of feminism.

A reconstruction of the system/lifeworld distinction along the lines of a theory of civil society corrects these two blind spots. On the one hand, it translates the concept of the lifeworld into the institutional articulation of a civil society secured by rights. On the other hand, it recognizes that there are receptors for the influence of civil society within political (and economic) society and that these can, within limits, be added to and democratized. Consequently, in this version of the dualistic conception of society, the dual logic of all the new movements can come into view. This approach enables us to see that movements operate on both sides of the system/lifeworld divide, and is thus able to accommodate the contributions of both paradigms of collective action.

This framework also yields a more synthetic interpretation of the meaning of "defensive" and "offensive" collective action than can be found in any of the approaches discussed above. On this account, the "defensive" aspect of the movements involves preserving *and developing* the communicative infrastructure of the lifeworld. This formulation captures the dual aspect of movements discussed by Touraine, as well as Habermas's insight that movements can be the carriers of the potentials of cultural modernity. This is the sine qua non for successful efforts to redefine identities, to reinterpret norms, and to develop egalitarian, democratic associational forms. The expressive, normative, and communicative modes of collective action have their proper place here; but this dimension of collective action also involves efforts to secure *institutional* changes within civil society that correspond to the new meanings, identities, and norms that are created.

The "offensive" aspect of collective action targets political and economic society—the realms of "mediation" between civil society and the subsystems of the administrative state and the economy. Certainly, this involves the development of organizations that can exert pressure for inclusion within these domains and extract benefits from them. The strategic/instrumental modes of collective action are indispensable for such projects. But the offensive politics of the new movements involve not only struggles for money or political recognition, but also a politics of influence targeting political (and perhaps economic) insiders and (self-limiting) projects of institutional reform. How else are we to understand attempts to make the subsystems more receptive to new issues and concerns, more responsive to the needs and self-understanding of actors in civil society, and more internally democratic than they are now? In other words, those elements of the new movements that target political society (and will one day perhaps target economic society as well) articulate a project of self-limiting, democratic institutional reform aimed at broadening and democratizing the structures of discourse and compromise that already exist in these domains.

A Feminist Critique of Dualistic Social Theory

While I believe that all contemporary social movements are amenable to analysis in these terms, I am going to focus on the feminist movement to make my point. Several interesting discussions of the relevance of Habermas's dualistic social theory to the contemporary women's movement have already appeared.[14] In the most comprehensive article on the subject of feminist critique of dualistic social theory, Nancy Fraser argues that, far from facilitating an understanding of feminism, Habermas's dualistic social theory (especially his distinction between system and lifeworld), is not only "gender-blind," but also "in important respects androcentric and ideological."[15] Fraser proposes a far more radical critique of dualistic social theory than the one I am proposing.

Fraser rejects Habermas's system/lifeworld distinction, arguing that there is no meaningful way to differentiate categorically between the spheres of paid and unpaid labor, between the family and the "official" economy.[16] Indeed, she argues that there is no warrant for assuming that a system-integrated organization of childrearing would be any more pathological than that of other work. This response, however, misses the real thrust of the distinction between system and social integration.

While Habermas, in his more Marxist moments, does try to distinguish between symbolic and material reproductive processes, the heart of the theory rests on the far more important distinction between modes of action coordination and not on the substantive elements of action itself. The claim, in short, which Fraser has not disproved, is that there is a fundamental difference between processes (cultural reproduction, social integration, socialization), social relations, and institutions in which the weight of coordination must be communicative and those that can be "media-steered" without distortion, such as markets or bureaucracies. This is not because labor or creative/productive activity takes place only in the second domain, but because meaning, norms, and identities cannot be maintained, reinterpreted, or created through functional substitutes for the coordinating accomplishments of communicative interaction. The heart of the difference between formally organized sets of social relations (subsystems) and others lies in the tendency of the former to neutralize the normative background of informal, customary, or morally regulated contexts of action that are tied to validity claims and to substitute for these contexts of interaction that are generated by positive law and are "media-steered."[17] The latter are coordinated by media that operate through linguistic codes; these codes, however, relieve actors of the necessity of mutually agreeing on the definition of the situation involved in every relevant interaction, thereby bypassing (or rendering impossible) the reference to normative validity claims. Meanings, norms, and identities are not created in such contexts but are used (or reinforced) for systemic purposes.

Viewing the family as an economic system would thus entail either a wholesale embrace of systems theory[18] (thereby rendering it immune to the kind of normative critique Fraser wants to make) or a misunderstanding of what a system is in Habermas's theory: a formally organized, media-steered set of social relations. If one intends to challenge the meanings, norms, and identities that are constitutive of gender inequality, then this is the wrong tack to take. The systems-theoretic approach obliterates the very dimension in which these are created and reproduced. Although families do perform economic functions, although they can be and are functionalized by the imperatives of the economic or the administrative subsystem, although there are strategic interactions within them as well as exchanges of services and labor for money or support, and although these are distributed along gender lines, families are not thereby economic systems. They are neither formally organized nor media-steered. By the same token, they cannot be described as administrative systems even though they are certainly imbued with power relations.[19]

The work performed by women within the family is unrecognized, unremunerated, and uncompensated, and it therefore disadvantages women even in the "official" labor market (reinforcing the image of dependency on a male "breadwinner"). Nevertheless it is unhelpful to describe childrearing as being just like the rest of social labor. The fact that it can and has been partially transferred to day-care centers or nurseries and remunerated does not mean that it can be formally organized in the way that other work can be, nor that it is either desirable or possible to transfer childrearing in its entirety to system-integrated institutional settings. Communicative coordination of interaction remains at the heart of childrearing and nurturing, as any parent, child-care worker, or nursery school teacher knows. Unless one is advocating the total institutionalization of preschool children and the total commodification of childrearing as the sole alternative to being raised by full-time mothers, then one must assume that children come home at some time of day—at which point they require attention and nurturing. Moreover, nurseries, day-care centers, and schools are themselves institutions within civil society. They have their economic and bureaucratic side, of course, but when organizational or economic requirements outweigh the communicative tasks of nurturing and teaching, they subvert the *raison d'être* of the institutions and have pathological consequences (unnurtured and untaught children).

While it is certainly conceivable that more household tasks can migrate from the home to the market, surely there is and ought to be a limit to this. I do not agree with the notion that all creative, productive, or reproductive activities should necessarily take the form of wage labor. Even when they do, this does not mean that the institutional frameworks in which these activities occur can be analyzed as economic systems. Only on the misleading assumption that all "social labor" is equivalent and thus equally amenable to or distorted by system integration could one consider primary socialization and nurturing in the same light as all other work. Only, in short, if one construes families simply as sites of unpaid, socially necessary labor time could the differences between interfamilial relations and social relations of production disappear. But this sort of assumption has been criticized by many feminists for overextending the categories of the Marxian critique of capitalism to issues they were not constructed to address.[20]

If one is willing to grant that a modern economy requires that some forms of labor be commodified and formally organized, the central question for critical theory is to how to distinguish the sorts of activities that should be left to the market mechanism or formally organized from those that should not be. There are two distinct issues here. For example, feminist critiques of "surrogacy contracts" challenge the appropriateness of exchanging babies for money (commodification) and treating pregnancy and childbirth on the model of a labor contract. Marketization in such cases would seem to distort the woman's relation to her body, herself, and her child, and it is not necessary to explicate this intuition on the basis of naturalist or essentialist arguments.[21] The idea of the communicative infrastructure of the social relations of civil society suffices to account for the distortions that arise from delivering these relations over to the market. And while day care and schooling involve paid labor (marketization of teachers' or child-care workers' services), this does not mean that these activities can or ought to be formally organized. They do not have the same form, purpose, or meaning as other wage labor. The public and private institutions in which child care and teaching take place are core components of civil society, despite the fact that the professional services involved are remunerated. In short, some criterion is necessary for assessing whether or not commodification or formal organization would have implications with respect to certain forms of activity or interactions that are unacceptable and unnecessary in a modern society. My theory of civil society offers a good start in this direction.

Instead of attempting to render the roles of worker and childrearer compatible by assimilating the latter to the former, an analysis that proceeds from the system/lifeworld distinction would lead one to challenge the gender subtext of both roles while insisting on their difference. Modernization has already involved the migration of work (including education) from the home to the market. But surely a large part of a specifically feminist solution to the double burden of the working mother, to the subordination and insecurity attached to the homemaker role and to labor market inequities, must entail the degendering of the childrearing, nurturing, and homemaker roles, along with a fight against the gendered division of labor in the workplace. Wages for housework and child care would only reinforce its gendered character and lock women even more strongly into low-paid service jobs. The domestic "division of labor" clearly entails a power relation based in part on women's economic dependency that deprives women of real choice and of equal voice in the distribution of such tasks; it both derives from and reinforces their inferior position in the labor market.[22] It is this relation that must be challenged.

But this approach does not rest on the strained analogy between families and economic systems, nor between childrearing and other productive labor. Instead, it involves a challenge to the patriarchal norms that define families and attach genders to household and other roles. Indeed, the very possibility of articulating and challenging the ways in which the modern capitalist economy and the equally modern nuclear family intersect (through gendered roles) presupposes their differentiation. Changes in the identity, normative conception, and internal role structure of families would not alter the fact that interfamilial relations including childrearing must be communicatively coordinated. Quite the contrary. One could not even criticize the contemporary family as unjust, as deformed by the unequal distribution of money, power, and asymmetric gender relations, if one did not presuppose its communicative infrastructure.[23]

The distinction between conventional and postconventional orientations captures a key dimension of power in existing gender norms. The forms that male dominance takes in the patriarchal nuclear family and the ways in which it structures job categories (and client relations in the welfare state) and the corresponding gender identities are modern in the descriptive, historical sense.[24] But they are neither rational nor modern in the normative sense—that is, in the way Habermas uses these words. The norms underpinning male dominance are an example of traditionalism par excellence; that is, they are based on a conventional normative "consensus" frozen and perpetuated by relations of power and inequality that lead to all sorts of pathologies in the lifeworld. The traditionalist attitude toward de facto norms based on such a consensus does not mean that the relevant norms are lingering forms of premodern status inequalities. It does mean that they are sealed off from critique and traditionalized, as it were. Indeed, they are based on a selectively rationalized civil society, and it is precisely the blockages to its further modernization in the normative sense that Habermas's theory tries to articulate. Moreover, the differentiation of the subsystems of economy and state from the lifeworld is a precondition for releasing the cultural potentials of modernity and for freeing communicative interaction from ritualistically reproducing sacralized, conventional norms. The lifeworld cannot be internally differentiated, the institutions of civil society cannot be modernized, subjectivity cannot be decentered, and roles cannot be challenged unless communicative interaction is unburdened from the task of coordinating all areas of life.

Nevertheless, there is more to male dominance than even a modern brand of traditionalism, and Fraser does a real service by signaling a missing dimension in Habermas's analysis of power. It *is* misleading to restrict the term "power" to hierarchically structured relations in bureaucratic settings without providing another term to articulate asymmetric social relations in other institutions. One would do better to distinguish among different kinds of power or, rather, among various *codes* of power and modes of the *operation* of power. Otherwise, one is left without the means to conceptualize the differential ability to impose norms, define identities, and silence alternative interpretations of femininity, masculinity, and needs. Traditionalism results from this ability but does not account for it. It is important that we know how the various forms of power operate in the construction of gender, how they permeate socialization processes, and how the norms and identities generated in civil society intersect with functioning of power as a medium in bureaucratic settings.

This would involve an analysis of power relations that is supplemental rather than antithetical to the conception of power as a coordinating medium. I have argued that formal organization is a precondition (and hence a mark of identification) of the construction of the autonomous subsystem of power.[25] It is a necessary prerequisite for power to function as a steering medium (and to be institutionalized as such). But it is neither the only mode in which power operates nor its only code. As many have pointed out, power generated outside of formal rules exists within organizations; power relations exist before the historical emergence of the medium of power, and power relations are operative in contexts that are not formally organized.[26]

Power can be defined generally as the transfer of selectivity (the ability to determine what can be done and said). Power operates through the conditioning of expectations (and of expectations of expectations), linking relatively preferred and relatively rejected combinations of alternatives of at least two persons.[27] This transfer presupposes both the availability of negative sanctions and a code (or several codes) of power. Many but not all codes of power incorporate forms of inequality that distinguish among individuals as higher and lower, superior and inferior.

In one of its guises, within formally organized contexts, power operates as a steering medium that can then be extended outward to functionalize relations and institutions of civil society that are not themselves formally organized and thereby achieve administrative goals.[28] As such, the medium of power uncouples the coordination of action from consensus formation in language and neutralizes the responsibility of participants in the interaction.[29] What counts here is not the presence of a rigid bureaucratic hierarchy or structure of domination in the sense of a clear chain of command[30] but the formalization of the action context such that abstract rules and impersonal roles (be they offices or functions) become at least the official channel (one among several) through which power (selection of what can or cannot be said or done) flows. Thus, the binary schematization of interactions in sets of formal codes (especially legal/illegal) produces an objectivating attitude toward the action situation, an abstraction from concrete persons, and a certain automatic quality to the continuation of the interaction.[31]

Power does not operate only as a steering medium.[32] There are, of course, power relations within institutional settings that are not formally organized and thus lack a necessary condition for the anchoring of the medium of power. Here, too, power operates through "binary codes" that transfer selectivity, expedite communication, and avoid the risks of dissent so long as they are not challenged. But these "codes" have a different structure from those attached to steering media in formally organized contexts. Most important, they do not fully replace ordinary language in its coordinating function; instead, they involve second-order processes of consensus formation in language. Nor do they involve depersonalized social relations. Habermas has analyzed prestige and moral authority in this way, distinguishing these "generalized forms of communication" from steering media. Prestige and moral authority can motivate action or compliance, but the validity claims underlying them can also be challenged; and if these do not survive critique, their normative basis and their power to motivate collapse. Moreover, moral authority and prestige remain strongly attached to particular persons and contexts.[33]

It is reasonable to assume that the list of "generalized forms of communication" could be expanded to include status, authority, and gender.[34] Moreover, in line with Habermas's distinction between normative and communicative action, I should distinguish between forms that allow communicative thematization and questioning up to a fixed point (such as traditional authority) and forms that are so constructed as to allow in principle for unrestricted thematization, questioning, and even criticism. It is also possible for the structure of a generalized form of communication to change, for example, from traditional to democratic authority, from status to merit, or from one conception of gender to another.

I maintain that *gender is a generalized form of communication* or, rather, the code of such communication. Existing gender codes, even if historically changing and in this sense hardly traditional, are so constructed as to stop questioning at a supposedly unchallengeable meaning complex that is defined as "natural." That power operates through gender codes, reducing the free selectivity of some and expanding that of others, is the most important and paradigmatic core of any theory that might be labeled feminist. Gender is not another steering medium, but rather the set of codes in and through which power operates. Outside formal organizations (where it can serve as a secondary code of the power medium), gender continues to displace ordinary language communication and facilitate the operation of power. However, the codification of gender does not fully uncouple interaction from the lifeworld context of shared cultural knowledge, valid norms, and responsible motivations. Gender norms and identities are based ultimately on the intersubjective recognition of cognitive and normative validity claims. While conventional understandings of gender also reduce the expenditure of interpretive energy and the risks attending mutual understanding, their ability to motivate action and compliance is still linked to the alternatives of agreement or failed consensus.[35] This "relief effect" is not neutral in relation to the intersubjective recognition of norms, identities, or meanings.

Of course, the peculiar power of conventional interpretations in this domain lies in the fact that the meanings and norms at stake are bound up with identities that are transmitted through primary socialization and reinforced in secondary socialization processes throughout one's adult life. Power operating in the code of gender delimits not only what one understands as natural/unnatural, natural/cultural, male/female, feminine/masculine, attractive/unattractive, and appropriate/inappropriate sexual objects and aims, but also constructs the meaning of bodies and operates upon them. Gender norms and identities are, in addition, reinforced by direct or indirect, positive or negative sanctions that can (but need not) be linked to unequal access to money and power in the form of media. They must therefore be challenged on two fronts: The conventional gender codes of power must be dissolved by actors who take the responsibility for creating new meanings and new interpretations into their own hands, while inequities in the distribution of money and power must be contested.

It is in this sense that gender identity links the public and private domains of civil society to each other and to the economy and the state administration.[36] Viewing gender as a generalized form of communication, a power code distinct from but reinforced by the media of money and power generated in the subsystems, gives us a rich theoretical framework for articulating the public/private distinction in gender terms.

The most significant flaw in Habermas's work is his failure to consider the gendered character of roles of worker and citizen that emerged along with the differentiation of the market economy and the modern state from the lifeworld. Feminist historians have documented the parallel construction of the roles of housewife and mother and the restriction of women to these roles (as nurturer), as the flip side of the transition from the family economy to the capitalist mode of production and the replacement of autocratic/monarchic with republican/liberal forms of constitutionalism.[37] As wage labor became dominant, the role of wage worker came to be understood as a gendered, male role, while the family was constructed to be a private sphere, the domain of women, in which no "real" work was done. The same holds true for the republican conception of the citizen-soldier, which by definition excluded women.[38] It is no accident that as the roles of male breadwinner and male citizen crystallized, a cult of domesticity emerged to provide the ideological components of the new wife and mother role. Of course, a father role also developed, but this was an empty role, another name for the breadwinner. Thus, as a generalized medium of communication, gendered power relations have been built into all of the roles developed in (a selectively rationalized) modern society.[39]

It should be obvious that this reconstruction of the gender subtext of the institutional articulation of modern capitalist societies into sets of public and private relations does not undermine the dualistic social theory I have been defending. Rather, it presupposes the argument that the lifeworld "reacts in a characteristic way" to the emergence of the economic and state subsystems by internally differentiating itself into the public and private spheres of civil society, into sets of institutions oriented to cultural transmission, social integration, socialization, and individuation.[40] In my analysis of civil society, the acquisition of actionable civil rights, however selective and problematic these may be, institutionalizes the public and private spheres of civil society and subjects the economy and the state to its norms. The norms at issue here are, of course, not the ones Fraser has in mind when she appropriates the conception of the multidirectional character of influence among the various public and private spheres of classical capitalism. Patriarchal gender norms are hardly "freedom-guaranteeing," and they have justified the exclusion of women from those rights and norms that were. By implication, the gender norms that shape the key social roles mediating among institutions must be subject to critique and replaced by nonpatriarchal identities and roles.

The same holds true for the welfare state systems Fraser analyzes. I have argued that the norms of civil and political society continue to exert influence on the economy and state through the mediating institutions of political and economic society. The "receptors" for societal influence in these spheres are, however, restricted in scope and highly selective with respect to which norms they mobilize or reinforce. Patriarchal gender norms are certainly among the latter, and they structure the roles and policies put in place by many welfare reforms. Since these norms (already backed up by inequalities in money and power) constitute women as dependents, it is not surprising that they comprise the bulk of those who become clients. The key question today is not whether but which lifeworld norms will be decisive."[41]

The colonization thesis highlights the problems associated with the opposite direction of interchange: the penetration by the media of money and power (and formal organization) into the communicative infrastructure of everyday life. This tends to reify and deplete nonrenewable cultural resources that are needed to maintain and create personal and collective identities. This includes the resources that are needed to create nonpatriarchal norms in the lifeworld and to develop the solidary associations and active participation that would help them assert their influence on the subsystems.

Habermas's sketchy but extremely suggestive analysis of the new forms of juridification utilized by welfare states highlights the ambiguities involved in the double process of interchange between system and lifeworld. On the one hand, juridification in the domain of the family involves the extension of basic legal principles to women and children who were formerly denied legal personhood by law under the doctrine of couverture (in Anglo-American countries at least). In other words, egalitarian principles replace patriarchal norms in the form of rights—of child against parents, of wife against husband, etc. Such new rights tend to dismantle the position of the paterfamilias in favor of a more equal distribution of competences and entitlements among family members. The direction of influence here clearly flows from civil society to the state, involving a choice of norms. It is these norms that are reinforced in civil society by the state as the end result of law making.

On the other hand, if the structure of juridification involves administrative and judicial controls that do not merely supplement socially integrated contexts with legal institutions but replace these by the operation of the medium of law, as is often the case under welfare law, then emancipation in the family is achieved at the cost of a new type of possible bond.[42] Experts (judges or therapists) become the adjudicators of the new rights and the conflicts around them. They intervene with their juridical or administrative means into social relations that become formalized, dissociated, and reconstructed as individualized cases to be handled administratively or juridically like any other set of adversary relations. Formal, individualizing, and hence universalizing judgments that cannot deal with contextual complexities disempower clients by preempting their capacities to participate actively in finding solutions to their problems. It is thus the medium of law itself that violates the communicative structures of the sphere that has been juridified in this way. This form of juridification goes beyond the external legal codification of rights. The administrative penetration of civil society it entails preempts the development of procedures for settling conflicts that are appropriate to structures of action oriented by mutual understanding. It blocks the emergence of discursive processes of will formation and consensus-oriented procedures of negotiation and decision making. It also necessarily abstracts away from the specific context, conditions, relations, and needs of each individual "case." It is precisely the disempowering effects of this sort of decontextualized, individualizing, and formalistic decision-making that feminist analysts of recent reforms in family law have described and criticized in some detail.[43]

Debate and confusion over the meaning and desirability of seeking rights in this domain have permeated the feminist discussion. I believe that the distinction between law as institution and law as medium, and the colonization thesis are helpful here. A theory of civil society constructed along these lines allows one to conceptualize all of the important aspects that makes the new "rights" so ambiguous. From this perspective, it becomes clear that the ambivalence of feminists vis-à-vis "equal rights" legislation in this domain is based on a real dilemma: The acquisition of formal equality through means and techniques that abstract away from particular contexts, level differences, and block the creation of egalitarian social relations within civil society is an ambiguous gain indeed. In a context not only of substantive inequality (the old Marxist insight) but also of contested and fragile identities, such means will either generate new dependencies or foster the resuscitation of the old patriarchal norms as a defense against the disintegrative side effects of state penetration. Traditional patriarchal forms of life have become formally delegitimated by the new rights for women and children, but the client/expert relations that proliferate in civil society via the medium of law neither abolish substantive inequalities in power or voice nor facilitate the creation of new meanings, identities, and norms. In effect, the new vertical relations between the legal subject and the judge or social worker substitute for the horizontal communicative interaction needed to generate new solidarities, egalitarian norms, and ways of life to replace the old ones. Consequently, autonomous processes of collective empowerment and the creation of nonpatriarchal identities in civil society are blocked.[44]

It would be extremely misleading, however, to assume that all welfare state reforms have the same structure or logic. Surely legal reforms that secure the freedom of wage workers to organize unions and bargain collectively, that protect them from being fired for such collective action, and that secure worker representation on company boards differ in kind from means-tested grants to single-parent households and from social services that "instruct" clients on how to function properly as childrearers and responsible providers according to some preconceived model.[45] The difference between these types of reforms is not fully captured by reference to the genders (or, for that matter, to the race) of the people they target. In addition to stating that women are the objects of one type of reform, men of the other, one ought to be able to say what it is about the reforms themselves that make some enabling and others debilitating.

Dualistic social theory allows one to do just this. The former set of reforms, unlike the latter, do not create isolated clients of a state bureaucracy, but rather empower individuals to act together collectively, to develop new solidarities, and to achieve a greater balance of power relations because they are addressed to an area that is *already* formally organized.[46] Such reforms create "receptors" in the economic subsystem for the influence of the norms and modes of action of civil society by putting procedures for discursive conflict resolution into place, thereby asserting control of the latter over the former without dedifferentiating them. The second type of reform does the reverse: It brings the full force of administrative agencies into areas that are not and should not be formally organized. This threatens the communicative infrastructure and autonomy of civil society and undermines the capacities of "beneficiaries" to act for themselves or to settle conflicts discursively. Yet one certainly would not want to argue that juridification, regulation, or monetary benefits in civil society by definition humiliate or disempower those whom they are meant to benefit. The question that arises is not whether juridification (the creation of new rights) or state intervention (the granting of new benefits) should occur in civil society, but which kind of legal rights, administrative relations, or monetary benefits ought to be established. Considering that women are the prime targets/beneficiaries of welfare in this domain, surely such a question is not "askew" of feminist concerns.[47]

A feminist version of the critique of the welfare state must involve its reflexive continuation.[48] Thus, the decolonization of civil society and its modernization (in the sense of replacing conventionally held patriarchal norms with communicatively achieved norms) are both feminist projects. So, too, is the development of egalitarian institutions that can influence the administrative and economic systems. The first project would permit juridification only in forms that empower actors in civil society without subjecting them to administrative control. The second would dissolve male domination in both public and private institutions. The third would entail structural reforms in economic and political society to make them receptive and complementary to the new identities and the newly democratized, egalitarian institutions of civil society.[49]

Dual Politics: The Example of the Feminist Movement

I am now in a position to present an alternative to Habermas's interpretation of the dualistic logic of contemporary feminist movements. I have argued that the primary targets of the new social movements are the institutions of civil society. These movements create new associations and new publics, try to render existing institutions more egalitarian, enrich and expand public discussion in civil society and influence the existing public spaces of political society, potentially expanding these and supplementing them with additional forms of citizen participation. In the case of feminism, the focus on overturning concrete forms of life based on male dominance and reinterpreting gender identities complements attempts to secure the influence of new, more egalitarian gender identities within the public spaces of civil and political society and to attain political inclusion on these terms.[50]

Given the dualistic institutional structure of the public and private spheres of modern civil society, there is no reason to view the first orientation as a retreat. To construe the defensive politics of feminism simply as a reaction to colonization, aimed only at stemming the tide of the formally organized systems of action, is quite misleading. So, too, is the pejorative tone of the label "particularist" for the concern with identities, conceptions of gender, new need-interpretations, and the like. These ought not be taken as a sign of a withdrawal into communities organized around naturalistic categories of biology and sex. Quite the contrary. Nor are they simply reactive. Rather, these concerns focus on the normative presuppositions and institutional articulation of civil society. The feminist intervention constitutes a challenge to the particularist sexist norms and practices that dominate in both public and private spheres. It attempts to initiate and influence discourses on norms and identities throughout society. Such projects are universalist insofar as they challenge restrictions and inequalities in the communicative processes (in public and in private) that generate norms, interpret traditions, and construct identities. To be sure, the content of new identities that emerge from such challenges are particular. No identity, collective or individual, can be universal. But some identities involve a greater degree of self-reflection and ego autonomy than others, and it is this condition that distinguishes those particular gender identities that are based on hierarchical sexist norms from those that are not.

Given the obvious permeability of political and economic institutions to societal norms, there is also no reason to foreclose the possibility of the development of egalitarian and democratic institutions capable of influencing and controlling the polity and the economy. Feminist movements contest the norms and structures of male dominance pervading civil society, but they also challenge the ways in which these inform the structuration of the subsystems in general and social policy in particular. The "offensive" dimension of feminist politics does indeed target the state and the economy, pressuring for inclusion on equal terms.[51] It is "emancipatory and universalist" as Habermas rightly argues, but universalism and the egalitarian inclusion of women in the world of work and politics involve a challenge to the male standards behind the allegedly neutral structures of these domains. Once the "typical worker" is no longer construed as the male breadwinner, the structure of labor time, the length of the working day, the nature of benefits, and the worth of jobs must be suitably revised. And once the "responsible citizen" is no longer construed as the male soldier, the inclusion of women in the political and state spheres must entail significant changes in these domains as well. In short, the offensive politics of "inclusion," if it is really to be universalist, entails institutional reform. The dual logic of feminist politics thus involves a communicative, discursive politics of identity and influence that targets civil and political society and an organized, strategically rational politics of inclusion and reform that is aimed at political and economic institutions.

Indeed, almost all major analyses of the feminist movement (in the United States and Europe) have shown the existence and importance of dualistic politics.[52] A brief look at the trajectory of the American movement will make this point.

Resource mobilization and political opportunity theorists argue that organization, networks, allies, the presence of a cycle of protest, and a reform atmosphere are central to the emergence and success of movements. The availability of these factors in the late 1960s and early 1970s has been well documented by analysts of the "second wave" of feminism.[53] So, too, has the impact on women of structural changes that facilitated their massive entry into the paid work force, the university, and the polity.[54] But neither structural change, nor the growth in the membership and political expertise of women's organizations, nor the existence of powerful allies sufficed to further women's rights or feminist agendas.[55] The resources, organization, and leadership for a women's movement had existed since the turn of the century; what had been missing was a mass constituency willing to support demands for women's rights that is, a feminist consciousness.[56]

Movement analysts also include the emergence of group consciousness, solidarity, and a sense of unjust discrimination among the preconditions to collective political action, although the form that such action takes varies with the structure of the state and the political institutions (unions, parties) in the country.[57] In the case of women, attaining group consciousness involved an explicit challenge to traditional norms that identified women primarily in terms of the roles of mother and wife and justified inequalities, exclusion, and discrimination. In short, the traditional understanding of women's place and identity had to be changed and new identities constructed, before challenges to sex discrimination could appear as a legitimate issue and women could be mobilized around them. Indeed, it quickly became evident to key sectors of the women's movement that there was a deeper problem underlying the otherwise inexplicable resistance to equal rights: Socially constructed conventional gender identities preserved male privilege and worked against women's autonomy and women's self-determination. Thus, before any standard offensive politics of reform and inclusion could be fruitful, a feminist consciousness and ideology had to be developed on the part of movement women and then communicated to others through a different politics of identity, one aimed at the public and private spheres of civil society.[58] Hence the focus on precisely those institutional arrangements and processes involved in the construction of gender identity and the slogan that "the personal is political."

It should come as no surprise, then, that the feminist movement adopted a dualistic strategy targeting both the state (and economy) and civil society. Nor is it surprising that this duality found organizational expression in two distinct, unconnected branches of the movement. The "older" branch (older in terms of median age of activists and also temporally first) included a range of interest groups focusing on political and economic inclusion and attempting to exercise influence throughout the legal and political system to fight discrimination and attain equal rights.[59] The "younger" branch, emerging from the New Left and the civil rights movement, formed into loosely connected autonomous "grass-roots" groups targeting the forms of male dominance within the private and public spheres of civil society. These were the groups that articulated the great mobilizing "gender" issues of abortion, contraception, rape, violence against women, and the like. Their focus on identity, self-help, consciousness raising, and proselytizing through the underground press, their own alternative publications, and the universities was aimed at spreading feminist consciousness and achieving institutional changes in social relations based on traditionalist, inegalitarian gender norms in civil society.[60] By the end of the 1960s, the two branches of the movement started moving closer together. Political "insiders" took up many of the issues articulated by grass-roots feminists, while the latter began to enter en masse into the local chapters of the national political organizations.[61] By the mid-1970s, "women's movement organizations took up every political avenue to change policy. They approached political parties, Congress, the courts and the executive branch; they used constitutional amendment, legislative lobbying, and political protest."[62] At the same time, the organizations that had originally restricted their activity to standard tactics of political pressure began to take up the methods of protest and persuasion initiated by the more radical groups.[63] As a result, despite its organizational diversity, one may speak of the contemporary feminist movement in the singular, composed of various associations and organizations engaged in a wide range of strategies all sharing a feminist consciousness.[64]

There can be no question that the dualistic strategy of the contemporary women's movement has had successes in political, cultural, and institutional terms. In 1972 alone, the U.S. Congress passed more legislation to further women's rights than had the previous ten legislatures combined.[65] Women's movement organizations helped trigger a wave of legislative action on feminist issues unequaled in U.S. history.[66] Between 1970 and 1980, women's access to and influence on political elites increased dramatically, and more women were elected and appointed to public office than ever before in American history.[67] In addition, the courts became an important and productive target of the movement in both of its forms and on both of its fronts. The landmark decision in *Reed* v. *Reed* in 1971 initiated a line of cases using the equal-protection clause of the constitution to knock down sexually discriminatory statutes in the labor market. The decision in *Roe* v. *Wade* in 1973 used the right of privacy to make abortion legal, thereby registering and furthering changes in gender relations in general and in a key institution of civil society, the family, in particular.[68] As most analysts stress, however, these political and legal successes had as their prerequisite and precondition success in the cultural sense—in the prior spread of feminist consciousness.[69] The point here is not the obvious one that a mass movement can be strategically helpful to new groups seeking power and influence; rather, that without a politics of identity aimed at the norms, social relations, institutional arrangements, and practices constructed in civil society, and without a politics of influence aimed at political society, success in the first respect would be unlikely and limited.[70]

The spread of feminist consciousness has been documented. The 1980 Virginia Slims Poll found that 64% of women favored efforts to change and strengthen the status of women, in contrast to 40% in 1970.[71] Moreover, by 1980 60% of the population believed that society, not nature, taught women to prefer homemaking to work outside the home.[72] In addition, 51% preferred a marriage in which husband and wife shared home responsibilities, and 56% favored shared responsibility for child care.[73] These statistics indicate cultural changes that go well beyond the acceptance of equal rights and inclusion of women in the political public sphere, although the latter is also accepted, at least in principle, by the majority of the population.[74]

A politics of influence informed by new conceptions of gender identity thus made it possible to turn access to political elites into the measures necessary to achieve feminist goals. And what was true for the United States has been true of Italy, Germany, England, and France as well.[75] To cite one example, Jane Jenson has shown that the insertion of the needs and interests of women onto the policy agenda in France became possible only after the women's movement took as its fundamental goal the specification of a new collective identity. She argues that "the fundamental contribution of the modern women's movement was its ability to alter the 'universe of political discourse' and thus to press its goals in ways quite different from those of earlier mobilizations of women."[76]

According to Jenson, the feminist movement changed the universe of political discourse that had excluded women by creating a new collective identity for them and by getting the political elites to accept this identity. Jenson also shows that reforms from above that extend women's rights do not, in the absence of a feminist movement, entail a change in the universe of political discourse nor a change in the identity of women. After World War II, women in France acquired the right to vote and more liberal access to contraception, but the traditional universe of political discourse that defined women as wives, as appendages of men, and as mothers was not altered by these reforms.[77] It was not until the feminist movement stepped into the cultural space opened up by the New Left in 1968, and began to take up in relation to women, critiques of everyday life and to demand the right to equality and autonomy, and redefined women's collective identity in feminist terms that the traditional universe of political discourse began to alter and reforms that were feminist in both intent and impact occurred.

It is telling that Jenson focuses on the debate around the legalization of abortion to demonstrate the impact of the women's movement on the universe of discourse. Indeed, most analysts of feminism agree that what is new and specific to the contemporary women's movement throughout the West, and what brought women into the public arena en masse, were the great mobilizing themes of abortion, violence against women (rape, wife-battering), sexual coercion, sexual harassment, and stereotyping.[78] Feminists demanded that the standards of justice be applied to all spheres of civil society, including the family. After formal citizenship rights had been granted to women, and alongside efforts to gain equal political rights, to end economic discrimination in pay and opportunity, and to fight sexual discrimination in and segmentation of the labor force, every modern feminist movement has mobilized primarily around these formerly "private," "nonpolitical," "civil society" issues.[79] And every modern feminist movement has explicitly attempted to reshape the universe of discourse so that women's voices could be heard, women's concerns perceived, women's identities reconstructed, and the traditional conceptions of women's roles, bodies, and identities, as well as the male dominance supported by it, undermined. To be feminist in character, new rights and institutional reforms had to reflect the changes in gender identity and in women's aspirations.

The abortion issue encompassed all of these concerns. It quickly became apparent that this issue threw down the gauntlet to the traditional universe of discourse because it signified a fundamental change in the definition and status of women.[80] The theme of freedom of choice and the demand for "control over our own bodies" expressed more than a desire for equal rights. They symbolized a demand for autonomy regarding self-formative processes, for self-determination, and for bodily integrity; in short, for the right for women to decide for themselves who they want to be including whether and when they choose to become mothers. Considered together with the thematization of violence against women, the demands for laws legalizing abortion and criminalizing marital violence and marital rape targeted a sphere of civil society that, under the guise of "privacy," had previously been removed from such scrutiny. On the one side, privacy as autonomy was being claimed by and for women; on the other, the notion that a social institution could be private in the sense of being immune to the principles of justice was seriously challenged.[81]

Challenges to the traditional identity and roles assigned to women articulated in the debates around the abortion issue influenced and altered the universe of political discourse: "for the first time, women alone and outside a family frame of reference became the subject of political discourse . . . the new discourse on abortion reform came to symbolize nothing less than a change in women's status and their relation to their own bodies and the state."[82] This discourse involved a conception of women as both autonomous and gendered (that is, with their own specific situation), as both different and yet worthy of equal concern and respect.[83] This is why the abortion issue cannot be construed in terms of the politics of inclusion along the lines of "bourgeois emancipation movements" that bring the excluded into the polity or economy on equal terms. Rather, it is an issue tied to the "new" dimension of the feminist movement, for it poses a fundamental challenge to traditional gender identities, to traditional conceptions of the family to patriarchal power, and to the standard liberal conception of the public and private spheres of civil society.

I have argued that Habermas's dualistic social theory has quite a lot to offer to feminist analyses of feminist politics. Thus, instead of focusing on its weaknesses, I have attempted to develop its strengths. According to the spirit if not the letter of his text, I have refined the theoretical framework such that it is able to encompass both the translation of the relevant dimensions of the lifeworld as civil society and the idea of "receptors" for the influence of civil society in the economic and political subsystems. My thesis is that this theoretical approach allows one to make sense of the double political task of the feminist movement: influencing publics, associations, and organizations in political society and the institutionalization of these gains (new identities, autonomous egalitarian associational forms, democratize institutions) within the lifeworld. Given the dearth of critical social theory today (it is no longer fashionable in the world of deconstruction), this, in my view, is no small achievement.

NOTES

1. My discussion perforce addresses Habermas's social theory developed in the early 1980s, for this was the last attempt on his part to develop a critical *social* theory until very recently. From the mid-1980s to the early 1990's Habermas turned his attention to elaborating the theory of discourse ethics. However, in his most recent book on legal theory, *Facticity and Validity* (Cambridge, MA: MIT Press: 1994) he has not only corrected for his earlier "gender blindness," but he has also made what I take to be an extremely important contribution to the "equality/difference" debate animating feminist legal theory in the U.S. (Ch. 9). He has also elaborated his social theory in terms of the category of civil society (Ch. 10). I regard these developments as a vindication of the claims made in the article.

2. See Jürgen Habermas, *The Theory of Communicative Action*, Vol. 2 (Boston: Beacon Press, 1985), pp. 332–403. For a critical discussion of Habermas's approach to social movements over the years, see Cohen, "Strategy or Identity," pp. 708–16.

3. See the concluding section of this chapter for a more complete discussion of the four components of the dual logic of contemporary movements.

4. Alain Touraine, *The May Movement* (New York: Random House, 1971); Jürgen Habermas, *Student und Politik* (Frankfurt: Suhrkamp, 1961), *Protestbewegung und Hochschulreform* (Frankfurt: Suhrkamp, 1969), and *Towards a Rational Society* (Boston: Beacon Press, 1970).

5. Jürgen Habermas, *Die neue Unubersittlichkeit* (Frankfurt: Suhrkamp, 1985), pp. 81–82, offers a reevaluation of his earlier political assessment of the New Left.

6. See Cohen, *Class and Civil Society*, pp. 194–228; Jean L. Cohen, "Why More Political Theory?" *Telos*, No. 40 (Summer 1979), pp. 70–94.

7. See the discussion in Habermas, *The Theory of Communicative Action*, Vol. 2, pp. 301–403.

8. Among the movements Habermas refers to as new are the feminist, ecology, peace, youth, minority, antinuclear, and citizen-initiative movements, *The Theory of Communicative Action*, Vol. 2, p. 393.

9. Habermas, *The Theory of Communicative Action*, Vol. 2, p. 395.

10. Ibid., *The Theory of Communicative Action*, Vol. 2, p. 396.

11. Thus, he rediscovers Tilly's "reactive" and "proactive" types of collective action.

12. In this regard, his analysis is less perceptive than that of Touraine, who saw that social movements targeting the norms and identities of civil society involve a struggle with a social adversary and that the stakes of the struggle are the future shape of the institutions of civil society.

82 / Jean L. Cohen

13. Habermas, *The Theory of Communicative Action,* Vol. 2, p. 392.

14. Nancy Fraser, "What's Critical about Critical Theory? The Case of Habermas and Gender," *New German Critique,* No. 35 (Spring/Summer 1985), pp. 97–131. For a different view, see Linda Nicholson, *Gender and History: The Limits of Social Theory in the Age of the Family* (New York: Columbia University Press, 1986).

15. Fraser, "What's Critical about Critical Theory?" p. 111.

16. Fraser, "What's Critical about Critical Theory?" pp. 99–103. She takes Habermas at his word that this distinction is tied to a substantive distinction between the symbolic and material reproduction of the lifeworld. She correctly argues that it is not possible to distinguish among activities on the basis of a "natural-kinds" distinction between the material and the symbolic, and she criticizes Habermas for relying on such assumptions. This criticism echoes our own; see Andrew Arato and Jean L. Cohen, "Politics and the Reconstruction of the Concept of Civil Society," in Axel Honneth et al., eds., *Zwischenbetracthungen Im Prozess der Aufklärung* (Frankfurt: Suhrkamp, 1989). It is not true, though, that dualistic social theory stands or falls with the reified distinction between the symbolic and the material.

17. Habermas, *The Theory of Communicative Action,* Vol. 2, p. 310. For a more detailed discussion of these points, see Ch. 9.

18. For an unconvincing attempt, see Niklas Luhmann, *Love as Passion: The Codification of Intimacy* (Cambridge, MA: Harvard University Press, 1987).

19. Fraser, however, also tends to conflate the level of analysis of coordinating mechanisms with the analysis of the various types of action. She thus insists that strategic and instrumental action occur in lifeworld institutions—in families—and that communicative action (based on patriarchal norms) occurs in the subsystems. But this is not a serious argument against the system/lifeworld distinction; indeed, it is often asserted by Habermas himself. All of the action types appear in all of the institutions. The abstract categories of system and lifeworld indicate only where the weight of coordination lies in a given institutional framework. I would also reject references to the family as an economic system for another set of reasons: The psychodynamics of identity formation in general and of gender identities in particular can hardly be analyzed in such terms.

20. See Alison M. Jaggar, *Feminist Politics and Human Nature* (Totowa, NJ: Rowman and Littlefield, 1988), pp. 51–83, 207–49. See also the classic article by Heidi Hartmann, "The Unhappy Marriage of Marxism and Feminism: Towards a More Progressive Union," in Lydia Sargent, ed., *Women and Revolution* (Boston: South End Press, 1981), pp. 1–42.

21. See Barbara Stark, "Constitutional Analysis of the Baby M Decision," *Harvard Women's Law Journal* 11 (1988), pp. 19–53.

22. Studies of the domestic division of labor indicate that many women want a more equitable division of domestic labor but can't achieve it because of differentials in power and in earning capacity. For a discussion of changing family

patterns and the ways in which women are deprived of equal voice in the family, see Kathleen Gerson, *Hard Choices* (Berkeley: University of California Press, 1985). See also Susan Okin, *Justice, Gender, and the Family* (New York: Basic Books, 1989), pp. 134–70.

23. Moreover, on our view, it is precisely because the family is a core institution in and of civil society (and neither a natural presupposition of civil society nor just one more component of an economic subsystem) that egalitarian principles can be applied to it to a far greater extent than to a firm or a bureaucracy.

24. For an interesting account of the emergence of modern gender roles in the United States in the nineteenth century, see Carl Degler, *At Odds: Women and the Family in America from the Revolution to the Present* (New York: Oxford University Press, 1980). Degler also gives a good account of the debate over the impact of the companionate family form and the cult of domesticity that formed around women's relegation to the roles of wife and mother in the second half of the nineteenth century (see pp. 210–328 especially).

25. See Jean L. Cohen and Andrew Arato, *Civil Society and Political Theory*, (Cambridge, MA: MIT Press, 1992), Ch. 9, note 17, p. 699.

26. See Niklas Luhmann, *Macht* (Stuttgart: Enke Verlag, 1975), pp. 47–48. Luhmann mentions only examples preceding the institutionalization of the medium of power, but he clearly concedes the possibility of the generation and utilization of power outside the political subsystem (p. 91 ff.; he explicitly mentions power in the family). Luhmann provides no reason against the existence of non-media regulated forms of power, despite his general identification of modernity with media-organized forms of interaction. As might be expected, Foucault's work excels in analyzing the nonsystemic, multiple forms of power.

27. Luhmann, *Macht*, pp. 7, 11–12, 22–24.

28. In a formal organization with several operative codes, there can be different forms of inequality—which may or may not converge in the hierarchical summit—as well as nonhierarchical power relations all operating at the same time.

29. Habermas, *The Theory of Communicative Action*, Vol. 2, p. 263. "If responsibility means that one can orient one's actions to criticizable validity claims, then action coordination that has been detached from communicatively achieved consensus no longer requires responsible participants."

30. Such would be the action-theoretic Weberian conception of domination.

31. Habermas, *The Theory of Communicative Action*, Vol. 2, pp. 268–70. Habermas explains in what ways power differs from money as a steering medium.

32. The codes responsible for the transmission of power can take the form of commands linked to threats and involve ordinary language communication. That is, power can operate as "domination" in the action-theoretic sense. It can also operate as a general form of communication; see below.

33. Habermas, *The Theory of Communicative Action*, Vol. 2, p. 275.

34. Luhmann, for example, under the analogous heading of the generalization of influence, speaks of authority, reputation, and leadership, all located at a level of functioning between power as a medium and direct commands. See Luhmann, *Macht*, pp. 75–76. This confirms our point that generalized forms of communication can act as forms of power. I insist, however, that the codes are never entirely fixed but are open to reinterpretation, challenges, and creative appropriatiation by actors.

35. They provide relief from lifeworld complexity but, unlike steering media, do not technicize the lifeworld. See Habermas's discussion in *The Theory of Communicative Action*, Vol. 2, p. 277.

36. Fraser suggests treating gender as a "medium of exchange" in order to account for the way in which it links the various institutional domains. Fraser, "What's Critical about Critical Theory?" pp. 113, 117. Of course, Fraser wants to interpret gender as a medium like money and power. She misses the distinction between steering media and generalized forms of communication and is thus led to the misleading view that gender as a power code functions in the same way as these other media. But this cannot be so, for the reasons given in the text.

37. For an overview of this process in the United States, see Julie Matthaei, *An Economic History of Women in America* (New York: Schocken Books, 1982); Degler, *At Odds;* Joan B. Landes, *Women and the Public Sphere in the Age of the French Revolution* (Ithaca, NY: Cornell University Press, 1988).

38. Landes, *Women and the Public Sphere,* Judith Shklar, *Men and Citizens* (Cambridge, England: Cambridge University Press, 1969).

39. It would, however, be misleading to deduce from the feminist perspective on differentiation discussed above that the institutional articulation of modern civil society is wholly negative. On the contrary, the cultural potentials of modernity have entered into its institutional articulation, albeit selectively. Hence the ambivalent character, reflected in the debates among feminist theorists, of the modern family. The "companionate" family composed of a male breadwinner, a female homemaker, and their children did produce intimacy, privacy, and a new focus on childhood individuality. It also constituted an ideological and institutional terrain in which women could begin to develop their own conception of self and the power to assert control over their bodies and lives. The restriction of women to the domestic sphere, however, went hand in hand with a denial of the most basic rights and of the status of autonomous individuality, personhood, and citizenship, which appeared incompatible with the role of nurturer. By the end of the nineteenth century, the development of the family wage system (fought for by organized male workers), the exclusion of women from the union movement, and the "protective labor laws" that excluded women from most jobs had locked women into a situation of dependency that has only recently begun to be seriously challenged, ideologically and structurally. The feminist perspective thus reveals the double character of the family that is parallel to the dualities of all the public and private institutions in modern civil society discussed in Ch. 9.

40. Fraser admits as much: "A gender-sensitive reading of these arrangements . . .

vindicates Habermas's claim that in classical capitalism the (official) economy is not all-powerful but is, rather, in some significant measure inscribed within and subject to the norms and meanings of everyday life" ("What's Critical about Critical Theory?" p. 118).

41. Fraser, "What's Critical about Critical Theory?" p. 124.

42. Habermas, *The Theory of Communicative Action*, Vol. 2, p. 369.

43. See Lenore Weitzman, *The Divorce Revolution* (New York: Free Press, 1985); Deborah L. Rhode, *Justice and Gender* (Cambridge: Harvard University Press, 1989); Martha Fineman and Nancy Thomadsen, eds., *At the Boundaries of Law* (New York: Routledge, 1991).

44. Oddly enough, it is precisely the idea of a threat to the communicative infrastructure of civil society, articulated in dualistic social theory, that Fraser objects to most. She contests the idea that there is any categorical distinction to be made between welfare reforms addressed to the paid workplace and those addressed to the internal dynamics of the family. For her, the "empirical" ambivalence of reform in the latter case stems from the patriarchal character of welfare systems and not from the inherently symbolic character of lifeworld institutions. Indeed, having rejected the very distinction between system and lifeworld as androcentric, she argues that there is no theoretical basis for differentially evaluating the two kinds of reforms; see Fraser, "What's Critical about Critical Theory?" p. 124. I do not agree.

45. This seems to be Fraser's own position when she points out that there are two different kinds of programs in welfare states: one "masculine," aimed at benefiting principal breadwinners, the other "feminine," oriented toward the "negatives of possessive individuals," to "domestic failures" ("What's Critical about Critical Theory?" pp. 122–23).

46. Habermas, *The Theory of Communicative Action*, Vol. 2, p. 35.

47. Indeed, if I ignore such issues, they will not disappear but will be (and have been) formulated in ways antithetical to feminism. I am thinking of the neoconservative critique of the welfare state, which aims at removing system integrative mechanisms from civil society while retraditionalizing it.

48. There is already an interesting debate among feminists on this issue. The literature is vast; for an entree into the discussion, see Linda Gordon, "What Does Welfare Regulate?" *Social Research* 55, No. 4 (Winter 1988), pp. 609–30, and Frances Fox Piven and Richard A. Cloward, "Welfare Doesn't Shore Up Traditional Family Roles: A Reply to Linda Gordon," *Social Research* 55, No. 4 (Winter 1988), pp. 631–48.

49. For example, once the typical worker is no longer construed as a male breadwinner but as a woman or man who is also likely to be responsible at some point for the care of children or elders, the necessity of revising the structure of labor and of labor-time becomes obvious, and the argument for day-care centers at the workplace, flexible work schedules, and parental leave, for example, becomes stronger. It is surely not accidental that feminists have begun to articulate and fight for these sorts of reforms. Clearly, such efforts must comple-

ment attempts at transforming the gender hierarchies within the institutions of civil society.

50. For a recent discussion of the need to apply norms of justice to the family in particular and to gender relations in general, see Okin, *Justice, Gender, and the Family.* Of course, there are many new movements that seek the opposite goal; the right-to-life movement, for example, has as a basic goal a retraditionalization of the core institutions of civil society.

51. This involves a wide variety of strategies ranging from lobbying Congress or the executive branch, rights-oriented politics focusing on the courts, and working in political parties, depending on the political opportunity structure.

52. For a hermeneutic, participant observation approach, see Sara Evans, *Personal Politics* (New York: Random House, 1979). For an analysis that draws on resource-mobilization theory as well as accounts of role strain and relative deprivation, see Jo Freeman, *The Politics of Women's Liberation* (New York: McKay, 1975). The essays in the volume edited by Mary Fainsod Katzenstein and Carol McClurg Mueller, eds., *Women's Movements of the United States and Europe* (Philadelphia: Temple University Press, 1987), focus on political opportunity structures and public policy; while Ethel Klein, *Gender Politics* (Cambridge, MA: Harvard University Press, 1984), focuses on the role of consciousness in feminist movements. Despite their varied foci, all of these works confirm our thesis that a dual logic was always operative in feminist movements.

53. While their emphases vary, most of the discussions of the origin of the "second wave " of feminism stress the following "structural" changes and technological developments that transformed the role of women in the twentieth century: advances in medical science that lowered the birth rate and the time devoted to childrearing, rising marital instability, labor-saving devices that gave women more time for tasks other than housework, improvements in educational opportunity, integration of women into the workforce, formal integration of women into the polity through acquisition of the right to vote, massive entry of women into universities, displacement of female functions outside the home through urbanization and industrialization, and increased government involvement in providing social services. On their own, however, structural changes cannot account for the genesis or logic of the movement; see Klein, *Gender Politics,* pp. 1–32.

54. Klein, *Gender Politics,* pp. 32–81.

55. A nationwide organizational base, resources, and leadership in the form of traditional women 's volunteer organizations (which were not originally feminist in ideology but focused on women's concerns) was built between 1890 and 1925, and these associations used their resources to promote women's rights up through the 1960s. As in the case of the nineteenth-century women's movement, the contemporary feminist movement emerged in the context of other vital social movements. Moreover, it took advantage of the general reform orientation of the Kennedy and Johnson years. In 1961, President Kennedy

established a Presidential Commission on the Status of Women, the first of its kind, and state-level organizations on women's status soon followed. See Evans, *Personal Politics,* and Klein, *Gender Politics.*

56.   As Ethel Klein aptly puts it, "This traditional lobby could not, by itself, succeed in passing a broad spectrum of women's rights legislation. The efforts of specifically feminist organizations, such as NOW, WEAL, NWPC, and radical women's groups, were critical to rallying the troops and forming the social movement needed to turn the concern for women's issues into action" (*Gender Politics,* p. 5). See also Freeman, *The Politcis of Women's Liberation,* pp. 28–29; Joyce Gelb and Marian L. Palley, *Women and Public Policies* (Princeton: Princeton University Press, 1982), p. 18.

57.   For a comparison of the forms taken by women's movements in various countries, see Joyce Gelb, "Social Movement 'Success': A Comparative Analysis of Feminism in the United States and the United Kingdom," in Katzenstein and Mueller, eds., *Women's Movements of the United States and Europe,* pp. 267–89; "Equality and Autonomy: Feminist Politics in the United States and West Germany," ibid., pp. 172–95; and Karen Beckwith, "Response to Feminism in the Italian Parliament: Divorce, Abortion, and Sexual Violence Legislation," ibid., pp. 153–71.

58.   The main exceptions in this regard are Sweden and Norway. Here, the existence of powerful social democratic parties constituted a different "political opportunity structure" than in the United States, France, and Italy. Many benefits for women were enacted through pressure within these parties and not through the activities of an autonomous feminist movement. However, debates have begun today in these countries as well over the desirability of a more autonomous civil society and of an autonomous feminist movement. See Sylvia Hewlett, *A Lesser Life* (New York: William Morrow, 1986), pp. 341–83; Helga Hernes, *Welfare State and Woman Power* (Oslo: Norwegian University Press, 1987).

59.   See Freeman, *The Politics of Women's Liberation,* pp. 48–50; Klein, *Gender Politics,* pp. 9–31; Gelb and Palley, *Women and Public Policies,* pp. 24–61; Ann N. Costain and W. Douglas Costain, "Strategy and Tactics of the Women's Movement in the United States: The Role of Political Parties," in Katzenstein and Mueller, eds., *The Women's Movements of the United States and Western Europe,* pp. 196–214.

60.   For an account of the emergence of this branch of the feminist movement, see Evans, *Personal Politics.*

61.   While the former at first eschewed the dramatic direct-action efforts of the latter groups and the latter had little interest in the lobbying efforts of insiders such as NOW, the sharp distinction between women's rights advocates ("liberal feminists") and women's liberation groups ("radical feminists") disappeared after 1968. NOW became involved in sponsoring mass protest actions; and when considerable numbers of militant feminists joined local chapters, it also embraced many of the issues of the early radicals (such as abortion) as well as their participatory ideology and their focus on self-determination and autonomy alongside equal rights. At the same time, by virtue of joining organizations such

as NOW, movement activists learned the importance of the politics of influence. For detailed analyses of this trajectory in American feminism, see Costain and Costain, "Strategy and Tactics of the Women's Movement in the United States," and Gelb and Palley, *Women and Public Policies.*

62. Costain and Costain, "Strategies and Tactics of the Women's Movement in the United States," p. 201.

63. As William Scott Heide, head of NOW in 1972, put it, "NOW has worked within and outside the system to initiate change and implement women's rights and laws and executive orders on public contracts. . . . Our tactics and strategy include polite letters, interruption of conferences and Senate committees, demonstrating and consultations, calling for and coordinating the August 26 Strikes for Equality, rhetoric and positive programs, sisterly and brotherly consciousness-raising, experiments with new organizational patterns and leadership styles" (cited in Costain and Costain, "Strategy and Tactics of the Women's Movement in the United States," p. 200).

64. Today the feminist movement is comprised of at least five types of groups: mass-membership organizations; specialized feminist organizations including litigation and research groups; professional lobbies; single-issue groups; traditional women's groups; and an electoral campaign sector that includes PACs and groups operating within the framework of the Democratic party. Feminist associations continue to flourish in civil society and to organize myriad newspapers, magazines, newsletters, direct actions, shelters for battered women, childcare centers, consciousness-raising groups, and so on. Despite the apparent decline in spectacular mass collective actions, the feminist movement continues to target the public sphere to influence consciousness and alter gender norms. The striking spread of women's studies in the universities and in law schools is also worth noting. See Gelb and Palley, *Women and Public Policies,* pp. 26–27; Jo Freeman, "Whom You Know v. Whom You Represent: Feminist Influence in the Democratic and Republican Parties," in Katzenstein and Mueller, eds., *Women's Movements of the United States and Europe,* pp. 215–46.

65. Gelb and Palley, Women and Public Policies, pp. 26–27; Freeman, "Whom You Know"; Klein, *Gender Politics,* pp. 29–33.

66. Costain and Costain, "Strategy and Tactics of the Women's Movement in the United States," p. 203.

67. Gelb and Palley, *Women and Public Policies,* pp. 26–27; Freeman, "Whom You Know."

68. *Reed v. Reed,* 404 U.S. 71 (1971); *Roe v. Wade,* 410 U.S. 113 (1973). Successes have sometimes been limited or followed by significant reversals. In the case of sex discrimination, feminists have failed to get sex included as a "suspect classification" under the fourteenth amendment or to secure passage of the ERA. In the case of abortion, since *Roe v. Wade* courts and legislatures have been cutting back on women's right to choose, and a vocal antiabortion movement has emerged. Moreover, within the feminist movement, debates have arisen around every "success" as the limits of legal reform along the lines of equal rights have become felt. None of this obviates our more general point.

69. I am not arguing that feminists or women initiated the reforms alluded to above. In many instances, reform processes were initiated by other interest groups for reasons having nothing to do with women's interests or feminist concerns. The institution of no-fault divorce in California and even the initiation of the reform of abortion laws are cases in point. Nevertheless, the dynamics of these reforms were informed by the feminist discourse and, soon thereafter, by feminist activists. See Weitzman, *The Divorce Revolution*; and Kristin Luker, *Abortion and the Politics of Motherhood* (Berkeley: University of California Press, 1984).

70. Until women came to be perceived as individuals, the politics of equal rights had no chance of success. And until the patriarchal structure of the domestic sphere and its negative influence on other domains of society was thematized and challenged, equal or equivalent rights could never be equal for women.

71. Gelb and Palley, *Women and Public Policies*, p. 45.

72. Klein, *Gender Politics*, p. 92.

73. Klein, *Gender Politics*, p. 92.

74. Things look different in practice, however. For a discussion of the gendered division of labor at home and at work and the difficulties this continues to impose on women, see Gerson, *Hard Choices*. For statistics on the continuing wage gap between women and men and the feminization of poverty in the United States, see Hewlett, A Lesser Life, pp. 51–138.

75. Katzenstein and Mueller, eds., *Women's Movements of the United States and Europe*, passim.

76. Jane Jenson, "Changing Discourse, Changing Agendas: Political Rights and Reproductive Policies in France," in Katzenstein and Mueller, eds., *Women's Movements of the United States and Europe*, pp. 64–65. By "universe of political discourse," Jenson means the set of beliefs about how politics should be conducted, the boundaries of political discussion, and the kinds of conflicts resolvable through political processes. The universe of political discourse functions as a gatekeeper to political action, selecting or inhibiting the range of actors, issues, policy alternatives, alliance strategies, and collective identities available for achieving change.

77. Jenson, *Changing Discourse, Changing Agendas*, pp. 68–80. Women got the vote in France in 1945 as a reward for service in the resistance, at a time when the feminist movement was moribund. The Loi Neuwirth of 1968 legalized contraception for married women but also restricted the advertising of contraceptives and their use by single women. The primary intent of the law was to help families control their fertility to meet family goals of material well-being and emotional support for children, not to give women a choice over whether or not to have children. Women were still defined within a family frame of reference.

78. Jenson, *Changing Discourse, Changing Agendas*, pp. 80–86.

79. Gelb and Palley, *Women and Public Policies*, p. 30. Feminists have also challenged male conceptions of the standards of justice.

80. The abortion debate has also challenged male conceptions of rights or, rather, of the person to whom rights apply. It should not come as a surprise that this debate has posed a fundamental challenge to the very conception of rights, since it has been notoriously difficult to conceive of a right to abortion along the traditional lines of a right to one's body as one's own property when in that body there is another potential person who clearly does not "belong to" one as property. But on a nonpossessive, individualist model of rights, it becomes clear that the legal personhood, moral subjectivity, and particular identity of women are at stake, and these outweigh the state's interest in fetal life in the first trimester.

81. See Anita Allen, *Uneasy Access: Privacy for Women in a Free Society* (Totowa, NJ: Rowman and Littlefield, 1988).

82. Jenson, "Changing Discourse, Changing Agendas," pp. 82–83. For an insightful analysis of the feminist discourse on abortion and its conflict with traditionalist discourses, see Luker, *Abortion and the Politics of Motherhood.*

83. By insisting that women be recognized as individuals, persons, and citizens as well as situated women, the contemporary feminist movement brings together the values of universalism, plurality, and difference. By implication, the concept of equality before the law itself is being altered, for it can no longer mean that equal rights and nondiscrimination apply only to those who are similarly situated. This is because women and men can never be similarly situated when it comes to the question of abortion or reproductive rights generally.

3

The Public and the Private Sphere: A Feminist Reconsideration

Joan B. Landes

After a quarter-century delay, Jürgen Habermas's *Strukturwandel der Öffentlichkeit* appeared finally in English translation in the MIT Press series "Studies in Contemporary German Social Thought," edited by Thomas McCarthy. Habermas's philosophical-historical critique of the concept and function of the public sphere in England, France, and Germany (with some parting glances at the United States) from the Renaissance to the twentieth-century served as a direct inspiration for the German New Left and opened up new lines of scholarship and political debate in Germany and Western Europe. The 1989 translation coincided with a series of events (radical transformations in Eastern Europe, the bloody suppression of the democracy movement in China, and the bicentennial celebrations of the French Revolution) which once again pointed to the pertinence of Habermas's diagnosis of civil society for democratic theory and practice. Originally submitted to the Philosophical Faculty at Marburg as the author's *Habilitationsschrift,* the book deserves to be celebrated as a classic: It has stood the test of time, surviving the fortunes of mercurial literary tastes and changing intellectual seasons; its new translation has widened markedly the author's circle of readers. Nowadays, one is just as apt to hear "Habermas talk" at humanities or legal studies meetings as among social scientists, philosophers, media critics, or feminist theorists.

In the spirit of dialogue, I approach *The Structural Transformation of the Public Sphere* from the interrelated standpoints of critical theory, political thought, and intellectual history, with a special interest in questions of gender. I will review the model of the public sphere that Habermas derives from eighteenth-century philosophy and society, as well as his account of the rise of democratic social institutions, "universalistic" cultural practices, and the structures of "bourgeois representation" during the age of Enlightenment and Revolution. I lay particular stress on recent scholarship concerning eighteenth-century France. In place of a language-centered model of representation, I will emphasize the multiplicity of representation in human communication. Likewise, I will ask whether Habermas's normative subject is sufficiently multidimensional, embodied, or gendered to account for the organization of power in different cultural settings. Nonetheless, in my estimation, Habermas's text sets a high standard for the kind of political communication research that can help to bridge present divisions between literature, political theory, and philosophy, on the one hand, and history, on the other. By isolating the public sphere as a structure within civil society, Habermas established a new field of research on the political, distinguishable from both a narrower definition of the state and from a more broadly conceived "political system." By focusing on the "structural transformations" of the public sphere, Habermas invited concrete investigations of specific forms of political and cultural life, the benefits of which continue to be realized.[1]

Ironically, this gifted historical-sociological account was produced by an author whose later works earned him a reputation for rigorous, abstract, "rationalistic" scholarship. In this context, an analogy with the recovery of Marx's "early writings" may be instructive. Marx had been dead for over half a century when the rediscovery of these writings prompted a fundamental philosophical reappraisal of his science. To be sure, *Strukturwandel der Öffentlichkeit* is among Habermas's most influential and widely translated books into languages other than English. Still, as Thomas McCarthy acknowledges, a more timely translation of Habermas's book "would likely have facilitated the reception of his thought among Anglo-American scholars by showing how the more abstract and theoretical concerns of his later work arose out of the concrete issues raised in this study."[2] While McCarthy's observations are to the point, the problematic of *Strukturwandel* can also be appreciated on its own terms, or at least somewhat independently of the trajectory taken in Habermas's later writings. The path taken by the independent European reception of the book leads towards feminist and critical theorists who are reconstructing the original model of the public sphere, and to those scholars who are charting the possibilities for what is variously called the "new historicism" or the "new cultural and intellectual history." In this regard, we might consider whether Habermas has set forth a program for what might yet become a "new historicism" in political or sociological theory.[3]

The Public Sphere as a Category of Bourgeois Society:
Defense of Modernity?

Construed as a narrative of modernity, *Strukturwandel* reads as a tale of the rise of the public sphere (against great political obstacles posed by censorship and other forms of political despotism practiced by the absolutist state); its triumph (in the vibrant institutions of a free press, clubs, philosophical societies, and the cultural life of early liberal society, and through the revolutionary establishment of parliamentary and democratic regimes); and its fateful decline (under the pressures of a late capitalist economy and state). In short, a sorrowful voyage from reason to mediatized consumption.[4] Are we then in the company of another "dialectic of Enlightenment"? Has the once autonomous and rational subject ended life as a candidate for Foucault's disciplinary society of total surveillance? Is this an early anticipation of Habermas's plaint against the "colonization of the lifeworld"; a Marxist protest against capitalist economic and state organization; or perhaps a civic republican defense of virtue against the evils of commerce?

Surely, Habermas shares with others a dark outlook on modern public culture. Those who would characterize him as a blind and bland proponent of modernity therefore risk misunderstanding the complexity of his vision and the novelty of his attempt to sketch an historically saturated discourse theory of society.[5] Nor is language in some abstracted sense Habermas's sole object of concern. Rather, he proposes to investigate the political effects of a specific discourse on society, along with the institutional (that is, social and cultural) preconditions for this discourse to have come into existence in the first place. By beginning with an etymology of the terms public and private, Habermas signals from the outset the inherited ideological weight of these categories. He observes how the vocabulary of Greek political categories stamped by Roman law characteristic of the Renaissance civic republican tradition continues to structure political scholarship on the topic of public life even in the late twentieth century.[6] Inviting his readers to examine their own unacknowledged premises about public and private matters, Habermas proceeds to a critical reconstruction of the category of the modern bourgeois public sphere by way of its immediate historical antecedents.

Just as feudal authority could not be made to fit the Roman law contrast between private dominion (*dominium*) and public autonomy (*imperium*), so too according to Habermas medieval "lordship was something publicly represented. This *publicness* (or *publicity*) *of representation* in late medieval society was not constituted as a social realm, that is, as a public sphere; rather, it was something like a status attribute." Hence, the lord "displayed himself, presented himself as an embodiment of some sort of 'higher' power."[7] Habermas calls attention to the features of visibility, display, and embodiment; that is, the "aura" that surrounded and endowed the lord's concrete existence. He observes that something of this legacy is preserved in recent constitutional doctrine where representation is deemed to be a public, never a "private" matter. Moreover, these medieval features of staged publicity are fundamental to the "re-presentative" public sphere of absolutist society within early modern territorial nation-states. The "re-presentative" public sphere was not a sphere of political communication, nor did it require any permanent location. Rather, it was marked by the staged performance of authority, displayed before an audience, and embodied in the royal subject. After the Renaissance, aristocratic society also came less to represent its own lordliness (its manorial authority) and to serve more as a vehicle for the representation of the monarch. Thus, the grand spectacle of absolutism required a repeated reenactment of the sources and conditions of public power through festivals, balls, banquets, coronations, and entry ceremonies in which the visual aspects of theater were in command.

Habermas relates the genesis of the bourgeois public sphere to changes in the social organization and communication networks of early modern territorial states: the growth of urbanism, capitalist commerce and stock markets, new systems for news and the mail, and finally, state administrations for taxation and "policing" subject populations. Consequently, civil society came into existence "as the corollary of a depersonalized state authority."[8] To a well-worn view of the privatization of economic production, Habermas adds a strong appreciation for the role performed by a new set of cultural institutions that flourished in urban centers: coffeehouses, clubs, reading and language societies, lending libraries, concert halls, opera houses, theaters, publishing companies, lecture halls, salons, and above all, journals and the commercial press. He charts the way in which state authorities first made use of the press as a vehicle for addressing its promulgations to the public, and he identifies the crucial position of a new stratum of the bourgeoisie within the educated, literate public of late seventeenth and eighteenth-century society. Thus, Habermas marks the emergence of a critical public within Old Regime society:

> Because, on the one hand, the society now confronting the state clearly separated a private domain from public authority and because, on the other hand, it turned the reproduction of life into something transcending the confines of private domestic authority and becoming a subject of public interest, that zone of continuous administrative contact became 'critical' also in the sense that it provoked the critical judgment of a public making use of its reason. The public could take on this challenge all the better as it required merely a change in the function of the instrument with whose help the state administration had already turned society into a public affair in a specific sense—the press.[9]

The bourgeois public sphere is conceived to be a sphere of private people coming together as a public through the "historically unprecedented" public use of their reason. This informal association of private persons mediated between, on the one hand, civil society (the economy or sphere of commodity exchange and social labor) and the family, and, on the other hand, the state (the realm of the police or state administration and the court). The bourgeois public sphere consists of both a literary/cultural and political public sphere. Habermas addresses the process whereby culture was constituted as an object for discussion and packaged for purchase. At the same time, he insists that the literary public sphere functioned as a precursor to the public sphere operative in the political domain. "It provided the training ground for a critical public reflection still preoccupied with itself—a process of self-clarification of private people focusing on the genuine experiences of their novel privateness."[10] Nor could this have occurred without the emergence of a new form of the private sphere—the patriarchal conjugal family's intimate domain—and the intensification of processes of (psychological) individualism. As a result, an audience oriented subjectivity on the part of private individuals promoted the commodification of culture and served the polemical functions of the political public sphere.

Anticipating what Stephen Greenblatt has termed "self-fashioning," Habermas describes the interplay between the codes of intimacy characteristic of fiction (the novel), the forms of subjectivity that were fitted to print, and the appeal of literature to a widening public of readers.[11] Likewise, by appropriating aspects of the Frankfurt School's account of "authority and the family," Habermas concludes that the experiential complex of audience-oriented privacy affected the political realm's public sphere. He thereby undermines Hannah Arendt's despairing survey of the emergence of the categories of the social and the private.[12] Accordingly, Habermas rejects the Greek model of a citizenry acting in common to administer the law and to ensure the community's military survival. Instead he locates the *specificity* of the modern public sphere in the civic task of a society engaged in critical public debate to protect a commercial economy. In contrast to the older *res publica*, he deems the bourgeois public sphere to be the site for the political regulation of civil society, and credits it with a willingness to challenge the established authority of the monarch. Such a public sphere was from the outset both private and polemical. Neither trait was characteristic of the Greek model of the public sphere:

> for the private status of the master of the household, upon which depended his political status as citizen, rested on domination without any illusion of freedom evoked by human intimacy. The conduct of the citizen was agonistic merely in the sportive competition with each other that was a mock war against the external enemy and not in dispute with his own government.[13]

In this manner, Habermas critically reconstructs the specific contours of the modern public sphere. He provides nuanced descriptions of the distinctive institutions of eighteenth-century French, British, and German society: e.g., *salons*, coffeehouses, and *Tischgesellchaften*. Acknowledging their differences, he nonetheless identifies a series of common institutional criteria that they shared. First, the ideal of equality was institutionalized and stated as an objective claim insofar as a kind of social intercourse occurred irrespective of social status so that the authority of the better argument could assert itself against that of social hierarchy. Second, cultural communities, stripped of their former "aura" and extracted from their ties to the Church's and court's re-presentative forms of publicity, established new meanings and new domains of common concern based on rational, verbal communication among private people. Third, no matter how inclusive the newly constituted public may have been in practice, the issues discussed became general in their significance and in their accessibility. In principle, everyone had to *be able to participate*.

On the basis of these social criteria, Habermas claims that the "liberal fiction of the discursive formation of the public will" was created.[14] In addition, political objections to the secret dictates of absolute sovereignty encouraged appeals to general, abstract, objective, and permanent norms: e.g., to constitutional law wherein "a rationality in which what is right converges with what is just; the exercise of power is to be demoted to a mere executor of the norm."[15] Against secrecy and will, the new rationality—anchored in the principle of critical public debate among private people—held out the goals of publicity and universality.

But Habermas also grants the practical limitations of the bourgeois model of the public sphere. From the outset, a tension arose between the formal criteria of abstract moral reason and the goals of substantive rationality. Ambivalences in the principle of privacy derived from the system of private property and from a family caught up in the requirements of the market. In addition, conflicts arose in the identity of the privatized individuals who occupied the public sphere, insofar as their status derived either from a position as property owners rather than from their basic humanity; e.g., a conflict between Rousseau's *bourgeois* and *citoyen*. Hence, class and its accoutrements (property, income, literacy, and cultural background) were major barriers to full participation in the bourgeois public sphere.[16] The bourgeois public sphere was for the most part a restricted male preserve, except for salon society that was shaped by women "like that of the rococo in general."[17] Still, Habermas suggests that the exclusion of women from English coffeehouses may have been an advantage insofar as "critical debate ignited by works of literature and art was soon extended to include economic and political disputes, without any guarantee (such as was given in the *salons*) that such discussions would be inconsequential, at least in the immediate context."[18] On the other hand, he distinguishes between the literary and the political sphere, observing that whereas women and dependents were factually and legally excluded from the political public sphere, "female readers as well as apprentices and servants often took a more active part in the literary public sphere than the owners of private property and family heads themselves."[19]

One Public or Many? Where are the Women?

By Habermas's own account, then, the oppositional bourgeois public sphere only partially achieved its stated goals of equality and participation. But he sees this as a limitation of actually existing society, not of the model of a universal public according to which pre-existing social inequalities are bracketed. Within the region of social discourse, he believes, a public body is created wherein the differential rights of private individuals cease to matter. Yet, there were strong requirements for admission to this club as to any other. Even if property did not become a topic for discourse, it remained the precondition for participation in the bourgeois public sphere. Furthermore, because the public sphere and the conditions for publicity presupposed a distinction between public and private matters, it was ill equipped to consider in public fashion the political dimension of relations in the intimate sphere. Equally disabling was the expectation that all those who engaged in public discourse would learn to master the rules of disinterested discourse. Under ideal conditions, then, the members of a theoretical public were to behave according to the bourgeois liberal principle of abstract equality. Just as the laws of market assumed a certain forgetfulness concerning the real existence of property, so too the laws of the public sphere were predicated on the principle of disinterestedness and on the observance of the norms of reason not power, rationality not domination, and truth not authority. Still, Habermas never asks whether certain subjects in bourgeois society are better suited than others to perform the discursive role of participants in a theoretical public.

In my study *Women and the Public Sphere in the Age of the French Revolution*, however, I argued that Habermas's formulation effaces the way in which the bourgeois public sphere from the outset worked to rule out all interests that would not or could not lay claim to their own universality.[20] The notion of an enlightened, theoretical public reduced to "mere opinion" (cultural assumptions, normative attitudes, collective prejudices, and values) a whole range of interests associated with those actors who would not or could not master the discourse of the universal. Moreover, the structural division between the public sphere, on the one hand, and the market and the family, on the other, meant that a whole range of concerns came to be labeled as private and treated as improper subjects for public debate. Habermas overlooks the strong association of women's discourse and their interests with "particularity," and conversely the alignment of masculine speech with truth, objectivity, and reason. Thus, he misses the masquerade through which the (male) particular was able to posture behind the veil of the universal.

In any event, none of this was the accidental consequence of the lesser status of women in pre-liberal society, to be amended in a more democratic order. Rather, the resistance of enlightened liberal and democratic discourse to femininity was rooted in a symbolization of nature that promised to reverse the spoiled civilization of *le monde* where stylish women held sway and to return to men the sovereign rights usurped by an absolutist monarch. Furthermore, when women during the French Revolution and the nineteenth century attempted to organize in public on the basis of their interests, they risked violating the constitutive principles of the bourgeois public sphere: In place of one, they substituted the many; in place of disinterestedness, they revealed themselves to have an interest. Worse yet, women risked disrupting the gendered organization of nature, truth, and opinion that assigned them to a place in the private, domestic but not the public realm. Thus, an idealization of the universal public conceals the way in which women's (legal and constitutional) exclusion from the public sphere was a constitutive not a marginal or accidental feature of the bourgeois public from the start.

From parallel vantage points, other feminist scholars have also challenged the presuppositions of an abstract, universal model of the public sphere. Mary Ryan queries whether "the olympian notion of a sphere of rational deliberation may be incompatible with genuine publicness, with being open and accessible to all."[21] She traces women's entrance into public spaces in nineteenth-century America despite the strong barriers confronting them in the officially sanctioned public sphere. Yet, the pressures of social diversity meant that the public sphere was subject to powerful gender, race, class and regional cleavages. Anna Yeatman challenges the one-sided model of individuality on which universal citizenship in the natural rights tradition has been grounded.[22] Nancy Fraser draws a lesson from several historical investigations of the public sphere, observing that because Habermas failed to examine examples of nonliberal, nonbourgeois, or competing public spheres, "he ends up idealizing the liberal public sphere." Fraser observes that "virtually from the beginning, counterpublics contested the exclusionary norms of the bourgeois public, elaborating alternative styles of political behavior and alternative norms of public speech"[23] that bourgeois publics in turn attempted to block. She concludes that in both stratified and egalitarian societies, a multiplicity of publics is preferable to a single public sphere; and that an adequate conception of the public sphere would countenance the inclusion, not the exclusion, of interests and issues "that bourgeois masculinist ideology labels 'private' and treats as inadmissable."[24]

A question arises as to whether a universalistic discourse model can — ☆ satisfy conditions of genuine equality. I have suggested that the virtues of universality and reason are offset by the role they play within a system of Western cultural representation that has eclipsed women's interests in the private domain and aligned femininity with particularity, interest, and partiality. In this context, the goals of generalizability and appeals to the common good may conceal rather than expose forms of domination, suppress rather than release concrete differences among persons or groups. Moreover, by banishing the language of particularity, the liberal public sphere has jeopardized its own bases of legitimation in the principles of accessibility, participation, and equality. Last, I have argued that style and decorum are not incidental traits but constitutive features of the way in which embodied, speaking subjects establish the claims of the universal in politics.[25]

In complementary fashion, Seyla Benhabib argues that a range of distinctions in the Western philosophical tradition—between justice and the good life, norms and values, interests and needs—have operated to confine women and typically female spheres of activity like housework, reproduction, nurturance and care for the young, the sick, and the elderly to the "private" domain. "These issues have often been considered matters of the good life, of values, of non-generalizable interests ... and treated, until recently, as 'natural' and 'immutable' aspects of human relations. They have remained pre-reflexive and inaccessible to discursive analysis."[26] Iris Young also protests that "the Enlightenment ideal of the civil public where citizens meet in terms of equality and mutual respect is too rounded and tame an ideal of public. This idea of equal citizenship attains unity because it excludes bodily and affective particularity, as well as the concrete histories of individuals that make groups unable to understand one another."[27] In this light, we might consider whether Habermas's ideal representation of the public sphere or his normative description of the subject are perhaps too tame to accommodate the dilemmas raised by feminist critics.

Subjects, Actors, and Spectators

According to Habermas, the modern bourgeois public sphere came into existence when private persons joined together to exercise their reason in a public fashion. Public opinion is the end product of all the dialogues between discoursing individuals, each one of whom is capable of reflexive self-questioning and successful at internalizing the rules of rational discourse. In contrast, Hannah Arendt conceives of the political realm of the polis as rising directly out of acting together, the "sharing of words and deeds" that in turn generates a "space of appearances."[28] Both Habermas and Arendt agree on the potential of words or discourse to generate power, and they set this potential of the public sphere apart from violence or force. But, Arendt locates power not merely in the associational space, but also in the competition for excellence that occurs among actors who are by definition moral and political equals.[29] She deems action to be the only sphere in which individuals may distinguish themselves, even to the point of "greatness;" they do so through word and deed when they narrate the distinctive story of their own lives.[30] Through story telling, then, men "create their own remembrance."[31] Indeed, the polis is "a kind of organized remembrance."[32]

Now, Habermas has distanced himself justifiably from Arendt's antimodernistic perspective; her seeming indifference to the emancipation of women, workers, and minorities; her uncritical attitude toward property relations in the polis; and her agonistic view of the public sphere. He grasps that Arendt's individuals are a rather narrow slice of the human population: in Athens, the propertied, free, slave-holding men who inhabited the world of the *polis*, in contrast to women and slaves who belonged to the *oikos*, the sphere of biological reproduction and property. Still, Habermas has learned a great deal from Arendt's discussion of the public sphere, and the two theorists share a strong appreciation for the political implications of speech and language.[33] But Habermas's individuals participate in the public sphere as speakers and readers (of novels and the press). In contrast, in Arendt's public sphere individuals perform deeds and narrate stories; they are not just talking heads but embodied, suffering subjects who move in the world in relation to others. Such a world is a "web of relationships" constituted by "enacted stories." Neither labor (the metabolic interaction with nature) nor work (the making of products), but action produces relationships that bind people together. Action discloses the agent in the act; otherwise it loses its specific character. So, Arendt believes, it is in performing rather than writing the story that each actor reveals his individuality. She even submits that actors are not the authors of their own stories:

> Although everybody started his life by inserting himself into the human world through action and speech, nobody is the author or producer of his life story. In other words, the stories, the results of action and speech, reveal an agent, but this agent is not an author or producer. Somebody began it and is its subject in the twofold sense of the word, namely, its actor and sufferer, but nobody is its author.[34]

Thus, Arendt appreciates several dimensions of the public sphere absent from Habermas's discursive model. Although she is nowhere concerned either with women or with the gendered construction of subjectivity, certain aspects of her discussion are worthy of feminist's attention. Arendt addresses

value of Arendt

the performative dimension of human action and human speech. She implies that insofar as persons display themselves in public, they do so as storytellers, revealing aspects of their selves by acting in and through their bodies. Perhaps most radically, Arendt suggests that the subject is displaced within a wider communication network. Still, let us not confuse her metaphors of the stage with a poststructuralist abandonment of the subject. Her foremost objective is to describe and exalt exemplary moral actions. In that respect, she sees the theater as the political art *par excellence*, the site where the political sphere of human life is transposed into art. And, she holds out a privileged role for historians who reconstitute stories already told and for political theorists who narrate exemplary stories about the political.[35]

A radically different perspective on the intimate relationship between theater and politics—and, politics as theater—is offered in Marie-Hélène Huet's *Rehearsing the Revolution: The Staging of Marat's Death, 1793-1797*. In a sense, Huet picks up where both Arendt and Habermas leave off. In place of "the message," on the one hand, or the endless circuit of opinion, on the other, Huet investigates the spectatorial function of the always already theatricalized public sphere. Drawing on Diderot's remarks in *Jacques le fataliste*, she discovers some striking parallels between the spectator of a judicial action and of an aesthetic work. First, Huet asserts it is not the message that interests the spectator: "What interests the spectator is the spectacle per se. His position as a receiver is established, constituted, made use of, independently of the significance of the message received. There is not one public thirsting for blood and tortures and another public eager for entertainments and pleasures; a public is formed the moment there is a spectacle." Second, like Diderot, Huet appreciates the possibility of a transmutation from the role of spectator-receiver to that of actor; for in retelling every spectator has the potential to act. As she observes, "Diderot is ... describing the formation of a *mise en scène*, a 'rehearsal' properly speaking, in which the spectator ultimately finds his justification: to have become an actor."[36]

In place of a retrospective ideological analysis of public participation, Huet pursues a semiotic approach. She underscores the implicit reversibility, as well as the incompleteness and alienation that constitutes the role of the spectator/receiver:

> Inherent in the notion of the spectator is that of the future actor; part of the pleasure of the spectacle lies in anticipation of another spectacle in which the spectator will finally be actor. To appeal to an audience is to appeal to this possibility of a spectator-actor exchange, and an audience that does not achieve this exchange, this cycle, this transformation, is a mutilated audience.[37]

Now, Huet is concerned specifically with the production of the French revolutionary public, which she sees as being "inscribed in a tradition that consists in repressing by means of the spectacle."[38] She observes how the legislation freeing the theaters was accompanied by new regulations, constant surveillance of audiences and plays, a Rousseauian preference for open air festivals and an accompanying suspicion of the closed theatrical chamber—emblem, it was believed, of counter-revolutionary designs. Although Huet cautions against conflating the revolutionary dynamic with political liberalism, her argument adds immeasurably to a general understanding of the performative dimensions of the bourgeois public sphere. Likewise, she challenges us to consider the alienated and mutilating features of the open spaces of public speech which Habermas and Arendt otherwise celebrate. In contrast to the latter, Huet focuses attention not only on the actors but on the shared forms of representation between theater and politics. In very different terms than Habermas, Huet describes the communication network of a theoretical public—that public which acts as both spectator and judge and presumes its judgment will always be right.[39] She concludes that during the Revolution this theoretical public was composed of the people who were invited by the legislators to the deliberations of the juries as a guarantor of justice and a protection of the innocent. Yet, she cautions, "they were carefully separated from the spectacle to which they were exposed, they were subjected to a rule of silence, and they were constantly held to the passive role of spectators."[40]

In a provocative essay, *The Body and the French Revolution*, Dorinda Outram adds a heightened concern with physicality and gender to structural accounts of political culture conceived solely in verbal terms. By way of a phenomenology of embodiment, Outram resituates many of the features of Huet's theatrical politics, Arendt's public sphere and its public actors, and Habermas's public opinion.[41] She argues that the construction and use of dignified bodies—in Arendt's terms, their "enacted stories"—became a source of authority in both the private and public realm. However, the other side of this new political culture of the body involved the sanctioning of physical violence in the revolutionary process and the planting of seeds of self-destructiveness in the individual. In place of an abstracted classicism or a celebration of agonistic relations for their own sake, then, Outram discerns that stoicism and other classical motifs were reworked by a new revolutionary class that faced the task of "creating a new political embodiment for the individuals concerned and a new audience for their politics."[42]

The Revolution's most essential feature may not have been the production of a new state, but rather the production of new public spaces dominated by the authoritative public bodies of individuals. Men created models of heroic masculinity through dignity, self-containment, and suicide. Not surprisingly, many historians have observed that the political culture of the Revolution aimed "to redistribute various attributes of the king's body throughout the new body politic." As Outram explains,

> The public space of France before 1789 had also focused on an image of heroic public dignity almost exclusively applied to monarchy and aristocracy: it was such images that the middle class had to re-create. The new public bodies which they created and filled with attributes of heroic dignity were in turn inconceivable without, and were created for, the audiences that mass politics made possible. They possessed the power, which the competing linguistic discourses obviously did not, to focus dignity and legitimacy in incontestable, because non-verbal, ways on the bodies of known individuals who acted as personifications of value systems.[43]

For Outram, the body is not an undifferentiated object and behavior is not indifferent. She argues that the victory of *homo clausus*, "the male type validated by his separation of affect from instinct, by body-separation from other individual human beings," was achieved over and against traits associated with the feminine and popular behavior encapsulated in the carnavalesque.[44] She views the Revolution as a contest between male and female, resulting in the validation of only male political participation, supported by images of heroic masculinity. In social and philosophical terms,

> *Homo clausus* legitimated himself by his superiority to the somatic relations enjoyed by other classes—aristocracy, peasants, and workers—and by the other gender. In other words, what he possessed was a body which was also a non-body, which, rather than projecting itself, retained itself. In doing so, it became the location of abstract value-systems, such as rationality and objectivity. As Pierre Bourdieu has remarked such a move is integral to the production of middle-class systems of cultural hegemony, which privilege over-arching *languages*, such as the language of objectivity and rationality, rather than privileging energy or displays of integration between body and personality: display is characterized as aristocratic, emotionality and subjectivity as feminine, physical energy as plebian.[45]

Unlike Habermas, then, Outram unequivocally links the production of new public spaces to a new gender division in bourgeois public culture. In contrast to Arendt's vision of the polis as a sphere of organized remembrance and her celebration of agonistic action, Outram underscores the fragility of the poses of heroic dignity: "unlike fully sacralized bodies which exist *above* time, desacralized ones exist *in* time. They can only really find validation through death—not through re-creation."[46] She proposes that personal autonomy has been purchased at the price of exclusion (of women and the lower classes); that the subject's "self image of rationality, reflexivity, universalism, autonomy, individuation, and emancipation always [contain] the potential for transposition into its direct opposite."[47] Thus, to Habermas's version of the modern subject, Outram holds up the mirror of Horkheimer and Adorno's "dialectic of Enlightenment;" and it is by no means inconsequential that in that mirror she finds the faces of women and workers.

Whose Opinion?

Revisionist historians of the Revolution have sketched an equally disturbing portrait of how revolutionary politics strove toward absolute consensus, monitoring and expelling all instances of division within the revolutionary public. Rather than a contest over interests, revolutionary politics became the site of symbolic legitimations.[48] Benjamin Nathans aptly relates the challenge that recent historiography poses to Habermas's model of the public sphere:

> One finds here a stunning reversal of Habermas's principle of general accessibility: rather than adjusting the public sphere (as embodied by the various clubs) to accommodate society, society was radically tailored by a series of brutal excisions and exclusions in order to fit the mold of a fictitious public of abstract individuals. The exclusion of 'enemies,' in fact, took the place of critical discussion as the mechanisms for establishing the 'general good.' Behind the fiction of a unified, authoritative public opinion, an anonymous oligarchy thus 'prefabricated consensus' in the form of an ideology that acted as a substitute for the nonexistent public competition of ideas.[49]

In fact, Habermas has observed that the discursively organized public under the terms of bourgeois representation claimed not to equate itself with *the* public "but at most claimed to act as its mouthpiece, in its name, perhaps even as its educator."[50] Yet, he holds out the possibility that a distance can be maintained between *the* public and its representative (the one who claims to speak in its name). In direct contrast, François Furct presents the problem posed by popular sovereignty as that of eccentricity: the center is always vacant. Revolutionary politics is inherently unstable: because the source of sovereignty resides everywhere and nowhere, there is a perpetual slippage between the public and its representatives. As he states, "the Revolution replaced the conflict of interests for power with a competition of discourses for the appropriation of legitimacy."[51] Furthermore, in their respective investigations of the art public and the revolutionary festival, Mona Ozouf and Thomas Crow exhibit the repressive potential of the didactic or educative role that Habermas assigns to the public's representative.[52] In addition, Sarah Maza reveals the way in which late Old Regime lawyers used the device of the *mémoires judiciares* to publish their (otherwise censurable) views and to influence the outcome of a given trial. Thus, by appealing to public opinion, they exploited the capacity of the public to serve as a tribunal for the nation.[53] These and other empirical studies construct a much more complex picture of the workings of the oppositional public sphere than Habermas allows. Indeed, Keith Baker and Mona Ozouf have even challenged the notion that the new public sphere offered a straight-forward alternative to the traditional system. They demonstrate that the monarchy was forced to compete for the judgment of public opinion, so that contestatory politics also shaped the regime's evolution.[54]

Yet, Habermas is not unaware of the conceptual and political problems posed by a concept of public opinion as transcendent reason. In an immensely rewarding chapter titled "The Bourgeois Public Sphere: Idea and Ideology," he charts the most conspicuous philosophical contributions to the concept of public opinion beginning with Hobbes, Locke, and Bayle, proceeding through the English and European thinkers of the eighteenth century (the physiocrats, Rousseau, Forster, Kant, and Hegel) and concluding with the critical reflections of Marx, Tocqueville, and Mill on a range of difficulties such as the role of property interest, class restrictions on the free circulation of opinion, the distorting functions of propaganda, the problems of majority rule, the issue of tolerance, and the compulsion toward conformity. His final appraisal, however, is that neither the liberal nor the socialist model were adequate for a diagnosis of the breakdown of the public sphere, especially in its loss of critical publicity deriving from both too much and too little publicity. As he remarks, "The *principle* of the public sphere, that is, critical publicity, seemed to lose its strength in the measure that it expanded as a *sphere* and even undermined the private realm."[55]

Analytically, this assessment only makes sense against the backdrop of the eighteenth-century model. There, Habermas locates a crucial tension between the principle of critical publicity, on the one hand, and a legislative model of opinion, on the other. In France, the former is associated with the physiocrats and the latter with Rousseau. Thus, he observes, "only when the physiocrats ascribed it to the *public éclairé* itself did *opinion publique* receive the strict meaning of an opinion purified through critical discussion in the public sphere to constitute a true opinion."[56] In contrast to their British contemporaries who understood the public spirit to be an authority that could compel lawmakers to legitimize themselves, the physiocrats still acceded to absolutism. Yet, conceptually they achieved a novel fusion of the older contradiction between *opinion* and *critique*. [57] On the other hand, Habermas argues that "Rousseau projected the unbourgeois idea of an intrusively political society in which the autonomous private sphere, that is, civil society emancipated from the state, had no place."[58] He situates the undemocratic foundations of "Rousseau's democracy of unpublic opinion" in the manipulative exercise of power:[59]

> The general will was always right, the notorious passage stated, but the judgment that guided it was not always enlightened. . . . A direct democracy required that the sovereign be actually present. The *volonté générale* as the *corpus mysticum* was bound up with the *corpus physicum* of the people as a consensual assembly. The idea of a plebiscite in permanence presented itself to Rousseau in the image of the Greek *polis*. There the people were assembled in the square without interruption; thus in Rousseau's view, the *place publique* became the foundation of the constitution. *Opinion publique* derived its attribute from it, that is, from the citizens assembled for acclamation and not from the rational-critical public debate of a *public éclairé*. [60]

We have seen that Habermas's neat analytical distinction between the publicity function of opinion and its tendency to absolutize itself has been challenged in recent studies of eighteenth-century political culture. While rejecting Rousseau's democracy of "unpublic opinion" and registering the limits of opinion in a class-bound society, Habermas still adheres to a physiocratic concept of publicity, not withstanding its appeal to a transcendent concept of reason. He most favors Kant's cosmopolitan version of enlightenment—stripped perhaps of some of its "moral" wrapping—predicated on free and open communication between rational beings, each of whom possesses knowledge of the world ("humanity"). These citizens, Kant tells us and Habermas concurs, are engaged in rational-critical discussions concerning the affairs of the commonwealth. They are citizens of a "republican constitution" who enjoy a sphere of private autonomy, the safeguarding of personal liberties, equality before the law, and legislation that conforms to the popular will. Notably, they are not storytellers but rather critical disputants who know how to use their reason on behalf of the common good. In Kant's estimation, "if we attend to the course of conversation in mixed companies consisting not merely of scholars and subtle reasoners but also of business people or women, we notice that besides storytelling and jesting they have another entertainment, namely, arguing."[61]

Print and Other Media: On the Multiple Forms of Representation
Kant's model of free publicity is a direct antecedent of Habermas's interest in communicative action: different versions of a language-based model of

human communication.[62] Yet in the last instance, we are dealing not only with a prejudice toward "linguisticality," but with a compelling account of the historical emergence of textuality as the dominant form of representation in the modern bourgeois public sphere, in contrast to visuality or theatricality in the "re-presentative" public sphere of the Old Regime. Now, there is much to commend this position. It calls attention to a dramatic shift in the organization of the system of representation which I likened to a shift from icon to text in my own study of the gendered public sphere. However, further consideration suggests that a singular emphasis on language may be misleading from both a methodological and an empirical perspective.

The privilege that Habermas accords to the institutions of the press and literature has been only partially sustained in subsequent examinations of the eighteenth-century public sphere. On the one hand, research on the French language press before and during the Revolution has augmented Habermas's appreciation for the central contribution played by the print media in the rise of public opinion.[63] Investigations of the workings of provincial academies, free-masonry and salon society, as well as the role of literary and art criticism have more than repaid Habermas's invitation for a text-centered criticism; and sustained his insight that reading practices are best understood not merely as a personal habit but as a new kind of institution.[64] Indeed, even those who view the Revolution as a "return to the oral" acknowledge that the culture of the spoken word "always rests on writing or printing."[65]

On the other hand, studies of the print media and political discourse have introduced complexities not originally entertained by Habermas. Robert Darnton's portrait of critical journalism in late Old Regime France—hack writers in the cafes of "Grub Street"—subverts any representation of the literary profession restricted to its most successful, enlightened publicists. By implication, Darnton also challenges Habermas's effort to link literary subjectivity and political criticism by presenting the *libelle*, not the confession, as the characteristic genre of the period.[66] Likewise, Bernadette Fort finds in the parodic art criticism of Darnton's Grub Street an appropriation of figures, forms, and strategies from popular theater and from carnival.[67] Contributors to Lynn Hunt's recent collection *Eroticism and the Body Politic* explore the intimate connections among political, sexual, and gender themes in printed and graphic political pornography within Old Regime and revolutionary France. Together, then, these studies offer a perspective on political representation that diverges in good measure from Habermas's explication of rational and introspective forms of political opinion.[68] In addition, other scholars point to the restrictiveness of a narrowly defined print model. The selections in *Revolution in Print* demonstrate the extent to which political messages were communicated through a range of media that employed mechanically reproduced words or images.[69] And, studies of the revolutionary graphic arts explore how political communication is manifested through visual as well as textual means.[70] In short, even in a period which saw the incontestable triumph of the print media, the production of complex representations involved as well the creative intermixing of media. Political arguments, we may want to allow, may be communicated in discursive and non-discursive forms, and the two may interact in unanticipated ways.

Furthermore, Habermas has noted but hardly accounted for the symbolic structure of bourgeois representation; that is, the ability of one to stand in for, substitute for, or otherwise represent an absent other who remains the only legitimate source of authority for that representative. To speak in the people's name, to act on its behalf, and to claim to do so on behalf of the universal or general good, all bespeak a fundamental alienation in the source and nature of power. As Michael Warner observes, the transition from what Habermas would term the "oppositional" bourgeois public sphere to the national state was grounded in a cultural formation of print discourse, and not just in the legitimacy of the people or the rule of law:

> It required assumptions between individual subjects and general sovereignty. These assumptions derived not just from any popular group, but from a model of a reading public. Through the new constitutionalism, the metapolitics of print discourse became entrenched as an ideology of legitimate power. If this is a way of saying that the modern state commits a kind of fraud in claiming to represent the people and the law, it is no simple fraud. For the fraud is only the pretense that representational democracy derives its legitimacy from the people and their law, when in fact it performs what it claims to describe. A way of representing the people constructs the people.[71]

In practice, democratic discourse has exhibited an unfortunate potential for substituting its own universal for the real competition of interests. Likewise, appeals to the universal have concealed the gendered division of space and power; and, the creation of open spaces for public speech has fostered a conception of a transcendent, theoretical public which sanctioned the silent participation of spectators. In any event, I have observed that not all speech-acts or styles of talking are necessarily equal. More generally, by privileging speech-acts Habermas distorts the performative dimension of human action and interaction. In the specific context of the bourgeois Revolution, for example, an analysis of the iconography of power in the new republic might want to describe the theatrics and arguments of the Assembly as well as its published laws and proclamations; and further, to explore the graphic arts as well as acoustic media—speech, song, and music—alongside printed and verbal discourse. Habermas may be right to assume that certain representations are privileged for the representation of power in a given regime—hence textual representations under the early bourgeois regime. On the other hand, a theory of "public representations" needs to account for the culturally variant ways that humans produce and make use of multiple representations. Pragmatics, the formal use of language in interaction, is best accompanied by a theory and observation of (stylized and informal) bodily gestures and postures. As Dorinda Outram insists, "words do not give up their full meaning without an account of the physical behaviour which accompanies them." We are in agreement, then, on the need to examine "both verbal and physical behaviour and both verbal and physical symbolism"; while recalling that "physicality [is] always mediated, for individuals, by words."[72]

Prospects for a Democratic Public Sphere

Of all Habermas's feminist critics, Benhabib is perhaps most optimistic that "the discourse model, precisely because it proceeds from a fundamental norm of egalitarian reciprocity and precisely because it projects the democratization of all social norms, cannot preclude the democratization of familial norms and of norms governing the gender division of labor. Once this is granted, the distinction between matters of justice and those of the good life, between generalizable interests and culturally interpreted needs, can be reconceptualized."[73] Benhabib is confident that once practical discourse is "feminized," the emancipatory aspirations of new social movements such as the women's movement can be best served by the radical proceduralism of the discourse model. In a more critical vein but with many of the same objectives in mind, Fraser exhorts that we need "a post-bourgeois conception that can permit us to envision a greater role for (at least some) public spheres than mere autonomous opinion formation removed from authoritative decision-making.[74]

By problematizing Habermas's initial conception of enlightened opinion and public space, I have sought to underscore just how radical the revisions proposed by Benhabib and Fraser would have to be in order to arrive at a process of deliberation and opinion formation from which no subject or person is barred. On the other hand, my intention is not to discount but rather to join in their efforts to democratize and feminize the public sphere. For Benhabib's discursive conditions to obtain, the constraints placed on opinion formation by the authoritative structures of a non-egalitarian polity and economy would need not only to be bracketed but eliminated entirely. Nor could the gendered construction of an embodied subjectivity and the body politic remain an unexamined premise. Likewise, we would have to allow for the intersecting and multiple media of representation in any given setting.

These are utopian but not impossible goals. There is ample evidence, despite the barriers posed by the hegemonic order, that a democratic politics in the present would have been from the outset a politics of the public sphere, not of the state. Habermas's alertness to a zone of democratic participation— neither state, economy, nor family—is as pertinent to today's circumstances as to those of the late eighteenth century. Paradoxically, we seem to be once again in a period where iconic relations on the model of the older "re-presentative" public sphere count for more stylistically and substantively than the symbolic, predominantly textual relations promoted by the early bourgeois public sphere. Yet, our task is surely not to resort to texts in place of images, but instead to comprehend and deploy all means of representation in a counterhegemonic strategy against established power wherever it resides.

NOTES

1. For an investigation of the public sphere under welfare state conditions and a consideration of the role of mediatized publics under late capitalism, see "The Phantom Public Sphere" issue of *Social Text* 25/26 (1990); and the forthcoming collection *Habermas and the Public Sphere*, ed. Craig Calhoun (Cambridge, MA: MIT Press, 1991), not available at this writing. For an excellent appraisal by a French historian, see Benjamin Nathans, "Habermas's 'Public Sphere' in the Era of the French Revolution," *French Historical Studies* 16:3 (Spring 1990), pp. 620–44.

2. Jürgen Habermas, *The Structural Transformation of the Public Sphere: An Inquiry into a Category of Bourgeois Society,* trans. Thomas Burger with the assistance of Frederick Lawrence. (Cambridge, MA: MIT Press, 1989 [Orig. 1962]), p. xi.

3. See *The New Historicism,* ed. H. Aram Veeser (New York: Routledge, 1989); Hans Kellner, *Language and Historical Representation: Getting the Story Crooked* (Madison: The University of Wisconsin Press, 1989); Dominick LaCapra, *Rethinking Intellectual History: Texts, Contexts, Language* (Ithaca, NY: Cornell University Press, 1983); idem., *History and Criticism* (Ithaca, NY: Cornell University Press, 1985); Dominick LaCapra and Steven L. Kaplan, *Modern European Intellectual History: Reappraisals and New Perspectives* (Ithaca, NY: Cornell University Press, 1982); Keith Michael Baker, *Inventing the French Revolution* (Cambridge, England: Cambridge University Press, 1990).

4. Habermas has been charged by some new style media critics with a one-sided dismissal of media structured by advertising and the capitalist profit motive. Pushing the argument further, a group of cultural analysts attempt to reappraise the relationship between performance and audience in light of what they see as a present-day crisis in the spectacle form itself. See e.g., Paolo Carpignano, et. al., "Chatter in the Age of Electronic Reproduction," *Social Text* 25/26 (1990), pp. 33–55.

5. See Jürgen Habermas, "Modernity—An Incomplete Project" in *The Anti-Aesthetic: Essays on Postmodern Culture*, ed. and intro. Hal Foster (Port Townsend, WA: Bay Press, 1983).

6. Since *Strukturwandel's* publication, a rich literature on the topic of civic republicanism has been produced, spurred on by J.G.A. Pocock's seminal study, *The Machiavellian Moment: Florentine Political Thought and the Atlantic Republican Tradition* (Princeton, NJ: Princeton University Press, 1975). Unfortunately, Habermas does not clarify well enough the role of republicanism. Some readers have perhaps mistaken some of what he says about civic republicanism for an argument on liberalism.

7. Habermas, *The Structural Transformation of the Public Sphere*, p. 7.

8. Habermas, *The Structural Transformation of the Public Sphere*, p. 19.

9. Habermas, *The Structural Transformation of the Public Sphere*, p. 24. Or, as Habermas also states: "The *publicum* developed into the public, the *subjectum* into the [reasoning] subject, the receiver of regulations from above into the ruling authorities' adversary." Habermas, *The Structural Transformation of the Public Sphere*, p. 26.

10. Habermas, *The Structural Transformation of the Public Sphere*, p. 29.

11. Stephen Greenblatt, *Renaissance Self-Fashioning: From More to Shakespeare* (Chicago: University of Chicago Press, 1980).

12. Against intimacy, or what she regards as the modern world's flight into the inner subjectivity of the individual, and the tendency for wealth to take over the public realm, Arendt contrasts the ancients' practice of hiding the body—hence labor and reproduction, women and slaves—as well as property within the sphere of the household (oikos). See *The Human Condition* (Chicago: The University of Chicago Press, 1958).

13. Habermas, *The Structural Transformation of the Public Sphere*, p. 52.

14. Jürgen Habermas, *Theory and Practice*, trans. John Viertel (Boston: Beacon Press, 1973), p. 4.

15. Habermas, *The Structural Transformation of the Public Sphere*, p. 53.

16. Habermas does cite one instance of a more broadly popular sphere, the English coffeehouse where the poor artisan, craftsman, and shopkeeper mingled with their betters. Habermas, *The Structural Transformation of the Public Sphere*, pp. 32–33. For another appraisal, see Terry Eagleton, *The Function of Criticism: From "The Spectator" to Post-Structuralism* (London: Verso/NLB, 1984).

17. Habermas, *The Structural Transformation of the Public Sphere*, p. 33.

18. Habermas, *The Structural Transformation of the Public Sphere*, p. 33.

19. Habermas, *The Structural Transformation of the Public Sphere*, p. 56.

20. Joan B. Landes, *Women and the Public Sphere in the Age of the French Revolution* (Ithaca, NY: Cornell University Press, 1988).

21. Mary Ryan, *Women in Public: Between Banners and Ballots, 1825–1880*

(Baltimore: The Johns Hopkins University Press, 1990), p. 13.

22. Anna Yeatman, "Beyond Natural Right: The Conditions for Universal Citizenship," *Social Concept* 4:2 (June 1988), pp. 3–32.

23. Fraser, "Rethinking the Public Sphere," *Social Text* 25/26 (1990), p. 61.

24. Fraser, "Rethinking the Public Sphere," p. 77.

25. In another context, Jane Mansbridge has observed how styles of deliberation may serve as masks for domination and render mute the claims of members of disadvantaged groups. See her "Feminism and Democracy," *The American Prospect*, No. 1 (Spring 1990), and discussion of Mansbridge by Nancy Fraser, "Rethinking the Public Sphere," p. 64.

26. Seyla Benhabib, "Models of Public Space: Hannah Arendt, the Liberal Tradition and Jürgen Habermas," unpublished paper, p. 29. Benhabib goes on to mention Habermas's defense against these charges. She agrees with him that in principle the distinction between "justice" and "the good life" in moral theory and the categories of "public" and "private" in sociological theory need not overlap, but she argues that they have done so in the modern social contract tradition from Locke to Rawls to which Habermas is indebted partly in his discourse theory of ethics. Cf. Benhabib, "The Generalized and the Concrete Other: The Kohlberg-Gilligan Controversy and Feminist Theory" in *Feminism as Critique; On the Politics of Gender*, eds. and intro. Seyla Benhabib and Drucilla Cornell (Minneapolis: University of Minnesota Press, 1987); and Nancy Fraser, "What's Critical about Critical Theory? The Case of Habermas and Gender" in *Feminism as Critique*.

27. Iris Marion Young, "Impartiality and the Civic Public: Some Implications of Feminist Critiques of Moral and Political Theory," in *Feminism as Critique*, p. 76.

28. Arendt, *The Human Condition*, p. 198.

29. Arendt seems to take for granted the conditions of slavery, labor, and gender division of labor which are the basis for the equality between free propertied male subjects in the sphere of the polis. On Arendt's anti-modernism, see Hanna Pitkin, "Justice: On Relating Public and Private," *Political Theory* 9:3 (1981), pp. 327–52; Seyla Benhabib's forthcoming *The Reluctant Modernism of Hannah Arendt*; George Kateb, *Hannah Arendt: Politics, Conscience, Evil* (Totowa, NJ: Rowman and Allanheld, 1983).

30. "Action can be judged only by the criterion of greatness because it is in its nature to break through the commonly accepted and reach into the extraordinary, where whatever is true in common and everyday life no longer applies because everything that exists is unique and sui generis." Arendt, *The Human Condition*, p. 205.

31. Arendt, *The Human Condition*, p. 208. On story telling, see Melvyn A. Hill, "The Fictions of Mankind and the Stories of Men," in *Hannah Arendt: The Recovery of the Public World*, ed., Melvyn A. Hill (New York: St. Martin's, 1979); Elizabeth Young Bruehl, "Hannah Arendt's Storytelling," *Social Research*, 44:1 (Spring 1977), pp. 183–90; Benhabib, "Models of Public

Space: Hannah Arendt, the Liberal Tradition and Jürgen Habermas."

32. Arendt, *The Human Condition*, p. 198. "It assures the mortal actor the reality that comes from being seen, being heard, and, generally, appearing before an audience of fellow men, who outside the *polis* could attend only the short duration of the performance and therefore needed Homes and 'others of his craft' in order to be presented to those who were not there." Ibid.

33. Cf. Jürgen Habermas, "Hannah Arendt's Communications Concept of Power," *Social Research* 44:1 (Spring 1977), pp. 3–24.

34. Arendt, *The Human Condition*, p. 184.

35. "Action reveals itself fully only to the storyteller, that is, to the backward glance of the historian, who indeed always knows better what it was all about than the participants," *The Human Condition*, p. 192.

36. Marie-Hélène Huet, *Rehearsing the Revolution: The Staging of Marat's Death, 1793–1797* (Berkeley: University of California Press, 1982), p. 33.

37. Huet, *Rehearsing the Revolution*, p. 34.

38. Huet, *Rehearsing the Revolution*, p. 35.

39. Dolf Sternberger observes that Arendt had in mind a model of the citizen in the polis performing a dual role of actor and spectator, though she draws none of the disturbing conclusions from this relationship that I have seen in Huet. In any event, Sternberger reproduces an important passage from the German edition of *The Human Condition* omitted in the English text. There, Arendt speaks of the citizen "in an auditorium in which everyone is watching and performing at the same time." Cited in Dolf Sternberger, "The Sunken City: Hannah Arendt's Idea of Politics," *Social Research* 44:1 (Spring 1977), pp. 134–35. It is interesting to consider Arendt's remarks here in light of Rousseau's estimation of the festival as a moment of pure transparency where there is no division between the roles of spectator and actor. On this theme, see Jean Starobinski, *Jean-Jacques Rousseau: Transparency and Obstruction*, trans. Arthur Goldhammer, intro. Robert J. Morrissey (Chicago: University of Chicago Press, 1988).

40. Huet, *Rehearsing the Revolution*, p. 37.

41. For an explicit and related critique of Habermas's theory of communicative competence, see Theodore Mills Norton, *Language, Communication, and Society: Jürgen Habermas, Karl-Otto Apel, and the Ideal of a Universal Pragmatics* (Ph.D. dissertation, New York University, 1981).

42. Dorinda Outram, *The Body and the French Revolution* (New Haven, CT: Yale University Press, 1989), p. 69.

43. Outram, *The Body and the French Revolution*, p. 4.

44. Outram, *The Body and the French Revolution*, pp. 16, 158.

45. Outram, *The Body and the French Revolution*, p. 158.

46. Outram, *The Body and the French Revolution*, p. 160.

47. Outram, *The Body and the French Revolution*, p. 164.

48. See François Furet, *Interpreting the French Revolution*, trans. Elborg Forster (Cambridge: Cambridge University Press, 1981); Lynn Hunt, *Politics, Culture and Class in the French Revolution* (Berkeley: University of California Press, 1984); Patrice Higonnet, "'Aristocrate,' 'Aristocratie': Language and Politics in the French Revolution," in *The French Revolution 1789–1989: Two Hundred Years of Rethinking*: a special issue of *The Eighteenth Century: Theory and Interpretation* (Lubbock: Texas Tech University Press, 1989); Keith Michael Baker, ed., *The Political Culture of the Old Regime* (Oxford: Pergamon Press, 1987).

49. Nathans, "Habermas's 'Public Sphere' in the Era of the French Revolution," pp. 643–44.

50. Habermas, *The Structural Transformation of the Public Sphere*, p. 37.

51. Furet, *Interpreting the French Revolution* p. 49. Cf. François Furet and Mona Ozouf, eds., *A Critical Dictionary of the French Revolution*, trans. Arthur Goldhammer (Cambridge, MA: The Belknap Press of Harvard University Press, 1989).

52. Mona Ozouf, *Festivals and the French Revolution*, trans. Alan Sheridan (Cambridge, MA: Harvard University Press, 1988); Thomas Crow, *Painters and Public Life in Eighteenth-Century Paris* (New Haven, CT: Yale University Press, 1985).

53. Sarah Maza, "Le Tribunal de la nation: Les Memoires judiciares et l'opinion publique à la fin de l'ancien régime," *Annales: Economies, Société, Civilisations* 42:1 (January–February 1987), pp. 73–90. Cf. Maza, "The Rose-Girl of Salency: Representations of Virtue in Prerevolutionary France," *Eighteenth-Century Studies* (Spring 1989), pp. 395–412. Mona Ozouf notices that the key word in late old regime evocations of public opinion was "tribunal," implying that all must appear before this infallible judge. This anonymous, impersonal tribunal was to be visible to all "'Public Opinion' at the End of the Old Regime," *The Journal of Modern History*, Vol. 60, Supplement (September 1988), pp. S1–S21.

54. Baker, *Inventing the French Revolution*; idem., "Politics and Public Opinion under the Old Regime: Some Reflections" in *Press and Politics in Pre-Revolutionary France*, eds. Jack R. Censer and Jeremy D. Popkin (Berkeley: University of California Press, 1987); Ozouf, "'Public Opinion' at the End of the Old Regime," p. 58 and passim.

55. Habermas, *The Structural Transformation of the Public Sphere*, p. 140.

56. Habermas, *The Structural Transformation of the Public Sphere*, p. 95.

57. Whereas Ozouf agrees with Habermas's attribution of a key place to the physiocrats, she places more emphasis than he on the absolutist or coercive strain in their thinking, deriving from their appeal to a transcendent Reason. See her "'Public Opinion' at the End of the Old Regime" and "Public Spirit" in *A Critical Dictionary of the French Revolution*.

58. Habermas, *The Structural Transformation of the Public Sphere*, p. 97.

59. Thus, Habermas distances himself from a dominant Rousseauist strain in so

many versions of Marxist, anarchist and radical political thought and practice.

60. Habermas, *The Structural Transformation of the Public Sphere*, pp. 98–99.

61. Kant, *Critique of Practical Reason*, cited in Habermas, p. 106.

62. Habermas distinguishes "discourse ethics" from Kant's ethics in "Morality and Ethical Life: Does Hegel's Critique of Kant Apply to Discourse Ethics?" See this and other contributions to *Moral Consciousness and Communicative Action*, trans. Christian Lenhardt and Shierry Weber Nicolsen, intro. Thomas McCarthy (Cambridge, MA: The MIT Press, 1990).

63. For two excellent overviews, see Jeremy Popkin, "The Press and the French Revolution after Two Hundred Years," *French Historical Studies* 16:3 (Spring 1990), pp. 664–83; idem, "The French Revolutionary Press: New Findings and New Perspectives," *Eighteenth-Century Life* 5 (1979), pp. 90–104. I also appraise these developments in a review essay on print culture during the French Revolution, *Eighteenth-Century Studies* (forthcoming). Notable studies to consult include: Robert Darnton and Daniel Roche, eds., *Revolution in Print: The Press in France 1775–1800* (Berkeley: University of California Press, 1989); Jack R. Censer, *Prelude to Power* (Baltimore: The Johns Hopkins University Press, 1976); Jeremy D. Popkin, *The Right-Wing Press in France, 1792–1800* (Chapel Hill, NC: The University of North Carolina Press, 1980); idem., *News and Politics in the Age of Revolution: Jean Luzac's Gazette de Leyde* (Ithaca, NY: Cornell University Press, 1989); idem, *Revolutionary News: The Press in France, 1789–1799* (Durhan, NC: Duke University Press, 1990); Jack R. Censer and Jeremy Popkin, eds., *Press and Politics in Pre-Revolutionary France* (Berkeley: University of California Press, 1987); Claude Labrosse and Pierre Retat, *Naissance du Journal Revolutionnaire 1789* (Lyon: Presses Universitaires de Lyon, 1989); Pierre Retat, ed., *La Révolution du Journal, 1788–1794;* Paris: CNRS, 1989; Klaus Herding and Rolf Reichardt, *Die Bildpublizitstik der Französischen Revolution* (Frankfurt: Suhrkamp, 1989).

64. Daniel Roche, *Le Siécle des Lumieres en Province: Academies et académiciens provinciaux, 1660–1783,* 2 vols. (Paris, 1978); Maurice Agulhon, *Pénitents et Francs—Maçons de l'ancienne Provence* (Paris: Fayard, 1968); Anthony Vidler, *The Writing of the Walls: Architectural Theory in the Late Enlightenment* (New York: Princeton Architectural Press, 1987); Thomas Crow, *Painters and Public Life in Eighteenth-Century Paris* (New Haven, CT: Yale University Press, 1985); Dena Goodman, "Enlightenment Salons: The Convergence of Female and Philosophic Ambitions," *Eighteenth-Century Studies* 22:3 (Spring 1989), pp. 329–50; Robert Darnton, *The Business of Enlightenment: A Publishing History of the Encyclopédie 1775–1800* (Cambridge, MA: Harvard University Press, 1979); outside France, see especially Elizabeth L. Eisenstein, *The Printing Press as an Agent of Change: Communications and Cultural Transformations in Early-modern Europe,* Vols. I and II (Cambridge: Cambridge University Press, 1979); Peter Uwe Hohendahl, *The Institution of Criticism* (Ithaca, NY: Cornell University Press, 1982); Michael Warner, *The Letters of the Republic: Publication and the Public Sphere in Eighteenth-Century America.* (Cambridge, MA: Harvard

116 / Joan B. Landes

University Press, 1990); Anna Lena Lindberg, *Konstpedagogikens dilemma: Historiska rötter och moderna strategier* (Lund, Sweden: Studentlitteratur, 1991).

65. Roger Chartier, cited in Popkin, "The Press and the French Revolution," p. 682. Cf. Roger Chartier, *The Cultural Uses of Print in Early Modern France,* trans. Lydia G. Cochrane (Princeton, NJ: Princeton University Press, 1987); Roger Chartier, ed., *The Print: Culture of Power and the Uses of Print in Early Modern Europe,* trans. Lydia G. Cochrane (Princeton, NJ: Princeton University Press, 1989); Roger Chartier and Henri-Jean Martin, eds., *Histoire de l'edition française: Le livre triomphant, 1660–1830* (Paris: Fayard/Promodis, 1990).

66. Robert Darnton, *The Literary Underground of the Old Regime* (Cambridge, MA: Harvard University Press, 1982).

67. Bernadette Fort, "Voice of the Public: The Carnivalization of Salon Art in Prerevolutionary France," *Eighteenth-Century Studies* 22:3 (Spring 1989), pp. 368–95.

68. Lynn Hunt, ed., *Eroticism and the Body Politic* (Baltimore: The Johns Hopkins University Press, 1991).

69. Darnton and Roche, eds. *Revolution in Print.*

70. See *French Caricature and the French Revolution, 1789–1799* (Los Angeles, Grunwald Center for the Graphic Arts, 1988); Antoine de Baecque, *La Caricature Revolutionnaire,* preface Michel Vovelle (Paris: CNRS, 1988); Claude Langlois, *La Caricature Contre-Revolutionnaire* (Paris: CNRS, 1988); Michel Vovelle, ed., *Les Images de la Révolution française* (Paris: Publications de la Sorbonne, 1988); Joan B. Landes and Sura Levine, eds., *Representing Revolution: French and British Images. 1789–1804* (Amherst: Mead Art Museum, Amherst College, 1989).

71. Warner, *The Letters of the Republic,* p. xiv.

72. Outram, *The Body and the French Revolution.* pp. 34, 151.

73. Benhabib, "Models of Public Space," p. 34.

74. Fraser, "Rethinking the Public Sphere," p. 76.

4
Women and the "Public Use of Reason"

Marie Fleming

Jürgen Habermas's first major work was a study of the historical emergence of the European liberal public sphere at the end of the eighteenth century and its subsequent transformation under the pressure of working-class politics.[1] Though published as long ago as 1962, the book remained virtually unknown on this side of the Atlantic until its recent (1989) appearance in English under the title *The Structural Transformation of the Public Sphere: An Inquiry into a Category of Bourgeois Society*.[2] Reacting to the critical attention[3] that has accompanied the English edition of his book, Habermas recently said that, on an empirical level, he has "learned most from the criticisms that point to the exclusionary mechanisms of the public sphere, liberal or postliberal."[4] Such criticisms are also, potentially, fundamental challenges to his 1962 finding that inclusiveness was the public sphere's crucial justificatory claim. At the very least, the theorization of exclusion which is taking place in several academic disciplines suggests that the public sphere of modernity, in its liberal (bourgeois) and subsequent forms, might be thought of as structured by a logic of inclusion and exclusion.

Even on Habermas's account, the bourgeois public had to survive the challenges of a "plebeian" public that functioned for a time during the French Revolution and that persisted in some form in the Chartist and anarchist movements of the nineteenth century.[5] He has recently been charged with having unjustifiably "idealized" the liberal public sphere by

overvaluing its principle of inclusiveness and by paying insufficient attention to the exclusionary mechanisms that were operative from the moment
of its historical constitution.[6] From that perspective Habermas's argument
directs attention to the powerful dynamic of a literate public and rein-
scribes, at the level of analysis, the historical repression of the illiterate
(uneducated) publics which also claimed to represent the "people." In the
new (and lengthy) foreword to the 1990 edition of his book (which was
released in Germany with the original text intact),[7] he agrees that, in 1962,
he underestimated the plebeian public sphere's significance by thinking of
it as "merely a variant" of the bourgeois one. However, he maintains that
the class- and culture-specific groups which challenged bourgeois hegemony already shared the communication structures that came to distinguish the late eighteenth and early nineteenth centuries. Though he would
now produce a more nuanced picture, he continues to hold to the "larger
outline of the process of transformation" that he developed in 1962.[8]

Habermas's analysis is similarly put to the test on the question of
gender exclusion. In the years since the first publication of his book, feminist writers[9] have raised troubling questions about the consequences for
democratic theory of the historical confinement of women to the domestic
space of the private sphere. Joan Landes, whose study of France was
conceptually indebted to Habermas's book, argues that the potential for a
more gender-balanced public, embodied in the women-friendly salons of
the eighteenth century, was lost with the institutionalization of bourgeois
norms at the time of the French Revolution.[10] Carole Pateman's recent
work can be read as an implicit attack on the premises of Habermas's
account. She argues that the bourgeois idea of a social contract, which was
designed to secure civil rights for men, has historically and logically
presupposed a sexual contract, which secures men's sex-right or political
right to women's bodies.[11]

In 1990, in response to questions about the gender dimensions of the
bourgeois public sphere,[12] Habermas concedes that "the exclusion of
women from this world dominated by men now looks different than it
appeared to me [in 1962]."[13] However, he undermines the basis for
Pateman's scepticism about modernity's potential by suggesting that her
critique still appeals to "rights to unrestricted inclusion and equality,
which are an integral part of the liberal public sphere's self-interpretation."[14] The argument implicit in this remark is that Pateman too is a
participant in the discourse of modernity, and in a performative sense, she
acknowledges its legitimacy.

Habermas's argumentative strategy raises further questions, however.
We still need to account for the exclusionary practices that barred women
from the public sphere, and we also need to theorize the changes that are

required to meet women's claims to "rights to unrestricted inclusion and equality." The model he developed some thirty years ago to explain the internal dynamic of the public sphere cannot simply be extended to meet newer feminist critiques: "if one seriously tries to make room for the feminist dynamic of the excluded other," he writes, ". . . the model . . . is conceived too rigidly." If his (1962) model is too rigid to account for gender, then the question of how it could be improved is somewhat of a mystery. "The tensions that come to the fore in the liberal public sphere must be depicted more clearly as potentials for a self-transformation." He defuses the issue by identifying gender exclusion, along with plebeian exclusion, as "aspects . . . whose significance [he had] underestimated." He also insists that "a mistake in the assessment of the significance of certain aspects does not falsify the larger outline of the process of transformation" that he presented in 1962.[15] In the last analysis he stands by that work and admits that the social theory which he has been elaborating over the last three decades has changed "less in its fundamentals than in its degree of complexity."[16]

Habermas has seriously underestimated the challenge of contemporary feminism, and he is mistaken in thinking that he can simply stand by the "larger outline" of his earlier analysis. In this essay I shall argue that his model of the internal dynamic of the public sphere not only is unable to point the way to gender freedom, but that it actually presupposes gender exclusion.

I shall dissociate the question of women's exclusion from that of the repression of the historically competing publics. I also want to distinguish my concerns from those of Landes. My focus is upon the gender dimensions of the newly emerging liberal public, and for my present purposes I classify the "pre-literate" salon-based publics along with the "illiterate" ones as explicitly in conflict with the bourgeois model.[17] More to the point for my analysis are the attempts, documented by Landes and others, of those women who actually sought—but were denied—inclusion into the bourgeois public that survived its competitors' challenges.[18] My general question is why women who did not challenge bourgeois ideals were denied the right to full and equal participation in the "public use of reason" that, according to Habermas, structured the liberal public sphere. By raising that question I hope to make explicit those aspects of the operation of the "public use of reason" that might otherwise remain obscure in the notion of alternative publics.

The first section of my essay is a critical examination of Habermas's discussion of the genesis of the "public use of reason." The second is a review of the model of the contradictory institutionalization of the public sphere that he developed in his book to explain why the liberal public sphere's internal dynamic could accommodate class-based challenges. In the third section, I show how that model is constituted by the category of gender, even though it rests formally upon the category of class. I conclude by suggesting the implications of my analysis for an understanding of the gender relations of modernity.

Genesis of the "Public Use of Reason"

Habermas begins his book, *The Structural Transformation,* with a detailed investigation of the historical and legal uses of the terms "public" and "private." The discussion ranges from the practices of antiquity, through the feudal ages, and into the bourgeois period. However, the discourse of public and private is inadequate to explain the bourgeois "public use of reason," and to make up this deficit he resorts to a structural argument based in gender relations. Though the structural argument actually disrupts his narrative of public and private, the diachronic dimensions of his argument remain dominant and the structural argument—despite its crucial importance—remains underthematized. My aim in this part of the essay is to show why Habermas's narrative requires supplementation by the structural argument.

According to his diachronic account, the "public use of reason" was historically rooted in the art of rational-critical public debate which bourgeois intellectuals had learned from encounters with courtly-noble society. The latter, having gained increasing independence from the court, became a cultural-political force in the "town" where it played an important role in the promotion of institutions devoted to reading and discussion—the coffee-houses, salons, and *Tischgesellschaften*. In the salons and their counterparts Habermas discerns institutional criteria that would distinguish the discourse of modernity. For example, the social intercourse of the participants embodied not so much a presupposition of equal status as a total disregard of status. "*Les hommes*, private gentlemen, or *die Privatleute* made up the public not just in the sense that power and prestige of public office were held in suspense; economic dependencies also in principle had no influence." The important point, he contends, is not whether the idea of the public was actually realized in the salons, coffee houses, and *Tischgesellschaften*, but that it became "institutionalized and thereby stated as an objective claim." Another feature of the new discursive activity was the problematization of areas of life formerly not subject to question. At a time when the rational orientation involved in capitalism demanded ever-greater information, it was only a matter of time before interpretation in philosophy, literature, and art would escape the monopoly held by church and court. "To the degree . . . to which philosophical and literary works and works of art in general were produced for the market and distributed through it, these culture products became similar to that type of information: as commodities they became in principle generally accessible." However exclusive the actual public, it was always embedded in "a more inclusive public of all private people, persons who—insofar as they were propertied and educated—as readers, listeners, and spectators could avail themselves via the market of the objects that were subject to discussion." Inclusiveness was also promoted by the emergence of a concert-going public, which developed when admission on the basis of payment turned musical performances into commodities. Music, like literature and philosophy, thereby assumed the form of cultural products freed of ties to a purpose set by court or church. The history of the theater is somewhat more complex, but here too, Habermas maintains, a "public in the strict sense of the word" could come into existence only when the theater declined as an expression of courtly publicity.[19]

Habermas views the culture of the "town" and the salons as a bridge between the collapsing courtly form of publicity and the new publicity connected with the emerging bourgeois public sphere. The commodification of culture, already a factor in the literary institutions of the urban nobility, was thus further intensified by bourgeois intellectuals who learned the art of rational-critical public debate in their adventures in the "towns." This bridging thesis presents difficulties, however, because it cannot explain the *specificity* of bourgeois publicity.

Habermas's initial attraction to the classical bourgeois public sphere was rooted in an effort to recover its emancipatory potential for critical theory.[20] It was his intention to use the emancipatory moment he was hoping to find, to develop a critical standard against which he could evaluate subsequent historical public spheres.[21] He also did not want to accede to the liberal view that prevailed after the extension of the franchise to working-class males, briefly, that political agreement is no more than a "strategically conducted struggle" of differences that are basically irreconcilable.[22] For these reasons he needed to show that bourgeois publicity involved something more than the rational-critical public debate which was essentially and internally related to the development of capitalism.

To recover the normative force of bourgeois publicity, Habermas stages what appears to be a counter-thesis, namely that the literary institutions of the bourgeois owed their existence to a decisive break with those of the urban nobility. This surprising turn in the argument actually re-directs the analysis—the emphasis is now on rupture rather than continuity and on the arbitrariness of historical forces rather than evolution. What distinguishes Habermas's synchronic account is the location of institutional changes at the level of the bourgeois household as the principal factor in the development of a bourgeois public. In his words, "the rational-critical public debate of private persons with one another flowed from the well-spring of a specific subjectivity ... [that] had its home, literally, in the sphere of the patriarchal conjugal family."[23] To draw together the diachronic and synchronic dimensions of the analysis, we might say that, as the bourgeois were making social and economic advances and as they were learning the art of rational-critical public debate, there also occurred deep structural changes at the level of gender relations. The patriarchal conjugal family became the dominant family type within the bourgeois strata, and its eventual consolidation as the norm led to the displacement of both the open "houses" typical of aristocratic life and the "extended families" of the countryside.

While the bourgeois "public use of reason" is explained with reference to the patriarchal conjugal family, this explanation requires not only a detour to a structural argument, but also a temporary departure from the discourse of public and private. Habermas now distinguishes between the *public* (in its literary and political forms), the *private* (economic), and the *intimate* (conjugal family). The idea of a third sphere makes it possible for him to argue that, while the bourgeois learned the art of rational-critical public debate from the urban nobility, the public sphere that they created—in literary works, but also in philosophy and law—became the expression of a sphere of subjectivity that was specifically bourgeois. To miss that point—as one might be inclined, given that Habermas himself privileges the diachronic aspects of his analysis—is to fail to see the importance of his argument that the bourgeois "public use of reason" was not, in essence, a continuation of the salon-based, rational-critical public debate.[24] According to Habermas, bourgeois subjectivity was structurally tied to a concept of "humanity" that originated as a feeling of "human closeness" in the innermost sphere of the conjugal family. That "closeness" was apparently related to the "permanent intimacy" characteristic of the new type of family life (in contrast to the "playful" intimacy of the urban nobility). The historical self-image of the bourgeois family was in serious conflict with its reality: though members of a family might view themselves "as persons capable of entering into 'purely human' relations with one another," the wife and children were, in fact, socially and economically dependent on the male head. These asymmetrical relations notwithstanding, "the ideas of freedom, love, and cultivation of the person that grew out of the experiences of the conjugal family's private sphere were surely more than just ideology." They also constituted an "objective meaning contained as an element in the structure of the actual institution, and without whose subjective validity, society would not have been able to reproduce itself."[25]

To demonstrate the emerging consciousness of a common humanity,

Habermas recounts the flood of letter exchanges and diaries of the eighteenth century that Michel Foucault would later situate in the tradition of a "confessional mode."[26] Habermas places these confessing activities in a different (and more positive) light with the suggestion that they were intrinsically "audience-oriented" and "experiments with the subjectivity discovered in the close relationships of the conjugal family." Taken together, these Habermasian and Foucaultian insights increase our understanding of a complex historical process. However, the significance of Habermas's point that there is a transfer of experience from the intimate to the public spheres gets lost as he now effaces the intersection of "intimate" and "public." On the surface, the experiences of the former spilled over into the latter, as author and reader engaged in "intimate mutual relationships" and "talked heart to heart" about what was "human." He relates that the bourgeois reading public sought insight about itself in the moral weeklies and Richardson's *Pamela*, as it would later on in the domestic drama and the psychological novel.[27] Foucault was similarly struck by the confusion of identity experienced by privatized individuals set adrift from the cohesiveness of tradition. The bourgeois could not, like the aristocrats they were displacing, simply refer to their superior "blood": according to Foucault, they constructed a body for themselves by looking "inward." The rest is "history." As Habermas reports, the reading public grew as public libraries were founded, book clubs and reading circles were established, and weekly and monthly journals increased their sales. A liberal political public sphere developed out of this liberal literary public sphere as the state-governed apparatus succumbed to the pressure of the newly confident bourgeois to debate publicly the general rules governing commodity exchange and social labor.[28]

If the bourgeois came to see themselves as authentically human, it follows that they would regard the beliefs they developed about themselves in the "psychological emancipation that corresponded to the political-economic one" as applying in principle to a "common" humanity. In a trivial sense, they could not help but profess that the "voluntariness, community of love, and cultivation" that they believed they had discovered in a process of self-clarification inhered in humankind as such.[29] But Habermas is not simply referring to beliefs about a humanity that might be found to be false. The concept of humanity, while historically produced, was itself part of a newly structured "public use of reason." Whatever the historical circumstances in which it emerged, the bourgeois experience of humanity was an event of world historical importance. For the first time there developed a concept of humanity that was not derivative (based on higher law) and that was in principle inclusive. Habermas notes that even though the public of the constitutional state was historically restricted, through property (and implicitly education) qualifications, it had a "strict" view of the public sphere: "in its deliberations it anticipated in principle that all human beings belong to it."[30] Whereas the publicity of representation typical of the court had been located in the person of the sovereign, the site of the new publicity was the "people." Early bourgeois writers soon identified this new publicity with openness and the "rule of law," the very opposite of the secrecy and arbitrariness typical of courtly practices.[31]

The Contradictory Institutionalization of the Public Sphere

Habermas offers the model of the contradictory institutionalization of the public sphere as a description of the public sphere's internal dynamic. I want to demonstrate why he thought that this dynamic logically held out the promise of a self-transformation that, paradoxically, could not help but remain true to the liberal ideal of humanity.

At the heart of the model is an ambivalence in the concept of law. As "an expression of will," the concept of law "included as an element the claim . . . to the exercise of domination," but as an "expression of reason" it retained "other, older elements of its origin in public opinion" and in fact aimed at the dissolution of domination. Cross-cutting this ambivalence between force and freedom is another one between a particular and a general interest, as reflected in the equation of bourgeois and homme— property owner and "human being." These ambivalences, which structure the model, also de-stabilize it, and this de-stabilization is sufficient to actualize its built-in mechanism for self-transformation—there are potentially ever new definitions of "human beings" and "universal interest." Therefore, while the historical transformation of the public sphere was initiated by the socialist rejection of the liberal equation of property owners and human beings and by the Marxist identification of new relationships of power between the class of property owners and the class of wage-earners, the rejection of a particular (bourgeois) claim to represent a general interest does not dislocate the internal dynamic of a public sphere committed to the idea of a general interest and to the non-coercive use of reason.

The counter-model does, however, reverse the liberal distinction between public and private. Whereas the liberal model required that private people come together as a public to secure their private sphere legally and politically, the "universal concern" of the mass of non-owners who gained access to the public sphere (through electoral reforms) is no longer the reproduction of social life under the conditions of private appropriation, but rather the reproduction of social life as such. The liberal "public of private persons" is thus transformed into a "public of citizens," and criticism and control by this new public extend to the formerly privately controlled area of socially necessary labour.

Habermas's class-based model reflects the historical fact that class conflict had to be built into the argument for the inclusion of non-owners. It does not, however, explain why the raising of the class issue failed to secure women's participation. That question is a potential challenge for his model, as he concedes in the new (1990) foreward to his book. With reference to Pateman's work,[32] he formulates the problem for contemporary feminism as follows: "The question is whether women were excluded from the bourgeois public sphere *in the same fashion* as workers, peasants, and the 'people,' i.e., men lacking 'independence.'"[33] He also seems to agree that women were in fact excluded in a different way. At least he reports on Pateman's findings without registering any objection on the substance of what she says:

> unlike the institutionalization of class conflict, the transformation of the relationship between the sexes affects not only the economic system but has an impact on the private core area of the conjugal family. This shows that the exclusion of women has been constitutive for the political public sphere not merely in that the latter has been dominated by men as a matter of contingency but also in that its structure and relation to the private sphere has been determined in a gender-specific fashion. Unlike the exclusion of underprivileged men, the exclusion of women had structuring significance.[34]

He has grasped the import of Pateman's thesis. However, though he notes her scepticism about the potential of a public sphere that continues to be marked by patriarchy, he also views her critique as premised on unredeemed claims to "rights to unrestricted inclusion and equality, which are an integral part of the liberal public sphere's self-interpretation."[35] That premise of Pateman's argument, as mentioned above, would situate her within the discourse of modernity. Habermas's point is that, if women appeal to the norms of that discourse, women's exclusion from the public sphere cannot be constitutive in the "Foucaultian" sense.

He clarifies what he means by distinguishing between two types of exclusion:

> We may use 'excluded' in Foucault's sense when we are dealing with groups that play a *constitutive* role in the formation of a particular public sphere. 'Exclusion' assumes a different and less radical meaning when the same structures of communication simultaneously give rise to the formation of several arenas where, beside the hegemonic bourgeois public sphere, additional subcultural or class-specific public spheres are constituted on the basis of their own and initially not easily reconcilable premises.

The "less radical" type of exclusion is a reference to remarks he made in the 1962 foreword to his book, in anticipation of criticisms that he did not consider alternative publics such as the Jacobins or the Chartists. As for "Foucaultian" or constitutive exclusion, Habermas did "not consider [that type] at all at the time."[36] He now (1990) explains it with reference to Foucault's idea that "the formative rules of a hegemonic discourse . . . [are] mechanisms of exclusion constituting their respective 'other'" and identifies, as a key component of constitutive exclusion, the absence of a "common language" between the participants of the hegemonic discourse and the "protesting others." In Habermas's view, the category of constitutive exclusion can be used to understand the events that led to the collapse of traditional societies. In the bourgeois revolutions, he writes, the "people," having been constituted as the "other" of aristocratic society, had had no choice but to "move and express themselves in a universe that was different and *other*." However, he denies the relevance of the category for analyses of modernity by arguing that the liberal public sphere had a built-in potential for self-transformation that made Foucaultian-type discourses structurally impossible.

> Bourgeois publicness . . . is articulated in discourses that provided areas of common ground not only for the labor movement but also for the excluded other, that is, the feminist movement. Contact with these movements in turn transformed these discourses and the structures of the public sphere itself from within. From the very beginning, the universalistic discourses of the bourgeois public sphere were based on self-referential premises . . . they differ from Foucaultian discourses by virtue of their potential for self-transformation.[37]

If, as Habermas contends, women's exclusion cannot be explained with reference to the constitutive (Foucaultian) type, and if, as he admits, it does not fit the model of the contradictory institutionalization of the public sphere, and if there is, as he insists, the structural possibility of self-transformation, we need to get a better idea of what is involved.

I shall take Habermas to mean that women's exclusion was constitutive, though in a way that avoids closure of the Foucaultian type. I propose that we think in terms of two types of constitutive exclusion: one that is logically constitutive (the Foucaultian type) and another that is historically constitutive. This allows us to view Habermas's position as involving the claim that, while women's exclusion was historically constitutive of a specific (liberal) public sphere, it was not logically constitutive because it belonged to the nature of the public sphere that emerged in modernity that it had the capacity to "correct" for the limitations of its historically gender-specific institutions. His response to feminists would then have to be interpreted as follows: a capacity for radical reconstitution—sufficiently radical to effect fundamental structural change—is a built-in feature of the public sphere of modernity.

If gender exclusion represents different problems from those pertaining to class, the resolution of those problems would also require a different view of the potential for self-transformation of the public sphere than the one Habermas offered in 1962. One way of looking at the matter is to suggest that because he leaves gender relations unaccounted for, his model cannot tolerate an argument based on gender conflict, just as classical liberal theory, which left class relations unaccounted for, could not allow for an argument based on class conflict. There is some point to this view, but the gender problem is not exactly parallel to the class one because the internal dynamic of the model relies on the category of gender in a complex way.

The Gender Basis of the Model of the Contradictory Institutionalization of the Public Sphere

As discussed above, Habermas traces the historical roots of the principle of inclusiveness to the bourgeois experience of intimacy. The intimate sphere is also of originary significance for the "public use of reason": it is the actual site of the "truth" of bourgeois ideology and is crucial to his understanding of how the public sphere's internal dynamic generates inclusions out of class-based exclusions. According to Habermas, the privatized individuals of modernity experienced a deep ambivalence in the intimate sphere which was carried over into the public one. The individual was both bourgeois and homme—compelled to identify himself as owner of goods and property, even as he claimed (at least implicitly) to be one human being among others. However, while the intimate sphere yields the "truth" for the public one, the gender relations of the patriarchal conjugal family become invisible in Habermas's model, as the extraction of that truth becomes a publicly resolvable question, spatially removed from the sphere of intimacy. To talk about exclusion now means to expose the false identification of the (political) public of "property owners" and the (literary) public of "common human beings."[38]

The relation between male and female in the patriarchal conjugal family, while connected to the ambivalence between bourgeois and homme, cannot simply be identified with it, as Habermas seems to suggest. In fact, *The Structural Transformation* shows why feminists should be wary of suggesting that women were regarded as "possessions" of the male head of the household, or his "property." If that were so, women would have been included in the "public of citizens" model in which participants are no longer property-owners, but "human beings." Moreover, many readers were women, and they were excluded, notwithstanding the fact that, as readers, they had learned the "public use of reason." Thus, even after ownership had ceased to be an issue as to the definition of a public person, there persisted a "specific form" of humanity—a male one—that falsely posed as a "common·humanity." But the gendered identity shared by the liberal public and its "socialist" successor cannot explain what it was about the gender relations of modernity that demanded women's exclusion. That exclusion was apparently connected to an experience called private autonomy that positioned bourgeois—and eventually all—males in the public sphere of speech and action and females in the intimate one. The general contours of this split have been documented, but its importance for modernity is only now beginning to be understood.

Habermas's expressed view is that private autonomy had originally derived from one's status as a private (economic) person and by virtue of one's control over the means of production, but that within a public of citizens (where one's public status is not tied to property) it had to be grounded in the public sphere. "Private persons came to be the private persons of a public rather than a public of private persons." Though he views this development as a reversal, the guarantee of the excercise of private autonomy—in the liberal model no less than in the socialist counter-model—is secured by one's participation in a public sphere. Moreover, either private autonomy means something very different in the counter-model—where it cannot refer to private control over the means of production—or its connection to the private (economic) sphere in the liberal model does not exhaust its meaning. That private autonomy cannot be reduced to the economic is suggested by the presence, in the counter-model, of what Habermas calls a "derivative" private autonomy. As the range of potentially public matters increases, a sphere of "informal and personal interaction of human beings . . . [is] emancipated . . . from the constraints of social labor (ever a 'realm of necessity') and become really 'private'." This "really 'private'" is the intimate sphere, which was obviously intended to survive the socialization of the means of production.[39] In Engels's words, "the relations between the sexes [would become] a purely private affair, which concerns only the two persons involved."[40] If the removal of the intimate sphere from legal regulations of every kind is the *ne plus ultra* of this "derivative" private autonomy, the "original" private autonomy was only contingently related to one's status in the private (economic) sphere.

When Habermas talks about a reversal of public and private in the context of the "public of citizens," we have to understand the term private in the sense of economic. This reading is consistent with the intentions expressed in his book, but it also suggests that the intimate sphere was not substantially affected by the reversal (of public and private) that accompanied the public sphere's structural transformation. With respect to the liberal public, Habermas states that "the individual's status as a free human being ... [was] grounded in the intimate sphere of the patriarchal conjugal family" and was legally guaranteed through such "basic rights" as "personal freedom" and "inviolability of the home." The legal securing of the "inviolability" of the home—which was not challenged in the transition to the new model—is a violent act perpetrated on those "human beings" legally confined to it, but this apparent "irrationality" goes beyond the obvious circumstance that the individual was a male head of the household or that the patriarchal conjugal family was already presupposed in the category of humanity, since, as Habermas relates (in passing), "family and property" were the "foundation of private autonomy."[41] If, as he also says, the intimate sphere (patriarchal conjugal family) is at the core of the private (property),[42] then the bourgeois family is at the core not only of property, but private autonomy itself. That seems to explain why there is a "derivative" private—or intimate—that is not in itself economic even when citizenship is no longer based on ownership.

Habermas's description of the bourgeois "public of private persons" bears a strong—but ultimately misleading—resemblance to his depiction of the Greek "public of private persons." It is an integral part of his argument that, in each case, the public sphere was institutionally both separate from and tied to a private one. According to the Hellenic model, public life, or the sphere of the *polis*, represented what was common to Greek citizens (adult free males). It was constituted in discussion and associated with the activities of the market place, but extended to responsibilities in courts of law and to the common action of athletic games and war. Women and slaves were confined to the private sphere of the household (*oikos*), but one should not—without qualification—accept the structural-functional argument that the labour of women and slaves was socially required to provide the necessary leisure, in order to allow the few to engage in public activities. As Habermas points out, "movable wealth and control over labour power" could not substitute for "being the master of a household and of a family," nor, conversely, could someone be excluded from the *polis* merely because he was too poor or had no slaves. While the patrimonial slave economy gave citizens freedom from productive labour, their status as citizens was strictly tied to their "private autonomy as masters of households."[43]

To some extent, bourgeois intimacy, which had no parallel in the Greek model, can be viewed as a camouflage for male domination. As Habermas reports, the bourgeois public owed its existence to "the background experience of a private sphere that had become interiorized human closeness," whereas the private status of the Greek master of the *oikos*, "upon which depended his political status as citizen, rested on domination without any illusion of freedom evoked by human intimacy."[44] However, despite the surface similarity of the institutional arrangements of Hellenic and bourgeois publics, the relatively static relation of public and private in the former case was radically transformed, in the bourgeois period, by the new sphere of intimacy. According to Habermas, the "experience of 'humanity' originated ... in the humanity of the intimate relationships between human beings who, under the aegis of the [patriarchal conjugal] family, were nothing more than human."[45] For the bourgeois, he claims, "humanity's genuine site" was the intimate sphere of the patriarchal conjugal family and not the public sphere itself, as one might be led to believe from a comparison of the Greek model.[46] In Habermas's analysis, the Hellenic dyad of public and private yields to the modern triad of public, private (economic) and intimate.

If the category of gender played a crucial and determining role in the elaboration of his public sphere model, why then did Habermas not theorize gender exclusion in 1962? It is not enough to say that the gender issue simply never entered his mind at the time—even if that is literally true— because by 1990 he had thought about the issue and he still held to the "larger outline" of his earlier analysis. Nor is it a straightforward matter of personal insensitivity to women's issues. In fact, he regards the feminist movement as a hopeful sign of a potential in liberal democracies for significant social and political change. I am also reluctant to reduce the matter to a male interest in preserving the idea of private autonomy. The difficulty can be traced to the tradition of ideology critique, in which Habermas's book is written.

Ideology critique "finds" the "standards" of reason "already given in bourgeois ideals" and takes them "at their word."[47] If the origin of ideology is, as Habermas claims, in the "identification of 'property owner' with 'human being as such' in the role accruing to private people as members of the public in the political sphere of the bourgeois constitutional state,"[48] ideology critique, as the other side of ideology, also has its origin in the identification of "property owner" with "human being as such"— notwithstanding the fact that it contests this identification as a false one. As a class-based analysis, ideology critique restricts its concern to the relation between public and private (economic) and cannot go beyond the "specific form" of humanity espoused by the bourgeois reading public. The intimate sphere, despite its importance for Habermas's explanation of the "public use of reason," falls away as he takes up anew the discourse of public and private.

Bourgeois subjectivity, with its "formal criteria of generality and abstractness,"[49] posed as the exact opposite of the particular and concrete that it associated with aristocratic privilege. This reversal of the aristocratic model required an expulsion, from the level of the law, of the concrete and particular, even though it fell to reason to secure what had been expelled.

> The bourgeois public's critical public debate took place in principle without regard to all preexisting social and political rank and in accord with universal rules. . . . These rules, because universally valid, secured a space for the individuated person; because they were objective, they secured a space for what was most subjective; because they were abstract, for what was most concrete.[50]

The problem is that, under the conditions of an abstract subjectivity, reason cannot make good its claim to "secure" the particular and concrete, except as absences. This aspect of the logic of public and private was to pose conceptual difficulties for postliberal publics, especially in the context of the advocacy of social rights, which seems to require something stronger than the idea of securing space for the private enjoyment of goods. In the case of the social-sexual arrangements of the bourgeois family, however, the idea of an absence takes on a different meaning altogether.

As the ground of the new public, the intimate sphere was legally secured by the liberal state. However, whereas the public and private (economic) spheres were subject, from the start, to a formal regulation which made it possible, in principle, to identify matters of public concern, the informal (non-legal) regulation of *internal* family relationships ensured that this sphere was basically resistant to the logic of public and private. The special (non-legal) status of the intimate sphere was also a feature of the new "public of citizens." As Habermas tells us, Marx and Engels, like their liberal counterparts, "considered a relationship to be actualized as 'private' only when it was no longer saddled with any legal regulations."[51]

The view that the intimate sphere is basically resistant to the logic of public and private is implicit in the argument of *The Structural Transformation*. However, this view persists, in somewhat different language, in Habermas's later (1981) thesis of "internal colonization."[52] The colonization thesis refers to the conditions of advanced capitalism, in which there is a contraction of the "public" sphere in the sense of reduced institutional opportunities for non-ideological participation and independent discussion, but a corresponding increase in state-administrative activities. As the subsystems of the economy and the state gain in complexity, he explains, they respond to social problems associated with capitalist growth by "penetrating" more and more deeply into the symbolic reproduction of the lifeworld. This penetration is understood as the formal intrusion of a process of juridification (an increase in positive law) in (once) informally regulated lifeworld structures, notably, but not restricted to, family and school. According to Habermas, the juridification of family and school creates dysfunctions in these lifeworld structures because they are not "constituted in legal form." He is not simply referring to the negative effects (in the sense of the creation of new dependencies) intrinsically related to the implementation of socially necessary welfare policy, but rather to the pathological effects of a process of juridification in areas of life (family and school) which are, by their nature, non-juridical: "in these spheres of the lifeworld, we find, *prior to* any juridification, norms and contexts of action that by functional necessity are based on mutual understanding as a mechanism for coordinating action." For Habermas, juridification of the (normally) informally regulated spheres of the lifeworld means "legally supplementing a communicative context of action through the superimposition of legal norms." As "communicatively structured" rather than "formally organized" areas of action, family and school "must be able to function independent of legal regulation" because socialization in these areas "*exists prior to and conditions* legal norms." As he sees it, juridification "should not go beyond the enforcement of principles of the rule of law, beyond the legal institutionalization of the *external* constitution of . . . the family or the school."[53]

This account is compelling as an explanation of the (well-documented) dysfunctions that occur in the lifeworld structures of the family (and school) when these "socially integrated contexts" are supplemented by legal-bureaucratic measures designed to respond to system imperatives. But it is also conservative insofar as it works as an argument for resistance to fundamental change at the level of family structures; Habermas merely calls for a de-juridification of the lifeworld with no consideration of the issues of justice which such juridification is meant to address. Nancy Fraser[54] has rightly argued that his colonization thesis is "gender-blind" and that we need a "gender-sensitive reading" of the developments he traces. Fraser's views are important and need to be addressed in detail, but I am not entirely convinced that the problem can be traced to Habermas's "categorial opposition between system and lifeworld institutions," if that means that we should abandon the opposition to the point where there is no philosophically interesting distinction between system and lifeworld. Rather than breaking down the opposition, as Fraser does, to show how economic (and implicitly political) categories can be applied to an understanding of the functioning of the family, I would like to heighten the opposition by making the connection between system (economy and state) and lifeworld (notably, family) more complex. My concern about breaking down the opposition is that, while it can lead to insightful analyses, it also tends to obscure features of sex-gender relations that cannot be viewed in terms of the economic and political. The problem for feminism, as I see it, is to find a way of addressing the gender issue while learning from what Habermas has to say about the freedom-denying consequences of the expansion of juridification into non-juridical areas of life.

Concluding Remarks

Feminists have known for some time that the issue of gender is larger than the question of formal rights to social and political equality and that it extends to the more complex questions of intimacy. That understanding has not always been effectively transmitted because the ideas of private and intimate have generally been run together. The private sphere has been conceived to include everything that is a non-public matter—hence the tendency to view gender in terms of the private (economic) or property. The occasional (non-systematic) reference by feminists to a domestic sphere—though the term is similarly overburdened with economic meanings—reflects the need for a concept that does not reduce the family to a microcosm of the subsystem of the economy. In my view, there are considerable advantages in keeping the intimate and private spheres conceptually distinct. In particular, we can isolate the gender issue of the (legally secured) social-sexual arrangements of modernity, which are not in themselves "constituted in legal form," from gender-related questions—for example, the enfranchisement of women—that can, and have been, successfully posed in the logic of public and private. The idea of an intimate sphere does not deny the connection of the family to the state and the economy—to the contrary, it is meant to theorize that connection. However, the idea leads to challenging questions for theory because questions related to intimacy are not simply a matter of personal decision (the family as an institution is formally secured), and they are not amenable—without a loss of freedom—to formal resolution (internal family relationships are by their nature informally regulated).

Up to a point then, my concerns cannot be equated with worries about whether or not Habermas has idealized the bourgeois public. I concur that the zeal with which he pursues the principle of inclusiveness seems to lead to a valorization of a "one" public which is increasingly suspect. I also sympathize with efforts to resist that valorization by directing attention to alternative "publics," whether historical or actual or potential.[55] At the same time we need to rethink the concept of public in relation to the gender issue. That will involve a new logic of gender relations. I cannot address the nature of that logic here, but, to judge from feminist researches in many fields, it would have to include a concept of humanity that can tolerate the idea of a "differentiated we." The category of gender must also become central to the philosophical discourse of modernity. If it is true that, for modernity, humanity's "genuine site" is the intimate sphere—and it is possible to show that Habermas's later work not only does not deny this important insight, but actually supports it—the claim to truth of the bourgeois concept of humanity cannot be redeemed, as he thought, in a public sphere that presupposes the historically specific sex-gender relations of modernity.

I began this essay with the question of women's historical claims to rights to inclusion and equality. These claims were not intended as radical. As a group, women shared in the values of literacy and did not challenge the identification of bourgeois and homme. However, the redemption of those claims demands a radical reconceptualization not only of sex/gender relations, but also of the public/private/intimate spheres in which those relations are socially and politically organized.

NOTES

1 Jürgen Habermas, *Strukturwandel der Öffentlichkeit: Untersuchungen zu einer Kategorie der bürgerlichen Gesellschaft* (Darmstadt and Neuwied: Luchterhand Verlag, 1962); the book was republished with a new Foreword by Suhrkamp Verlag in 1990).

2. Habermas, *The Structural Transformation of the Public Sphere: An Inquiry into a Category of Bourgeois Society*, trans. Thomas Burger (Cambridge, MA: MIT Press, 1989).

3. See the essays in Craig Calhoun, ed., *Habermas and the Public Sphere* (Cambridge, MA: MIT Press, 1992).

4. Habermas, "Concluding Remarks," in Calhoun, *Habermas and the Public Sphere*, p. 466.

5. See the 1962 Preface to Habermas, *The Structural Transformation*, p. xviii.

6. Geoff Eley, "Nations, Publics, and Political Cultures: Placing Habermas in the Nineteenth Century," in Calhoun, *Habermas and the Public Sphere*, p. 289 ff., esp. p. 306. Cf. Nancy Fraser, "Rethinking the Public Sphere: A Contribution to the Critique of Actually Existing Democracy," in the same volume, p. 109 ff.

7. The 1990 Foreword to *Strukturwandel* appears in translation as "Further Reflections on the Public Sphere," in Calhoun, *Habermas and the Public Sphere*, p. 421 ff.

8. Habermas, "Further Reflections," pp. 424–30.

9. Some of this research has been explicitly related to Habermas's philosophy and social theory. Cf. Nancy Fraser, "What's Critical About Critical Theory?" The Case of Habermas and Gender," in Seyla Benhabib and Drucilla Cornell eds., *Feminism as Critique* (Minneapolis: University of Minnesota Press, 1987), p. 31 ff.; Seyla Benhabib, "The Generalized and the Concrete Other: The Kohlberg-Gilligan Controversy and Feminist Theory," in *Praxis International* 5:4 (January 1986), p. 402 ff.; Marie Fleming, "The Gender of Critical Theory," in *Cultural Critique* 13 (Fall 1989), p. 119 ff.; Joan B. Landes, *Women and the Public Sphere in the Age of the French Revolution* (Ithaca, NY: Cornell University Press, 1988).

10. Landes, *Women and the Public Sphere*. Cf. Dena Goodman, "Public Sphere and Private Life: Toward a Synthesis of Current Historiographical Approaches to the Old Regime," *History and Theory* 31:1 (1992), p. 1 ff., who is critical of Landes's use of the terms public and private in the context of the Old Regime.

11. Carole Pateman, *The Sexual Contract* (Stanford: Stanford University Press, 1988).

12. See Mary P. Ryan, "Gender and Public Access: Women's Politics in Nineteenth-Century America," in Calhoun, *Habermas and the Public Sphere*, p. 259 ff.; Seyla Benhabib, "Models of Public Space: Hannah Arendt, the Liberal Tradition, and Jürgen Habermas," in the same volume, p. 73 ff.; Eley, "Nations, Publics, and Political Cultures," p. 307 ff.

13. Habermas, "Further Reflections," p. 427.

14. Habermas, "Further Reflections," p. 429.

15. Habermas, "Further Reflections," p. 430.

16. Habermas, "Further Reflections," p. 422.

17. Habermas's distinction between "preliterate" and "literate" publics allows the former to be collapsed into the latter. My employment of that distinction resists the sublation of the one type of public sphere into the other.

18. See Landes, *Women and the Public Sphere*, p. 93 ff. Cf. Ryan, "Gender and Public Access."

19. Habermas, *The Structural Transformation*, pp. 36–40.

20. This motivation is noted by Eley, "Nations, Publics, and Political Cultures," pp. 292-93 and Craig Calhoun, "Introduction," in *Habermas and the Public Sphere*, p. 2. See also Peter Uwe Hohendahl, "The Public Sphere: Models and Boundaries," in the same volume, p. 99 ff.

21. Habermas has since tried to develop that critical category through the analysis of "everyday communicative practices." See his remarks in "Further Reflections," pp. 442–43.

22. See Habermas, "Further Reflections," pp. 446–47.

23. Habermas, *The Structural Transformation*, p. 43.

24. The diachronic dimensions of Habermas's analysis are emphasized in

Thomas McCarthy's remarks in his introduction to Habermas's *The Structural Transformation* and in Eley, "Nations, Publics, and Political Cultures." Cf. Calhoun, "Introduction," who summarizes Habermas's structural argument in the context of an overview of the book.

25. Habermas, *The Structural Transformation*, pp. 44–48.

26. Cf. Michel Foucault, *History of Sexuality: An Introduction*, Vol. I (New York: Vintage Books, 1980).

27. Habermas, *The Structural Transformation*, pp. 48–51.

28. Habermas wants to show the logical priority of the literary public sphere over the political one. At the level of practice, the situation was more complex, and the two might not be easily distinguished. Subsequent historical research which points to that complexity would not necessarily invalidate Habermas's point. For a recent discussion of Habermas's reception in the field of history, see Anthony J. La Vopa, "Conceiving a Public: Ideas and Society in Eighteenth-Century Europe," *The Journal of Modern History* 64:1 (March 1992), p. 79 ff.

29. Habermas, *The Structural Transformation*, pp. 46–47.

30. Habermas, *The Structural Transformation*, p. 85.

31. See the discussion in Habermas, *The Structural Transformation*, p. 89 ff.

32. Habermas refers to Carole Pateman, "The Fraternal Social Contract," in John Keane, ed., *Civil Society and the State* (London: Verso, 1988), p. 101 ff. Cf. Pateman, *The Sexual Contract*.

33. Habermas, "Further Reflections," p. 427. Emphasis in original, here and elsewhere.

34. Habermas, "Further Reflections," p. 428.

35. Habermas, "Further Reflections," p. 429.

36. Habermas, "Further Reflections," p. 425.

37. Habermas, "Further Reflections," p. 429.

38. Habermas, *The Structural Transformation*, pp. 55–56.

39. Habermas, *The Structural Transformation*, pp. 128–29.

40. Friedrich Engels, "Principles of Communism," quoted in Habermas, *The Structural Transformation*, p. 129.

41. Habermas, *The Structural Transformation*, p. 83.

42. Habermas, *The Structural Transformation*, p. 55.

43. Habermas, *The Structural Transformation*, p. 3.

44. Habermas, *Structural Transformation*, p. 52.

45. Habermas, *Structural Transformation*, p. 48.

46. Habermas, *Structural Transformation*, pp. 51–52.

47. Habermas, "The Entwinement of Myth and Enlightenment," in his *The*

Philosophical Discourse of Modernity, trans. Frederick Lawrence (Cambridge, MA: MIT Press, 1987), p. 116.

48. Habermas, *The Structural Transformation*, p. 88.

49. Habermas, *The Structural Transformation*, p. 55.

50. Habermas, *The Structural Transformation*, p. 54.

51. Habermas, *The Structural Transformation*, p. 129.

52. Habermas, *The Theory of Communicative Action*, Vol. II, trans. Thomas McCarthy (Boston: Beacon Press, 1987), esp. p. 356 ff. (first published in Germany in 1981).

53. Habermas *The Theory of Communicative Action,* Vol. II, pp. 368–71.

54. Nancy Fraser, "What's Critical about Critical Theory?" in Benhabib and Cornell, *Feminism as Critique*, p. 31 ff.

55. See esp. the discussion in Fraser, "Rethinking the Public Sphere."

5

From Communicative Rationality to Communicative Thinking: A Basis for Feminist Theory and Practice

Jane Braaten

The feminist critique of science and reason has figured centrally in the development of feminist theory in the last twenty years. The principal targets of this critique are the apparent links between traditional conceptions of reason on the one hand, and androcentric theories of autonomy, models of political legitimacy, and ideals of community on the other. Although Jürgen Habermas rejects the "philosophy of the subject," which locates the foundations of knowledge in the thinking subject, some of these objections still apply to his theory of communicative rationality. I argue that it is his limitation of a critique of reason to a theory of justification, rather than the content of that theory, that constitutes the crucial point of divergence from feminist conceptions of reason and knowledge. While Habermas is correct in seeing a relation of dependence between conceptions of knowledge and ideals of community, feminist theory tends to reverse the traditional relation of dependence, deriving criteria of rationality and knowledge from substantive ideals of solidarity and community, rather than vice versa. I will discuss these ideals, and outline a conception of feminist thinking—communicative thinking—rooted in a feminist understanding of solidarity.

Feminist theory is inherently a *critical* sort of theory. For those who understand "critical theory" as inquiry rooted in what Kant called *Kritik,* or Habermas the "philosophy of critique,"—a tradition whose critical, self-reflective moment begins in Kant's Copernican turn—this statement provokes the question of foundations. The philosophy of critique is above all concerned with foundations of all possible theory and of critical philosophy itself. For Kant, the question of foundations was motivated by the twin challenges of dogmatism and scepticism. For Hegel, this question is made critical by the historicity of the understanding; for Marx, foundational questions become questions about history, and they call for the analysis of lived *practical* historical experience for answers. Socialist and Marxist feminism have shared the Marxist concern to relocate the foundations of theory in lived experience, while remaining aware of the historical (and particularly the en-gendering) conditions of this experience.[1]

Though Marxist analysis has been useful in providing a foothold for the development of an epistemology that begins with the experience of the oppressed, its reliance on the fundament of the 'logic' of production—the theory of the forces and relations of material production—and its intrinsic focus on the male worker, has posed obstacles for the use of Marxist theory as a systematic analysis of patriarchy, women's oppression, and the possibility of women's emancipation.[2] Attempts to supplement Marxist analysis with analyses of patriarchy have met with a dawning awareness that "women's experience" has few common denominators, and the question has arisen of whether any *systematic* analysis of women's experience is possible. It is not clear that there is a sufficient common basis in women's experiences to support a full systematic analysis of patriarchy. Feminist theory has responded to the call for more open, less presumptive, less segregated communication about women's experiences—a form of communication that is not only comfortable with the diversity of those experiences but committed to a solidarity that is founded upon that diversity.[3]

The debate about what this commitment entails for the possibility of feminist analyses of systematically oppressive structures is not an easy one. Oppression takes many faces, and some of those faces are our own, depending upon the privileges we enjoy relative to others. Not only have the dimensions of women's oppression multiplied, but those dimensions are charged with vulnerability and defensiveness, even within the women's movement. The need for a reexamination of how we as feminists communicate and how we think about what we hear is more sharply felt now than ever before. In this chapter, I shall frame my reflections within the critical philosophical tradition of the critique of reason, and specifically, in a dialogue with Jürgen Habermas's theory of communicative rationality. What I wish to emerge from this dialogue is a picture of feminist reasoning—what I will call communicative thinking—and an understanding of feminist solidarity upon which communicative thinking is based. I shall also raise the issue of the rational "basis," or foundation, of feminist thinking, as well as the complementary issues of a peculiarly feminist scepticism.

From those thinkers in the tradition of critical philosophy and critical theory, Habermas is an especially promising partner in dialoging, since his critique of the legacy of the Cartesian "philosophy of the subject," his requirement of the plurality of participants in dialogue, and his insights into the interdependence of conceptions of knowledge and conceptions of community resonate with aspects of feminist epistemology. Admittedly, judging from his publications, his acquaintance with both feminist theory and activism appears to be minimal, and his social categories mirror gender divisions just as unreflectively as Marx's does. Nancy Fraser criticizes Habermas's analysis of the welfare state on the grounds that his distinction between material reproduction and symbolic reproduction reifies gender divisions, and as a result, he "fails to understand precisely how the capitalist workplace is linked to the modern restricted male-headed nuclear family."[4] Though they are pertinent to a broader analysis of Habermas's work, I will set these issues aside and focus for the most part only on his defense of the theory of communicative rationality.[5] Habermas's analysis of communicative rationality, and its conceptual development in terms of the ideal of consensus, can be useful in investigating the nature of feminist thinking, analysis, and solidarity. Because the need for further exploration of communicative thinking and analysis is so evident in the building of solidarity between diversely identified women, I will identify and examine the points of convergence and divergence of Habermas's conception of communicative rationality with that project.

In the following section, I will present Habermas's conception of communicative rationality as one that is developed in tandem with conceptions of autonomy, social relationship, and community. Habermas's communicative theory of epistemic justification provides the content of a concept of autonomy as the ability to participate in argumentation (communicative competence), of a concept of social relationship as the mutuality of shared grounds, and of a concept of community as a community of the communicatively competent. Though Habermas departs from Kantian "philosophy of consciousness," these concepts of autonomy, relationship, and community are essentially Kantian. I raise the question of whether this Kantian conceptual development is appropriate for feminist epistemology.

In the second section, I compare the historical and critical motivations of Habermas's and feminist critiques of reason and knowledge. Where Habermas sees the construction of a theory of mutual understanding to be crucial in an age that has abandoned the search for ultimate foundations, but must forge a rational basis for interaction and cooperation, the critical focus of feminist epistemology lies in the connections between traditional conceptions of reason and patriarchy. I look for points of divergence and convergence between these two projects and argue that the sceptical issues facing each of them are fundamentally distinct. Habermas, with traditional epistemology, is concerned with defending the possibility of science and moral law against the new historicism of late modernity. Thus his conception of justification takes priority over his conception of intersubjectivity and community. Feminist epistemology rejects the sceptical roots of this project and seeks instead a vision of reasoning that is derivative of ideals of solidarity and community. Contrary to Habermas, feminism gives visions of solidarity and community a foundational role in developing conceptions of thought and analysis. This may be the most philosophically contentious claim in this paper, since it amounts to the introduction of substantive social values as constitutive values of reasoning, unlike the traditional values of truth and right, which are widely thought to transcend substantive commitments.

In the third and final section, I take up the question of what those visions of solidarity and community entail, and suggest a form of communication, thought, and analysis (communicative thinking) derived from the solidarity of diversely identified communities. I address Iris Young's argument that the ideals of community and friendship impose unreasonable requirements on radical political movements and the forms of association that they wish to realize. She argues that an ideal of "city life" better captures the ideal of a politics committed at the same to particular communities and to mutual support between communities. I use the ideal of solidarity implicit in this image of city politics to outline a conception of feminist thinking as focused on specialized and local projects, while also informed by cross-communication between projects, aware of their diverse impacts.

Communicative Rationality, Autonomy, and Community

Habermas uses the concept of consensus to articulate an ideal of socialization and enculturation, an ideal of the just society, and an epistemological theory of justified belief. For Habermas, the coincidence of these various functions in one particular type of social relationship—a rationally grounded consensus—is no accident. Defining the ideal consensus as one in which no point of view is excluded or arbitrarily discounted, Habermas argues that the confidence that one has in being freely and openly convinced of the best argument is also the basis of genuine social mutuality and trust, as well as that of democratic and just institutions.

The ideal of consensus also holds sway in much of feminist practice. The consensual method of feminist practice shares with Habermas's ideal consensus the interest in overcoming relationships of dominance and submission, in sharing power, and opening discussion to all perspectives. However, the feminist practice of consensus, unlike Habermas's ideal discourse, only occasionally takes the rarified form of theoretical-scientific or ethical-judicial discourse (the two forms of universal consensus-oriented discourse). Normally, except perhaps in the academy, the feminist effort to arrive at consensus is meant to elicit more individual truths and needs, in order to shape and consolidate consensual support for substantive practical and political goals. This does not entail a rejection of the ideal of universal truth in relation to scientific claims or issues of justice. Nor does it entail that feminists have no stake in how claims about scientific truth and universal principles of justice are adjudicated. It simply means that procedures for testing scientific theories or the formal virtues of a principle of justice do not figure centrally in reaching consensus on practices and goals that feminists consider. But if Habermas's consensual procedure is designed for purposes that might really be peripheral to feminist ends, then how pertinent can it be to our conception of feminist communication, thinking and analysis? And if feminist thought is not principally scientific-theoretical, or ethical-judicial in Habermas's sense, then what is it? Bearing these questions in mind, let us examine his vision of communicative rationality.

Habermas's interest in overcoming domination is expressed in his requirement that a consensus is valid only insofar as each individual participant is "motivated," by consideration of the full range of observations, interpretations, analyses, counter-examples, and replies offered to accept the "forceless force of the better argument." Thus, rational consensus is based not on the power or charisma of individuals, but upon the most cogent position. The cogency of a position, in turn, is decided on the grounds of the strength and consistency of the inductive relation between observation and theory, and ideally, because there are no further possible reasons for conflict with the consensual position. Because acceptance of a consensual position is based only on this activity of collective hypothesis generating, testing, and accepting or rejecting (without any coercive or otherwise undue pressure from anyone), each participant is fully autonomous, while at the same time maximally respectful of the other participants in dialogue. As in Kant's Kingdom of Ends, autonomy coincides both with freedom from coercion (or self-legislation) and with community.

Habermas's implicit claim that the ideal speech situation represents the ideally emancipated, coercion-free form of human interaction rests upon specific concepts of autonomy and coercion, community and social disintegration. His conception of autonomy owes a great deal to the work of Jean Piaget and Lawrence Kohlberg, who had their own allegiances to Kant. It is a conception of cognitive and intellectual autonomy or 'maturity' (*Mündigkeit*) whose opposite, heteronomy, is less a state of constraint in the usual sense than of intellectual immaturity (*Unmündigkeit*). As in Piaget's and Kohlberg's work, autonomy amounts to freedom of thought from prejudice and the cognitive deficits of incomplete logical development.[6] It is an intellectual ability to put any and every hypothesis or ethical principle to a systematic test. Coercion (*Zwang*) or "force," then, is any interference with cognitive autonomy whose origins are ultimately social or historical (e.g. deceit, obviously, but Habermas might also include such things as poor education and mass media production techniques), rather than physiological (brain tumors, etc.).

Likewise, Habermas constructs a specific conception of community, or as he calls it, "communication community." Community is analytically distinguished both from administrative or corporate organizations and from solidarity. "Communication community" refers to all actual and potential co-participants in communicative action and in principle encompasses all human beings capable of communicative action.[7] Participants in functionally or strategically organized institutions, such as government regulatory commissions or corporate directorships, are not in this capacity members of the communication community. They are members only in virtue of their ability to participate in discourse—the systematic contestation of truth, justice, and cultural integrity claims. Thus, Habermas's concept of community, again echoing the Kingdom of Ends, is tied to an essentially justificatory activity and abstracts from geographical, cultural, racial, religious, class, familial or tribal, ancestral, ideological, organizational, or otherwise affiliative associations.

Habermas's concept of solidarity is narrower than his concept of community. It evolved out of his reading of Emile Durkheim and George Herbert Mead.[8] Durkheim understood solidarity in the context of traditional and tribal societies as ordered group membership, the value or meaning of which is expressed in religious ritual. Integrating Mead's analysis of communication as a process of individual socialization and enculturation, Habermas identifies solidarity as a dimension of the "reproduction of the lifeworld," or the passing of culture, social order, and personal identity from one generation to another in communicative action. Specifically, solidarity is membership in "legitimately ordered interpersonal relations," where legitimacy is judged by commonly recognized norms of association.[9] In the modern context, which has by and large abandoned "nonrational" traditional and religious morality, these norms of legitimate interpersonal relations are "rationalized."[10] In other words, they are procedurally justified principles of justice and legal principles, intended to apply to all concerned alike. As general principles, Habermas concedes, they are "less and less tailored to concrete forms of life."[11]

In summary, Habermas's theory of rationality embodies interdependent concepts of rational justification, of the autonomous rational agent, and of community and solidarity. In the process, each of these terms acquires a highly technical definition, and one that does not necessarily converge with its usage in feminist theory. What I have tried to show in presenting these concepts is that while the consensus theory departs from Kant in theorizing reason as inherently dialogical, it retains the Kantian association of community with autonomy, of autonomy with rationality, and of rationality with the ability to discover laws both natural and ethical. Questions remain as to whether and how this conceptual apparatus compares to feminist ideas about knowledge and community. In the next section of this paper, I argue that however attractive Habermas's definition of the ideal speech situation may be for its emphasis on exposing the forces of domination in human interaction, his reliance on procedures of epistemic justification in developing this ideal as an ideal of community countervails the basic premises of feminist epistemology. To give Habermas his due, I must point out the importance to my argument of his insight, that an understanding of emancipatory thought and reason is inseparable from analysis and evaluation of forms of relationship. Along the way, I will look more closely at points of convergence and divergence between Habermas's and feminists' conceptions of reason and community.

Reason and Community

Explaining the motivation for his inquiry in the introduction to Part I of *The Theory of Communicative Action,* Habermas wrote: "The philosophical tradition, insofar as it suggests the possibility of a philosophical worldview, has become questionable. Philosophy can no longer refer to the whole of the world, of nature, of history, of society, in the sense of a totalizing knowledge."[12] Contemporary philosophy confronts a "postmetaphysical, post-Hegelian" breakdown of First Philosophy, and has abandoned "all attempts at discovering ultimate foundations."[13] In this cognitively and culturally decentered age, Habermas argues, "interest is directed to the formal conditions of rationality in knowing, in reaching understanding through language and in acting."

Although it has abandoned "First Philosophy," the project of developing a theory of argumentation, of "reaching understanding through language," has roots in the last two centuries. Habermas, in the tradition of critical philosophy, believes that the task of a critique of reason is inescapable in modern society. With Hegel, Habermas believes that the age of modernity "has to create its normativity out of itself."[14] Conscious of itself as a "new age," open to the future, having "broken with what was hitherto the world," "modernity sees itself cast back upon itself without any possibility of escape."[15] For Habermas as for Kant, the critique of reason is motivated by modernity's sceptical threat of uncertainty, and the dogmatic threat of prejudice, threats that represent enslavement, disintegration, and injustice. For Kant, the positive aim of critique was the discovery of laws—of thought, of nature, and of action—that answer the sceptic without lapsing into dogmatism. Though Habermas rejects Kant's assumption that critique should seek its foundations in the subjective conditions of possible experience, he accepts Kantian outlines of possible knowledge, in his Piagetian-Toulminian understanding of truth as scientific knowledge, and his baldly Kantian ethical theory (redeveloped via Kohlberg).[16]

It could be argued that feminism faces a parallel challenge to "create its own normativity out of itself." As feminists, we find ourselves in a position of radical uncertainty and orientation to the future that could be likened, if only broadly, to Hegel's "new age." One expression of this uncertainty might be found in a question raised by Joyce Trebilcot: "Do I contemplate these ideas in feminist consciousness or as I have been taught in patriarchy to do? Do I think the succession of ideas myself or do I follow patriarchal patterns of words drummed into me?"[17] One could read Trebilcot's question as a sceptical question, expressing a need to move outside of the dogmatics of patriarchy. In raising it, she calls into question the nature of theorizing in general, asking whether the activity of theorizing is not intrinsically a patriarchal tool of domination. She suggests that storytelling is a more appropriate (because more truthful and honest) way of creating connections of understanding and purpose between women. Rather than contribute to a general ideology in which the truths of individual women are lost or erased, stories contribute a variety of analyses.

It is revealing that this expression of feminist scepticism is directed against the activity of theorizing itself. Similar sceptical sentiments towards theory are present in much feminist writing, though they do not always target the same concepts or methods. Theory and analysis are also challenged from a postmodern perspective, e.g., by Jane Flax and Susan Bordo.[18] Jane Flax discerns in the pursuit of theoretical foundations the privileging of a standpoint that is dishonestly abstract, disembodied, and ahistorical. Susan Bordo adopts a postmodern incredulity towards generalizations and general analytic categories (including the category of gender), on the grounds that generalizations marginalize the voices and experiences of those persons who are different from their authors. Habermas would agree with these objections insofar as the theory criticized by Flax and Bordo does not fulfill his requirements of consensual theory. However, one of his consensual requirements, that a final consensus be universal, has appeared to many of his postmodern critics to be all but indistinguishable from the ill-fated Hegelian absolutism. The attractiveness of Habermas's recognition of social plurality and its role in knowledge formation is offset by an anticipated end to plurality, in the form of final epistemic justification.

There is no doubt that Trebilcot's, Bordo's, and Flax's criticisms of theory-construction diverge from Habermas's own conception of critical inquiry. But it is doubtful that these perspectives can be a substantial guide to conducting feminist analysis. On the one hand, Trebilcot's insight into the importance of women's truth-telling and analysis of personal life histories is right on the mark. I shall argue below that her insistence upon rooting feminist analysis in women's stories is essential in conceiving feminist thinking. On the other hand, her objections to theory are self-contradictory: either she admits that systematic analysis (theory) is necessary and expects it to come from the stories themselves, or the nature of analysis or theory is invested with dangers of such diabolical dimensions that any analysis done in the process of story-telling would be implicated as well. Bordo's and Flax's reservations in generalizations are well-motivated insofar as they caution against normalizing the dominant and marginalizing the powerless. But generalizations and principles as such are hardly pernicious, and as Christine Pierce argues, their use is necessary in making arguments such as these e.g., "Generalizations tend to marginalize the powerless."[19] More likely, it is what we count as the test of principles and generalizations that needs work. Nonetheless, these authors develop two themes which cannot be ignored in a feminist conception of reason and knowledge: we must seek out and listen to the stories of women, and we must be mindful of difference.

Other feminist challenges have targeted not theory as such, but the traditional philosophical project of the critique of reason. Robin Schott's book, *Cognition and Eros* criticizes the notion of the "purity" of reason, exploring the division, created by European philosophy from Plato to Kant, between reason and eros.[20] If Kant were to successfully complete this division, she argues, reason itself had to become ascetic. Schott argues that Kant's distillation of pure reason (both theoretical and practical) is not merely coincidental with his religious and personal asceticism. Rather, an ascetic distance between the reasoning and knowing subject on the one hand and those dimensions of the self and the world that conflict with a sustained "fear of God in the heart" on the other is constitutive of reason and knowledge. Sensual pleasure and pain, for example, do not contribute for Kant either to scientific or to moral knowledge, and the senses which are predominantly occupied with conveying impressions of pain or pleasure (touch, smell, and taste) are therefore inferior to sight as sources of knowledge.[21] Schott finds it revealing that Kant should choose to distinguish sense impressions that can contribute to empirical observations from those that cannot by the extent to which the resulting experience is "admixed" or tainted with impressions of pleasure or pain. Here the divergence of Kantian scepticism and feminist scepticism becomes clear: where Kant was sceptical of erotic connection, feminism is sceptical of the *denial* of erotic connection and the ways in which this denial has structured our most basic conceptual resources.

Does this analysis of Kant's concept of reason as ascetic carry over to Habermas's theory of rationality? I believe that it does, insofar as Habermas's conception of reason still relies so heavily upon the concept of epistemic justification in developing the concepts of autonomy and community. On the one hand, Habermas defends his consensus theory of reason and knowledge on the ground that the mutuality of understanding is the basis of all fully human social relationships. There is no fully human (i.e., fully rationalized) social relationship, Habermas argues, without mutuality of understanding, on the basis of shared grounds.[22] Here again we see the immanent interdependence of his concept of consensus with a concept of community. On the other hand, however, Habermas limits the community of mutual understanding to a justified consensus—the mutuality is a mutuality of shared justifications—and his community is one of agents whose autonomy and mutuality both are constituted by nothing other than justificatory competence. It is in this ultimate reliance on a procedure for epistemic justification as the guarantor of autonomy, community, and knowledge that we can see, once again, the illusions wrought by early modern scepticism. Where Kant once sought and Habermas still seeks to rebuild, in the shape of systematically justified beliefs, the confidence and social bonds of a subject sundered from itself and its community, feminism protests against the premises of this project. We wonder whether critical philosophy does not have it backwards: whether knowledge is not created out of solidarity, rather than the reverse.

Sympathetic readers of Habermas would plausibly object that in drawing parallels to Kant, I have played down the importance of mutuality in Habermas's account of the possibility of knowledge. Habermas emphasizes that the very ability to perform any kind of speech act, specifically, an illocutionary act, rests upon the speaker's essentially social ability to position himself or herself as a co-participant in a communicative relationship—to say, "*I* address this speech act to *you*. How do *you* respond?" The issue lies in how Habermas understands this social ability. For Habermas, this ability is not a simple, basic capacity to enter into relationship; it has an internal structure, which he calls the "validity basis of speech." The validity basis of speech is the set of rules of justificatory argumentation. It is the mutual recognition of and compliance with these rules, Habermas argues, that secures the possibility of relationship.[23] The successful speech act, then, establishes a relationship between the speaker and the hearer only insofar as the epistemic confidence of each requires the justified agreement of the other.

This argument provides the crucial premise for Habermas's contention that an orientation to rational consensus is present in every speech act. If no relationship is possible without shared recognition of the norms of communication, and the norms of communication are given in the validity basis of speech, then every act of communication must invoke them. It is this argument, then, that claims for the validity basis of speech its alleged "quasi-transcendental" status. Many of Habermas's critics have challenged the universality claimed for the validity basis of speech. Here, I will raise the issue of whether there are universal norms of communication aside, focusing on the claim such norms (if there are any) must be norms of epistemic justification. It is this second, stronger claim rather than the first that ties the act of communication to the notion of an ideal community composed specifically of communicatively competent persons (i.e., persons competent in the procedures of epistemic justification). Specifically, I wish to challenge two premises of this second claim. The first premise is that the ideal of a community held together by shared techniques of justification is an adequate one in articulating the ideals of social association.

Of course, Habermas's concept of consensus was never intended to embody a substantive vision of societal institutions and associations. Rather, the ideal of consensus is an ideal of a universal "community" of agreement upon basic epistemic and ethical questions, leaving questions of individual and group identity and association, and specific social institutions, to the domain of local consensus on social and cultural values.[24] My complaint may thus seem to miss the point of Habermas's consensus theory. Nonetheless, the point, which is similar to objections raised by others, bears repeating: The notion of the communication community is maximally thin in content, however committed it may be to justice for all.[25] The usual rejoinder to this observation is that, that's the way it goes when you're working out general guiding principles: they bear little concrete content, and this is a difficulty that you'll have to face unless you want to do without them. Rather than protest against the thinness of science and ethical-judicial reasoning as such, I wish to contest their status as the sole fundamental constitutive activities of community, solidarity, and society. It is possible to concede Habermas's assertion that a distinctly modern rationality has taken shape vis-à-vis questions of truth and justice in theoretical-scientific and ethical-juridical discourse, without granting his view that it constitutes the basis for the entire edifice of socialization, social integration, and enculturation. To concede that competence in the art of justification may be crucial to deciding fundamental issues of truth and justice is not to concede that justification is the foundation of all forms and dimensions of relationship. Mimesis, sympathy, and affection have at least as much claim to this status. Below, I explore the possibility that substantive ideals of solidarity and community can serve as the central constitutive values of feminist reasoning, as truth and justice are the constitutive values of science and philosophical ethics, respectively. To designate a value as a constitutive value of an activity or form of inquiry is to claim that it belongs to the set of characteristic aims of that activity or inquiry; in the absence of that aim the activity would simply not be *that* activity, as modern science would not be modern science without its aim of constructing a true theory of the universe.

The second questionable premise evokes the precedents of modern philosophy: the assumption that the possibility of intersubjectivity in general must be grounded in the possibility of accepting and rejecting arguments. Epistemic confidence in a shared objectivity is not the answer for feminism (as it was for Descartes and Kant) to the question of the possibility of intersubjectivity. Indeed, as I shall argue below, feminist critics of reason tend not to regard the possibility of intersubjectivity as a problem at all and protest those aspects of traditional epistemology that do. Feminist epistemology tends to argue that the subject comes to the specialized activity of justifying knowledge claims as an already socially embedded being. In contrast, the abstracted form of social relationship established, according to Habermas, by the successful illocutionary act—a mutuality of shared justifications—entails the inessentiality of any social embeddedness with which every subject might come to the social relationship. It is a form of relationship from which the substantive and "erotic" dimensions are subtracted. The question raised here is whether it is necessary to subtract them in the first place, unless one's interest is solely in formal or analytic issues.

Rather than rely upon a theory of justification to develop the idea of community, many feminist writers on knowledge start the other way around. Visions of community and solidarity, of friendship, of self located by solidarity, serve to affirm and cultivate the ways in which we are learning how to communicate, to analyze, to self-critically reflect; in other words, to reason and know. Some forms of feminist knowledge building stress the essential continuity of friendship or solidarity and the knowledge at the basis of the feminist movement. There is the communicative knowledge of particular others created in the kind of storytelling that Trebilcot describes, and the knowledge of interactive "world-travelling" of women whose sources of identity are deeply different, described in Maria Lugones's work.[26] From the multifaceted diversity of the particular experiences shared in these acts of communication, there are larger pictures to be drawn. Patterns in the nature of oppression become visible, and our own experiences of enslavement are transformed before our eyes from private cages to cells in a mass detention system. At the same time, we learn that this detention system is not one-dimensional, and that it has no single point of origin. The patterns of oppression that emerge into view also reveal norms of affiliation and desire that, while weighing heavily on one woman, embody the conditions of liberation for another. We learn that we need to see the territorial boundaries that we have established among ourselves as women; their nature, their justice or injustice, and the gates that are left open and closed by them. The fabric, weak or strong, of our shared stories and of our careful analysis of our own stories in relation to those of other women, is part of the fabric of our solidarity. In this sense, feminist knowledge is the creation of solidarity-building.

Other feminist writers challenge the assumption, which I have so far left untouched, that the constitutive values of science-as-usual and those of feminist thinking belong to independent domains of discourse. These writers argue that social ideals are always present in scientific inquiry and theory, and that a feminist science would reflect feminist social goals. Evelyn Fox Keller has employed the comparison between the anxious solipsistic self of early modernism and the communicatively identified self of feminism to articulate a feminist conception of "dynamic" objectivity, illustrating its emergence in the work of several women in science.[27] Instead of looking for relations of hierarchy and control within nature and between the observer and nature, Keller argues, dynamic objectivity approaches the natural world as something that tends to behave in ways that are unpredictable from a "master control" perspective. Focusing specifically on some of the human sciences (paleontology, human genetics, and neuroendocrinology), Helen Longino has illuminated the intricate dependence of scientific research programs, *and* the constitutive values of scientific method, upon shared commitments to particular social and cultural values.[28] When those values are patriarchal, she argues, accepted methods of scientific inquiry follow suit, avoiding questions about variables that might threaten assumptions about man as the toolmaker, the harem-collector, and the conqueror. Both Keller's and Longino's arguments develop the view that one's visions of and assumptions about forms of social association are fundamental to one's vision of inquiry and knowledge, and both urge the adoption of feminist values of relationship in mapping the dimensions of scientific inquiry.

Keller's and Longino's arguments can be of help in further refining my characterization of feminist epistemology. My claim is not that an ideal of solidarity *replaces* that of truth as a "criterion" of knowledge (a claim that would make little sense), but that ideals of community and solidarity figure centrally in articulating the ideal of knowledge, namely truth. In other words, truth is not a value or ideal that is empty of substantive (and specifically, social) content. Again, this reverses Habermas's conceptual scheme, which relies upon a vision of interpersonal argumentation (truth-seeking) to articulate the ideal community.

In summary, there is some convergence in feminist epistemology with Habermas's insight that ideals of community are developed in tandem with conceptions of reason and knowledge. Habermas's argument that the knowledge that belongs to the subject is knowledge only in virtue of that subject's relation to a community of knowers is consistent with what most feminist writers on knowledge have proposed. However, feminist critics of epistemology have rejected the sceptical issues and anticipated resolutions central to epistemology since Descartes, issues still present in Habermas's defense of the possibility of science and universal ethical laws against the solipsistic and sceptical threat of relativism.[29] Feminist theorists have rejected this project because it presupposes the very isolation of the subject that the project itself seeks to overcome. But if the alleged isolation and detachment of the knowledge-seeking subject is not a threat countenanced by feminism, then what interest do women have in developing a conception of reason and knowledge at all? Is epistemology to feminism what social science was to Marx—a web of obfuscation, constructed to make the unreal seem real, and the real seem unreal? Perhaps, if the only point to having a theory of knowledge were to overcome the legacy of Cartesian scepticism. However, other options have emerged. In the final section of this paper, I wish to draw upon these insights about the dependence of thought, analysis and knowledge for feminist visions of solidarity, but first, it is necessary to further explore the content of feminist solidarity.

Feminist Solidarity and Communicative Thinking
To even suggest that there is a feminist conception of solidarity might seem presumptuous. Therefore I will first consider what "feminist solidarity" might mean.

Feminism is an unprecedented social, political, economic, and cultural movement in its scope and ambitions. It is not geographical, ethnic, racial, national, class, religious, sexually-oriented, or physiological by identity, and its own parameters is therefore constantly in question (who is simply a woman?). The identity (identities?) and commitments of the feminist movement are still in the making. Our conceptions of desirable forms of political association (nation-states, anarchist decentralization, consensually operated communities, all-women communities, feminist political parties, tribal self-determination, urban coalitions) have not gelled into a world-historical manifesto on behalf of all women or, for that matter, all women from Manhattan. Unlike Marxist proletarianism, sisterhood is sceptical of guarantees of historical-rational progression; nor does it place its unquestioning confidence in ideals (such as a female "essence") defined as prior to or outside of such a progression. Many of us, then, are not sure how important it would be to have such a manifesto. Is it because the demands of working from within, for difficult but clearly visible changes like those called for in the fight against sexual harassment, founding a women's economic development network, keeping a women's clinic open, or regaining our sanity with a cherished group of friends, are simply too distracting?

It is worth exploring the possibility that this apparent lack of clarity concerning ideals of political and social association disguises the clearest of intentions. Perhaps, in our myriad engagements and affiliations, we are practicing an unfamiliar rational competence, one that is attuned to the undeniable *complexity* of what is right in front of us. We are aware that changes are accomplished with a thousand tiny steps, and that the consequences of each step can multiply in unpredictable directions, for better and for worse. We have seen, in the history of modernism and colonialism, how sweeping changes in the name of liberation have sullied the hands of the liberators with ruin in countless unforeseen ways. These are not grounds for rejecting the use of any form of critical systemic analysis, but they are grounds for caution, for working from where we are, with what we have, remembering the variety of the incredible stories told by individual women.

In her book, *Justice and the Politics of Difference,* Iris Young voices one such (very important) cautionary note, a protest against the anti-urban character of so many feminist (as well as neoconservative) ideals of community and friendship.

> Contemporary political theory must accept urbanity as a material given for those who live in advanced industrial societies. Urban relations define the lives not only of those who live in the huge metropolises, but also of those who live in suburbs and large towns. Our social life is structured by vast networks of temporal and spatial mediation among persons, so that nearly everyone depends on the activities of seen and unseen strangers who mediate between oneself and one's associates, between oneself and one's objects of desire.[30]

Moreover, Iris Young argues, the desire for community among the members of radical organizations "channels energy away from the political goals of the group," "produces a clique atmosphere," often "reproduces homogeneity," and may pose as a reason to disband any group that fails to achieve it.[31] She proposes instead an ideal of city life nurturant of diversity while cooperative in providing infrastructural services justly conceived, distributed, and administered. Her intention is not to deny the need for community and friendship, but to express doubt that sustainable forms of political association can require the transparency and affection of face-to-face relationships.

Many questions persist concerning the viability of the city and its reciprocal complements: suburbs, exurban housing tracts, large corporate agriculture and the demise of the farm town, massive waste of resources, massive transport costs, and so on. But at least one of Young's implicit points proves useful in focusing the ideal of feminist solidarity: one can love a city, love the fact of its diversity, contribute to the mutual support of its diverse populations, without sustaining affectionate and personally supportive relationships with all of the individual people whose paths one crosses. (At the same time, it is unlikely that mutual support can be sustained without many relationships that cross communal boundaries.) It suggests a vision of solidarity in which the enclave or project one is most devoted to is recognized at the same time as uniquely appropriate for her or him as an individual, and as one among uncountably many foci of devotion and belonging that deserve mutually cooperative attention. Solidarity need not be conceived as a one-dimensional, all-or-nothing relationship. In recognition of the diversity and complexity of the feminist movement, there must be room in the idea of solidarity for multiple identification with diverse projects, while each of us is focally committed to the integrity of our own.

Young's reflections on the politics of polis may also be helpful in working out the dimensions of the activity of feminist thinking, as other feminist ideals of association have been. Unlike institutional approaches to urban and regional planning and management, which begin and end with issues of revenue sources, her critique follows the structures of urban decision-making into their phenomenological consequences. For example, she describes how the zoning of businesses and residences plays itself out in time spent in a car; the privatization of the suburban household (and consequent loss of opportunity for spontaneous interaction with others); the proximity or remoteness of grocery stores, the availability of public space for a quiet walk or a lunch hour outdoors; the loss of neighborhoods to a stadium, freeway, or business park; and the withdrawal of resources from the inner cities. She proposes that city-dwellers have the opportunity to participate in regional planning:

> Social justice involving equality among groups who recognize and affirm one another in their specificity can best be realized in our society through large regional governments with mechanisms for representing immediate neighborhoods and towns.[32]

Her critique bears some similarities to Habermas's critique of the colonization of the lifeworld, or the encroachment of the imperatives of profit-oriented and centralized management upon our cultural and social resources. However, unlike Habermas's fatalist view that the functioning of the economic-bureaucratic "system" is phenomenologically opaque, her proposal for regional governance insists on the transparency of cause and effect between the functional imperatives of the business and administrative system and their social, aesthetic, political, and economic projections in the lifeworld.[33] This insistence is especially plausible when its focus is local or specific rather than global. It is paralleled in the work of feminist writers such as Nancy Fraser (in her critique of the management of Aid to Families with Dependent Children or AFDC) and Dolores Hayden (in her historical documentation of feminist urban planning and architecture, and in her own urban activism in Los Angeles).[34] Interestingly, and as Young does not point out, one of the motivations for her's and Hayden's proposed changes to regional decision-making is the desire to preserve or establish the preconditions of community and friendship, by rescuing public space, and instituting the possibility of collectively designing the landscapes of our "immediate neighborhoods and towns." While community may not be the basis of political action, it is certainly one of its ends.

Within the framework of Habermas's theory of rationality, such thought and analysis might be characterized as "interpretive" thought ("aesthetic-cultural" discourse), since it involves so much identification and interpretive analysis of needs and interests from within the holistic experience of one's particular locale in the lifeworld. But categorizing it as distinctly value-interpretative discourse ignores the insistent linkage of questions of justice, cause and effect, bureaucratic functional organization, quality of life, with the need for community in feminist analysis and practice. In our concern for our diverse and mostly local projects, we cannot afford to ignore the logic of profit, the functional logic of administrative organizations, or the causal consequences of our choices when discussing such things as what services to offer through a campus women's center. Answers to concerns about the justice of serving some needs and not others may hinge on the possibility of opening bureaucratically closed doors or raising funds, and answers to concerns about racial exclusion in a local women's organization may depend upon what ways are available to overcome geographical and economic racial segregation.

The conception of feminist thinking that emerges here and in the previous section is a multifaceted one, but always one that is derived from the nature and complexity of the forms of association that we work within and those we are attempting to realize. Because our projects develop within diverse contexts to meet diverse needs, it seems at first glance hardly appropriate to identify any one set of "principles of reason" to frame their rationality. We specialize: the skills of a feminist therapist of victims of abuse are not those of a feminist urban planner. However, moving forward means developing synthetic perspectives on the nature of these projects and the needs that spawn them. The planner needs to think about the indirect contributions to violence of architecture, landscape, and land use planning, and the therapist needs to understand the patterns of traffic in her client's locale. Our specialties need the enrichment of cross-talk. For this reason, it might be appropriate to call this kind of thinking "communicative thinking."

The synthetic and communicative mapping of the dimensions of our work certainly branches into many of traditional domains of rational procedure, both theoretical and organizational. There would be no feminist microbiology, philosophy, critical legal studies, and urban planning if it did not. Communicative thinking is no wholesale abandonment of the resources of what Habermas calls communicative and functional rationality, or of the resources of the specific rationalized procedures and techniques comprised in the institutions with which we must interact. To the contrary, these are resources necessary to our survival. But survival is not success, and the successes that these traditional and institutional rational procedures are designed to achieve are not, by and large, the aims of feminism. Thus, while making the necessary use of these resources, we must also forge analytic, imaginative, and synthetic resources of our own. I conclude with a few suggestions.

First, as in Young's analysis of urban planning, communicative thinking insists upon the transparency of the multiple causal projections of the institutions of the welfare state into our lives, and on possible ways of reworking these institutions to meet the needs of women. Understanding these patterns of cause and effect is not a matter of distilling mathematically elegant and parsimonious laws of human nature, as it tends to be for modern science's vision of the human sciences, but of analyzing the confluence of the multiple and changeable consequences of institutional choices that make their appearance in our lives.

Second, if we are to make these causes and effects transparent, we need to resist one of the concomitants of specialization: identification with the mainstream aims of the institutions in which we work and upon which we depend. As anyone knows, this is far easier said than done; few of us enjoy the privilege of being paid for advocating the destruction of patriarchy or racism, and few of us can afford to retreat forever to a cabin in Vermont. Many of us have no choice but to contribute indirectly to patriarchy in some of our actions, and the cognitive and moral dissonance this brings with it is weighty. Communicative thinking must address these issues with imagination and flexibility, and specifically, provide a mode of communication that recognizes the reality of the effects this dissonance has on our thought and motivation, while supporting our efforts to reduce our dependence upon hegemonic structures.

Third, our lives are positioned differently, and thus it is also essential to communicative thinking, as *communicative,* to recognize the different ways the institutions of welfare state capitalism impact women. The functional rationality of the AFDC program, for example, appears differently in the life of a working single mother a stone's throw away from unemployment and poverty, than in the life of the professor of social work who studies the program. The labyrinthine red tape and paramilitary organization of the Immigration and Naturalization Service may enforce the boundaries of existence for a garment worker in Los Angeles, while the California Assemblywoman's office analyes immigration statistics. In tracing the multidimensional projections of our institutions into the lives of women, we need also to recognize that the proportions and intensity of those projections vary greatly.

Fourth, for this reason, communicative thinking is rooted in the myriad details of the stories of women's lives. When the remarkable stories of women's lives are kept in mind, it is not so easy to forget the powerless and the silenced in formulating analyses, and in generalizing from experience.

Communicative thinking is thinking that not only seeks out these stories at conferences, in feminist journals, novels, magazines, and galleries, but remembers them and reflects upon them. Remembering and synthesizing from women's stories also creates the bonds of solidarity that Young discovers in the ideal of city life. Though we find each other's stories sometimes overwhelmingly unlike our own, our knowledge of them creates the possibility of mutual support.

Fifth, as feminist thought has always been defiantly holistic, communicative thinking is holistic, but this holism is not one that seeks to offer a univocal axiomatic structure or a regimented semantics. It seeks intricacy, complexity, and multidimensionality, not as ends in themselves, but because understanding the nature and contexts of our real ends, however specific, requires it. While this holism is opposed to reductive unity, it is also opposed to the fragmentation of women. This holism is a defiant attitude towards the alienation and value-confusion imposed by fragmenting logics of consumerism, the profit imperative, and bureaucratic procedure. It is opposed to the segregating logic of distribution of opportunity by race, "management" and zoning of race in city bureaucracy, and stereotyping of race by conceptual opposition to the police, law, and order.

Sixth, the test of the epistemic rationality of communicative thinking is not principally of the formal virtues of its structure or in any narrowly instrumental success but of the integrity of its ideals of solidarity and community, as they are assessed and tested in the course of practice. Knowledge of contemporary society that succeeds only by virtue of capturing "laws of behavior" is not enough; a critical understanding of the "causal structure of the social world" must be reflectively aware of the role of existing and ideal forms of association in shaping that understanding.

Seventh, it follows that communicative thinking approaches the values of truth and of the just social life as interarticulated values. As the work of Evelyn Fox Keller and Helen Longino suggests, the form taken by our knowledge of the world is constrained and informed by social ideals, and the imagined range of possible forms of association is shaped by one's enculturated consciousness of the natural and social world. Mindfulness of issues of justice thus animates a critical understanding of the contemporary social world. Communicative thinking cannot (and need not) ignore questions about justice that happen to be formal or general. Feminists engaged in their projects cannot often afford to dither with the formal virtues of abstract principles of justice, when there is a need for substantive norms of justice formulated from within those projects. The feminist movement needs to focus on issues of the substantive content of justice as Young does, for example, in challenging the presumption that justice is a question of distribution rather than of oppression and domination.[35]

Finally, I should point out that this essay does not repudiate Habermas's theory of communicative rationality. Indeed, I have set some important questions relevant to this issue aside: 1) whether communicative thinking might not be encompassed within Habermas's 'aesthetic-cultural' domain of discourse; 2) how the substantive constitutive ideals of feminist thinking interact with the formally defined ideals of traditional epistemology; and 3) whether substantive ideals of social association must or need not be rejected as grounds for conceptions of reason just because they are "substantive." Although these questions require further debate, I have presumed that their answers are not crucial here. First, Habermas's conception of aesthetic-cultural discourse has received little of his attention and is delineated only in extremely vague terms.[36] Second, the holism of communicative thinking is consonant with dialogue and correction from diverse domains of discourse, so long as they do not entail a commitment to the substantive values of patriarchy. Third, it is not clear that the constitutive values of epistemic enterprises aimed specifically at axiomatizable forms of theory must be as privileged as they have been in twentieth-century epistemology. It could be argued that conceptions of truth and justice as axiomatic systems of principles and observations are no more or less committed to substantive values (such as "creating a normativity" for a society committed to overcoming Cartesian scepticism) than conceptions that begin with social-ecological ideals, to construct visions of truth and justice grounded in the multiple experiences of subjects who need and offer each other cooperation and respect.

I have chosen Habermas's theory as a participant in dialogue, in order to focus the image of feminist epistemology as part of a feminist critical theory. Along the way, I have employed several of Habermas's insights and distinctions. Perhaps the most crucial of my Habermasian premises is adapted from his sociological interest in distinguishing domains of rationality as the bases of distinct domains of action, less concerned with the technical details of successful probability assignment (as in standard Anglo-American theories of rationality) than with the characteristic aims of distinct types of rational action. My principal point of departure from Habermas is in suggesting that substantive feminist ideals of solidarity and community can be constitutive ideals of a feminist rational discourse.

NOTES

1. See e.g., Nancy Hartsock, *Money, Sex and Power* (Boston: Northeastern University Press, 1985).

2. See Juliet Mitchell, *Woman's Estate* (New York: Pantheon Books, 1971); Alison Jaggar, *Feminist Politics and Human Nature* (Totowa, NJ: Rowman and Allenheld, 1983); Nancy Hartsock, *Money, Sex and Power*; Heidi Hartmann, "The Unhappy Marriage of Marxism and Feminism: Towards a More Progressive Union," in Lydia Sargent, ed., *Women and Revolution: A Discussion of the Unhappy Marriage of Marxism and Feminism* (Boston: South End Press, 1981) pp. 1–41; Iris Young, "Socialist Feminism and the Limits of Dual Systems Theory," *Socialist Review* 10:2–3 (March – June 1980), pp. 169–88; and "Beyond the Unhappy Marriage: A Critique of the Dual Systems Theory," in L. Sargent, ed., *Women and Revolution*, pp. 43–69.

3. See Elizabeth Spelman, *Inessential Woman: Problems of Exclusion in Feminist Thought* (Boston: Beacon Press, 1988); Maria Lugones, "On the Logic of Pluralist Feminism," in Claudia Card, ed., *Feminist Ethics* (Lawrence, KS: University of Kansas Press, 1991), pp. 35–44; Iris Young, *Justice and the Politics of Difference* (Princeton, NJ: Princeton University Press, 1990).

4. Nancy Fraser, *Unruly Practices: Power, Discourse and Gender in Contemporary Social Theory* (Minneapolis, MN: University of Minnesota Press, 1989), p. 127.

5. Habermas's theory of communicative rationality is defended in "What is Universal Pragmatics?" in Habermas, *Communication and the Evolution of Society*, (Boston: Beacon Press, 1979); "Wahrheitstheorien," in *Vorstudien und Ergänzungen zur Theorie des kommunikativen Handelns* (Frankfurt am Main: Suhrkamp Verlag, 1984); *The Theory of Communicative Action*, Vol. I trans., Thomas McCarthy, (Boston: Beacon Press, 1984), pp. 273–337; and "Discourse Ethics: Notes on a Program of Philosophical Justification," in *Moral Consciousness and Communicative Action*, trans., Christian Lenhardt and Shierry Weber Nicholsen, (Cambridge, MA: MIT Press, 1990), pp. 43–115.

6. See e.g., Habermas, *The Theory of Communicative Action*, Vol. I, pp. 68–69.

7. This reflects Habermas's usage of the term; he offers no formal definition of the term. See Habermas, *The Theory of Communicative Action*, Vol. II, pp. 55, 94–111. For example, consider the following passage from p. 97: "Let us imagine individuals being socialized as members of an ideal communication community; they would in the same measure acquire an identity with two complementary aspects: one universalizing, one particularizing. On the one hand, these persons raised under idealized conditions learn to orient themselves within a universalistic framework, that is, to act autonomously. On the other hand, they learn to use this autonomy, which makes them equal to every other morally acting subject, to develop themselves in their subjectivity and singularity. . . . Membership in the ideal communication community is, in Hegelian terms, constitutive both of the I as universal and the I as individual."

8. See Habermas, *The Theory of Communicative Action*, Vol. II, pp. 3–111.

9. Habermas, *The Theory of Communicative Action*, Vol. II, p. 142, Figure 21; See pp. 137–42.

10. Habermas *The Theory of Communicative Action*, Vol. II, p. 147.

11. Habermas, *The Theory of Communicative Action*, Vol. II, p. 146.

12. Habermas, *The Theory of Communicative Action*, Vol. I, p. 1.

13. Habermas, *The Theory of Communicative Action*, Vol. I, p. 2.

14. Habermas, *The Philosophical Discourse of Modernity*, trans., Frederick Lawrence, (Cambridge, MA: MIT Press, 1987) p. 7.

15. G.W.F. Hegel, "The Preface to the *Phenomenology*," in W. Kaufmann, ed., *Texts and Commentary* (New York, 1966), p. 20. As quoted in Habermas, *The Philosophical Discourse of Modernity*, p. 6–7. See also the Introduction to Part I of Habermas, *The Theory of Communicative Action*, Vol. I, for a defense of the necessity of a theory of rationality for critical sociology.

16. See Habermas, *The Theory of Communicative Action*, Vol. I, pp. 22–42; Habermas, *Moral Consciousness and Communicative Action*, pp. 116–94.

17. Joyce Trebilcot, "Ethics of Method: Greasing the Machine and Telling Stories" in Claudia Card, ed., *Feminist Ethics*, pp. 45–51.

18. Jane Flax, "Postmodernism and Gender Relations in Feminist Theory," *Signs: Journal of Women in Culture and Society*, 12:4 (Summer 1987), pp. 621–43; Susan Bordo, "Feminism, Postmodernism, and Gender-Scepticism," in Nancy Nicholson, ed., *Feminism/Postmodernism* (New York: Routledge, 1990) pp. 133–56.

19. Christine Pierce, "Postmodernism and Other Skepticisms," in Claudia Card, ed., *Feminist Ethics*, pp. 60–77.

20. Robin Schott, *Cognition and Eros: A Critique of the Kantian Paradigm* (Boston: Beacon Press, 1988).

21. See Schott, *Cognition and Eros*, pp. 103–105.

22. This argument is made in "What is Universal Pragmatics?" in Habermas, *Communication and the Evolution of Society*.

23. Habermas, *Communication and the Evolution of Society*, p. 63.

24. Habermas includes a third domain of communicative rationality, aesthetic-cultural rationality, that is not oriented to universal consensus. It is within this domain of discourse that substantive principles of justice and right are, presumably, negotiated. Habermas has variously characterized this discourse as one that raises claims of personal truthfulness, dramaturgical and aesthetic authenticity, and cultural integrity. (See Habermas, *The Theory of Communicative Action*, Vol. I, p. 326, 334; Habermas, *Moral Consciousness and Communicative Action*, p. 104.) However it is characterized, aesthetic-cultural agreement does not admit of consensus and thus is not, strictly speaking, knowledge. For this

reason, I exclude aesthetic-cultural discourse in my presentation of Habermas's theory of knowledge.

25. Parallel objections to the abstractness of Habermas's discourse ethics have been systematically developed by Albrecht Wellmer and Seyla Benhabib. See Albrecht Wellmer, *Ethik und Dialog* (Frankfurt am Main: Suhrkamp Verlag, 1986); Seyla Benhabib, *Critique, Norm and Utopia* (New York: Columbia University Press, 1986).

26. Maria Lugones, "On the Logic of Pluralist Feminism," in Claudia Card, ed.; "Playfulness, 'World'-Travelling, and Loving Perception," *Hypatia* 2:2 (Summer 1987), pp. 3–19.

27. Evelyn Fox Keller, *Reflections on Gender and Science* (New Haven: Yale University Press, 1985).

28. Helen Longino, *Science as Social Knowledge* (Princeton, NJ: Princeton University Press, 1990).

29. See e.g., the dialogue with the sceptic in "Discourse Ethics," in Habermas, *Moral Consciousness and Communicative Action*.

30. Iris Young, *Justice and the Politics of Difference*, p. 237.

31. Iris Young, *Justice and the Politics of Difference*, p. 235.

32. Iris Young, *Justice and the Politics of Difference*, p. 248.

33. See Habermas, *The Theory of Communicative Action*, Vol. II, p. 355.

34. See Nancy Fraser, *Unruly Practices*, pp. 144–83; Dolores Hayden, *The Grand Domestic Revolution: A History of Feminist Designs for Amercian Homes, Neighborhoods and Cities* (Cambridge, MA: MIT Press, 1981); *Redesigning the American Dream: The Future of Housing, Work, and Family Life* (New York: W.W. Norton, 1984).

35. See Iris Young, *Justice and the Politics of Difference*, p. 3.

36. Habermas's aesthetic-cultural discourse appears to be principally concerned with issues of personal and cultural identity. But its definition as any discourse concerned with nonuniversal values and norms is unhelpfully broad, and gives few clues as to how such discourse might be conducted.

6

Feminist Discourse/Practical Discourse

Simone Chambers

At his most ambitious, Habermas claims that the ideal of a consensually steered society is inherent to discourse ethics.[1] What would such a society look like? What would it require of citizens? What place does or should consensus have in our pluralistic world? Although not for the most part inspired by Habermas, many feminist activist groups have consciously adopted procedures of consensual will-formation. This paper investigates the dynamics of small-group consensual will-formation in the hope that such real-world undertakings can shed light on some of the above questions.

I begin by describing a discursive experiment undertaken by a group of feminist antinuclear activists. These activists worked out and implemented a set of concrete guidelines for consensual will-formation. One of the most interesting aspects of these guidelines is that, in drawing them up, participants realized that fulfilling the conditions of discourse meant more than simply adhering to certain procedural rules. Rules limit action. Successful discourse requires more than external limits on action; participants must adopt particular and concrete attitudes towards each other. In achieving attitudes productive for discourse, an ethic of care which accentuates responding to others (a reaching out to others) is more helpful than an ethic of justice which stresses not interfering with others (a limitation of the self). Thus, I argue that the feminist experiment in consensual will-formation points to the necessity of learning how to be discursive actors as opposed to strategic actors.

To what extent can the dynamics of a small-scale activist group be reproduced at the level of society at large? The most obvious objection to this type of move is that it is unrealistic given the diversity and plurality of modern liberal democracies. I argue that although the consensual "way of life" adopted by the activists is an unrealistic model on a larger scale, discourse and consensual will-formation are not incompatible with pluralism as such. However, a further problem arises: from a goal-oriented perspective of coming to a hard-and-fast collective decision, consensual will-formation is highly inefficient. As participation becomes wider and more diverse, discourse becomes less efficient. This leads to the conclusion that beyond small and relatively homogeneous groups, discourse cannot serve as an efficacious or even realistic method of decision-making. This does not mean, however, that discourse has no role to play in democratic politics. I argue that the proper domain of consensual will-formation is cultural reproduction. A consensually steered society is one in which public opinion, rather than public decisions, is reproduced and altered discursively.

A Discursive Experiment

An illustration of what I consider to be a successful feminist discursive experiment can be found in the practices and procedures adopted by the Women's Encampment for a Future of Peace and Justice established at the Seneca Army Depot. The Seneca Peace Camp began its life in the summer of 1983 and was inspired by the Women's Peace Camp at Greenham Common, which, two years earlier, had captured the attention of the international press and feminist activists from around the world. Women from all walks of life, ideological perspectives, and feminist orientations came together under the banner "a future of peace and justice." The ambition of the organizers went far beyond testing discursive procedures: it was visualized as a "bold experiment in a communal life of non-violence where women cooperate and share decision-making through consensus." The Peace Camp was to provide "a place where women gain strength and courage from one another, where women continue their commitment to non-violence and feminism."[2] All aspects of the Camp were organized in such a way as to avoid hierarchies and leadership/non-leadership stratification. The highly communal, egalitarian, and consensual nature of the Camp as a whole was itself the product of consensual will-formation. This highlights the two separate roles that discourse played at the Peace Camp: 1) a foundational role legitimizing the organizational structure and decision procedures to be adopted; and 2) an ongoing conflict resolution and decision procedure.

While the Camp was being conceived and set up, a discourse began about how it would be organized and how decisions would be made.[3] In these initial "foundational" meetings, the focus was on discussing, airing, and collectively evaluating options. It was accepted as unproblematic that the goal of these meetings was to construct a consensus. However, it became evident that an initial and widespread commitment to consensus formation did not necessarily mean a commitment to adopting procedures of consensual will-formation for the Camp itself. A general agreement that the Camp should be run in a highly democratic way was already in place but there was no agreement as to the form that democracy should take. In addition to consensus formation, administrative decision-making, and simple majority rule, Robert's Rules of Order were discussed.[4]

Many women were hesitant about adopting discursive procedures. They argued that women would be more familiar with "mainstream" procedures, that consensus formation was a very demanding form of decision-making, and finally that discourse would involve an extensive preliminary learning process to prepare women for a constraint-free format.[5] Whereas the arguments in favor of mainstream procedures focused on questions of efficiency, practicality, and expediency, the arguments in favor of consensus formation focused on which decision-procedure would embody and further the goals of personal growth, solidarity, and individual and collective empowerment. In the end, the internal goods gained through the experience of discourse were deemed more important and—despite the initial misgivings on the part of many participants—a consensus was reached that decisions should be reached by consensus. It is important to note here that the women at the Seneca Peace Camp could have come to a consensus that some form of majority rule would better suit their needs and interests.

Once the women decided that consensus was to be their decision-procedure, they set about constructing guidelines for actual implementation. These were published in a fifty page pamphlet entitled *Resource Handbook for the Women's Encampment for a Future of Peace and Justice*. In addition to principles of consensus formation, the *Resource Handbook* also included a great deal of information and history about the Seneca Army Depot itself and feminist antimilitary activity. With regard to consensus, the *Resource Handbook* defended "the fundamental right of . . . all people to be able to express themselves in their own words and of their own free will." It went on to state that "the fundamental responsibility of consensus is to assure others of their right to speak and be heard. Coercion and trade-offs are replaced with creative alternatives and compromise with synthesis."[6]

The similarities between this view of consensus formation and Habermas's are striking: the conditions of practical discourse are designed precisely to guarantee that all participants have the right to speak and be heard. The most important conditions are as follows: every actor affected by the norm may enter discourse; each participant must be allowed an equal opportunity to speak and be heard; anything may be questioned, challenged, and defended; no one may use force or deception to sway participants.[7] Under these conditions and motivated by a desire to reach agreement, participants attempt to build a consensus. The consensus legitimizes the norm because in being "immunized in a special way against repression and inequality," the outcome represents what all want.[8]

The picture, then, is of a constraint-free dialogue in which closure cannot be enforced unilaterally. However, unilateral blockage is possible because in trying to reach an agreement which represents what *all* want, each individual has a veto power. This in turn implies that successful discourse will only take place when participants are sincerely committed to the process and the search for common ground. A strategic as opposed to discursive actor can hold up proceedings indefinitely. In a world where negotiation, instrumental trade-offs, and strategic bargaining are the most common routes to reaching collective "agreement," it is not surprising that the women of Seneca Peace Camp understood that discourse was going to require an extensive learning process. What they set out to do was to describe what this learning process would involve, and from it, we can learn a great deal. They did not simply lay out rules of discourse which should not be broken, but attempted to specify the concrete attitudes, sentiments, and modes of talk that are necessary to be a discursive as opposed to a strategic actor.

These concrete attitudes, sentiments, and modes of talk were drawn from female communicative experiences. Despite many similarities between the Peace Camp's idea of discursive will-formation and Habermas's, these women were not influenced or inspired by Habermas and the philosophy of discourse ethics. Instead, their inspiration came from the tradition of cultural feminism. As one commentator put it "the same values that Gilligan identified as 'female' were considered the basis of the alternative world toward which the encampment was striving."[9] The organizers themselves put it this way:

> Feminism is a value system which affirms qualities that have traditionally been considered female: nurturance of life, putting others' wellbeing before one's own, cooperation, emotional and intuitive sensitivity, attention to detail, the ability to adapt, perseverance. These traits have been discounted by societies which teach competition, violent conflict resolution, and materialism.[10]

Many of the above-mentioned qualities are necessary for productive discourse. An ethic of care, which places communication, a reaching out to make connections, and mutual and sympathetic understanding at the center of moral problem solving, can give content to the abstract and formal rules of discourse.[11] This, of course, does not mean that only women are capable of productive discourse. It does mean that female moral experience has an important contribution to make in giving content to the abstract formalism of discourse ethics.[12]

Discursive Attitudes and Sentiments

The *Handbook* listed five major requirements which each participant should attempt to fulfill: responsibility, self-discipline, respect, cooperation, and struggle. The requirement of responsibility stated that "participants are responsible for voicing their opinions, participating in the discussion, and actively implementing the agreement."[13] This is an aspect of discourse that is often ignored. When Habermas speaks of the conditions of discourse, he often talks in terms of non-interference as opposed to positive requirements. For example, he says: everyone *may* enter discourse; no one *may* interfere with a participants rights to speak and be heard; anything *may* be questioned.[14] It is conceivable that all these conditions are met and yet the discourse itself falls short of a full participatory discussion. That I may enter the debate does not mean that I will enter the debate; that I am given the equal opportunity to speak and be heard does not mean that I will avail myself of that opportunity; that I may question and challenge anything does not mean that I will actually question and challenge. Successful discourse involves more than ensuring that people who want to engage in discourse may engage in discourse. Successful discourse involves fostering the desire to participate; it involves, as the women at the Seneca Peace Camp saw, a positive responsibility to engage in the process.

If the emerging consensus is to represent "what all want," then it is essential that as many voices are heard in the debate as possible. A practical discourse is made up of a web of talk. The more people caught in that web, the better the guarantee that all possible objections to the proposed claims have been given a hearing. Thus, the question of who enters the debate goes beyond whether individuals or groups have been systematically excluded from the process. The major barrier to discursive resolution in liberal democracies usually comes in the form of political apathy rather than conscious suppression. People have little interest in many decisions which affect them and are willing to allow others to debate those issues and find solutions. Thus, to the rule that no one may be excluded from discourse must be added the positive requirement that people ought to be encouraged to include themselves in the debate. This calls for an active reaching out to others which is never fully or adequately addressed in the formal language of proceduralism.

Next, the *Handbook* informed participants that self-discipline would be needed if the process was to be successful and advised that "blocking consensus" should only be done for principled objections. Object clearly, to the point, and without putdowns or speeches. Participate in finding an alternative solution."[15] It is interesting that the women of Seneca Peace Camp understood constructive opposition as a form of self-discipline. It requires a *self*-discipline because it asks participants to put aside the desire "to get one's way." Objections may reflect a particular or private interest but not an interest in winning the argument. Further, the reason for an objection cannot be *simply* that the proposal does not further an individual's particular interest. For example, one of the most hotly debated issues at the Peace Camp was whether or not to include men. Women who had male partners equally committed to the peace movement could not argue for inclusion solely on the grounds: "I want the company of my partner." Instead, they had to explain why the inclusion of men would also be in everyone's interest. Why is personal preference not a valid ground for objection? If the goal is agreement, then sincere discursive actors must move beyond the individual utility maximization model of action. They should not come to the table with the attitude: "I want X and my wanting X is, in and of itself, a good enough reason to try and hold out for X." Again, this is a form of self-discipline because it requires participants to argue in terms of what will contribute to consensus and not in terms of how to further their own interest. In addition to reasonable grounds for objections, the *Handbook* also speaks about the tone of objections. Here discourse is being envisioned between real people with real feelings and reactions to each other. An adversarial attitude, even when defending "principled" objections, can destroy the process.

The third requirement asked participants to "respect others and trust them to make responsible input."[16] At a minimum, respect involves allowing participants to speak their minds. This also requires a form of self-discipline. Participants must refrain from monopolizing the conversation and must understand that silence is often just as important to the discursive process as talk. But, in addition to the negative requirement that individuals be given the space and opportunity to speak, productive discourses contain the positive requirement that individuals listen to each other, respond to each other, and justify their positions to each other. To treat each other as equal dialogue partners means that we must start from the assumption that each participant has something potentially worthwhile to contribute to the discourse; that each participant deserves to have her claims considered. A dismissive or condescending attitude toward interlocutors can silence them just as effectively as shouting them down. Thus, the "egalitarian reciprocity" of discourse must express itself in something more than an equal distribution of opportunities to speak and be heard. In *treating* people as equal dialogue partners, participants must do more than refrain from cutting a speaker off. Participants must adopt attitudes that encourage and foster equal dialogic opportunities.

Cooperation is the fourth requirement stipulated in the *Handbook*. It asks participants to "look for areas of agreement and common ground and build on them. Avoid competitive, right/wrong, win/lose thinking."[17] As with Habermas's conception of practical discourse, the organizers at Seneca understood that successful discourse requires that participants be motivated by a desire to reach agreement. This desire must outweigh any desire to have one's own position win the day. Without the desire to reach agreement, one cannot explain why participants would be motivated to reevaluate their positions and be persuaded by argument.

Finally, the *Handbook* suggests that struggle and disagreement can be positive learning experiences and need not destroy the solidarity of the group. It counsels participants to "use disagreements and arguments to learn, grow, and change. Work hard to build unity in the group, but not at the expense of the individuals who are its members."[18] Learning from discourse is part of being a discursive as opposed to strategic actor. Successful discourse requires that participants are open-minded in the sense of being willing to reevaluate their positions and change their minds. As Seyla Benhabib has pointed out, unless one assumes that a harmony of interests already exists prior to discourse and that discourse simply tears away the mask hiding that harmony, then one must assume that people enter discourses with real disagreements and emerge from the process having changed their previously held beliefs.[19] Strategic actors will also change their position in the course of negotiation; however, this does not necessarily indicate a "change of heart." A strategic actor will settle for what she can get and not necessarily what she wants. A consensus is supposed to reflect what all want. This implies that what one wants is altered and changed through discourse. A willingness to "learn, grow, and change" is an essential aspect of the discursive process.

What we see is that discourse requires that participants possess a willingness to get involved, to use reasons that appeal to the other's point of view, to treat each with respect, to grow, learn, and change, and finally an interest in reaching agreement. This last is the most important for if possessed it can lead to a learning process in which the other aspects of discursive action are acquired. If we sincerely engage in the search for agreement it will become apparent that some attitudes are conducive to this end and some are not.

> Should one party make use of privileged access to weapons, wealth, or standing, in order to wring agreement from another party through the prospects of sanctions and rewards, no one involved will be in doubt that the presuppositions of argumentation are no longer satisfied.[20]

Although the discursive attitudes outlined above are necessary for any successful discourse whether it be among like-minded antinuclear activists or unlike-minded citizens, when we try to visualize the place and scope of discourse in a larger political context the Seneca model has only limited applicability.

Consensus and Pluralism

The women at Seneca were trying to create a "communal life of non-violence"—an "alternative world." Another way to put this is that they were trying to create an ideal way of life. This is not a realistic or even desirable goal for society at large. Many if not most citizens would find Seneca communal life unbearable and an infringement on their right to choose their own way of life. Some critics have suggested that this is precisely the problem with discourse ethics: it projects an ideal society that would look something like the ideal communication community. We would strive in all spheres of life to achieve consensus, to resolve disagreement, to find a commonly grounded way of life.[21] This is a misreading of the social and political ideal contained in discourse ethics.[22]

The rules of practical discourse are not guidelines for all social interaction; they are guidelines for collective deliberation regarding disputed norms—not rules of action but rules of argumentation. Discourse ethics might contain the ideal of a consensually *steered* society but not the ideal of a fully rational and entirely consensual society.[23] The women at Seneca chose a peace camp as their form of protest; that is, they chose to set up a microcosmic "way of life." Nowhere does discourse ethics imply that such a choice is right for everyone or that any one way of life is "uniquely capable of rational justification."[24] Indeed, discourse ethics implies that "ways of life" are not the sort of things we will, as members of large modern democracies, ever agree on.

There is, however, a slightly different version of this criticism that is more plausible. Even if we admit that practical discourse is a model of argumentation only and not a model way of life, there still appears to be a questionable and utopian privileging of agreement over disagreement.[25] This privileging of consensus (the reaching of full understanding between actors) puts into question the place of pluralism, diversity, and difference within discourse ethics. Are these pathologies to be overcome? If the Seneca peace camp is taken as the model for society-wide discourse, then this appears to be the correct conclusion. Again, some critics have thought this to be the implication of Habermas's position.

The most extreme criticisms equate consensus-formation with an updated but still dangerous collectivism. The worry of some liberal pluralists, for example, is that the search for consensus and generalizable interests has authoritarian or, at least, paternalistic implications: it implies that a great many people in our competitive, market-oriented societies who continue to disagree with each other are laboring under a form of false-consciousness.[26] Talk of false-consciousness is anathema to many liberal pluralists wed to the idea that an individual's true interests are simply what that individual believes her true interests to be. From the postmodern perspective the criticism is sometimes no less extreme as, for example, when consensus is equated with a collective subjectivity that is inherently totalitarian.[27] Less extreme is the argument, put forward most notably by Foucault, that the search for consensus through discourse is a type of disciplinary action ("consensual disciplines") aimed at taming and bringing order to a world of unruly differences.[28] The suspicious harbor a fear that rational consensus represents a dangerous homogenization of differences. The experiment at Seneca does support some of this: a number of antinuclear feminists left the camp after a short stay complaining that they could not deal with the communal orientation of the camp.

Does the cooperative search for agreement devalue heterogeneity, difference, and nonconformity? This way of construing the search for agreement ignores the fact that disagreement, conflict, dispute, argumentation, opposition—in short, nay-saying—is an essential aspect of the discourse process. Pluralism, diversity, and difference, far from being antithetical to discourse ethics, furnish the very conditions which make universalized norms possible. Habermas, for example, notes that:

> as interests and value orientations become more differentiated in modern
> societies, the morally justified norms that control the individual's scope
> of action in the interest of the whole become ever more general and
> abstract.[29]

Norms become more general and abstract because their justification must satisfy a wider and more profound set of criticisms and objections in a pluralistic, democratic society. Points of agreement within a highly homogeneous and conventional society will not be subjected to the same range and depth of scrutiny. And as society moves from a conventional to a post-conventional stage, those norms which cannot withstand the critical force of pluralism, diversity, and difference will pass away. Only those norms that represent principles generalizable within pluralism, that is, which can generate the support of all, will survive.

But even if there is no conflict in principle between consensual will-formation and pluralism, is there a practical conflict? We may agree in theory that the more varied our private interests and conceptions of the good, the more general and impartial will be those points upon which we do agree. But it might also be that, as a practical matter, the more pluralistic our society becomes, the fewer points there are upon which we *can* agree. It is the case, as Habermas acknowledges, that the area has grown in which private conceptions, and not consensually based general norms prevail.[30] Does this mean that the area where consensus is possible has correspondingly shrunk and will continue to shrink as we explore new lifestyles and develop ever more divergent visions of the good? According to Habermas, one can assume that the expanding diversity of particular lifestyles and conceptions of the good decrease the chances of finding anything to agree on only if one believes that there is a zero-sum relationship between these two aspects of collective life:

> But there are enough counter-examples—from traffic rules to basic institutional norms—to make it intuitively clear that increasing scope for individual options does not decrease the chances for agreement concerning presumptively common interests. The discourse ethical way of reading the universalization principle does not rest—even implicitly—on assumptions about the quantitative relation between general and particular interests.[31]

As Rawls points out, pluralism is simply a fact about us, and pluralism is characterized by irreconcilable disputes and differences of opinion on a plethora of deep issues. However, it is important to remember that "irreconcilable" does not necessarily describe each particular dispute, but a general state of affairs: there will always be things that people disagree about; they will not always be the same things. What is disputed and contested today may not be disputed and contested tomorrow. And what is uncontroversial today may tomorrow give rise to bitter dispute.

Discourse ethics does not project the ideal of a dispute-free world nor does it devalue contestation. Not only is such a world unattainable, it is also undesirable. Diversity and difference lead to criticism and criticism is our avenue to well-founded general norms. But, while discourse ethics does not devalue contestation—indeed, it points to the critical and productive force of contestation—it does not "valorize" contestation either.[32] Contestation, nay-saying, and struggle are not ends in themselves. Practical discourse is not an agonistic forum, but a dialectical forum where the clash of opposing forces can move participants forward.

Efficiency

There is a price to pay for the pursuit of this dialectical forum. That price is inefficiency. Consensual will-formation takes a long time. When a decision has to be made, stamina sometimes is as important as argument. Although the ideal of consensus guided all policy-making at the Seneca Peace Camp, "in reality decisions were often made on the basis of who could survive the longest in meetings that stretched on for hours or days."[33] As many of the organizers had anticipated, consensual decision-making was a difficult, drawn-out process, frustrating those who were more interested in acting than talking. If a relatively small group, united by a common goal, found discourse an unwieldy tool of decision-making, can we even begin to envision the wider discourse to which Habermas alludes? A consensually steered society implies a discourse that includes all its members. Is this plausible? I want to suggest that the implausibility of the Seneca model for the society at large does not point to the implausibility of practical discourse as such. It points instead to implausibility of discourse as a *decision* procedure within democratic politics.

Discourse is constraint free. This means that no one may force closure. The conversation continues until (ideally) every single participant is in full agreement. The larger and more diverse the group the more difficult and drawn out the process. Now clearly this is not a realistic model for all the decisions we associate with democratic government. The question then becomes which decisions should be made discursively and which by more efficient means? One answer is that the more the issue is a foundational one dealing with the legitimacy of the rules the more we are under an obligation to include all citizens.

But, in what sense is a face-to-face conversation between all citizens a feasible model of democratic legitimation? We cannot all sit in a circle facing each other as did the activists at Seneca. Nor can we be expected to devote the kind of time necessary to such an undertaking. Do we imagine a series of participatory face-to-face constituent assemblies? In large modern democracies this does not seem plausible. The problem here is that we are imagining practical discourse as a decision procedure with a determinate outcome. Thinking of discourse in this way will always bring us back to small, manageable groups like the women at Seneca Peace Camp. A decision procedure implies a set of rules which govern closure. These rules tell us when the process is over—what counts is a fair decision that can be acted upon. Now, as a decision rule, discourse stipulates that full, rational agreement under the ideal conditions of discourse of all affected by a norm constitutes the point of closure. However, when translated into the real world of politics it turns out that this point can never be definitively reached. Because real agreements can never be perfectly universal they never settle a question once and for all. Through the idea of an ideal communication community we can imagine the conditions of a perfectly rational consensus and therefore the criteria of universal validity. But, as we can never attain the ideal in the real world, the process is one of degrees of approximation. Discourse is not a contract where there is a privileged moment of promising which is then binding on all parties for perpetuity.

Discourses must be understood as open ended and fallible. This means that discourse is ongoing and conclusions and agreements reached by means of discourse are always open to revision.

Once we move beyond small groups, the notion of consensual will-formation cannot be understood as the outcome of one conversation, but must be seen as the cumulative product of many crisscrossing conversations over time. The point is simply to highlight the diffuse nature a real practical discourse must have if it is to underwrite a legitimate social norm. On this reading, then, practical discourse is a long-term process through which citizens construct common understandings, not a decision procedure. Unconstrained discourse is highly inefficient. The closer our conversations come to embodying this ideal, the more inefficient they are. The more general the norm under discussion, the more diffuse, fragmented, and complicated the web of discourse and the longer the process is likely to take. In this light, it becomes difficult even to talk about a decision being taken in discourse; instead, we must visualize discourse as a process through which collective interpretations are constructed. If we cannot come to decisions in discourse, then what role does discourse play in democratic politics? In conclusion I would like to briefly sketch the idea of a discursively formed public opinion as an answer to this question.

Public Opinion Formation

Following Durkheim and Weber, Habermas argues that social and political institutions cannot be maintained solely through force or strategic manipulation.[34] Although the threat of sanctions or the prospect of rewards are often part of what motivates citizens to play by the rules, by themselves such inducements cannot guarantee mass loyalty and stability. Stability requires that "reasons for obedience can be mobilized" which "at least appear to be justified in the eyes of those concerned."[35]

> Laws need to be inter-subjectively recognized by citizens; they have to be legitimated as right and proper. This leaves culture with the task of supplying reasons why an existing political order deserves to be recognized.[36]

When the reasons culture supplies are no longer convincing, then the fragile maintenance system of a norm falls apart. At this point a process must be undertaken whereby mobilization is either regenerated or shifted to an alternative norm. Mobilizing reasons for obedience is achieved through the communicative practice of convincing each other that there really are (or are not) good grounds to recognize a norm. Without such a regenerating process, not simply at our disposal but constantly in use, the shared background to our social world would fall apart.

There are two aspects to a discursive theory. First, there is the recognition and analysis of the real-world processes through which a citizen body generates the recognition necessary to sustain a stable system of justice. Culture and communication underpin this process. This analysis brings out the consensual foundation to all stable systems of rules and norms. Overlaid upon this social analysis is the theoretical/ethical analysis, which points to the optimal conditions under which this process ought to take place if the outcomes are to represent what is in the common interest. Thus rationalism is introduced not as a rational plan for society but as a process of rationalizing the consensual foundations to society.

It is not controversial to hold that stable political systems require some underlying belief in the legitimacy of the system; what is more controversial is to hold that this legitimacy must be rationally constructed through a democratic public debate. One need only think of Madison's remark that frequent appeals to the public would destroy "that veneration which time bestows on everything, and without which perhaps the wisest and freest governments would not possess the requisite stability."[37] Madison is echoing the conservative view that stability is maintained through non-cognitive, affective motivations such as reverence, respect, and patriotism. But the rise of pluralism in the modern world has made reliance on such shared community feelings increasingly implausible. Pluralism does not necessarily undermine the substance of traditional ways, rather it undermines "the *sanctity* . . . of a politics attached to traditional ways."[38] Pluralism challenges the authority of tradition more than its content. When this authority is challenged then reverence and respect must be earned; it cannot simply be assumed to be the natural by-product of the passage of time.

The historical circumstances that we, in modern liberal democracies find ourselves in, points to the conclusion that we can no longer depend on unquestioned veneration for our stability. We no longer share a common religious view nor a comprehensive moral outlook. The authority of tradition has been greatly weakened in a world where "nontraditional" perspectives are gaining an ever-stronger voice. We have very little homogeneity to fall back on to do the work of keeping our world together when a normative dispute arises. Thus, we must construct a consensus; we can no longer appeal to one that is ready-made.[39] The conditions for producing, reproducing, or changing a consensus in the modern political world point to the necessity of rationalizing and democratizing our public debates.

As a rationalized version of the processes through which culture and social integration are reproduced, discourse does not take place in any specially designated institutions. It can take place wherever public opinion is formed and this means at all levels of society—from one-on-one debates in informal settings to debates in Parliament.[40] What this means is that the defining characteristic of discourse cannot be found in any one set of institutional rules. Certain institutional rules can be necessary conditions for discourse but not sufficient conditions. For example, at the most general level, institutionalized rights are part of the context which can enable us to pursue discursive solutions. The legal protection of free speech is part of such an enabling context. But the First Amendment does not enforce the reciprocal requirements of practical discourse. It does not require us to *listen* to what others have to say; it does not require us to attempt to *understand* the other's point of view; it does not require us to *refrain* from manipulating or deceiving others; it does not require us to be *swayed* only by the force of the better argument. Only we can require these things of ourselves; institutions cannot force us to do them.

In distinguishing discursive democracy from republican or communitarian ideals of democracy, Habermas points out that discourse does not depend on a shared community ethos or the creation of a collective subject that acts as one.[41] These are unrealistic ideals in a modern pluralistic context. Instead, discursive democracy depends, on the one hand, on institutionalizing the procedures and conditions of communication and, on the other, the interplay between institutionalized decision-making and informally yet rationally shaped public opinion. In avoiding the pitfalls of communitarianism and the need for a high level of civic virtue, Habermas over stresses the purely procedural requirements of discursive democracy. Discourse does depend on institutionalizing the procedures and conditions of communication. But discourse also depends on citizens participating in institutionalized as well as informal discourse as discursive actors. If citizens do not possess this willingness, then no matter how well designed institutional arrangements are for the purposes of discourse, discourse will not take place. Everyone might have the opportunity to speak, but if no one is listening, the result is chaos. Habermas does not deny that discourse requires an interest in mutual understanding, but he never deals fully with the possibility that citizens might generally lack such an interest or not possess the competencies to pursue such an interest. In a world where negotiation, instrumental trade-offs, and strategic bargaining are the most common routes to reaching collective "agreement" and resolving disputes, it is plausible that the most serious barrier to discourse can be found in the conversational habits that citizens have become used to.

Discourse ethics replaces the image of public debate as a marketplace of ideas between elites in which interests and understandings compete with each other for domination with the idea of public debate as a democratized forum in which we cooperatively construct common understandings and work through our differences. Part of this transformation can take place by opening up opportunities to participate, by including excluded voices, by democratizing media access, by setting up "town meetings," by politicizing the depoliticized, by empowering the powerless, by decentralizing decision-making, by funding public commissions to canvas public opinion, and so on. But all such initiatives will fail to produce a discursively formed public opinion if citizens are unwilling to or uninterested in acting discursively.

Despite their commitment to process over end-result, the women at Seneca Peace Camp had to come to decisions. Choices had to be made, actions had to be organized, policies had to be decided. Closure had to be achieved in a relatively clear and unambiguous way. But an ongoing public discourse in which deep collective understandings and interpretations are reevaluated and altered does not require closure in the same way. Indeed, closure is undesirable in this context. The ideal of a consensually steered society is the ideal of a society that is committed to a certain type of political culture. Implementing practical discourse, then, is not so much a matter of setting up a constitutionally empowered "body" of some sort as it is of engendering a practice. It involves fostering a political culture in which citizens actively participate in public debate and consciously adopt the discursive attitudes of responsibility, self-discipline, respect, cooperation, and productive struggle necessary to produce consensual agreements. It is utopian to believe that we will ever be as considerate, respectful, and caring of each other while working through normative *disagreements* as is required by the ideal of discourse. But it is not unrealistic to hope that habits of argumentation change, nor is it unrealistic to explore ways of changing them. The road from public debate in which strategic actors compete in a marketplace of ideas to public debate in which discursive actors democratically work through their differences is a long one. Its length, however, is a poor argument for not setting out on the journey.

NOTES

1. Jürgen Habermas, "Reply to My Critics" in *Habermas Critical Debates*, eds. John B. Thompson and David Held (Cambridge, MA: MIT Press, 1982), p. 262.

2. Loise Krasniewicz, *Nuclear Summer: The Clash of Communities at Seneca Women's Peace Encampment* (Ithaca, NY: Cornell University Press, 1992) p. 3. See also, Mima Cataldo et. al., The Women's Encampment for a Future of Peace and Justice (Philadelphia: Temple University Press, 1987) p. 4.

3. The core group of organizers were drawn from the Upstate Feminist Peace Alliance (UFPA). Once the idea of a peace camp was discussed at the New York City Conference on Global Feminism and Disarmament many women from the Women's International League for Peace and Freedom (WILPF) also joined ranks. See Cataldo, et. al., The Women's Encampment, pp. 4–5.

4. Perigrine Schwartz-Shea and Debra D. Burrington, "Free Riding, Alternative Organization and Cultural Feminism: The Case of Seneca Women's Peace Camp" Women and Politics 10:3 (1990) p. 7–9.

5. Cataldo, et. al., *The Women's Encampment* p. 13.

6. *Resource Handbook for the Women's Encampment for a Future of Peace and Justice* (New York: Romulus, 1983) p. 42.

7. Habermas, *Moral Consciousness and Communicative Action* (Cambridge, MA: MIT Press 1990) p. 89.

8. Habermas, *Moral Consciousness and Communicative Action*, p. 89.

9. Krasniewicz, *Nuclear Summer*, p. 48.

10. *Resource Handbook*, p. 32.

11. Carol Gilligan, *In a Different Voice* (Cambridge, MA: Harvard University Press, 1982).

12. Seyla Benhabib, *Situating the Self* (New York: Routledge, 1992). Nancy Fraser, "Towards a Discourse Ethic of Solidarity," *Praxis International* 5:4 (1986), pp. 425–29. Nancy Fraser, "What's Critical About Critical Theory? The Case of Habermas and Gender" in *Feminist Interpretations and Political Theory*, eds., Mary Lyndon Shanley and Carole Patement (University Park: Penn State University Press, 1991), pp. 253–76. Nancy Love, "Ideal Speech and Feminist Discourse: Habermas Re-Visioned," Women and Politics 11:3 (1991) pp. 101–22.

13. *Resource Handbook*, p. 42.

14. Habermas, *Moral Consciousness and Communicative Action*, p. 89.

15. *Resource Handbook*, p. 42.

16. *Resource Handbook*, p. 42.

17. *Resource Handbook*, p. 42.

18. *Resource Handbook*, p. 42.

19. Seyla Benhabib, *Critique, Norm, and Utopia: A Study of the Foundations of Critical Theory* (New York: Columbia University Press, 1986), p. 312.

20. "Reply," pp. 272–73.

21. For an interpretation of Habermas along these lines see, for example, Stephen Lukes, "Of Gods and Demons: Habermas and Practical Reason," in *Habermas: Critical Debates*, p. 144. Also Wolfgand Schluchter, *Religion und Lebensfuhrung* (Frankfurt: Suhrkamp, 1988) vol. 1, pp. 322–33.

22. One source of this misunderstanding can perhaps be found in Habermas's earlier (1971) reference to the ideal speech situation as prefiguring a form of life (Vorschein eines Lebensforms). J. Habermas and N. Luhman, Theorie der Gessellschaft oder Socialtechnologie—Was leistet die Systemforschung? (Frankfurt: Suhrkamp, 1971), pp. 140–41. He has since retracted this formulation in a number of places: "Reply," p. 262 and Habermas, *Autonomy and Solidarity* (New York: Verso, 1986) p. 260. However, even before the

retractions, there was no evidence that the ideal speech situation was intended as something to be realized in an ideal communication community.

23. Habermas, "Reply," p. 262.

24. Lukes, "Of Gods and Demons," p. 145.

25. Habermas himself has said that he takes "the type of action aimed at reaching understanding to be fundamental" and starts from the assumption that "other forms of social action—for example, conflict, competition, strategic action in general—are derivatives of action oriented to reaching an understanding. See Habermas, *Communicative Action and the Evolution of Society*, trans. Thomas McCarthy (Boston: Beacon, 1979) p. 1.

26.. Quenten Skinner, "Habermas's Reformation," *New York Review of Books*, (October 7, 1982), pp. 35–38.

27. Jean-Francois Lyotard, *The Postmodern Condition*, trans. Geoff Bennington and Brian Massuni (Minneapolis, MN: University of Minnesota Press, 1985), p. 66.

28. Michel Foucault, *Foucault Reader*, ed. Paul Rabinow (New York: Pantheon Books, 1984) p. 380, "The Order of Discourse," in *Untying the Text*, ed. Robert Young (London: Routledge and Kegan Paul, 1981), p. 66.

29. Jürgen Habermas, *Moral Consciousness and Communicative Action*, p. 205.

30. Habermas, *Moral Consciousness and Communicative Action*, p. 205.

31. Habermas, "Reply," p. 257.

32. For a reading of Foucault that places the valorization of contestation at the center of the French philosopher's thought see Leslie Paul Thiele, "The Agony of Politics: The Nietzschean Roots of Foucault's Thought," *American Political Science Review*, Vol. 84, No. 3 (September 1990), pp. 907–26.

33. Krasniewicz, *Nuclear Summer*, p. 57.

34. Habermas, *Communicative Action and the Evolution of Society*, pp. 178 ff.

35. Habermas, *Moral Consciousness and Communicative Action*, p. 62.

36. Habermas, *Theory of Communicative Action*, trans. Thomas McCarthy (Boston: Beacon Press, 1987), Vol. II, p. 188.

37. Alexander Hamilton, James Madison, and John Jay, *The Federalist Papers* (New York: Penguin, 1987), No. 49.

38. Michael Oakeshott, "Rationalism in Politics" in *Rationalism in Politics and Other Essays* (London: Metheun, 1962), p. 22 (my emphasis).

39. Habermas, *Theory of Communicative Action*, Vol. II, pp. 342–43.

40. Habermas, *Faktizitat und Geltung* (Frankfurt: Suhrkamp Verlag, 1992), pp. 361–66.

41. Habermas, *Faktizitat und Geltung*, pp. 361–66.

7

The Debate over Women and Moral Theory Revisited

Seyla Benhabib

The contemporary debate over women and moral theory, which was prompted in 1982 with the publication of Carol Gilligan's *In A Different Voice,* has generated an impressive literature of a truly multidisciplinary nature. Reflecting back on the various themes and disagreements of this debate, we can isolate several reasons why Gilligan's work, in addition to its intrinsic merits, insights, and elegance, would become the focus of such an intense, and interestingly enough, nonacrimonious controversy.

In A Different Voice reflected a coming of age of women's scholarship within the domain of "normal science," in Thomas Kuhn's sense of the word. Like Nancy Chodorow's *The Reproduction of Mothering* in socialization theory, Evelyn Fox Keller's *A Feeling for the Organism* and *Reflections on Gender and Science* in the social studies of science, and Genevieve Lloyd's *The Man of Reason* in the history of philosophy, Gilligan's work showed the consequences of raising the "women's question" from within the parameters of established scientific discourse. Once women are inserted into the picture, be it as objects of social-scientific research or as subjects conducting such inquiry, established paradigms are unsettled. The definition of the *object domain* of a research paradigm, its units of measurement, its method of verification, the alleged neutrality of its theoretical terminology, and the claims to universality of its modes and metaphors are all thrown into question.

Gilligan's work in cognitive and moral development theory recapitulated an experience that women's historians had first encountered in their own field. Joan Kelly Gadol has described this in a 1975 article entitled "The Social Relations of the Sexes: Methodological Implications of Women's History" as follows:

> Once we look at history for an understanding of women's situation, we are, of course, already assuming that women's situation is a social matter. But history, as we first came to it, did not seem to confirm this awareness . . . The moment this is done—the moment that one assumes that women are a part of humanity in the fullest sense—the period or set of events with which we deal takes on a wholly different character or meaning from the normally accepted one. Indeed, what emerges is a fairly regular pattern of relative loss of status for women in periods of so-called progressive changes. . . . Suddenly we see these ages with a new double vision—and each eye sees a different picture.[1]

Gadol writes of a "doubled vision," each eye seeing something different. Gilligan writes of hearing a different voice. In each case, the experience is the same. The women's question—women as objects of inquiry and as subjects carrying out such inquiry—upsets established paradigms. Women discover difference where previously sameness had prevailed; they sense dissonance and contradiction where formerly uniformity had reigned; they note the double meaning of words where formerly the signification of terms had been taken for granted; and they establish the persistence of injustice, inequality, and regression in processes that were formerly characterized as just, egalitarian, and progressive.

In the following discussion I shall isolate two broad ranges of issues from among the complex set of problems within and outside the confines of feminist theory which Gilligan's work has given rise to. While the second half of this chapter will look at the methodological status of the category of "gender" and at the question of "difference" in Gilligan's research on women and moral theory, in the first half I shall continue to explore the implications of Gilligan's research for universalist moral philosophy.

Universalist Moral Philosophies and Carol Gilligan's Challenge

Undoubtedly, Gilligan's work invoked the widespread recognition and controversy that it did because it reflected the coming-of-age of women's scholarship within the paradigms of normal science. Equally significant, however, was that the kinds of questions which Gilligan was asking of the Kohlbergian paradigm were also being asked of universalist neo-Kantian moral philosophies by a growing and influential number of critics. As I have explored previously, these communitarian, neo-Aristotelian, and even neo-Hegelian critics of Kantianism like Michael Walzer, Michael Sandel, Alasdair MacIntyre, and Charles Taylor—like Gilligan herself—questioned the formalism, cognitivism, and claims to universality of Kantian theories. Just as Gilligan challenged the separation of form from content in the evaluation of moral judgment, so too, MacIntyre argued that out of the pure form of moral law alone no substantive moral principles could be deduced.[2] Just as Gilligan reported her female subjects' sense of bewilderment in view of a language of morals which would pose even the most personal of all dilemmas like abortion in terms of formal rights, so too, Michael Sandel maintained that a polity based on the procedural and juridical model of human relationships alone would lack a certain solidarity and depth of identity.[3] And just as Gilligan doubted that the Kohlbergian model of the development of moral judgment could claim the universality that it did in view of the difficulties this model encountered in accounting for women's judgment and sense of self,[4] others like Taylor and Walzer questioned whether the form of moral judgments of justice could be so neatly isolated from the content of cultural conceptions of the good life.[5] There was a remarkable convergence then between the Gilligan-type feminist critique of Kantian universalism and the objections raised by these other thinkers.[6]

But exactly what implications should one draw from Gilligan's findings, which themselves have been moderated over time, for universalist moral philosophies? Does Gilligan's work suggest and even warrant replacing an ethics of justice with an ethics of care? My own position on this complex issue is that Gilligan's work to date does not provide us with sufficient reasons to want to reject universalist moral philosophies. Gilligan has not explained what "an ethic of care" as opposed to an "ethical orientation to care reasoning" would consist in, nor has she provided the philosophical argumentation necessary to formulate a different conception from the Kohlbergian one of the moral point of view or of impartiality. Many of her formulations suggest that she would like to see the ethics of justice be complemented by an ethical orientation to care.[7] These approaches are complementary and not antagonistic. Undoubtedly, one can also attempt to formulate a "feminine ethic of care,"[8] but this is not an implication supported by Gilligan's own work. Precisely because I do not think that a moral theory adequate to the way of life of complex modern societies can be formulated without some universalist specification of impartiality and the moral point of view, I find it more fruitful to read Gilligan's work not as a wholesale rejection of universalism—for which there is little evidence in her own texts—but as a contribution to the development of a non-formalist, contextually sensitive, and postconventional understanding of ethical life. I shall attempt to specify this claim by taking my cue from a penetrating analysis of the relation between the justice and care perspectives provided by Lawrence Blum.

In a recent article on "Gilligan and Kohlberg: Implications for Moral Theory," Blum outlines a hypothetical response to Gilligan that could be given by defenders of the "impartialist conception of morality." Impartialism is understood in this context to characterize not only Lawrence Kohlberg's view of morality, but to have been "the dominant conception of morality in contemporary Anglo-American moral philosophy, forming the core of both a Kantian conception of morality and important strands in utilitarian (and, more generally, consequentialist) thinking as well."[9] Impartialism demands that the moral point of view articulate impersonality, justice, formal rationality, and universal principle. Blum then suggests that the relation between impartialist moralities and a morality of care can be conceived of in eight different ways:

1. One can deny that the care orientation constitutes a genuinely distinct moral position from impartialism. "Acting from care is actually acting on perhaps complex but nevertheless fully universalizable principles, generated ultimately from an impartial point of view."[10]
2. While care for others, it may be argued, constitutes a genuinely important set of concerns and relationships in human life, nevertheless such concerns are more personal than moral ones.[11]
3. This position admits that concerns of care and responsibility in relationships are truly moral (as opposed to being merely personal), but it claims that they are secondary to, parasitic upon, and/or less important than principles of impartiality, right, and universality.[12]
4. Care, it is said, is genuinely moral and is a moral orientation distinct from impartiality, but it is inadequate because it cannot be universalized. An ethics of care, it may be argued, is ultimately inadequate from a moral point of view for the objects of our care and compassion can never encompass all of mankind, but must always remain particularistic and personal. An ethics of care can thus revert to a conventional group ethics, for which the well-being of the reference group is the essence of morality. This reference group may be the family, the nation, a particular affinity group, let us say a political or an artistic avant garde, to whom the individual owes special allegiance. An ethics of care yields a non-universalizable group morality.
5. According to this position, the difference between an ethics of care and one of impartiality is in the "objects of moral assessment" or in the "construal of the domain of the moral." While care is concerned with the evaluation of persons, motives, and character, impartiality is concerned with the evaluation of actions, principles, and rules of institutional life.
6. While care and responsibility are appropriate moral responses in certain situations, it is claimed, considerations of an impartialist right set the constraints within which care is allowed to guide our conduct.

"Considerations of impartiality trump considerations stemming from care; if the former conflict with the latter, it is care which must yield."[13]

7. While considerations of care are genuinely moral, nevertheless their ultimate justifiability "rests on their being able to be validated or affirmed from an impartial perspective."[14] This can be seen as an elaboration of position 6.

8. In the final, most mature stage of moral reasoning the perspectives of "justice and care" will be integrated to form a single moral principle.[15]

Using this scheme, I shall first look more closely at Habermas's response to the challenge posed by Gilligan's work; in the second place, I shall suggest how on my own understanding of discourse ethics as a conversational model of enlarged mentality, a different response to Gilligan becomes not only possible but also desirable.

In "Moral Consciousness and Communicative Action," Jürgen Habermas suggests that Carol Gilligan, particularly in her article coauthored with J.M. Murphy on "Moral Development in Late Adolescence and Adulthood: A Critique and Reconstruction of Kohlberg's Theory," fails to disentangle the complex set of problems which arise when, in the transition from adolescence to adulthood, the everyday lifeworld of our community loses its prima facie validity for the individual and is judged from a moral point of view. Habermas writes:

> Thus the formation of the moral point of view goes hand-in-hand with a differentiation within the sphere of the practical: *moral questions*, which can in principle be decided rationally in terms of criteria of *justice* or the universalizability of interests are now distinguished from *evaluative questions*, which fall into the general category of issues of the *good life* and are accessible to rational discussion only *within* the horizon of a concrete historical form of life or an individual life style. The concrete ethical life of a naively habituated lifeworld is characterized by the fusion of moral and evaluative issues. Only in a rationalized lifeworld do moral issues become independent of issues of the good life.[16]

How does this observation bear on Gilligan's and Murphy's argument for the necessity of formulating a "postconventional contextualist" position which will take into account the dilemmas of applying ethical principles in complex life-situations? On Habermas's reading of her, "Carol Gilligan fails to make an adequate distinction between the *cognitive problem* of application and the *motivational problem* of the anchoring of moral insights."[17] For both the cognitive problem of how to make contextually sensitive moral judgments and the motivational problem of how to act in concrete life situations according to principles the validity of which one hypothetically acknowledges, only arise when the moral point of view has been abstracted from the certainties of a shared way of life and this way of life has been submitted to the hypothetical test of impartiality. In other words, although Gilligan and Murphy put their fingers on an important problem—namely, how moral agents who have attained a postconventional stage of moral reasoning behave and judge in concrete life-situations—their insights bear on the "application" of a universalist and post-conventional morality to life situations; the program of a "post-conventional contextualism" has no relevance then for the justification or delineation of the moral domain. Habermas agrees with one of Kohlberg's early objections to Gilligan that her work confuses "issues of justice" with those of the "good life," thus blurring the boundaries of the moral domain.[18] "In terms of the conduct of an individual life, this corresponds to the distinction between self-determination and self-realization," writes Habermas. "Typically questions of preferences as to forms of life or life goals (ego ideals) and questions of the evaluation of personality types and modes of action only arise after moral issues, narrowly understood, have been resolved."[19]

With this response, Habermas maintains that the kind of issues raised by Gilligan belong not to the center but to the margins of ethical theory, and that they are "anomalies" or problems of an otherwise adequate scientific paradigm. Using Blum's scheme, we can say that for Habermas the relations between the justice and care orientations follow positions 1 and 2. That is, issues of care and responsibility toward others which arise out of the special relations in which we stand to them are "evaluative questions of the good life," concerned with forms of life or with life goals and with the "evaluation of personality types and modes of action." In modern societies in which moral questions of justice have been distinguished from evaluative questions of the good life, relations and obligations of care and responsibility are "personal" matters of self-realization. Since much of this discussion of Gilligan is couched in the language of Habermas's own terminology deriving from his social theory, an example may help us understand Habermas's position better.

Take the generally accepted principle that younger members of a family should not continue the family business or the father's profession but should pursue the career and way of life most compatible with their abilities and talents. Historically, this principle originates with the eventual development of a universal market economy and with the continuing decline of the family household as an economic unit of production in the modern world. Whereas in most pre-capitalist economic formations and even in some forms of merchant and industrial capitalism, generations within a single household acted as an economic unit, let us say in the form of the family business or the family firm, with the spread of capitalism and the continuing decline of the feudal estates system sons no longer followed in their fathers' footsteps and did not assume the family vocation or business. Eventually, it became accepted that children, primarily male children, could and should follow the vocation most suitable to their talents. The moral expectations which governed family life in most western countries up until the late 1920s or 1930s, let us say, have been subject to a differentiation. The choice of a career by the younger generation is no longer a "moral" issue of obligation owed to other family members, in particular to the *pater familias*, but an "evaluative" matter of the good life. Now for the modern liberal family the question whether the less talented first-born son should get to attend an expensive private college as opposed to sending the more talented younger daughter to medical school may continue to be a moral problem, for this involves a question of justice, of conflicting interests over scarce resources. But neither the one child's decision to study business administration nor the other's decision to study medicine are moral issues; they have become evaluative matters of the good life.

Yet this conclusion is profoundly counterintuitive and remote from everyday moral reality. If my example captures Habermas's meaning correctly, then there is something profoundly odd in his insistence that these issues are "personal" as opposed to "moral"; in fact, this claim runs just as contrary to our moral intuitions as Kohlberg's assertion that "the spheres of kinship, love, friendship, and sex that elicit considerations of care are usually understood to be spheres of personal decision-making, as are, for instance the problems of marriage and divorce."[20] These issues are obviously both personal and moral. Even in highly rationalized modern societies where most of us are wage-earners and political citizens, the moral issues which preoccupy us most and which touch us most deeply derive not from problems of justice in the economy and the polity, but precisely from the quality of our relations with others in the "spheres of kinship, love, friendship, and sex." We may lament the sterility of our political lives as citizens and long for a more vibrant and compelling civic life; certainly I have argued for this position at various points. We may strongly oppose the fact that our economic arrangements are so unjust and so immoral from the point of view of satisfying the basic needs of millions upon this earth, but none of this detracts from the fact that for the democratic citizen and economic agent, the moral issues that touch her most deeply arise in the personal domain. How can Habermas and Kohlberg defend such a counterintuitive position, counter that is, to the phenomenology of our moral experience? Let us look more closely at the argument distinguishing moral issues of justice from evaluative matters of the good life.

My thesis is that Habermas and Kohlberg conflate the standpoint of a universalist morality with a narrow definition of the moral domain as being centered around "issues of justice." These, however, are different matters. How we define the *domain of the moral* is a separate matter than the kinds of *justificatory constraints* which we think moral judgments, principles, and maxims should be subject to.[21] Universalism in moral theory operates at the level of specifying acceptable forms of the justification of moral principles, judgments, and maxims. "Universalism" in morality implies first of all a commitment to the equal worth and dignity of every human being in virtue of her or his humanity; secondly, the dignity of the other as a moral individual is acknowledged through the respect we show for their needs, interests, and points of view in our concrete moral deliberations. Moral respect is manifested in moral deliberations by taking the standpoint of the other, as a generalized and concrete other, into account. Third, universalism implies a commitment to accept as valid intersubjective norms and rules of action as generated by practical discourses, taking place under the constraints specified above. The universalizability procedure in ethics specifies a model of individual and collective deliberation and imposes constraints upon the kinds of justification leading to certain conclusions rather than specifying the moral domain. An example may help explain matters.

Suppose in a family of three siblings one of the brothers is struggling financially and is unable to make ends meet. The moral standpoint of care, which Gilligan, Blum, and myself acknowledge, would say that there is a *prima facie* moral claim here, namely the claim whether we, as the more successful members of the family, have a moral obligation to help this brother. This moral obligation arises out of the special nature of the relationships in which we stand to this particular individual. The obligation may or may not be construable as one of justice. If we, as the older brothers, got to where we did in life by helping ourselves to a family inheritance and leaving the younger brother destitute, then the moral situation is also one of justice and of what is morally owed to the youngest sibling. But if we owe our position in life to nothing but our own hard work and good fortune, then the obligation owed to the other sibling is not a matter of justice. From a Kantian point of view, this obligation would be construed as one of "benevolence." Indeed, it has been frequently maintained with respect to Gilligan's work that the ethic of care and responsibility covers the same domain that Kant himself had classified as "positive duties" of benevolence or altruism. The domain of the moral, it is maintained, is distinct from supererogation or altruism although such acts may crown a virtuous character.[22]

As opposed to this classification of issues of care as issues of supererogation and altruism, I would like to argue, again with Gilligan and Blum, and against Habermas and Kohlberg, that obligations and relations of care are genuinely moral ones, belonging to the center and not at the margins of morality. If in the situation described above, the involved family members do not see or even acknowledge that there is a moral situation, in other words if they cannot cognize this situation as being "morally relevant," then they lack moral sense. But strictly speaking, the morally relevant situation is not a situation of justice. There would be nothing "unjust" in the decision of the two elder brothers not to help the younger one, but there would be something morally "callous," lacking in generosity and concern in their actions. Unlike Habermas and Kohlberg, I am not ready to say that "callousness, lack of generosity, and concern," are evaluative but not moral categories; that they pertain to the quality of our lives together rather than to the general procedures for regulating intersubjective conflicts of interests. Such a claim is an unnecessary and unwarranted narrowing of the domain of the moral, and does not follow from a universalist moral position. A universalist moral position of enlarged mentality provides us with a procedure for judging the validity of our judgments in this context as well.

What a commitment to universalism in ethics requires from us in this context is to act in such a way as is consistent with respecting the dignity and worth of all the individuals involved and a willingness to settle controversial matters through the open and unconstrained discussion of all. What does this mean concretely? The successful siblings and the younger brother should be willing to engage in a discourse about the needs of the one and the responsibilities and expectations of the others. Respect for the worth and need of the youngest brother as a generalized and concrete other would require no less. The outcome of such a discourse, however, is not dictated by the procedure of the discourse itself. It is indeed possible for all involved to see that the financial help of the elder brothers is undesirable at this point because it may reinforce patterns of dependency, create resentment, etc. It is also possible to decide that with some help at this crucial juncture the youngest brother may be on his way toward a more self-sufficient existence. Procedures do not dictate specific outcomes; they constrain the kinds of justification we can use for our actions, judgments, and principles. Discourse ethics is a deontological and universalist moral theory where conceptions of the right do constrain the good. Here is where I depart from a care perspective and rejoin the universalists.

So far, I have argued that the definition or specification of the domain of the moral and the level of justification or argumentation required by a commitment to universalism must be distinguished from each other. If universalism is interpreted procedurally, as it must be, then such a procedure can be applied to test the validity of moral judgments, principles, and maxims even in situations that, according to Habermas's and Kohlberg's definitions of them, appear to be concerned with "evaluative questions of the good life" rather than with "moral matters of justice." Questions of care are moral issues and can also be dealt with from within a universalist standpoint. Such a universalism supplies the constraints within which the morality of care must operate.

If we return to Lawrence Blum's scheme discussed above, then my position would be captured by theses 4, 6, and 7. Care issues are genuinely moral, yet the care perspective does not amount to a moral theory with a distinct account of a moral point of view (thesis 4 above). Considerations of a universalist morality do set the constraints within which concerns of care should be allowed to operate and they "trump" over them if necessary (thesis 6 above); and considerations of care should be "validated or affirmed from an impartialist perspective" (thesis 7). Let me return to the example given above to explicate these more clearly. Now suppose the members of this family are part of the clan of Don Corleone (the Godfather) and belong to the Mafia. The Mafia is an organization based on care and mutual responsibility toward members of one's own clan or extended family, yet this morality of care is accompanied by a morality of injustice and contempt towards the lives, dignity, and property of non-group members. Theorists of care must specify the criteria according to which such clans as the Mafia are to be considered "immoral" from the standpoint of a morality of care. I consider Kantian universalism to be indispensable at this point. A morality of care can revert simply to the position that what is morally good is what is best for those who are like me. Such a claim is no different from arguing that what is best morally is what pleases me most.

Thesis 6 says that a universalist morality should set the constraints within which concerns of care can operate. In the case of our example this would mean that the elder brothers cannot recommend to the younger one, from a moral point of view, that the murder of X would be an appropriate way to put his financial life in order; nor would any other recommendation which violated the dignity and worth of another person be consistent with the moral point of view. The right limits the precepts of virtuous conduct and good judgment. It would not be moral to recommend to the younger brother, for example, that he marry a rich woman and thus put his life in order since this would be treating the woman involved as a means to an end and would be incompatible with her human dignity.

As thesis 7 states, considerations of care "must be validated or affirmed from an impartialist perspective." The principle that "family members should show support, concern, and care for one another" is, in my view, justifiable for all and not only for some, because if we could enter into a practical discourse and consider whether a world in which families exercised no solidarity would be more acceptable for all involved than a world in which families did show such support and solidarity, we could all agree that the latter alternative would be in the interests of all involved. There is a distinction between saying that "Jewish, Irish, or Italian family members should show support, concern and care for one another" and the claim that whoever we are and whatever our background, a world in which families or family-like household arrangements showed support, concern, and care for one another would be preferable to a world in which this were not the case. The latter is a universalizable moral claim whereas the former remains an ethnocentric articulation of a group morality which can cut both ways: group solidarity may often be achieved at the expense of moral disregard and contempt for individuals who are not group members.

Suppose, however, a more strictly Kantian theorist questioned us about the status of the claim "a world that would be preferable to." Is this a utilitarian or a consequentialist claim? Am I arguing that the sum of all happinesses and well-being in such a universe would be greater than in another? At some level, of course, these considerations about morally intact families derive from a concern for human well-being and flourishing. Meta-theoretically I am committed to the position that the discursive procedure alone and not some additional moral principles of utility or human well-being define the validity of general moral norms. Yet as a discourse theorist who is also a feminist, the needs and well-being of the concrete other are as much of a concern to me as the dignity and worth of the generalized other.

In this respect as well, Habermas and Kohlberg have dismissed all too quickly a central insight of Gilligan and of other feminists: namely, that we are children before we are adults, and that the nurture, care, and responsibility of others is essential for us to develop into morally competent, self-sufficient individuals. Ontogenetically, neither justice nor care are primary; they are each essential for the development of the autonomous, adult individual out of the fragile and dependent human child. Not only as children, but also as concrete embodied beings with needs and vulnerabilities, emotions, and desires we spend our lives caught in the "web of human affairs," in Hannah Arendt's words, or in networks of "care and dependence" in Carol Gilligan's words. Modern moral philosophy, and particularly universalist moralities of justice, have emphasized our dignity and worth as moral subjects at the cost of forgetting and repressing our vulnerability and dependency as bodily selves. Such networks of dependence and the web of human affairs in which we are immersed are not simply like clothes which we outgrow or like shoes that we leave behind. They are ties that bind; ties that shape our moral identities, our needs, and our visions of the good life. The autonomous self is not the disembodied self; universalist moral theory must acknowledge the deep experiences in the formation of the human being to which care and justice correspond. Gilligan formulates the interdependence of justice and care thus:

> Theoretically, the distinction between justice and care cuts across the familiar divisions between thinking and feeling, egoism and altruism, theoretical and practical reasoning. It calls attention to the fact that all human relationships, both public and private, can be characterized *both* in terms of equality and in terms of attachment, and that both inequality and detachment constitute grounds for moral concern. Since everyone is vulnerable both to oppression and to abandonment, two moral visions— one of justice, and one of care—recur in human experience. The moral injunctions, not to act unfairly toward others, and not to turn away from

someone in need, captures these different concerns.[23]

The continuing challenge posed by Gilligan's findings to universalist moral philosophies is how to acknowledge the centrality of justice as well as care in human lives and how to expand the moral domain to include consideration of care without giving up the justificatory constraints imposed upon the articulation of the moral by universalism.

There is a belated acknowledgment of some of the issues raised by the Gilligan debate in Habermas's article "Justice and Solidarity: On the Discussion Concerning 'Stage 6.'" Commenting on Kohlberg's last efforts to integrate justice and benevolence into a unified moral perspective, Habermas writes:

> Thus, the perspective complementing that of equal treatment of individuals is not benevolence but solidarity. This principle is rooted in the realization that each person must take responsibility for the other because as consociates all must have an interest in the integrity of their shared life context in the same way. Justice conceived deontologically requires solidarity as its reverse side. . . . Every autonomous morality has to serve two purposes at once: it brings to bear the inviolability of socialized individuals by requiring equal treatment and thereby equal respect for the dignity of each one; and it protects intersubjective relations of mutual recognition requiring solidarity of individual members of a community, in which they have been socialized. *Justice* concerns the equal freedom of unique and self-determining individuals, while *solidarity* concerns the welfare of consociates who are ultimately linked in an intersubjectively shared from of life. . .[24]

The similarities in these two formulations are striking. Gilligan writes of "equality and attachment," of the need "not to act unfairly toward others" and not "to turn away from someone in need." Habermas writes of "solidarity," of the interest each has in protecting "intersubjective relations of mutual recognition."[25] Certainly, there are differences of emphases as well. For Habermas, justice is tempered by "mutual recognition" (*Anerkennung*) among individuals of each others' welfare; for Gilligan justice must be tempered by care and a mutual acknowledgment of dependence and vulnerability. Yet in both formulations, the ideals of moral autonomy and justice are traced back to their foundations in fragile human relations and thus "reduced to size." The generalized other of the justice perspective is always also a concrete other, and we can acknowledge this concreteness of the other by recalling those human relations of dependence, care, sharing, and mutuality within which each human child is socialized. If feminist theory has reminded universalist moralities in the Kantian tradition of the need to compensate "for the vulnerability of living creatures who through socialization are individuated in such a way that they can never assert their identity for themselves alone . . .,"[26] then a significant paradigm shift is occurring in such theories—a paradigm shift which I describe as a movement away from a legislative and substitutionalist universalism model towards an interactive universalism.

Gender and Difference in the Gilligan Debate

Carol Gilligan's work challenges universalist moral theories in the Kantian tradition to expand their definition of the moral domain, to question their ideals of the autonomous self in the light of the experiences of women and children, and to acknowledge that a universalist moral theory must also heed the voice of the "excluded others." In recent years the debate over women and moral theory has also been at the center of the general concern within feminist theory with the question of "difference." Some of the most vehement criticisms of Gilligan's work have been voiced by feminists who have taken her to hypostatize illegitimately the "voice" of professional, heterosexual, white women to be the voice of all women.[27] Whereas for established academic disciplines the very fact of "difference" is a subversive issue, for feminist theory the existence of difference, the unravelling of its ideological construction, and the explication of its social and historical constitution are the central tasks.

Is a "different" voice really the women's voice? Can there be a "woman's voice" independent of race and class differences, and abstracted from social and historical context? What is the origin of the difference in moral reasoning among men and women which Gilligan has identified? Does not Gilligan's analysis of women's tendency to reason from the "care and responsibility" approach merely repeat established stereotypes of femininity? To untangle the many issues involved, I shall distinguish between the methodological, the reductionist, and the postmodernist approaches to the question of women's difference in moral theory.

Methodological Aspects

In subsequent reflections on her work, Gilligan noted that she had deliberately called her work "in a different voice" and not a "women's voice."[28] She was not concerned to identify "sex difference" in "moral reasoning," as some of her critics maintained. Rather, she compared women's experience with psychological theory—the subtitle of her book—in order to show that the exclusion of women and their experiences from mainstream developmental theories in psychology generated a number of models and hypotheses which were neither "universal" nor "neutral."

"Gender" was not an analytical and methodological category guiding Gilligan's early work. For her the empirical identification of gender difference appears to have preceded the use of gender as an explicit research category. By "gender" I mean the differential construction of human beings into male and female types. Gender is a relational category. It is one that seeks to explain the construction of a certain kind of difference among human beings. Feminist theorists, whether psychoanalytical, postmodern, liberal, or critical, are united around the assumption that the constitution of gender differences is a social and historical process, and that gender is not a natural fact. Furthermore, although there is some disagreement on this issue, I would agree with the recent work of Londa Schiebinger, Judith Butler, and Jane Flax that the opposition of sex and gender itself must be questioned.[29] It is not as if sexual difference were merely an anatomical fact. The construction and interpretation of anatomical difference is itself a social and historical process. That the male and the female of the species are different is a fact, but this fact itself is also socially constructed. Sexual identity is an aspect of gender identity. Sex and gender are not related to each other as nature to culture. Sexuality itself is a culturally constructed difference.

It is the absence of gender as a research category in Gilligan's work that has created some of the most serious misgivings about her conclusions. Linda Kerber comments on this issue in her remarks entitled "Some Cautionary Words for Historians":[30]

> A *Different Voice* is part of a major feminist redefinition of social vocabulary. What was once dismissed as gossip can now be appreciated as the maintenance of oral tradition; what was once devalued as mere housewifery can be understood as social reproduction and a major contribution to the gross national product. Gilligan is invigorating in her insistence that behavior once denigrated as waffling, indecisive, and demeaningly "effeminate" ought rather to be valued as complex, constructive, and humane. Yet, this historian, at least, is haunted by the argument that we have heard this argument before, vested in different language. Some variants of it are as old as western civilization itself; central to the traditions of our culture has been the ascription of reason to men and of feeling to women. . . . Ancient tradition has long been reinforced by explicit socialization that arrogated public power to men and relegated women to domestic concerns, a socialization sometimes defended by arguments from expediency, sometimes by argument from biology. Although now Gilligan appears to be adding arguments from psychology, her study infers at times that gendered behavior is biologically determined and at others that it, too, is learned, albeit at an earlier stage of socialization than previous analysts had assumed.

Kerber's point is well taken. However, it is hardly convincing that Gilligan thought that the styles of moral reasoning she identified in her research and the preferences of women to reason more frequently in one style rather than in another reflected some ontological and universal essence called "femaleness." The problem of gender difference is much more complicated in her work, and ultimately rests with the ahistoricity of the cognitive-developmental framework within which Gilligan—at least initially—set out her research. This theory, as developed by Piaget and Kohlberg, is concerned with ontogeny, i.e., individual development, and not with phylogeny, i.e., species development. This theory generates a model for explaining how the development of the moral judgment of the child and of the adolescent is a maturation process, involving an interaction between the potentials of the human mind to structure experience and the environment. This interaction between self and world create certain incongruities and crises as the child grows. These cannot be resolved within an earlier pattern of moral reasoning but require the movement unto "higher" stages of moral reasoning. The "higher" stages of moral reasoning, Kohlberg maintains, are not simply developmentally later; they are also more "adequate" to the resolution of moral dilemmas from a cognitive and philosophical point of view.

The subject of this theory is by definition gender-neutral; for these abilities are said to be species-specific. Of course, this theory has a gender-subtext. Since moral learning results from certain kinds of activities, we might well ask what these are for young boys and girls. Are children's games gender neutral? Remember Piaget's remark that in their game of marbles, boys show a degree of precision and complex attention to rules and a propensity for rule-governed negotiations, which he finds lacking in girls' games.[31] Furthermore, since this theory claims that the development of "higher" levels of moral reasoning is tied to the opportunities of the self to assume different roles in social life, we might well expect that in a gendered universe, the kinds of roles men and women will assume will be different.

Gilligan rejected the gender neutrality of the Kohlbergian model at a different level. Instead of focusing on the gender subtext of activities and social roles, she focused on personality patterns. Gilligan relied on Nancy Chodorow's work in *The Reproduction of Mothering*. Briefly, Chodorow maintains that processes of separation and individuation which each human child must go through, proceed differently for males and females. In the case of the male child, separation and individuation involve the establishment of a gender identity which is the opposite of the primary nurturant figure, the woman, although not necessarily of the biological mother. To become a boy means to become not only other than mama, but different than her; it involves repressing those aspects his person most closely identified with the mother. For girls, to become a girl means to become different than mama but also like her. Gender identity is established by two-and-a-half to three years old. In a patriarchal society, based on the denigration and oppression of women, gender identity goes hand in hand with the internalization of those attitudes that also devalue and denigrate women.

Gilligan and Chodorow agree that the consequence of this psychosexual development of the young child are certain personality patterns among the adults of the species. The male has a more firmly established sense of ego boundaries; the distinction between self and other is more rigid. For females the boundaries between self and other are more fluid. Women are more predisposed to show feelings of empathy and sympathy for the other. Each of these personality patterns brings with it certain deformations as well. Males experience closeness and bonding as a threat to their person, whereas females have a hard time establishing a firm sense of identity and individuality over and against the claims of others.

This psychosexual model, as we know by now, is not a theory which explains the emergence of gender difference; it simply gives us a scheme for its "reproduction." In this model the mothering figure is already a female; the father is absent during the first three years of the child's life. It is also assumed that mothering is socially denigrated by the larger societal context so that the young male child learns to associate this activity with negative characteristics and values or at least with highly ambivalent ones. Chodorow's model presupposes gender difference in its characteristically modern form; it does not explain its historical and social constitution. This model presupposes the patriarchal denigration of female gender attributes; it explains their reproduction but not their historical origin. To the extent to which Gilligan relied on this model, she also did not explain the social construction of gender: on the one hand she identified its neglect by mainstream psychological theory, and on the other hand called attention to its persistence within these theories as a continuing but inexplicit subtext.

Linda Kerber is right that gender difference is left unexplained in Gilligan's work. For this task we have to move from moral theory to a social theory of gender relations; we have to leave behind psychological theory for a historical sociology of the development and constitution of gender. Gender as an analytical category thus subverts established disciplinary boundaries.

Reductionist Objections

While feminists and women's historians like Linda Kerber criticized Carol Gilligan's work methodologically for neglecting the historicity of her results and for ignoring the historical determinants of women's difference which she had identified in moral theory, others argued that the kind of "difference" which Gilligan had described as being primarily, even if not exclusively, female was *oppressive*. Claudia Card and Catharine MacKinnon have voiced the view that the morality of "care and responsibility" is a version of Nietzschean slave morality.[32] Card writes: "Study of Women's values could profit from Nietzsche, whose writings on ethics speak directly to the consequences of domination and subordination for the development of character and ideals. Although his target was Christian ethics, his ideas are applicable to recently identified women's values."[33] Following Nietzsche, Card pleads for a consideration "of the underside of women's ethics."[34] For Nietzsche morality is a sublimation of the life drive of the stronger to dominate the weaker; the origins of morality are the internalized controls imposed upon the strong by the weak such that the weak will not be damaged.[35]

MacKinnon does not go back to Nietzsche but to the Marxian theory of class struggle. Just as the "ruling ideas" are the ideas of the "ruling classes," so too dominant moral conceptions are the result of a system of gender and class oppression of compulsory heterosexuality. Gilligan, in MacKinnon's view, ultimately has done little else but raise to scientific status the "good girl" image which heterosexual culture has of women and whose purpose is to "domesticate" women by portraying them as "gentle, caring, and responsible." She states:

> On the other hand, what is infuriating about it (which is a very heavy thing to say about a book [*In A Different Voice*] which is so cool and graceful and gentle in its emotional touch), and this is a political infuriation, is that it neglects the explanatory level. She also has found the voice of the victim—yes, women are a victimized group. The articulation of the voice of the victim is crucial because laws about victimization are typically made by people with power, and come from the perspective with power. . . . But I am troubled by the possibility of women identifying with what is a positively valued feminine stereotype. It is the 'feminine'.[36]

These feminist appropriations of Nietzschean and Marxian views reduce normative problems of justice and morality in complex societies to simple patterns of interest and power camouflaging. Both views are ultimately profoundly anti-political: for Nietzsche the ultimate vision is that of an aesthetic utopia of wisdom, in which a wise old sage, Zarathustra, reaches a state of autonomy beyond community. But if instead of parroting the master thinkers of the past, one would apply feminist methodology to Nietzsche's final moral utopia, one would discover here once more a version of the autonomous, male ego—certainly now presented not as the stern Kantian legislator but as the artistic, poetic, multifaceted, but all-too-masculine hero— Zarathustra "who is lamb and lion" at once.[37] This archaic ideal of the beautiful and wise male hero is hardly what the contemporary debate on women and moral theory should lead to.

Nietzsche's reductionist treatment of morality in his early writings is coupled with the aesthetic utopia of a beautiful male in his later work who lives "beyond good and evil." The reductionist Marxian theory of morality which views it as being a mere expression of the interests of the ruling classes is, in turn, inseparable from the utopia of a society of total reconciliation. Just as with the elimination of class conflict, all interpersonal conflict and conflict over scarce resources will also come to an end, so too with the elimination of the current regime of gender, or in MacKinnon's language, with the end of the regime of "compulsory heterosexuality," "gender difference" will cease to exist.[38] The "rule of men over women" will be replaced by the "administration over things." In the case of MacKinnon then the utopia is not that of an archaic beautiful male but the image of a totally rationally ruled, self-transparent society of perfect power. If, on the other hand, one accepts that neither interpersonal conflict nor economic scarcity nor the sources of human vulnerability and need are likely to be wholly eliminated, even in a more just society, moral theory cannot be rejected as simply representing the ruling idea of heterosexual males. There will always be need to regulate the sources of human conflict and dispute, and to protect the commitments of a shared human existence. A statement like the following which proceeds from a series of dogmatic oppositions, as between morality and politics, liberalism, and radicalism, indicates very clearly that MacKinnon's understanding of politics, as well as of morality, shares more with the authoritarian utopias of Leninist politics than it does with the tradition of critical Marxist theory: "In my opinion," she writes, "to take the differences approach is to take a moral approach, whereas to criticize hierarchy is to take a political approach. To take a difference view is also to take a liberal view (although that view, of course, includes conservatism as well), and to take the view that we are dealing with a hierarchy is to take a radical approach. I also think that to make issues of gender turn on the so-called gender difference is, ultimately, to take a male perspective. I therefore call the differences approach masculinist. The position that gender is first a political hierarchy of power, is in my opinion, a feminist position."[39] The flip side of the denial of politics is an authoritarian politics which will put an end to all difference, controversy, conflict, and violence among humans.[40]

Postmodernist Reservations

Claudia Card and Catharine MacKinnon would dispense with the ideal of autonomy and may be even of morality altogether. Postmodernist feminists, by contrast, strive to develop a "decentered" and "fractured" concept of the self in place of the "connected" or "relational" self which they find to be privileged in Gilligan's work.

Jane Flax and Iris Young, inspired by postmodernist critiques of the "identitary self," have challenged the "relational" self. The western philosophical tradition, they argue, has always prized identity over difference, unity over multiplicity, permanence over change. The subject of western philosophical discourse is constituted at the price of repressing difference, excluding otherness and denigrating heterogeneity. From Plato to Descartes to Kant the self is the unitary, identical substratum; reason reigns over the passions, the I reigns over the will; otherness must be suppressed.

Young argues that the view of the empathetic, connected self presupposes a state "in which persons will cease to be opaque, other, not understood, and instead become fused, mutually sympathetic, understanding one another as they understand themselves. Such an ideal of shared subjectivity, or the transparence of subjects to one another, denies difference in the sense of the basic asymmetry of subjects."[41] Not only is intersubjective transparency presupposed: but equally objectionable is the fiction of the subject as the unified center of desire; but "because the subject is not a unity, it cannot be present to itself, know itself. I do not always know what I mean, need, want, desire because these do not arise from some ego origin. . . . Consequently, any individual subject is a play of differences that cannot be comprehended . . . the subject is [a] heterogeneous presence."[42] Young concludes that the Cartesian/Kantian concept of the unitary self, as well as the feminist theory of the relational self, perpetrate a "metaphysics of presence" and a "logic of identity."

Young's position is that Gilligan's view of the self, far from challenging traditional views of autonomy and selfhood in the western philosophical tradition, continues their fundamental assumptions in presupposing that subjects can truly understand one another and that the individual is a coherent subject of desire. But Young's claim that mutual care and responsibility must presuppose a "transparency" of understanding is exaggerated. Such a perfect understanding or meeting of minds would perhaps be a fair criticism of the Kantian view of noumenal selves, but neither my concept of the "concrete other," which Young also criticizes, nor Arendt's view of the "enlarged mentality" must presuppose that there is ever a state of perfect understanding. Young is not heeding the distinction between "consensus" and "reaching understanding" introduced above. Admittedly, rationalistic theories of the Enlightenment and in particular Rousseau's theory of democracy were based on the illusion that a perfect consensus was possible; but a dialogic model of ethics defended envisages a continuous process of conversation in which understanding and misunderstanding, agreement as well as disagreement are intertwined and always at work. The very commitment to conversation as the means through which the enlarged mentality is to be attained suggests the infinite revisability and indeterminacy of meaning.

The objection that the self, viewed as a unified center of desire, is a fiction again overstates the issue. Young seems to celebrate heterogeneity, opacity, and difference at the cost of belittling the importance of a coherent core of individual identity. Not all difference is empowering; not all heterogeneity can be celebrated; not all opacity leads to a sense of self-flourishing. We do not have to think of "coherent identities" along the lines of the sameness of physical objects. We can think of coherence as a narrative unity. What makes a story can be the point of view of the one who tells it, the point of view of the one who listens to it, or some interaction between the meaning conveyed and the meaning received. Personal identity is no different. As Arendt has emphasized, from the time of our birth we are immersed in "a web of narratives," of which we are both the author and the object. The self is both the teller of tales and that about whom tales are told. The individual with a coherent sense of self-identity is the one who succeeds in integrating these tales and perspectives into a meaningful life history. When the story of a life can only be told from the perspective of the others, then the self is a victim and sufferer who has lost control over her existence. When the story of a life can only be told from the standpoint of the individual, then such a self is a narcissist and a loner who may have attained autonomy without solidarity. A coherent sense of self is attained with the successful integration of autonomy and solidarity, or with the right mix of justice and care. Justice and autonomy alone cannot sustain and nourish that web of narratives in which human beings' sense of selfhood unfolds; but solidarity and care alone cannot raise the self to the level not only of being the subject but also the author of a coherent life-story.

NOTES

1. Joan Kelly Gadol, "The Social Relations of the Sexes: Methodological Implications of Women's History," *Women, History and Theory* (Chicago: The University of Chicago Press, 1984), pp. 2–3.

2. Alasdair MacIntyre, *After Virtue*, pp. 44 ff.

3. Michael Sandel, "The Procedural Republic and the Unencumbered Self," *Political Theory*, Vol. 12, No. 1 (1984).

4. Gilligan has been remarkably silent on the issue of the cultural and ethnic relativity of the Kohlbergian paradigm.

5. Taylor, "Die Motive einer Verfahrensethik," *Moralitat und Sittlichkeit*, Wolfgang Kuhlmanm, ed. (Suhrkamp: Frankfurt, 1986), pp. 194–217; Michael Walzer, *Interpretation and Social Criticism* (Cambridge, MA: Harvard University Press, 1987).

6. The commonalities and the tensions in these approaches have been explored in the Introduction to *Feminism as Critique*, Seyla Benhabib and Drucilla Cornell, eds.

7. Owen Flanagan and Kathryn Jackson give a very clear and helpful overview of the problems involved in Gilligan's various formulations to date concerning the two perspectives. They write: ". . . her recent work still shifts between the ideas that the two ethics are incompatible alternatives to each other but are both adequate from a normative point of view; that they are complements of one another involved in some sort of tense interplay; and that each is deficient without the other and ought to be integrated." See "Justice, Care, and Gender: The Kohlberg-Gilligan Debate Revisited," *Ethics* 97 (April 1987), pp. 622–37, here p. 628.

8. See Nel Noddings, *Caring, A Feminine Approach to Ethics and Moral Education* (Berkeley: University of California Press, 1984). Noddings's dichotomous reasoning which sharply distinguishes between "law and justice" as male

and "receptivity, relatedness, and responsiveness" as female is deeply at odds with Gilligan's and my attempts to overcome these sharp dichotomous in a more integrated approach to moral reasoning and moral judgment. See, Noddings, p. 2 ff. for a particularly sharp statement.

9. Lawrence A. Blum, "Gilligan and Kohlberg: Implications for Moral Theory," *Ethics* 98 (April 1988), p. 472.

10. Blum, "Gilligan and Kohlberg," p. 477.

11. Lawrence Kohlberg himself has at different points in the debate subscribed to a version of most of the positions to be presented in this enumeration. Some of the ambivalences in his responses to Gilligan have been outlined above.

12. Blum, "Gilligan and Kohlberg," p. 478.

13. Blum, "Gilligan and Kohlberg," p. 479.

14. Blum, "Gilligan and Kohlberg," p. 481.

15. Blum, "Gilligan and Kohlberg," p. 482. Blum here refers to Kohlberg's position in "Synopses and Detailed Response to Critics," p. 343.

16. Jürgen Habermas, "Moral Consciousness and Communicative Action," *Moral Consciousness and Communicative Action,* p. 178.

17. Habermas, "Moral Consciousness and Communicative Action," p. 179.

18. Habermas, "Moral Consciousness and Communicative Action," p. 180.

19. Habermas, "Moral Consciousness and Communicative Action," p. 180.

20. Kohlberg, "Synopses and Detailed Response to Critics," pp. 229–30.

21. There is a brief acknowledgment of this point in Habermas's article, "Justice and Solidarity. On the Discussion Concerning 'Stage 6'": "But justifications through procedural ethics apply just as naturally to principles of distributive justice. . . ; or to principles of care and aid to those in need of help; to conventions of self-restraint, consideration, truthfulness, the duty to enlighten others, and so on." *The Philosophical Forum*, Vol. xxi, Nos. 1 and 2 (Fall-Winter 1989-1990), p. 43. This point though remains undeveloped and its import unclear, for, if procedural ethics applies to issues of distributive justice as well as to principles of care and various forms of self-regarding virtues, then the moral domain is not only concerned with issues of justice but with evaluative matters pertaining to the good life as well. Or does Habermas mean that procedural ethics applies to such phenomena as "consideration, truthfulness," and the like, *insofar as*, and only insofar as, these can be reconceptualized as matters of justice? While it is not difficult to imagine how care and aid toward others as well as truthfulness can be moral phenomena of justice *and* matters of the good life for the individual and for the collectivity, it is more difficult to see how "considerateness" and "self-restraint" can be classi-fied as phenomena of justice. Habermas cannot have it both ways: on the one hand, he insists that there is a clear distinction between matters of justice and issues of the good life, and that discourse ethics concerns the former alone; on the other hand, he wants to define the discourse principle, not as delimiting the moral domain, but as specifying levels and forms of justifiable moral argument. As I

argue in the text, it is the latter position that is most defensible, while the former claim must be dropped. The issue is not the definition of the moral domain, of what are and are not moral questions; obviously both matters of justice and questions of the good life are moral matters. Rather, the question is how to circumscribe the domain of individual autonomy (legally and politically) in which choices concerning different forms of the good life are exercised in such manner as would be compatible with universalistic principles of justice.

22. See G. Nunner-Winkler, "Two Moralities? A Critical Discussion of an Ethic of Care and Responsibility versus an Ethic of Rights and Justice," in W.M. Kurtines and J.L. Gewirtz, eds., *Morality, Moral Behavior, and Moral Development* (New York: Wiley, 1984), pp. 348–61.

23. Carol Gilligan, "Moral Orientation and Moral Development," in *Women and Moral Theory*, E.F. Kittay and Diane T. Meyers, eds. (Lanham, MD: Rowman and Littlefield, 1987), p. 20.

24. Habermas, "Justice and Solidarity," p. 47.

25. The theme of "mutual recognition" and the significance of these relations of recognition for moral theory are at the center of Axel Honneth's *Habilitiationsschrift*.

26. Habermas, "Justice and Solidarity," p. 46.

27. See Linda Nicholson for an early statement of this criticism, "Women, Morality and History," *Social Research*, Vol. 50, No. 3 (Autumn 1983), pp. 514–37.

28. Carol Gilligan, Ellen C. Dubois, Mary C. Dunlop, Catharine A. MacKinnon, Carrie J. Menkel-Neadow, "Feminist Discourse, Moral Values and the Law—A Conversation," The 1984 James McCormick Mitchell Lecture, *Buffalo Law Review*, Vol. 34, No. 1 (Winter 1985), p. 39.

29. See Londa Schiebinger, "Skeletons in the Closet. The First Illustrations of the Female Skeleton in Eighteenth-Century Anatomy," *The Making of the Modern Body: Sexuality and Society in the Nineteenth Century*, Catherine Gallagher and Thomas Laquer, eds. (Berkeley: University of California Press, 1987), pp. 42–83; Judith Butler, "Variations on Sex and Gender. De Beauvoir, Wittig and Foucault," *Feminism as Critique*, Benhabib and Cornell, eds., pp. 128–43; Jane Flax, "Postmodernism and Gender Relations in Feminist Theory," *Signs*, Vol. 12, No. 4 (1987), pp. 621–43.

30. L. Kerber, "Some Cautionary Word for Historians," "On In a Different Voice: An Interdisciplinary Forum," *Signs*, Vol. 11, No. 2 (Winter 1986), pp. 304–10, here p. 306; see also Linda Nicholson "Women Morality and History," *Women and Morality*, Special Issue, *Social Research*, Vol. 50, No. 3 (Autumn 1983), pp. 514–37 for similar concerns about Gilligan's work.

31. Jean Piaget, *The Moral Judgment of the Child*, Marjorie Gabain (New York: Free Press, 1965), p. 77.

32. See Claudia Card, "Women's Voices and Ethical Ideals: Must We Mean What We Say?" *Ethics*, Vol. 99, No. 1 (October 1988), pp. 125–36. Card's concern with the way in which an ethics of care may hide or silence feelings of aggression and manipulation among the cared for parties, and the way in which a too sacri-

ficial ethics of care may be profoundly distortive of personality—think of extreme forms of motherly love and maternal solicitude—is welcome. Nonetheless, she is unfair to Gilligan in maintaining that she idealizes the "care approach." Gilligan herself calls attention at various points to the dangers of self-effacement and self-denial which particularly women are prone to, cf. *In A Different Voice*, pp. 64 ff; 123 ff. See also Catharine A. MacKinnon, et. al., "Feminist Discourse, Moral Values and the Law—A Conversation, *Buffalo Law Review*, pp. 25 ff.

33. Card, "Women's Voices," p. 130.

34. Card, "Women's Voices," p. 135.

35. F. Nietzsche, *The Genealogy of Morals*, trans. Francis Golffing (New York: Doubleday and Co., 1956), pp. 170 ff. It is astonishing that not more caution would be exercised by feminists in appropriating Nietzschean categories, since Nietzsche's "naturalistic" categories of human difference as between the "weak" and the "strong"—not to mention his actual and profound dislike of women— are quite incompatible with the fundamental premise of feminist theorizing that "difference"—not only between men and women, but between the "weak" and the "strong", the "Jew" and the "Aryan"—is not a natural but a social-cultural construction.

36. MacKinnon, et al, "Feminist Discourse, Moral Values and the Law—A Conversation," pp. 73–74.

37. Mark Warren uses the apt phrase of "neoaristocratic conservatism" to characterize Nietzsche's political ideology but distinguishes between Nietzsche's insights into power relations and his political views, see *Nietzsche and Political Thought* (Cambridge, MA: MIT Press, 1988), p. 3. Despite elegant and cogent treatments of Nietzsche's political thought, as that of Warren's, I remain skeptical about his relevance for feminist theory and believe that appropriations of Nietzsche by feminists, as I have also argued against Judith Butler, cause more trouble than insight.

38. See her statement, "Dominance and submission made into sex, made into the gender difference, constitute the suppressed social content of the gender definitions of men and women." MacKinnon, et. al., "Feminist Discourse, Moral Values and the Law," p. 27.

39. "Feminist Discourse, Moral Values and the Law," pp. 21–22.

40. For an analysis of the often contradictory visions of the political in Marx's work and in the Marxist tradition, see Jean Cohen, *Class and Civil Society: The Limits of Marxian Critical Theory* (Amherst: The University of Massachusetts Press, 1982); Dick Howrad, *The Marxian Legacy*, (Minneapolis, MN: University of Minnesota Press, 1988) and S. Benhabib, *Critique, Norm and Utopia: A Study of the Foundations of Critical Theory*, Part 1.

41. Iris Young, "The Ideal of Community and the Politics of Difference," *Social Theory and Practice*, Vol. 12, No. 1 (Spring 1986), p. 10.

42. Young, "The Ideal of Community and the Paths of Difference."

8

Discourse in Different Voices

Jodi Dean

A twofold claim underlies Habermas's assertion that discourse ethics provides a procedural reconstruction of the moral intuitions of competent subjects; namely, that discourse ethics presents a theory of *morality* and that this theory is situated at the *post-conventional* level. First, moral intuitions are those that tell us "how best to behave in situations where it is in our power to counteract the extreme vulnerability of others by being thoughtful and considerate."[1] This idea of extreme vulnerability refers to the notion of the person or subject of discourse ethics. Emerging out of a communicative engagement with many voices, the subject of discourse ethics "exists in relation." It depends for its very being on the lives and experiences of those around it. The fragility and insecurity of the self results from the fact that our very identities require relationships of mutual recognition for sustenance. Moralities protect both of these–the dignity of fragile individuals and the mutual ties and relationships in which individual identities are constructed and situated. Second, the claim for post-conventionality refers to the idea that the ethics of traditional and religious communities can no longer tell us what we should do and how we should live. Traditional beliefs no longer have the binding capacity to anchor us within a given social world. In a disenchanted and pluralized age, considerations of duty and obligation, of virtue and the good life, present themselves as so many unanswered questions always in need of justification. So, if our moral intuitions are not merely remnants of an earlier age, the rationality of norms must itself be proven. We have to understand if and why norms deserve respect, why we should follow them. Arising from the presuppositions which competent speakers have to make when they engage in action oriented toward reaching understanding, discourse ethics provides a way to answer these questions via a procedure for the testing of normative validity claims. As such, it endeavors to break beyond the boundaries of the substantive ethics of particular communities to suggest a formal and universal theory of morality. In so doing, it retreats from the ethical concern with the good life, confining itself to issues of justice as those moral questions answerable on the basis of good reasons. Post-conventionality, then, involves an acceptance of the limits of morality understood in terms of the conditions under which norms can be said to deserve recognition.

To be sure, as a post-conventional account of morality, discourse ethics cannot say why we should act in accordance with rationally valid norms, nor can it itself fulfill the conditions necessary to guarantee that each affected by a norm is able to participate in practical discourse.[2] These motivational questions become issues of socialization and personality formation on the one hand, and the appropriate social and democratic institutions on the other. From the standpoint of personality formation, Habermas has drawn from Lawrence Kohlberg's stage theory of moral development, using it as indirect confirmation of discourse ethics insofar as it provides an empirical test of discourse ethics' status as a rational reconstruction of the moral judgment of competent subjects.[3] Rational reconstructions—ethics, logic, philosophy of language—attempt to give an account of the "know-how" of competent subjects, the pretheoretical knowledge of how to form a sentence, say, or make a moral judgment. Always hypothetical, the coherence of rational reconstructions with empirical findings counts only as indirect corroboration. Failure to cohere disproves the rational reconstruction, but coherence itself does not guarantee validity. In fact, Habermas emphasizes the hypothetical status of *all* rational reconstructions, writing: "There is always the possibility that they rest on a false choice or example, that they are obscuring and distorting correct intuitions, or, even more frequently, that they are overgeneralizing individual cases. For these reasons, they require further corroboration."[4]

Now, Habermas's attempt to draw out the action-theoretic underpinnings of the Kohlberg stage sequence and use them as support for discourse ethics seems to falter in precisely these dimensions. Indeed, it calls discourse ethics' ability to include the concerns of women into doubt: the work of Carol Gilligan calls Kohlberg's theory into question in terms of the issue of sexual difference.[5] In other words, her research suggests that Kohlberg's model provides a false example for discourse ethics, one which obscures and distorts some correct intuitions and overgeneralizes individual cases, the cases of men.

Gilligan's discovery of a moral voice that expresses the feelings and concerns of women has been heavily discussed, generating new research and becoming an important element in feminist theory construction.[6] Although some feminist critics have warned against accepting a difference long used to exclude women from the moral domain and others have stressed the restricted domestic origins of women's morality, many feminists have embraced Gilligan's discussion of the moral strengths of care and responsibility as an ethic which reinforces their experiences as women.[7] Gilligan's supporters have emphasized her depiction of women's type of moral reasoning as relational and contextual. Further, they have often employed it as a critique against formal and abstract moral theories. They argue that since women stress the context in which a moral dilemma is situated, theories which depict morality in exclusively principled terms bar women from the moral domain—or misconstrue the moral domain entirely—by discounting their type of judgment.[8] Presumably, then, if Gilligan were right, her conclusions would undermine discourse ethics' claim to present a rational reconstruction of our post-conventional moral intuitions.

However, since the publication of *In a Different Voice* Gilligan's subsequent research has led her to reconsider her earlier findings, dropping those elements which suggested a feminine contextualist morality in contrast to a masculine universalist one. In light of this reevaluation, I want to emphasize three ways in which Gilligan's work still suggests the need for a revised conception of moral development if discourse ethics is to be capable of including women and of providing a justification of moral principles which protect vulnerable identities. My use of Gilligan, however, should not be taken to mean that I endorse a version of feminine difference and specificity that is somehow essential to all women. Rather, in confronting Habermas's account of moral development with their research, I am seeking to expose the limits and biases hidden in his account. This strategy is what Mary Joe Frug terms "a progressive Gilligan reading." Frug writes:

> a progressive reading would interpret Gilligan's use of sex differences as a methodology for challenging gender, as an example of how contingently formed gender identity can be strategically deployed to unsettle existing inequities between the sexes. Sex differences, pursuant to a progressive reading, are context-bound. They are associated with language, more than individual identity, so that to the extent that language can be transformed, gender identity also can be transformed.[9]

Using this strategy, I argue, first, that Gilligan's insight into the problems facing women at the conventional level reveals the blind spot in Habermas's use of the neutral, third-person, or observer perspective. Habermas's assumption that the observer perspective is "neutral" causes him to conflate it with the perspective of the generalized other, a move which prevents him from noting the different meanings of the conventional level for men and for

208 / Jodi Dean

women. Second, I emphasize the gendered nature of authority which remains obscured in Habermas's account. Drawing from the research of Lyn Mikel Brown, I examine the ways in which girls are diminished and devalued at the conventional level. Third, I show how Gilligan's research suggests the need for a more differentiated account of moral development that includes the capacity to recognize the other as a subject deserving of equal respect. In taking over Kohlberg's stage sequence, Habermas falls into a gendered and dualistic treatment of action in terms of competition or cooperation. This causes him to push empathy outside of the structure of moral development and ignore the possibility of learning in the dimension of recognition. Indeed, one of the most striking aspects of Habermas's account of moral development is the way in which the absence of women occasions a description of moral argumentation at odds with the discourse ethics ideal. I try to fill in this gap by introducing the category of connection. Finally, I conclude by offering a suggestion as to how the transition to the post-conventional level is possible and what sort of interpretation of discourse ethics it entails. In so doing, I hope to strengthen the plausibility of discourse ethics as a rational reconstruction of the post-conventional morality of women as well as men.

The Different Voice

Gilligan's claims about a different moral voice have changed over the last decade in response to critics and as a result of the further development of her own research. I want to highlight two aspects of this change: the empirical, which includes the evidence for the different voice and the issue of developmental stages, and the theoretical, which centers on the conceptual use of the terms justice and care. From an empirical perspective, Gilligan's early stage sequence was frustratingly ambiguous. The origin of these stages in the deliberations of women troubled over an abortion decision lent them a degree of particularity that made comparison with Kohlberg difficult and hindered generalization beyond Gilligan's original sample. It was not clear how these stages would play themselves out in women who personally do not have to face the experience of abortion. Now, this argument corresponds with Gilligan's later assessment of her stage sequence. She writes:

> The development sequence I had traced . . . did not jibe with my observations of younger girls. In short, the sequence that I had traced by following the adolescent girls and adult women through time and through crisis did not seem to be rooted in childhood. Instead, it seemed a response to a crisis, and the crisis seemed to be adolescence. Adolescence poses problems of connection for girls coming of age in Western culture, and girls are tempted or encouraged to solve these problems by excluding themselves or excluding others—that is, by being a good woman, or by being selfish.[10]

Rather than indicating an alternative notion of morality with its own developmental logic, the moral issues revealed in *In a Different Voice* reflect the particular problems women face in dealing with issues which force them to confront gendered role expectations.

On the theoretical level, in her early work Gilligan employed an extremely rigid and atomistic conception of justice, setting it off against an exaggerated notion of care and connection. She interpreted the ethic of justice as premised on the values of autonomy and equality, with autonomy implying that persons are separate and detached.[11] Furthermore, she argued that the ideal of autonomy excluded difference: insofar as selves are said to be autonomous, they are considered as fundamentally alike, as possessing a set of general characteristics. This assumption of similarity is reinforced in the justice perspective's emphasis on equality. Equality requires that "everyone should be treated identically" and is embodied in the concept of rights. Since rights guarantee that the autonomy of each individual will be respected, that the claims and interests of each will be weighed, justice reasoning focuses on the identification and prioritization of these rights and claims.[12]

Gilligan sharply distinguished the ethic of care (or the ethic of responsibility; she uses the terms interchangeably) from the morality of justice. From the care perspective:

> ... the moral problem arises from conflicting responsibilities rather than from competing rights and requires for its resolution a mode of thinking that is contextual and narrative rather than formal and abstract. This conception of morality as concerned with the activity of care centers moral development around the understanding of responsibility and relationships just as the conception of morality as fairness ties moral development to the understanding of rights and rules.[13]

Her shift from competing rights to conflicting responsibilities began with the discarding of the notion of autonomy. Rather than stressing our ultimate similarity as autonomous individuals, Gilligan argued in her early work and continues to stress that an understanding of the moral features within a given dilemma requires the recognition of the difference between self and other. Once we have recognized the essential difference of the other, she claimed, we cannot appeal to the fundamental similarities of individuals to ground a notion of basic rights when making a moral judgment. Neither can we justify treating everyone identically by evoking some standard of equality, since we no longer have a basis for determining which characteristics are to be given equal consideration. Instead, the recognition of difference leads to an appreciation of the ties and relationships binding us to one another. Not only do we find connection with an other essential to our own experience of self, but we perceive that, given the very fragility of connections predicated on difference, our relationships can only be sustained by attention and response.[14] For Gilligan, then, the fact of our mutual dependence itself takes on normative significance in moral dilemmas. She stressed that from this initial recognition of the interdependence of self and other the ethic of care proceeds to an emphasis on nonviolence, found in the injunction "that no one should be hurt." So, when viewing a dilemma from the perspective of care one tries to identify the needs of those concerns and attempts a creative "solution responsive to the needs of all."[15] Finally, Gilligan argued that in the process of caring for others as well as for oneself, one becomes aware of multiple truths and the contextually relative nature of moral judgment.[16]

Now, this stark opposition between justice and care appears as a parody because of the depiction of the extremes of justice. Clearly, justice, like care, relies on the presumption of relationships and connections among people. As Susan Moller Okin points out, Gilligan conflated the principled conception of rights and justice with individualism and selfishness.[17] Similarly, Habermas observes that Gilligan focuses on the problems of moral rigorism and intellectualism which emerge at the post-conventional level, but that she tends "to misconstrue these *deficiencies* as characteristic of a *normal* stage of post-conventional formalism."[18] In her more recent work, Gilligan has taken these critiques into account. She writes:

> ... one can see "bad justice" in the rigid or blind adherence to moral principles of rules and "good justice" in the attentiveness to differential power and the potential for oppression which it creates. And one can see "bad care" in the strategies of exclusion which often are valorized in the name of care–the sacrifice of self or of other–just as one can see "good care" in the search for inclusive solutions that are responsive to everyone involved."[19]

Thus, Gilligan has moved away from the stark juxtaposition between justice and care to claim that care, too, can be principled.[20] While she acknowledges "the universal ground of moral problems in the often divergent aims of equality and attachment," that is, in the childhood experiences of both boys and girls which lead to the moral understanding of fairness and of care, she chooses to focus less on issues of justification than on practical dilemmas of application.[21] Gilligan writes:

> To move away from the framing of moral questions in terms of the contrast between a unitary view of moral truth and endless moral relativism, we have shifted the focus of attention from abstract moral truths to the observable world of social relationships where people can describe something that happened which they thought was unfair or situations in which someone did not listen.[22]

Gilligan's new focus elucidates the strengths of the early argument. Now her emphasis on the context-sensitivity of moral judgments can be seen not as opposed to the universalist claims of the justice perspective, but as an explication of the types of considerations involved in the application of moral principles. Furthermore, her attention to relational and evaluative concerns, rather than the result of a failure to distinguish between issues of justice and issues of the good life, can be interpreted as reflecting a concern with the relationships of mutual recognition necessary for moral development, on the one hand, and an awareness of the ethical context in which application discourses are always situated, on the other.[23]

This helps to clarify the contrast she draws in *In a Different Voice* between the emphasis on "right answers" she sees as constitutive of the justice perspective and the fluidity which gives the ethic of care its moral strength. The former is "geared to arriving at an objectively fair or just resolution to moral dilemmas upon which all rational agents could agree"; while the latter "focuses instead on the limitations of any particular resolution and describes the conflicts that remain."[24] To this extent, the care perspective draws attention to the problems arising in the application of norms in complex situations, problems only capable of resolution when "dialogue replaces logical deduction as the mode of moral discovery, and the activity of moral understanding returns to the social domain."[25] Gilligan's current understanding of the ethic of care underlies a commitment to a communicative process of investigation and discovery, of learning about the interests and concerns of the other while simultaneously gaining awareness of the complexities of relationships and one's own needs and responsibilities.

Gilligan's recent research signifies a substantial rethinking of her earlier claims: a new way of interpreting the empirical position of her earlier findings and an abandonment of a contextual relativist position in favor of a differentiated understanding of the relationship between the application and justification of universal principles. Furthermore, her communicative reinterpretation of care and her focus on the relationships of mutual recognition necessary for moral development now cohere with the conception of morality found in discourse ethics. Indeed, Gilligan's assertion that the recognition of difference leads us to an appreciation of our intersubjective ties suggests precisely that understanding of universality through plurality which underlies discursive universalism. However, Gilligan's work does more than confirm the status of discourse ethics as a rational reconstruction of the moral intuitions of competent subjects. In fact, it indicates the ways in which Habermas's reconstruction remains blind to the concerns of women and, hence, calls for a series of revisions.

The Observer Perspective and Moral Development

Turning to Habermas's account of moral development, I want to look at his effort to clarify some of the conceptual problems in Kohlberg's theory. Drawing from Selman's stages of perspective taking, Habermas endeavors to provide a more plausible grounding for the logic of moral development and to show how the demanding process of ideal role-taking which underpins practical discourse is possible at the post-conventional level. While the post-conventional stage cannot be understood as a natural stage like the first two stages,[26] Habermas tries to show how the reconstruction of moral development in action-theoretic terms lends support to discourse ethics as the most convincing account of the universal core of our moral intuitions.

Beginning with the complex structure of perspectives which characterizes a decentered understanding of the world, Habermas distinguishes between world perspectives and speaker perspectives.[27] With regard to world perspectives, he presents the ways in which participants in communicative action can refer to three different worlds and the different sorts of attitudes they can take toward these worlds. First, they can present facts with reference to conditions and events in the *objective world*. Second, they can establish and renew interpersonal relationships with reference to the *social world* of legitimately ordered interactions. Third, speakers can represent themselves and their experiences by referring to the *subjective world* to which they as individuals have privileged access.[28] Additionally, competent speakers have the capacity to adopt three different attitudes toward the world. They are able to take an objectivating attitude toward existing states of affairs, a norm-conformative attitude toward legitimately ordered personal relations and an expressive attitude toward their own subjective experiences. Moreover, they are also able to vary these attitudes with respect to each of the three worlds.[29] Turning to the speaker perspectives, when participants in communicative action want to come to an understanding with one another over something in one of these three worlds, they must also be able to take the attitudes which are connected with the communicative roles of the first, second and third person (that is, speaker, hearer, and observer).[30] The crux of Habermas's argument is that the development of this complex structure of perspectives provides the necessary key for justifying the developmental logic of Kohlberg's moral stages.

Habermas claims that this perspective structure stems from two roots: the observer perspective, which the child develops through engagement with the physical environment, and the reciprocally interconnected "I-you" perspectives which arise in the course of symbolically mediated interaction with reference-persons. Moreover, he tries to explain how the shift from the pre-conventional to the conventional level is occasioned by the introduction of the observer perspective in a way that makes possible the completion of both the system of speaker and the system of world perspectives. The basic idea is that although children at the preconventional level may be capable of correctly using third-person pronouns, extending the reciprocal connection between speaker and hearer to the reversible action perspectives of ego and alter and taking an objectivating attitude toward the external world, it is not until early adolescence that they become able to apply the objectivating attitude of a third person to an interpersonal relationship with another participant in interaction. At this point, then, they conjoin the performative attitude of the "I-you" perspective "with the neutral attitude of a person who is present but remains uninvolved, in other words, the attitude of a person who witnesses an interactive event in the role of a listener or viewer."[31] This thus permits the shift to the conventional level to be understood in terms of the completion of the system of speaker perspectives as it is actualized as a system of action perspectives. Not only can the young adolescent take the reciprocal roles of a speaker and hearer in communicative action, but he can now also interchange the participant perspectives with the third-person perspective of an observer.

While the introduction of the observer perspective enables the young adolescent to perceive his relationship with another as an element of the objective world, this is not the same thing as understanding it as part of the social world of legitimately ordered interactions. In other words, a bit more is involved in the completion of the system of world perspectives. To explain this, Habermas first distinguishes between two forms of reciprocity capable of embodying the "I-you" perspective structure. *Nonsymmetrical reciprocity* refers to the complementarity of different behavioral expectations, as seen the unequal and authority-governed relations in the family. *Symmetrical* or *interest-governed reciprocity* applies to egalitarian friendships where behavioral expectations are of the same kind. Accordingly, in actions coordinated under conditions of authority-governed complementarity, one person controls or sets the terms of the interaction. When conditions of interest-governed reciprocity hold, participants mutually control the interaction.

Next, Habermas introduces two types of action available at the preconventional level which must be coordinated at the conventional level: cooperation-oriented action and conflict-oriented action. In cases of conflict in symmetrical relationships, children can behave either cooperatively or competitively; that is, either by trying to come to an understanding or by engaging in strategic action and, possibly, using deception in order to realize their interests. In instances of conflict in authority-governed interactions, children do not have this option. Unable to use deception, they are left with trying to avoid threatened sanctions (being punished).[32] Accordingly, this implies a polarization between actions oriented toward success and actions oriented toward understanding which simultaneously compels and normalizes the choice between an action orientation with and one without the possibility of deception. Since strategic action thus already exists as an option in the competitive realm (because the child can see the reciprocity of action perspectives in both the speaker and hearer positions), the problem with the transition to the conventional level becomes one of developing the capacity to coordinate one's interactions in ways which are neither governed by authority nor by immediate self-interests. Or, to put it somewhat differently, the child has to develop the capacity to see why he *should* choose a type of action which does not include the option of deception.

Again, this developmental move results from the insertion of the observer perspective. Habermas claims that at the preconventional level the child understands both friendships and relations with authority figures as relationships of exchange. At the conventional level, however, the child is able to see beyond the simple reciprocity of immediate relations. As Habermas explains:

> Only when A in his interaction with B adopts the attitude of an impartial member of their social group toward them both can he become aware of the *interchangeability* of his and B's positions. A realizes that what he thought was a special behavior pattern applicable only to this particular child and these particular parents has always been for B the result of an intuitive understanding of the norms that govern relations between children and parents in general.[33]

As the child internalizes concrete behavioral expectations, then, he comes to understand that his interaction with a parent is part of general pattern of behavior shared by members of their social group: both parent and child are, generally speaking, acting in accordance with social roles. Since the child realizes that any member of their social group could take the position of either A or B, he understands the interchangeability of these positions as stemming from the collective will, the norms and expectations, of their social group.[34] At this point, having internalized the authority of the group, the adolescent understands that he is expected and obliged to observe his social role and that he is entitled to expect the same from others. The group's sanctions become his own standards of behavior which he applies against himself. Thus, with the emergence of the social world in this stage, the system of world perspectives becomes complete.

Having explicated the logic of development underlying the move from the preconventional to the conventional stage, Habermas addresses the shift to the post-conventional stage. This shift has three key components. First, when compared to the quasi-naturalness with which social agents accept the legitimacy of the norms and institutions into which they have been socialized, the hypothetical attitude toward the world necessary for argumentation appears as a dramatic break. While they had previously taken the validity of the social norms of their group for granted, actors now look at them critically, questioning their worthiness to be recognized.[35] Second, Habermas argues that the systems of world and speaker perspectives completed at the conventional level become conjoined at the post-conventional stage. Thus, the reversible system of speaker perspectives establishes the conditions for agreement in argumentation—a valid norm must be acceptable from the perspective of each of the three positions. Likewise, the various attitudes toward the world are available as themes for argumentation and offered up as claims to be criticized and defended. Third, and finally, the split between normatively regulated and strategically regulated action which occurred at the conventional stage is overcome. Of course, this does not mean that social agents no longer have the option of behaving strategically toward one another or that persons at a postconventional level always coordinate their actions communicatively. Rather, the overcoming of this split refers to the idea that in argumentation the success-orientation of competitors is included in a form of communication which continues action oriented toward reaching understanding with other means. As Habermas writes: "In argumentation, proponents and opponents engage in a *competition with arguments* in order to convince one another, that is, in order to reach a consensus."[36] So long as arguments are not reduced to means of mere influence as opposed to reasons offered in an effort to convince, discourse can be used to coordinate action.

A Different View: Looking Behind the Neutral Observer

My critique of Habermas's account singles out three elements: the claimed neutrality of the observer perspective, the lack of differentiation in the notion of authority-governed complementarity, and the limits placed on the interpretation of moral development by the construction of competition and cooperation as binary oppositions. A consideration of these concepts in light of the experiences of girls and women reveals their inability to accommodate sexual difference. Indeed, in relying on a reading of moral development which has dismissed women's moral experience, Habermas's account obscures the different developmental issues faced by women and men in each transitional phase. Thus, he can neither recognize his elision of the observer perspective into that of the generalized other, the organized expectations of a social group, nor can he suggest a more differentiated account of authority governed complementarity which makes clear the masculinity of the conventional generalized other. Indeed, once sexual difference is introduced into the stages of moral development, the need for the category of connection as a supplement to competition and cooperation becomes clear if discourse ethics is to be seen as a reflective continuation of action types emerging at the preconventional and conventional stages. In brief, by attending to the importance of relationships of mutual recognition we can better understand how the hypothetical attitude required of participants in argumentation demands the radical questioning of gendered and hierarchical roles if each is to recognize the other as a subject deserving equal respect.

Beginning with the perspective of the neutral observer, we see that, as he moves from the description of the objectivating perspective acquired by the child through engagement with external nature to the discussion of the role of the objectivating standpoint in the completion of the system of speaker perspectives, Habermas "quietly alters" the meaning of the observer perspective. What was previously rooted in the first-person perspective of a person perceiving the world of physical events is moved out of the body of the child and into the body of a third person. But sexual difference disrupts the "neutrality" of the observer perspective at two points. First, in representing a member of the child's social group, the body of the third-person is a sexed and gendered body. Second, as the object of the onlooker's gaze, the child's body itself is seen as sexed; the onlooker sees a "her" or a "him." This is hardly surprising since learning social roles at the conventional level essentially involves learning sex roles. Indeed, although he ignores the differing repercussions for boys and girls, in an earlier essay Habermas at least acknowledges that one acquires a gendered role identity at this stage.[37] In any case, the sex of the observer poses a question: is the child similarly or differently sexed than this third person?[38]

To be sure, sexual difference is not the only difference that disrupts the neutrality of the observer perspective. Racial difference in a racist society also comes into play in particularly powerful ways. As Patricia Williams writes, "blacks in a white society are conditioned from infancy to see in themselves only what others, who despise them, see."[39] While I am not focusing on the racial dimension of the observer, my hope is that the thematization of the exclusion of sexual difference will expose the false neutrality of the observer perspective to such an extent that the necessity of acknowledging the situatedness of this perspective is revealed. The identification of the notion of sexual difference, in other words, works as a critical tool, alerting us to possibility of other sorts of exclusions enacted in the name of neutrality.

My claim is that under familial, social, and cultural conditions where men dominate, calling the third person "neutral" occludes its masculinity. To be sure, this perspective is not inherently masculine. As Habermas generally uses the term, the third-person or observer perspective refers to a particular sort of cognitive operation involving the ability to distance one's self from a situation, generalize from the particular issues involved, and judge or assess them.[40] However, in his account of the development of the stages of perspective taking, Habermas replaces the third-person observer perspective with the perspective of the generalized other, the organized responses and expectations of the social group. In fact, his account of the completion of world perspectives relies on this switch, since he is trying to show how the child generalizes from particular interactions with parents to see them as part of a larger normative pattern. The perspective of the generalized other, then, provides a place for the third-person to stand, a particular set of shared norms and expectations which make assessment possible by furnishing the framework and standards for judgment. At the conventional level, the observer becomes engendered through its equation with the generalized other—and thus represents a masculine perspective. The child is either like this third male person or different from him. Clearly, this affects the development of children growing up female differently from the way it affects children growing up male.

To be sure, the child's acquisition of the "I-you" perspective at the preconventional level is also significantly affected by gender, namely, in the differing experiences of male and female children in their interaction with their fathers and mothers. Jessica Benjamin has looked at the denial of the mother's subjectivity in traditional patriarchal family structures, analyzing its impact on the process of individuation for boys and girls. For both sexes, the father represents the liberator, the way beyond dependency and identification with the mother into the outside world of agency and the recognition of one's independence and individuality; corresponding to this idealization of the father is a devaluation of the mother.[41] But, as the culmination of the pre-oedipal struggle to separate from the parents and grasp the sexual meaning of the difference between child and parent and mother and father, the oedipal phase presents the following limit: "identify only with the same-sex parent."[42] The boy repudiates the mother, denying her power and transferring it to the idealized father and denying her subjectivity. The girl has to "overcome the primary identification with the mother and replace it with more generalized gender identifications that do not equate all femininity with the mother. If the girl tries to differentiate exclusively by repudiating the mother in favor of the father . . . she never really separates from the mother."[43] Well before they even reach the conventional stage children have a differentiated conception of themselves in relationship to each parent and conceive the father to have authority over the mother.

This leads to the second problem in Habermas's account of moral development. The child is aware of two different types of authority-governed complementarity: that of parent over child and that of male over female. The transition to the conventional level is thus a fundamentally different experience for girls than what it is for boys. Each child realizes that what might have a particular sort of interaction within her or his family is actually part of the generalized pattern of behavior of their social group. But, while the self-identity of boys is reinforced in a culture which values masculine roles, the girls' sense of self is diminished. As Lyn Mikel Brown writes in her description of research on the moral development of girls from the second through the tenth grades:

> This fifth grade girl has begun to see and question the consequences of a cultural norm that suggests, because of "like everything about names and stuff," her mother is less than who she could be; who, according to the culture itself, "is not even alive." These girls seem caught between their own relational experiences of female adults as powerful and trustworthy and a growing awareness that such experiences are not reflected in the wider society. Perhaps, then, things aren't as they seem. What can it mean that those with whom they have felt the strongest bonds and with whom they have felt their strongest trust and value are made to "look like [they're] not even there?"[44]

The work of Gilligan and Brown draws attention to the struggle between "self-silencing" and speaking in one's own voice which occurs as girls take on feminine role definitions. The dilemmas Gilligan describes in *In a Different Voice* involve the difficulties women confront as they try to measure up to the societal expectations of the caring, maternal woman while nonetheless attempting to remain "responsive to themselves." Similarly, Brown charts the preoccupation with being "nice" and "polite" which appears in girls' narratives of their moral experience. While second grade girls understand being nice in terms of simple reciprocity—"if I'm nice to them, then they will be nice to me," the fifth graders see being nice as a safeguard "against oppression, mean treatment, or isolation, while being polite . . . should mitigate, even erase, the meanest and most hurtful behavior."[45] Moreover, by the time girls have reached the fifth grade, they have also begun to associate being nice with not mentioning things like unfairness or detachment: "they sometimes choose to silence themselves rather than to speak if by doing so they will risk exclusion or if speaking could be perceived as mean or thoughtless."[46] At seventh grade, girls see being nice as the key to social acceptability, learning that "to include their own real wishes and needs is to be called 'selfish.'"[47] Finally, facing the pressure of the feelings and thoughts they suppressed in order to be nice, girls in the tenth grade doubt their own voices, questioning the legitimacy of their ideas and expressing self-doubt, confusion, and ambivalence.[48]

Because of the gendered inequality of our social and cultural institutions in which masculine roles are authorized and feminine roles are simultaneously devalued and glorified as instances of silent self-sacrifice, the internalization of the authority of the group which occurs at the conventional level reinforces the self-esteem of boys and diminishes that of girls. Moreover, what they both learn is not that each role is in principle "interchangeable," but that some roles are better, i.e., worth more, than others. In fact, once the gendered subtext of authority governed complementarity is brought into the picture, the more reflective form of reciprocity characterized by the formal symmetry of rights and duties at the conventional level appears fundamentally asymmetrical: the contents of social roles are distributed on the basis of men's authority over women. To be sure, this does not mean that women themselves do not dominate; they, too, exercise authority over children, over other women, those disadvantaged by class and ethnicity, and, sometimes, over men of their own race and class. My point here, however, is that the hierarchy of sex roles instantiates a basic inequality at the conventional level that remains occluded when it is viewed primarily in terms of an increased reflexivity of reciprocal action perspectives.

A third problem with Habermas's account of moral development becomes clear once we acknowledge the inability of the action categories of cooperation and competition accurately to conceptualize the loss of voice girls experience at the transition to the conventional stage. In order to clarify this point, I want, first, to note the way in which Habermas's taking over of Kohlberg's framework leads to a distortion of the importance of relationships of mutual recognition in discourse ethics; second, to suggest an alternative formulation which adds the concept of connection to the categories of competition and cooperation; and, third, to look at Gilligan's and Brown's findings in light of this more complex model.

First, Habermas wants to show how each stage is the reflective continuation of action perspectives acquired at the previous level. Yet, his action categories at the preconventional level are limited to those of cooperation and competition. Accordingly, at the conventional level he is left with the opposition between strategic and norm-guided interaction which he seeks to overcome at the post-conventional level. Argumentation is thus supposed to synthesize two orientations which Habermas usually seeks to separate—the success orientation constitutive of strategic action and the orientation toward understanding constitutive of communicative action.[49] On the one hand, since argumentation is supposed to exclude attempts merely to influence one's opponent rather than convince her, it remains unclear how the split between strategic and norm-governed interaction is overcome at the post-conventional level. Presumably, Habermas means to suggest that norms are no longer taken as given but brought into question via reflection. Yet, with this move the meaning of "strategic" changes to refer to a purely cognitive competence; but such a cognitive understanding of "strategic" does not provide a way for overcoming the distinction between norm-governed and strategic action. On the other hand, even if it somehow were clear how this distinction were to be surmounted, it is difficult to see what Habermas wins with such a move. Indeed, he seems to lose more than he wins in that the notion of a "contest with arguments" filters out the element of intersubjective recognition usually associated with ideal role-taking.

Second, because he begins with the binary opposition between cooperation and competition at the preconventional level, Habermas is forced to bring in empathy "from behind." Although he neglects empathy in his discussion of the stages of perspective taking, he sees sympathy for the fate of one's neighbor as "a necessary emotional prerequisite for the cognitive operations expected of participants in discourse."[50] Further, he finds it "unlikely that one will be able to achieve this significant cognitive act [ideal role-taking] without that sensitive understanding which becomes real empathy and opens one's eyes to the "difference," that is the peculiarity and the inalienable otherness of a second person."[51] Finally, he claims that "without empathetic sensitivity by each person to everyone else, no solution deserving universal consent will result from the deliberation."[52] What is gained simply through a competition with arguments, then, may not be *worth* recognizing. Yet, for all its importance, Habermas fails to consider how the empathetic component of perspective taking emerges in the course of moral development. Empathy thus appears more as a some sort of motivational supplement than a constitutive component of intersubjective relationships.

To suggest how Habermas's account might be filled out, I want to introduce the notion of an orientation toward connection. This orientation suggests itself because of the character of the relationship of mutual responsiveness between the child and her primary reference persons. Rather than simply experiencing interactions with authority figures or friends as "relations of exchange," the child also experiences them as relations of attachment. In an article written with Grant Wiggins, Gilligan argues that "through the attachment or connection they create between them, child and parent come to know one another's feelings and in this way discover how to comfort as well as how to hurt one another."[53] Benjamin also emphasizes the pleasure in being with the other which stems from the emotional attunement of child and parent: "Already at one year the infant can experience the wish to fulfill his own desire (say, to push the buttons on the stereo), and the wish to remain in accord with his parents' will. Given such inevitable conflict, the desire to remain attuned can be converted into submission to the other's will."[54] So not only is the child in a position of inequality and dependency, but she is also attached to her parents, wanting their approval and recognition. In instances of conflict, the child's desire for connection can be manipulated by parental authority. The parent may "make the child feel that the price of freedom is aloneness, or even, that freedom is not possible. Thus, if the child does not want to do without approval, she must give up her will."[55] The lack of symmetry in the authority governed relationship between the child and her parents, then, in this case in the child's dependency on her connection with her parents, follows the same pattern in instances of conflict which Habermas describes. Yet, the issue involved is not merely avoiding punishment, but maintaining connection.

Things look somewhat different, however, when we turn to the desire for connection in symmetrical relationships. Gilligan stresses the way girls' play manifests an emphasis on the relationship among those playing, keeping it intact as opposed to making the game itself the focal point of interaction.[56] In these symmetrical relationships the possibility of deception in instances of conflict which Habermas discusses also appears, but this time as an element in the maintenance of connection. So here it is not only a way to achieve one's particular goals, but also a device used to continue the relationship. Brown describes the negotiating strategies of second graders when they face conflicts with their friends, strategies which may include deception—as in the case of a little girl who puts on a disguise to avoid a friend whom she sees as wanting to play with her too much—but which are centered around trying to come to an understanding in a way that avoids conflicts and includes everyone. While the fifth graders exhibit a more developed insight into the complexities of relationship and are able to understand conflicts from the perspectives of the various participants involved, their efforts to avoid conflict and maintain connection often lead them to associate "disagreement with fighting and loss of relationship" which pressures them "not to confront and work through differences."[57] Even more so, the attempts of the seventh graders to find inclusive solutions where there are no "winners or losers" reflect, on the one hand, a nuanced understanding of "public and private selves" and the variety of ways in which words and actions can hurt, but also a readiness to lie, remove themselves from the situation, or remain silent, on the other. By the tenth grade, although the girls again show an increase in social-cognitive complexity, they struggle to maintain connections with others to such an extent that they trust neither their perceptions nor their feelings and fear the potential costs of honesty to themselves and their relationships.[58]

What is striking in this account of the efforts girls go to in order to maintain connection is the shift from the willingness to deceive another to the willingness to deceive or deny themselves. It is as if the honest recognition of their feelings and perceptions of their relationships would leave them detached and abandoned, disconnected and alone. But they are, of course, recognized to a certain extent. That is, they are recognized within the context of the structured expectations of women's social roles. Brown's research suggests that by the tenth grade, girls have internalized expectations of role recognition. Like Gilligan's, her findings indicate that at the conventional level women learn that keeping a relationship intact requires conforming to the social expectation that women nourish relationships, even when it requires them to be suppress part of themselves.[59] Habermas claims that at the conventional level complementary and symmetrical roles are synthesized at the cost of a polarization between strategic and normatively regulated interaction. While this may be the case when the categories of cooperation and competition frame the description, once connection is introduced additional costs come to light, namely the cost to one's own sense of self when social norms can only be internalized through the denial of one's own understandings and perceptions.

Deploying the research on girls' development to reveal the gaps in Habermas's discussion indicates that recognition and its place in relationships of mutual interconnection embody capacities essential to morality's function in protecting vulnerable identities, capacities occluded when an orientation toward connection is left out of the description of moral development. Brown's study shows that social cognitive complexity, although it may be a precondition for the perspective taking necessary at higher stages of moral development, is neither constitutive of nor sufficient for moral understanding. Along with Gilligan's, her work draws attention to the importance of connection in the development of a moral sensibility. As the problems confronting the tenth-grade girls in Brown's study and the women in Gilligan's attest, there is a substantial difference between understanding a moral situation and being able to *trust* one's understanding of the moral situation—and this is not a difference between what I "ought" to do and what I "would" do in a situation (a confusion for which Habermas faults Gilligan),[60] but a difference between having a perception and having the confidence to acknowledge that perception as one's own. Indeed, the latter requires relationships of mutual recognition where one acquires a sense of confidence in one's own voice.[61] Although he associates this capacity more with the general category of ego development than with moral development per se, Habermas appeals to this sense of self-recognition and self-trust in an earlier essay. He argues that:

> . . . ego-identity requires not only cognitive mastery of general levels of communication but also the ability to give one's own needs their due in these communicative structures; as long as the ego is cut off from its internal nature and disavows the dependency on needs that still await suitable interpretations, freedom, no matter how much it is guided by principles, remains in truth unfree in relation to the existing system of norms.[62]

As I have described it, the orientation toward connection can be interpreted in terms of increasingly reflexive forms of recognition. Accordingly, at the preconventional level children recognize others particularly or naturally, that is in terms of the immediacy of face-to-face interactions.[63] With the shift to the conventional level, recognition appears in terms of social roles. I have stressed that for women this stage is characterized by a split between norm conformity and self-trust. At the post-conventional level, then, the orientation toward connection requires overcoming role recognition in favor of the mutual recognition of subjects deserving equal respect.

Mutual Recognition: Looking Beyond the Generalized Other

Although it might be clear that post-conventional morality requires recipro-cal recognition, how it is possible to break out of the restrictions of role recog-nition which characterize the conventional stage, remains problematic, to say the least. I hope that by exploring the gaps between the observer and gener-alized other perspectives I might be able to suggest a plausible route. I begin by first looking at three ways in which we can find elements of indetermina-tion in position of the generalized other.

First, as I said above, the generalized other refers to the organized set of expectations of a social group. Mead offers the examples of the shared expec-tations institutionalized in the policeman or the state's attorney.[64] Using the example of the police, we could probably assume that the sort of expectations involved concern those of enforcing law and order or, perhaps, protecting property and securing the peace. Yet, from the perspective of poor urban blacks, say, these same expectations may take on a very particular meaning. We might understand law and order as a system which keeps us in our place, reinforcing our inequality. Protecting property might involve making sure that we don't walk or drive into white neighborhoods. Securing the peace could evoke images of being beaten into submission—even after we have the strength to do nothing but submit. Thus different interpretations of the gener-alized other are available. The way the expectations organized in the gener-alized other are interpreted, the meanings they have for different members, is not fixed.

Second, the exact content of these expectations is not fixed. While we can assert with a high degree of confidence that the conventional expectations of sex roles involve the hierarchical domination by men and the concomitant subordination of women, further specificity is difficult. So although girls inter-nalize the awareness that some feminine roles are more worthy than others, their actual role choice remains indeterminate. For example, how does a girl interpret being a "good mother?" Is it the woman who stays at home, baking cookies—or is she a suffocating, overly attentive mother? Is it the Super-Mom of media hype—or is she a cold careerist barely able to manage a couple of hours of "quality" time? To be sure, these and other idealizations of Woman exert a pressure on girls and women to be the impossible. Nonetheless, these reflections point to the possibility of variability within the social role expec-tations which constitute the generalized other.

Third, there is not simply *the* generalized other, but a number of different generalized others. We internalize the expectations of more than one group. Indeed, the recognition and reinforcement we receive through one set of connections helps provide us with a standpoint for interpreting, and often combatting and rejecting, the distorted recognition or even lack of recognition we experience in other groups. For example, Janie Victoria Ward describes the role of the conventional generalized other in the process of identity formation in black girls. She writes:

> As the black child sees herself as others see her, she knows that she is viewed in this society as a member of a devalued group. Transmitted daily to black children are messages that black people are undesirable, inadequate, and inferior. Therefore, if she is black, she is undesirable, inadequate, and inferior.[65]

Yet, when the black child can call upon positive experiences from within the black community, when she feels reinforced and recognized in her connection with black family members and friends, she can use this perspective to reject conventional expectations: "I am not what you believe black people to be, *and I am black.*"[66] Clearly, learning sex roles can also be seen in such a light. bell hooks describes the way she countered "the right speech of womanhood," the speech which from the conventional perspective of the community provided a sort of background music which could be tuned out, claiming an authorship rooted in her valuation of speech among black women.[67] The presence of generalized others, of groups with expectations and norms other than or beyond those of the conventional generalized other, provides us with a third perspective in the concept of the generalized other.

Thus interpretations of the generalized other are variable, the shared norms and expectations organized in the perspective of the generalized other are in some sense indeterminate, and the *position* of the generalized other can actually be broken down into a series of perspectives out of which generalized others are constructed. This openness means that we can never completely assume the perspective of the generalized other. Instead, we take over an interpretation of it, an interpretation which arises out of our understanding of ourselves in the context of the relationships in which we are situated. Of course, becoming aware of the interpretations which we take over, and recognizing them as interpretations which can be questioned, requires a critical distance, that is, the perspective of a third person toward the perspective of the generalized other itself. In fact, it is this degree of reflection which makes possible the shift to the post-conventional level for this is the hypothetical attitude which we adopt when we question the norms and conventions of our social world. The gap between the perspectives of the generalized other and the third-person observer tells us how it is possible to break out of the confines of role recognition demanding that we take seriously the reciprocal recognition of each as a subject deserving of equal respect.

Awareness of sexual difference requires that we rethink the logic of moral development, attending to the importance of our interconnections if we are to recognize each other as subjects deserving of equal respect. Further, taking a hypothetical attitude toward the generalized other is an essential aspect of post-conventional morality. If we are to move beyond complementary forms of recognition to achieve the more reflective form of reciprocity, we have to continuously struggle against restrictive interpretations of the generalized other, to become aware of the differences among our expectations, and to assert the importance of the various groups of which we are apart. Achieving such recognition in practice remains dependent on our critical efforts and political engagement. We must fight against those cultural interpretations which limit our ability to see beyond conventional hierarchical and gendered notions of roles, rights, and duties. We must question given sets of expectations, exposing the power differentials within them in order to create spaces for new expectations, for the expectations that we think should be shared. Finally, we must work to provide opportunities for the emergence of a variety of groups and relationships founded on this recognition.

NOTES

1. Jürgen Habermas, "Morality and Ethical Life," *Moral Consciousness and Communicative Action*, trans. Christian Lenhardt and Shierry Weber Nicholsen, (Cambridge, MA: MIT Press, 1990), p.199.

2. "Morality and Ethical Life," pp. 207–209. See also Klaus Günther, *Der Sinn für Angemessenheit: Anwendungsdiskurs in Moral und Recht* (Frankfurt: Suhrkamp Verlag, 1988), p. 205.

3. See Jürgen Habermas, "Interpretive Social Science vs. Hermeneuticism," *Social Science as Moral Inquiry*, Norma Haan, Robert N. Bellah, Paul Rabinow and William M. Sullivan, eds. (New York: Columbia University Press, 1983), p. 260.

4. Jürgen Habermas, "Reconstruction and Interpretation in the Social Sciences," *Moral Consciousness and Communicative Action*, p. 32.

5. Carol Gilligan, *In A Different Voice* (Cambridge, MA: Harvard University Press, 1982).

6. Recent research occasioned by Gilligan's findings on women's moral and psychological development includes: Mary Field Belenky, Blythe McVicker Clinchy, Nancy Rule Goldberger, and Jill Mattuck Tarule, *Women's Ways of Knowing* (New York: Basic Books, Inc., Publishers, 1986); Ann Ferguson, "A Feminist Aspect Theory of the Self," *Women, Knowledge and Reality*, Ann Garry and Marilyn Pearsall, eds. (Boston: Unwin Hyman, 1989), pp. 93–107; Carol Gilligan, Nona P. Lyons and Trudy J. Hamner, *Making Connections* (Troy, NY: Emma Willard School, 1990); Carol Gilligan, Janie Victoria Ward, and Jill McLean Taylor, eds., *Mapping the Moral Domain* (Harvard University: Center for the Study of Gender, Education and Human Development, 1988); and Ruthellen Josselson, *finding herself* (San Francisco: Jossey-Bass Publishers,

1990). Examples of feminist incorporation of Gilligan's ideas include: Annette C. Baier, "Hume, the Women's Moral Theorist," *Women and Moral Theory*, Eva Feder Kittay and Diana T. Meyers, eds. (New Jersey: Rowman and Littlefield, 1987), pp. 37–55; Seyla Benhabib, "The Generalized and the Concrete Other," *Feminism as Critique*, Seyla Benhabib and Drucilla Cornell, eds. (Minneapolis: University of Minnesota Press, 1987), pp. 7–95; Jessica Benjamin, *The Bonds of Love* (New York: Pantheon Books, 1988); Sharon Bishop, "Connections and Guilt," *Hypatia* 2:1 (Winter 1987) pp. 7–23; Jean Bethke Elshtain, "Feminist Discourse and Its Discontents: Language, Power and Meaning," *Signs* 7:3 (Spring 1982) pp. 603–21; Barbara Houston, "Gilligan and the Politics of a Distinctive Women's Morality," *Feminist Perspectives*, Lorraine Code, Sheila Mullet, and Christine Overall, eds. (Toronto: University of Toronto Press, 1988) pp. 168–89; and Joan C. Tronto, "Women and Caring: What Can Feminists Learn About Morality from Caring?" *Gender/Body/Knowledge*, by Alison M. Jaggar and Susan R. Bordo eds. (New Brunswick: Rutgers University Press, 1989), pp. 172–87. For a selected bibliography, see Mary Jeanne Larrabee, "The Care Ethics Debate," *Newsletter on Feminism and Philosophy* 90:2 (Winter 1990) pp. 103–09.

7. For feminist critiques of aspects of Gilligan's research see Lorraine Code, "Experience, Knowledge and Responsibility," *Women, Knowledge and Reality*, pp. 157–92; Sandra Harding, "The Curious Coincidence of Feminine and African Moralities," *Women and Moral Theory*, pp. 296–315; Linda K. Kerber, Catherine G. Greeno, Eleanor E. Maccoby, Zella Luria, and Carol B. Stack, "On *In a Different Voice*: An Interdisciplinary Forum," *Signs* 11:2 (Winter 1986) pp. 304–33; Debra Nails, "Social-Scientific Sexism: Gilligan's Mismeasure of Man," *Social Research* 50, 3 (Autumn 1983) pp. 643–64; Susan Moller Okin, "Thinking Like a Woman," *Theoretical Perspectives on Sexual Difference*, Deborah Rhode, ed. (New Haven: Yale University Press, 1990), pp. 145–59; and, Mary Ann O'Laughlin, "Responsibility and Moral Maturity in the Control of Fertility—Or A Woman's Place is in the Wrong," *Social Research* 50:3 (Autumn 1983), pp. 556–75. For a discussion of the American and German debates around "the different voice," see, Andrea Maihofer, "Ansatze zur Kritik des moralischen Universalismus," *Feministische Studien* 1 (1988), pp. 32–52.

8. For a critique which stresses the later with regard to discourse ethics see especially Maihofer, "Ansatze zur Kritik des moralischen Universalismus."

9. Mary Joe Frug, *Postmodern Legal Feminism* (New York: Routledge, 1992), p. 40.

10. Carol Gilligan, "Teaching Shakespeare's Sister," in *Making Connections: The Relational World of Adolescent Girls at Emma Willard School*, Carol Gilligan, Nona P. Lyons, and Trudy J. Hamner, eds. (Troy, NY: Emma Willard School, 1990), p. 9.

11. Gilligan, *Voice*, p. 174; Gilligan, "Remapping the Moral Domain: New Images of Self in Relationship," *Mapping the Moral Domain*, p. 6. As Jessica Benjamin and others have pointed out, this critique of the autonomous individual—quite widespread among feminists—closely parallels the Marxian critique of the bourgeois individual elaborated by the early Frankfurt school, *Bonds of Love*, p. 187.

12. Gilligan, "Adolescent Development Reconsidered," *Mapping the Moral Domain*, p. xxi.

13. Gilligan, *Voice*, p. 19.

14. Gilligan, "Remapping the Moral Domain," p. 6.

15. Gilligan, "Adolescent Development Reconsidered," p. xxi.

16. Gilligan, *Voice*, p. 166.

17. Okin, "Thinking Like a Woman," p. 24.

18. Habermas, "Moral Consciousness and Communicative Action," *Moral Consciousness and Communicative Action*, p. 180.

19. Carol Gilligan, Lyn Mikel Brown, and Annie G. Rogers, "Psyche Embedded: A Place for Body, Relationships and Culture in Personality Theory." Presented as Henry A. Murray Lecture in Personality, Michigan State University, April 8, 1988, pp. 36–37. (Manuscript.)

20. Carol Gilligan and Grant Wiggins, "The Origins of Morality in Early Childhood Relationships," *Mapping the Moral Domain*, p. 129.

21. Gilligan and Wiggins, "The Origins of Morality," p. 136.

22. Gilligan, Brown and Rogers, "Psyche Embedded," p. 17.

23. For a discussion of the place of application discourses in discourse ethics, see Klaus Günther, *Der Sinn für Angemessenheit* (Frankfurt: Suhrkamp Verlag, 1988).

24. Gilligan, *Voice*, p. 22.

25. Gilligan, "Do the Social Sciences Have an Adequate Theory of Moral Development?" *Social Science as Moral Inquiry*, p. 45.

26. Habermas argues that although post–conventional judgments demonstrate a reflective attitude toward moral norms which distinguishes them from lesser degrees of reflection at the preconventional and conventional stages, the differences among theories of the moral point of view cannot be interpreted as representing different psychological levels. Furthermore, post-conventional research subjects have to be understood as operating at the same level as the researcher herself. They are thus all engaged in an effort to provide an account of those moral intuitions to which they all have equal access. The description of the post-conventional level, remains a philosophical rather than a strictly empirical problem. Jürgen Habermas, "Justice and Solidarity," *The Philosophical Forum* XXI, 1–2 (Fall-Winter 1989–1990), pp. 32–35.

27. Habermas, "Moral Consciousness," pp. 138–139.

28. Habermas, "Moral Consciousness," p. 136.

29. Habermas, "Moral Consciousness," p. 139.

30. Habermas, "Moral Consciousness," p. 139.

31. Habermas, "Moral Consciousness," p. 146.

32. I am not exactly sure why Habermas claims that children cannot resort to

deception in authority-governed relationships. However, I interpret Habermas to mean that insofar as the interaction is steered by the authoritative partner, the dependent partner has not other option than trying to avoid punishment. To be sure, deception may be one way of avoiding punishment, but in this case it would not be a way of attempting to influence the interaction itself, just the consequences which arise from it. Additionally, Habermas acknowledges that, of course, competitive interactions occur within the framework of the family (presumably along with the option of deception), but in these instances the child behaves as if the relationship were symmetrical, "Moral Consciousness," p. 148.

33. Habermas, "Moral Consciousness," p. 154.

34. See also Habermas's discussion in *The Theory of Communicative Action. Volume Two. Lifeworld and System: A Critique of Functionalist Reason*, Thomas McCarthy, trans. (Boston: Beacon Press, 1987), pp. 33–40.

35. Habermas, "Moral Consciousness," pp. 125–26.

36. Habermas, "Moral Consciousness," p. 160.

37. Jürgen Habermas, "Moral Development and Ego Identity," *Communication and the Evolution of Society*, trans. Thomas McCarthy (Boston: Beacon Press, 1979), p. 91.

38. Obviously, sexual difference is not the only difference which disrupts the neutrality of the observer perspective. Racial difference in a racist society also comes into play in particularly powerful ways—"blacks in a white society are conditioned from infancy to see in themselves only what others, who despise them, see." Patricia Williams, *The Alchemy of Race and Rights* (Cambridge, MA: Harvard University Press, 1991), p. 62.

39. Patricia Williams, *The Alchemy of Race and Rights* (Cambridge, MA: Harvard University Press, 1991), p. 62.

40. See *Erläuterungen zur Diskursethik* (Frankfurt: Suhrkamp Verlag, 1991), pp. 95–96, 143.

41. Benjamin, *Bonds of Love*, pp. 100–103. She writes, "The asymmetry of the father's role for boy and girl toddler, the fact that little girls cannot as readily utilize the father in their separation from the mother or defend against feelings of helplessness, has, with few exceptions, been accepted as inevitable in psychoanalytic literature," p. 103.

42. Benjamin, *Bonds of Love*, p. 171.

43. Benjamin, *Bonds of Love*, p. 169.

44. Lyn Mikel Brown, "Narratives of Relationship: The Development of a Care Voice in Girls Ages 7 to 16," Doctoral Thesis, Harvard University Graduate School of Education, 1989, p. 99. (Unpublished manuscript.)

45. Brown, "Narratives of Relationship," p. 209.

46. Brown, "Narratives of Relationship," p. 209.

47. Brown, "Narratives of Relationship," p. 210.

48. Brown, "Narratives of Relationship," p. 213. It is worth noting that Brown's

seventh graders had a mean global stage score of 3 and the tenth graders of 3(4) on the Kohlberg scale. See the footnote, pp. 199–200.

49. See Jürgen Habermas, "Handlungen, Sprechakte, sprachliche vermittelte Interaktionen und Lebenswelt," *Nachmetaphysisches Denken* (Frankfurt: Suhrkamp Verlag, 1988), pp. 68–72.

50. Habermas, "Moral Consciousness," p. 182.

51. Jürgen Habermas, "Morality, Society and Ethics," *Acta Sociologica* 33:2, 1990, p. 112.

52. Habermas, "Morality and Ethical Life," *Moral Consciousness and Moral Development*, p. 202.

53. Gilligan and Wiggins, "The Origins of Morality in Early Childhood Relationships," p. 124.

54. Benjamin, *Bonds of Love*, p. 31.

55. Benjamin, *Bonds of Love*, pp. 35–36.

56. Gilligan, *Voice*, p. 10.

57. Brown, "Narratives of Relationship," p. 93.

58. Brown, "Narratives of Relationship," p. 187.

59. While there are certainly differences in the role expectations of women of color, bell hooks' account of the way she was taught "to talk a talk that was in itself a silence" and the way her own interests were considered unimportant or frivolous—"one's time could be 'better' spent sweeping, ironing, learning to cook"—indicate that the denial of self expected of women at the conventional level is also part of the experience of black women, *Talking Back: thinking feminist, thinking black* (Boston: South End Press, 1989) 7.

60. Habermas, "Moral Consciousness," 179.

61. See also Axel Honneth, "Integritöt und Mißsachtung," *Merkur* 12 (December 1990), 1047.

62. Habermas, "Moral Development and Ego Identity," p. 78.

63. My use of the term "natural recognition" is meant to correspond to Habermas's discussion of natural identity as the first stage in the development of ego-identity. See "Moral Development and Ego Identity," pp. 84–85.

64. George Herbert Mead, *Mind, Self & Society* (Chicago: The University of Chicago Press, [1934] 1962) p. 261.

65. Janie Victoria Ward, "Racial Identity Formation," *Making Connections*, p. 219.

66. Ward, "Racial Identity Formation," p. 219.

67. hooks, *Talking Back*, p. 6.

9

Autonomy, Recognition, and Respect: Habermas, Benjamin, and Honneth

Johanna Meehan

In his work on moral development, Jürgen Habermas focuses on the cognitive steps which make it possible for a child to move from a conventional understanding of right and wrong to a post-conventional stage where norms require discursive justification. His account, influenced by Lawrence Kohlberg's, details the cognitive skills required in recognizing, raising, and redeeming moral claims. This child navigates from conventional to post-conventional morality by learning to problematize normative claims and generate and offer arguments in support of them in discourses with others. The child Habermas describes, is a child whose ego-identity is essentially intact even at the earliest moral stage charted, though its moral development may be far from complete. Habermas assumes the development of this identity, though he has never explored the process of its constitution and distinguishes sharply between the acquisition of ego-identity, the skills involved in social-role-taking, and those involved in moral reasoning. I will argue in what follows that Habermas's focus on the cognitive aspect of moral development can be traced to this sharp distinction between cognitive development and the establishment of ego-identity, which like his "knife-sharp" distinction between norms and values, cannot be sustained. Because children establish their identities in relationships with others, the nature of these relationships structures the formation of their own identities and their projected construction of the other. These phenomena are captured to some extent in Pierre Bourdieu's notion of the habitus, which illuminates how self/other understanding, is embedded in a way of being with

232 / Johanna Meehan

others which is not added to our self-understanding, or to our understanding of others, but is instead constitutive of them. If the habitus in which one becomes a self is one where identity is valenced by disparate power relationships, then those social relationships inscribe themselves upon its inhabitants long before disputes about norms arise and skew those disputes in a way that remains opaque to some or even to all the participants in the discourse. While I believe this kind of skewing does occur and is seen in the politics of sexism, racism, anti-Semitism, and homophobia, for example, I do not claim that we are so hopelessly embedded in our identities or lifeworld to the extent that it is useless to engage in the discursive negotiation and redemption of norms. I think Habermas is right to locate justice in the institutionalization of reflective, public discourse, but I argue that it is a goal made distressingly elusive when the full extent of the intersubjective constitution of ego-identity is recognized. Such a recognition also points to the significance of normatively guided relationships between caregivers and children and the social structuring of those relationships, and raises questions as to what constitutes recognition, what constitutes mutual recognition, and about the role recognition plays in social relationships.

Since the publication of Carol Gilligan's, *In A Different Voice*, the identification of moral maturity with the achievement of ego independence by deontological theories like Habermas's have been called into question. In her recent book, *The Bonds of Love*, Jessica Benjamin argues that this ideal of ego maturity arises from a psychoanalytic model which identifies autonomy with domination and associates maleness with autonomy and difference, and femaleness with dependence and sameness. Benjamin traces the psychosexual construct of gender in the context of patriarchy calling into question the model of autonomy that underlies current psychoanalytic and psychological models, including those used by moral development theorists. In condemning the notion of autonomy, Benjamin, by implication, dismisses Habermas's moral theory. While agreeing that his account of moral development is incomplete, her dismissal of his position is wrongheaded and reflects her failure to recognize the significance of the norms which structure non-dominative relationships. Habermas's move to redefine moral autonomy in terms of communicative rationality leads him to a conception of autonomy much closer to Benjamin's own than to the more traditional psychoanalytic models she rejects. In actuality, their analyses complement each other, and Axel Honneth's notion of respect, which describes the capacity to relate to one's self and to others in relationships of mutual recognition, a capacity that originates in an ego constituted in the psychological context of such relationships, serves as at least an initial reflection on the psychologically and normatively structured conditions that make relationships of recognition possible. This concept of respect, or one like it, could thus provide a bridge between

Benjamin's and Habermas's positions by clarifying the structure and preconditions for realizing noncoercive relationships of mutual recognition in the inter-psychic, intersubjective, and social/political worlds.

Benjamin's Argument

Freudian pyschoanalytic theory views the acquisition of ego identity as a project which is initiated at birth and realized in the context of a never completely resolved conflict between the needs for attachment *to* and separation *from* the original and compelling power of the infant-mother bond. Freud's account posits an infant whose self-identity is initially merged with that of its primary caregiver, assumed by Freud to be the child's biological mother. In this intrapsychic narrative, the focus is on the child's dawning sense of his/her separateness from the physical, and then from the psychic identity of the caregiver. The infant is seen to be advancing along a course from an original oneness to a state of separateness.

Benjamin argues that we should reject this, what we might call "trajectory" model of development, and replace it with an account that fully appreciates the relational aspects of the developmental project. Self-identity cannot be achieved by a development of the infant by itself, for self-identity is founded on the *mutual* recognition of subjects. The intrapsychic view of the infant subject must, Benjamin claims, be exchanged for a intersubjective perspective. Since the infant's sense of self emerges from the context of relationship with the primary caregiver, the process of differentiation from others must be seen on a continuum of relatedness:

> The intersubjective view maintains that the individual grows in and through the relationship to other subjects. Most important, this perspective observes that the other whom the self meets is also a self, a subject in his or her own right. It assumes that we are able and need to recognize that other subject as different and yet alike, as an other who is capable of sharing similar mental experience. Thus the idea of intersubjectivity reorients the conception of the psychic world from a subject's relation to its object toward a subject meeting another subject.[1]

From birth, the relationship of child to primary caregiver and of primary caregiver to child, is a relationship which necessitates a recognition which in turn points to an original distinction of self and other, acknowledged and bridged by both child and mother in the act of recognition.

Recent studies of newborns indicate that the extent to which they recognize the mother and/or other primary caregivers is much greater than was previously thought; this recognition, different from mere reaction, is only possible between subjects who also recognize a distinction from and between others. In even very early infant/mother interactions, Benjamin argues, there is empirical evidence that, the mother can already identify the first signs of mutual recognition in the interactions between she and her infant.

The psychoanalytic literature has failed to adequately acknowledge the mutuality of mother/infant relationships this research suggests, though it has long been recognized as crucially important in infant development theory, where it has been referred to it as emotional attunement, affective mutuality, sharing states of mind, etc.[2] Despite this ego, psychologists have continued to adopt the "trajectory" model of development deriving:

> the idea of separation from oneness: which contains the implicit assump-
> tion that we grow out of relationships rather than becoming more active
> and sovereign within them, that we start in a state of dual oneness and
> wind up in the state of singular oneness.[3]

Benjamin argues that the assumption of an original symbiotic unity is as problematic as the assumption that the telos of the ego trajectory is the achievement of an identity defined in complete separation from the other.

She advances her argument on several different fronts. First, she argues that evidence of the newborn's recognition of the mother undercuts the claim that the infant experiences the symbiosis with the mother ascribed by the Freudian psychoanalytic model.[4] In Freud's account, child and mother both experience the merging of self and other. He describes the child's experience of this unity in terms of a primary narcissism. The mother's unity with the child on the other hand, is described as a blissfully satisfying regression achieved in part by recreating the bond she had with her own mother, and achieving psychic wholeness through the child which functions as a phallic substitute. In identifying the experience of mother and child, Freud does not recognize the distinction between mother and child, and thus forecloses the conception of *two* selves meeting in relationship.

Benjamin also questions the psychological telos to which Freud's perception of the infant-mother bond leads him. Because he does not view the mother as a subject, in relationship to whom *the child* becomes a subject, Freud cannot construct a narrative of the mother-child relationship as one of ever more mutual recognition. Instead, ego formation is seen as a desperate struggle to assert difference in the face of an always threatening maternal sameness. The Freudian child must establish autonomy by denying the subjectivity of the mother by establishing his[5] identity over and against hers. While needing to assert himself in a dynamic which necessitates his domination of the mother, the child cannot completely obliterate her, for that would destroy the very source of the recognition he is attempting to compel. In destroying her, he destroys himself; in allowing her a subjectivity, his own is threatened. "Mutual" recognition is impossible in this Freudian frame as it is in the Hegelian one which it echoes; any balance is temporary and only tenuously maintained.

In this psychoanalytic narrative, the infant is the developing male self and the mother is the "other" who must be made to recognize this nascent male subject whose self-identity rests precisely on his denial of the subjectivity of the other. Thus, the denial of *the other's* subjectivity becomes a necessary moment and gives rise to the fiction of the bourgeois autonomous subject giving birth to itself, a fiction the psychoanalytic tradition shares with the philosophical one. The concept of autonomy which these narratives reflect identifies self-determination with freedom from the control, the manipulation or the determination of others. Benjamin, like Adorno and Horkheimer before her, argues that with this ideal of autonomy we merely reverse relationships of domination rather than escaping them. In seeking to conceptualize freedom, the Freudian psychoanalytic tradition again like the philosophical one, has seen relationship itself as a threat to the realization of freely constituted subjectivity. In its account of autonomy, self-identity, and agency are only achieved by denying the significance of and the dependence upon the other.

The thrust of Benjamin's critique of autonomy is directed at the patriarchally constructed and maintained gender system the psychoanalytic narrative reflects, which casts men as subjects, women as objects, and objects as mothers. Benjamin argues that in this narrative of the dynamics of self/other/male/female relationships, the ideal of male autonomy recreates a version of the Hegelian master/slave dialectic, where the infant male, the nascent subject, plays Hegel's master, necessarily resulting in the casting of the mother both actual and internalized, as the slave. The female child, in turn, internalizes the father as the master and constructs femaleness, her own and that of the maternal caregiver, as lack.

Benjamin concludes that the process of ego identity formation must be reconceptualized by replacing the ideal of "autonomy" with that of "mutual recognition." Mutual recognition, unlike autonomy, requires sustaining connection to another as one individuates in the process of ego identity formation. Full mutual recognition is achieved when both selves in a relationship maintain a balance between assertion of self/other and denial of other/self. The establishment of self-identity does and should involve the recognition of the other *as* other, and the recognition of the dependence of the self's identity on the other's recognition of it. Ideal subjecthood requires a relational dynamic whose ideal expression involves this fully mutual recognition which is possible only if the dependence and independence of *both* members of the relationship are recognized. As Benjamin puts it. "The need for recognition entails this fundamental paradox: at the very moment of recognizing our own independence, we are dependent upon the other to recognize it."[6] The subject's subjectivity involves another subject who must be recognized if the nascent self is to fully constitute itself as a self.

Benjamin's arguments, while complex, are clear and to my mind are up to this point quite convincing. She expounds a normative critique of our ideal-ization of autonomy and argues that its attainment involves a gender struc-ture especially costly to women. At this juncture however, she moves in a direction which strikes me as somewhat unfortunate.[7] She abandons her clearly normative claims about what we *ought* to adopt as the ideal of ego achievement, and moves, through an assessment of the empirical evidence, to the claim that ego development not only *ought* to proceed along a course of normative development, but that it does in fact do so. While moving from to ought is not necessarily problematic, Benjamin loses sight of the distinction between the normative and the empirical and in so doing fails to recognize the role that norms play in structuring and maintaining relations marked by mutual recognition. This failure, in turn, explains her otherwise surprising dismissal of Jürgen Habermas's moral theory.

Benjamin's failure to recognize the role norms play in interaction can be clearly seen in her discussion of the empirical literature on infant-mother rela-tionships. Her condemnation of current notions of autonomy as implicitly idealizing relationships marked by inadequate ideals of recognition, is followed by an analysis of work on the dynamics of infant-mother play. Describing films made of mothers interacting with their three- and four-month old babies, she argues that what is depicted are complex self-other interactions where mothers do not merely mimic their babies facial and hand movements, but introduce changes which the babies then mimic, respond to, adapt, and change, whereupon the "attuned" mother then responds to the baby's responsive adaptation. Good primary caregivers use the interpretations of the movements and expressions of the babies in their care in order to adapt their play so that it is pleasing to the child. In the infant-caregiver relation-ship, the onus of the work of mutual engagement falls heavily on the caregiver and the engagement is not mutual in the fullest sense, since it is many years before the child can learn to return the recognition of the caregiver's gaze. The ideal of caregiver-maintained attunement can perhaps be best understood, Benjamin suggests, in light of filmed instances where this attunement is not achieved:

> We also observe how mutual regulation breaks down and attunement fails: when baby is tired and fussy, when mother is bored and depressed, or when baby is unresponsive and this makes mother anxious. Then we will see not just the absence of play, but a kind of anti-play in which the frus-tration of the search for recognition is painfully apparent. The unsuccess-ful interaction is sometimes almost as finely tuned as the pleasurable one. With each effort of the baby to withdraw from the mother's stimulation, to avert his gaze, turn his head, pull his body away, the mother responds by "chasing" after the baby. It is as if the mother anticipates her baby's withdrawal with split-second accuracy and can only read his messages to

give space as a frustration of her own efforts to be recognized. . . . Here in the earliest social interaction we can see how the search for recognition can become a power struggle: how assertion becomes aggression.[8]

True attunement, in contrast, is not this chase, not this power struggle, but rather involves a "recognition" of the infant's subjectivity, needs, and preferences by a caregiver who structures interaction on the basis of this recognition.

One could take Benjamin's point here to be a clarification of how mutual recognition functions in an infant-adult relationship, thus providing a model of the realization of recognition; or one could take Benjamin to be pointing to some natural impulse of caregivers which primes them to adopt recognition as the telos of infant-caregiver relationships. While I think Benjamin uses the films to depict worse, better, and ideal interaction, I don't think she intends to suggest that there is a natural impulse or ability involved in realizing fully mutual recognition. Alison Weir, however, reads Benjamin as making precisely this latter point, and she vigorously objects to it:

Benjamin makes the mistake of assuming that . . . human beings are born ready-made subjects with the capacity to recognize themselves and others as subjects. . . . But the assumption that to recognize the other is a social need or a normative ideal in no way entails the assumption that we are born with the ability to do so.[9]

While I think Weir is right to see a confusion in Benjamin's argument and while I share her rejection of any claim that the ability to engage in relationships of mutual recognition is natural, I think Benjamin only inadvertently suggests such a claim, unlike Weir, I do not believe that rejecting this entails rejecting Benjamin's claim that the notion of autonomy operative in the classic psychoanalytic narrative involves an identity that is constituitively determined in relation to a dominated other.

One motivation for Benjamin's appeal to these filmed studies of children and their caregivers is to argue that mutual recognition is, in fact, a normative ideal of infant-development literature that has been eclipsed by the ideal of autonomy in the psychoanalytic literature. The normative model of maternal engagement which infant-development theorists adopt, reflects an evaluation of the sensitivity of caregivers to self-other boundaries that determine the teaching and learning of the early lessons of mutuality. In normatively evaluating relationships in terms of the caregiver's ability to recognize and sustain self-other distinctions and boundaries in their relationships with children, these theorists challenge the accuracy and desirability of the Freudian view of the mother-infant relationships as completely symbiotic. Infant researcher Daniel Stern, for example, argues against the Freudian vision of the merging of mother and child, claiming that while the very young infant is never completely undifferentiated from the mother, it is "primed from the beginning to be interested in and to distinguish itself from the world of others."[10]

Benjamin points out that in the Freudian account, the symbiotic unity of a mother-infant *must* be disrupted to allow for the child's individuation. This logically leads to Freud's claim that separation is the essential moment of the child's establishment of autonomy. In contrast, a psychological model which adopts as its normative ideal a simultaneous responsiveness to the connectedness as well as to the distinctness of the infant from the start, opens up the possibility of recognizing the achievement and significance of attachment as well as of separation:

> Once we accept the idea that infants do not begin life as part of an undifferentiated unity, the issue is not only how we become free of the other, but how we actively engage and make ourselves known in relationship to the other.[11]

Though much infant-development literature implicity at least, adopts as its normative standard a relational ideal of mutual recognition, it does not provide a critique of social roles generally or of gender roles specifically. Benjamin uses the achievement of the capacity and opportunity to engage in relationships marked by mutual recognition as a measure to assess the unhappy role the gender-system plays in setting up sexual relationships of failed recognition, relationships characterized by domination, and not by reciprocity. Problems arise when Benjamin expands her argument and claims that the binary logic involved in the production of the gendered subject does not merely determine the structure of the individual psyche but:

> ... has its analogue in other long-standing dualisms of western culture: rationality and irrationality, subject and object, autonomy and dependency.[12]

These oppositions, so constitutive of gender, are "replicated in intellectual and social life . . .(eliminating) the possibilities of mutual recognition in society as a whole."[13] In identifying rationality with domination and maleness, Benjamin is forced to discount the role rationally articulated and justifiable norms play in establishing and evaluating relationships of mutual recognition. It is just this association of rationality with domination that prompts Weir to dismiss Benjamin's reconstruction of subjectivity, pointing to the problems inherent in her account of the genesis of failures of mutual recognition located in the establishment of male identity:

> So, male identity is established through separation from the mother, which produces objectification and the development of rationality, all of which are equated with domination.[14]

Identifying rationality with domination implies that mutual recognition does not or should not involve rationally mediated relationships. The process of ego formation thus becomes a directly affective process where one's subjectivity is constituted in an immediate identification or disidentification with the other. Weir rejects this account on two grounds. First, because it fails to recognize the extent to which ego identity is socially and symbolically mediated and thus fails to acknowledge the role that rationality plays in the understanding and taking up of the roles constitutive of identity. And second, because it fails to recognize the role social norms play in the demand for and the creation of relationships based on recognition.

In conceptualizing recognition as a purely affective relationship and by identifying rationality with an objectification of the other involving domination, Benjamin cannot account for the role that norms play in identity formation and dismisses Habermasian theory as merely reinscribing a patriarchal view of rationality in the moral and social domain. This unfortunate move springs from her oscillation between an empirical and normative analysis, which leads to her failure to examine the normative structure of the relationships crucial to identity formation. I would also argue, however, that Habermas's normative account of relationships presumes an adult whose subjectivity has originally been constructed in the crucible of the relationships of mutual recognition Benjamin describes, or at least one whose subjectivity has been radically reconstructed in light of an understanding of the failures of those relationships.

Habermas's account of the intersubjectively acquired ability to navigate in a post-conventional world of norms assumes an autonomous human being whose ego-development is complete, though its moral development may not be. Benjamin's, argument, however suggests that the concept of self embedded in psychoanalytic and moral theory relies on a model of autonomy that establishes relationships of domination as essentially entangled in identity formation. Since one's ego identity is intersubjectively constituted all the way down, human beings are subject to distortion, to psychic blightings which can be reflected in even our ideals of moral engagement. Benjamin argues that Habermas's account of moral judgment and justification reflects just this kind of problem, insofar as the over-valuing of the rational and the universal springs from the over-valuation of separation over attachment and hence the domination of women by men:

> (Habermas) merely displaces the problem of rationalism—the inability to recognize the other—to the area of symbolic interaction and moral discourse. And there, the same issue arises as in science: only formal procedures and abstraction allow a universal form of recognition, but these negate the recognition of the other's particular subjectivity.[15]

If this is the case, those engaged in supposedly ideal discourse, by virtue of the constitution of their identities, are incapable of relationships with others not shot through by domination: gender domination, race domination, ethnic domination. Any and every kind of domination does in fact occur and could have been expected to occur. The norms which guide interaction and serve to arbitrate conflicting moral claims arrive, in a sense, after the moment of self/other engagement. My constitution of my self and the other, while not fixed, lies below the ground of disputed norms. My subjectivity must allow for the mutual recognition of the other, or I inevitably construct the other as master or slave, limiting the extent to which truly ideal discourse is possible. Subjectivity, constituted in the context of mutual respect, makes possible the self's recognition of the other and is therefore a precondition for normative engagement with others. Affective recognition is as Weir puts it, a "necessary though not sufficient criteria for intersubjectivity."[16]

Habermas

It is precisely Habermas's recognition of the fundamentally intersubjective nature of subjectivity, coupled with his normative ideal of noncoercive discourse, that makes his work attractive, and I would argue that his position remains attractive even if we accept Benjamin's critique of patriarchy and autonomy. Habermas's appreciation for the intersubjective constitution of identity is expressed in his belief that we become selves through social interaction; we are not first individuals and then social agents who relate to each other; personal identity essentially involves social identity and the constitution of the self is concomitant with the establishment of relationships in the context of a shared lifeworld. This requires us not only to take up the perspective of the other participants in interaction, but also to recognize the norms which shape these relationships.

While Habermas's work for the last twenty years has been to reclaim the normative structures of practical reason which structure identity formation and social roles, he has never really offered a reflective reconstruction of self/other identity formation though he has acknowledged that becoming a moral subject requires relationships of the sort Benjamin describes. In a recent essay for instance, Habermas argues that the moral intuitions reconstructed in his discourse ethics, are available to "anyone who has grown up in a reasonably functional family, who has formed his identity in relations of mutual recognition."[17] While Habermas recognizes that the ability to adopt the perspective of the generalized other can only arise in the context of an ego developed in affective relationships of mutual recognition he does not examine the connection of that affective ability to the developmentally later ability to construct a non-dominated other. He shares with George Herbert Mead a notion of a self constituted intersubjectively all the way down, both focus on the child's ability to rationally construct itself relationally to others. They assume that the ego-development Benjamin describes is a distinct prior stage necessary to, but not essentially tied up in, the abilities required for adopting "the moral point of view." Indeed, Habermas, in the earlier context of the Gilligan/Kohlberg debate, argued that ego development should not be confused with moral development, thus splitting off the formation of self-identity from the acquisition of the abilities to recognize and use moral concepts.[18] But the force of Benjamin's argument, lies precisely in her contention that one becomes a subject only through relations where one is encountered as a subject, where one learns to construct self and other in relationships free from domination. This suggests that the individual and the other it generalizes can be constructed in a dialectic of domination long before its ability to decipher, offer, and defend the norms which structure moral arguments and social practices. I would argue that our construction of certain social others—women, specific racial groups, homosexuals, and others—involve a dynamic of dominative affective identity formation which precedes and determine, the normative considerations relevant to these others.

Clearly, the psychic construction of one's own subjectivity and that of others points to the inherent vulnerability of the social interactions in which we constitute our identity and that of others, a vulnerability which Habermas has argued motivates and sustains the moral character of our social engagements. This vulnerability extends deeper than the relationships between different subjects, for not only am I vulnerable to the mistreatment of others, but my very identity as a subject and my continued sense of self-worth rests on my being recognized as such—and on my recognizing others as I am recognized. Sexism, racism, homophobia, and personal relations of failed recognition are to be decried *first* because they threaten the conditions for mutual recognition necessary to the constitution of our identities as subjects, and *then* because they violate social and moral norms.

Benjamin's concept of mutual recognition suggests the need for an account of the psychological conditions necessary for the constitution of a subject capable of a truly moral rational construction of the other. The political thrust of her argument is directed at revealing the degree to which the patriarchal sex/gender system makes dominative relationships the rule rather than the exception. She describes an alternatively structured relationship where the normatively structured psychological relationship of infant and caregiver constitutes a child able to escape the self/other construction of Hegel's master and slave. Similar critiques of domination can and have been made vis-à-vis racial groups. While the need for such critiques might suggest that Habermas's confidence in the postmodern intuition of the claims of practical reason might be misplaced, I wish to make a different point here.

In his essay "Justice and Solidarity," Habermas made the following distinction:

> Justice concerns the equal freedoms of unique and self-determining individuals, while solidarity concerns the welfare of consociates who are intimately linked in an intersubjectively shared form of life—and thus also to the maintenance of the integrity of this form of life itself. Moral norms cannot protect one without the other: they cannot protect the welfare of one's fellow man and of the community to which the individuals belong.[19]

I take Habermas to be acknowledging that justice is only possible in the context of the social bonds constituted in my recognition of myself and all others as members of my community as equally worthy of respect. But in order to experience this solidarity, I must be able to constitute the identity of all others in developmentally significant relationships of mutual recognition. The importance of these early relational experiences for individuals' later recognition of moral norms requires that much greater attention be paid to the dynamics of this development than Habermas or most other moral theorists, with the exception of Axel Honneth, have done.

In a recent article Honneth recognizes this need, and in the course of reflecting on the origins and nature of respect, implies that its roots must be traced back to infant/caregiver relationships. Respect, he argues, is a precondition for moral subjectivity. But if respect is a precondition for moral subjectivity, which I believe it is, then primary attachments marked by mutual recognition are the preconditions for respect. Honneth's account of respect can function as a preliminary bridge between an account of the constitution of a non-dominative subjectivity and Habermas's account of the ability to recognize and justify moral claims.

Honneth argues that moral theory ought to include a normative ideal of respect because:

> . . . the experience of disrespect poses the risk of an injury that can cause the identity of the entire person to collapse.[20]

His analysis of respect derives from a consideration of the nature of disrespect. In our everyday language, he argues, we use the term "disrespect," to describe roughly three kinds of violations to the integrity of other persons, two of which are significant for this discussion. One involves violations to the physical integrity of others; the paradigms instances of such violations are torture and rape. The other involves exclusions of subjects from membership in a social or moral community. Violations of the first sort deprive a person of their bodily integrity by infringing on the right to relate autonomously to their own body. Violations of the second sort affect a person's normative understanding of self because they are "structurally excluded from the possession of certain rights within a given society"[21] and thus are denied the "ability to relate to (themselves) as a partner to interaction in possession of equal rights on par with all other individuals."[22]

One learns to recognize, to offer, and to demand respect in the context of emotional attachments to primary caretakers. Infants bring the possibility of a subjectivity to the world that can be "confirmed," that is, recognized or in some sense supported through emotional approval or encouragement—what Sara Rudick calls a preservative love, which cares for a child's body as well as a child's developing self.[23] This kind of recognition makes possible a kind of confidence in being a relational self:

> I am referring to the underlaying layer of an emotional, body-related sense of security in expressing one's own needs and feelings, a layer which forms the psychological prerequisite for the development of all further attitudes of self-respect.[24]

Torture and rape constitute violations to the body that tear at this confidence in self, constructed from the loving interactions of a caregiver who fosters and preserves the body by administering to its needs and recognizing its vulnerability and its sovereignty. As attacks on this core sense of the physical integrity of self, they attack bodily boundaries, the most primary of self-other boundaries and necessary for the establishment of the self. One can establish these boundaries and maintain them only if those who care for the child's body establish and maintain them in relationships of trust. Recent literature on incest survivors indicates that these (for the most part) women, share two somewhat common experiences. One is the sense that they lack a self—these women report difficulty in feeling that they have a continuous underlying personal identity and experience their subjectivity as disturbingly discontinuous and empty. They also report a deep sense of a split between self and body such that their own bodies seem no more related to them that the body of any one else. There is also evidence that such childhood sexual abuse can lead to a pattern of promiscuous adolescent sexuality that could in this context be seen, at least in part, as springing from a sense that one's own body is not worthy of respect.[25] These experiences of violation to bodily integrity can produce an adult whose relational capacities are potentially impaired in two ways: first, insofar as she may be unable to develop a trust in an other which normally arises from the other's recognition and respect for the infant's body, and second, insofar as she is unable to construct her subjectivity as equally worthy of the respect accorded to others.

The second form of disrespect Honneth identifies arises when some people are excluded from the legal and moral community. It has the effect of depriving these individuals "the status of full-fledged partners to interaction who possess the same moral rights (as others)." Such a person is simultaneously denied rights and denied the respect of others, and, in being denied this respect, and to the extent that respect is an intersubjectively realized project, is denied the grounds to self-respect. The other's failure to respect me denies me the socially constituted grounds for finding myself worthy of esteem. In his book, *Faces at the Bottom of the Well*, Derrick Bell suggests that this is one of the most vicious costs of racism.[26] In *The Alchemy of Race and Rights*, Patricia Williams describes how her sense of herself was radically thrown into question by her childhood discovery that her black skin meant that she was included in a group whose full subjectivity was radically limited by the racist construction of African-American identity.

The capacity to respect others which leads to an ability to conceive of all people as fully equal members of the moral and social community is in part rooted in childhood. For while the child's subjectivity needs to be recognized in order to be realized, the child must also be taught to accord the same recognition to other subjects. When the fabric of a child's relationship to self and to other is woven in threads of domination, the seeds of disrespect and domination are sown, and children may grow to be adults whose very construction of others undercuts the possibility of respect. Racism is one instance of this kind of moral failure; sexism is another. Williams and Bell describe the social and psychological dynamics of the former, and Benjamin describes the dynamic between the child and a mother whose subjectivity is limited by distorted and inegalitarian gender relations as an instance of the latter kind of failure.

Seyla Benhabib also traces the capacities necessary for instantiating a discursive ethical theory for reciprocal moral relations and for raising and redeeming claims to recognition which arise through the moral lessons of childhood:

> Discourse ethics projects such moral conversations, in which reciprocal recognition is exercised, onto a utopian community of humankind. But the ability and the willingness of individuals to do so begins with the admonition of the parent to the child: "What if others threw sand in your face or pushed you into the pool, how would you feel then?"[27]

Only when I am a subject, and only with those whose otherness I identify as properly that of a subject, can I join in relations of solidarity.

The violations which threaten subjectivity all involve denying some a subjectivity claimed by others. This denial can produce emancipatory movements which reflect the demands of the morally and politically disenfranchised. Political movements are, as Honneth puts it, "born in the struggle for recognition."[28] The need and ability to achieve recognition involves not only the ability to rationally construct and defend norms, but in addition a conception of self and of the other constituted in relationships marked by respect.

Moral progress may be motivated by the demands for recognition, but the ability to recognize the other is a precondition for this progress.

Ultimately the real force of Benjamin's argument lies in her understanding that patriarchally structured gender relationships which idealize autonomy—the construction of self and other as subject and non-subject—are built into the very identity of the participants in that relationship. Thus, not only does the ideal of emancipation require, as Habermas has claimed, the normative reconstruction of our notions of justice and the good life, but of the very constitution of psychic identity as well. While Benjamin fails to acknowledge the extent to which relationships marked by recognition are structured by abstract moral norms of reciprocity and symmetry, Habermas fails to explore the extent to which social norms depend on a relationally and affectively constituted ego. Ego-identity formation cannot be decisively separated from moral development as cognitive and affective development are entwined in the process of the constitution of the infant's subjectivity. Respect entails constructing the other as a subject worthy of the recognition accorded to all subjects; it precedes the normative consideration of the forms that recognition should take. Thus, I would argue not only is respect a precondition for normative engagement with others not identical to the norms that guide that engagement, but in addition it can only arise in the context of non-dominative relationships of primary attachment, or perhaps through radical reflection and self-reconstruction.

NOTES

1. Jessica Benjamin, *The Bonds of Love: Psychoanalysis, Feminism, and the Problem of Domination* (New York: Pantheon, 1988), p. 20.

2. Benjamin, *The Bonds of Love*, p. 16.

3. Benjamin, *The Bonds of Love*, p. 18.

4. Benjamin's argument supports claims of feminist critics like Madelon Sprengnether who argue that Freud's description of the mother-infant bond collapses the distinction between the child's experience of the relationship and the mother's experience of the relationship; see Madelon Springnether, *The Spectral Mother* (Ithaca, NY: Cornell University Press, 1990).

5. I use the masculine pronoun because though Freud suggest that the same dynamic is undergone by the female child, this view was an extrapolation from the male model of development he took as normative. Benjamin and others are also committed to a tale of ego development where the gender of the child has an impact on the way this dialectic of self and other is played out.

6. Benjamin, *The Bonds of Love*, p. 32.

7. I owe some of the following reflections to Allison Weir whose critique of Benjamin

recently appeared in *Thesis Eleven*. While I find the general direction of Weir's critique to be congenial to my own, I think Weir goes too far, dismissing the whole of Benjamin's argument, whereas I find her critique of autonomy and the way it plays itself out in contemporary gender roles revealing and persuasive.

8. Op. cit. Jessica Benjamin, *The Bonds of Love*, pp. 27–28.

9. Allison Weir, "The Paradox of the Self: Jessica Benjamin's Intersubjective Theory," *Thesis Eleven*, No. 32, 1992.

10. Benjamin, *The Bonds of Love*, p. 18.

11. Benjamin, *The Bonds of Love*, p. 18.

12. Benjamin, *The Bonds of Love*, p. 184.

13. Benjamin, *The Bonds of Love*, p. 184.

14. Weir, *Thesis Eleven*, 32, 1992, p. 10.

15. Benjamin, *The Bonds of Love*, p. 191.

16. Weir, *Thesis Eleven*, op. cit., p. 15.

17. Habermas, "Lawrence Kohlberg and Neo-Aristotelianism," in *Justification and Application: Remarks on Discourse Ethics*, draft, trans. Ciaran Cronin, p. 112.

18. Habermas, "Moral Consciousness and Communicative Action," pp. 175–82 in *Moral Consciousness and Communicative Action*, Jürgen Habermas, Christiona Lenhardt and Shierry Weber, trans., (Cambridge, MA: MIT Press, 1990).

19. Habermas, "Justice and Solidarity," in *Hermeneutics and Critical Theory in Ethics and Politics*, (Cambridge, MA: MIT Press, 1990), p. 47.

20. Axel Honneth, Integrity and Disrespect: "Principles of a Conception of Morality Based on the Theory of Recognition" pp. 189 in *Political Theory*, Vol. 20, No. 2, May 1992.

21. Honneth, *Political Theory*, p. 190.

22. Honneth, *Political Theory*, p. 191.

23. Ruddick Sara, *Maternal Thinking, Towards a Politics of Peace*, (New York: Ballantine Books), p. 74.

24. Honneth, *Political Theory*, p. 193.

25. N.B. Judith Herman, *Father-Daughter Incest*, (Cambridge, MA: Harvard University Press, 1978), Christopher Bagley and Kathleen King, *Child Sexual Abuse: The Search for Healing* (London: Tavistock/Routledge, 1990). Sue E. Blume, Secret Survivors: Uncovering Incest and Its Aftereffects in Women. (New York: John Wiley and Sons, 1990).

26. Derrick Bell, *Faces at the Bottom of the Well*, (New York: Basic Books, Harper, 1992), Preface.

27. Seyla Benhabib, "In the Shadow of Aristotle and Hegel: Communicative Ethics and Current Controversies in Practical Philosophy," in *Hermeneutics and Critical Theory in Ethics and Politics* (Cambridge, MA: MIT Press, 1990).

28. Honneth, *Political Theory*, p. 200.

10

Discourse Ethics and Feminist Dilemmas of Difference

Georgia Warnke

Since its beginnings, feminist theory has been involved in what Christine Di Stefano has called "dilemmas of difference."[1] Liberal feminists have stressed the equality of men and women and, hence, the unimportance of differences based on gender. But liberal feminists have also assumed that women hold certain interests in common. For this reason, they have presumed both the difference between men and women as political subjects and the importance of a separate feminist political practice. To this extent, as Deborah L. Rhode points out, "liberal feminism assumes the very sense of shared identity it seeks in large measure to transcend."[2]

Other theorists no longer attempt to transcend this shared identity, but instead stress both the importance of differences based on gender and the "false universalism" at the base of traditional moral, social, and political theories. The claim made by "relational feminists" such as Carol Gilligan, and by postmodern feminists such as Linda Nicholson and Nancy Fraser, is that these theories simply generalize the concerns and interests of men. They cannot be corrected either by merely expanding the conception of a human being to include women or by removing the most egregiously demeaning of their references to women's moral and intellectual capacities. Rather, proper attention to women's concrete lives and to the moral and intellectual capacities they actually have necessarily leads to radically different moral theories, conceptions of social relations, and political ideals. Thus, Gilligan points to an ethics of care that is based on women's particular form of socialization and

248 / Georgia Warnke

emphasizes the maintenance of interpersonal connections rather than simply the protection of individual rights.[3] Fraser questions traditional divisions between public and private domains because of the way these seem to be entwined in women's lives[4] and others point to a new form of community in which work, welfare, and political contexts are radically restructured to allow for the incorporation of caretaking values.[5]

But these "difference feminists" seem to have it no easier than liberal feminists. In the first place, if the stress on difference is meant to point up women's nurturing capacities and orientation to maintaining relationships then, whether these are meant to be biologically or socially induced, this emphasis seems to lead to just those restrictions on employment and opportunity that allowed for the original exclusion of women from public life.[6] The dilemma of difference here is that the sense of shared identity that difference feminism seeks to defend seems to be precisely that which traditional sexism has enforced.

In the second place, the emphasis by difference feminists on the way in which traditional theories falsely generalize the concerns and interests of men seems to apply to their own accounts of women's gender difference. Feminists have themselves questioned whether the theories of socialization and women's psychology on which they have relied simply generalize the experiences of a certain group of American and European, white, middle-class women. Does the object-relations psychology, for example, on which Gilligan and others depend simply extrapolate from a peculiarly modern and Western form of the family? Do distinctions between public and private spheres or between different sorts of labor simply over-generalize historical circumstances such as women's greater responsibility for child care and the devaluation of the domestic sphere?[7]

The logic that difference feminism pursues seems to be one of self-destruction. If we begin by emphasizing women's gender difference, we must also recognize differences between different groups of women, between rich and poor, European and non-European, heterosexual and lesbian. But once we recognize these differences, we are led to still further differences between rich European women and poor European women or between middle-class American women and middle-class Argentinean women and so on. Fraser and Nicholson point out that many feminists have given up on the project of "grand social theory"[8] in favor of particular investigations into varieties of social identity, forms of sexism, and the different permutations that relations between gender, race, class, ethnicity, and age can take. But these investigations do not resolve the dilemma that arises here. For if gender difference is no longer considered fundamental, can there be any identity to the category of woman so that women as a group can form the locus of feminist interests and political practice? If there are only rich and poor women, European and non-European women, and if these groups themselves break down into smaller groups depending on race, class, ethnicity, and age, what happens to a specifically feminist or women's perspective? Does the logic difference feminism takes up not lead, in the end, to the critique of all theory, including feminist theory, as the imposition of a false universalism on social experiences that are radically individual?

In this paper I want to assess the dilemmas of difference I have sketched by way of an examination of Jürgen Habermas's discourse ethics. This theory is of interest here, I think, for two reasons. First, it tries to resolve at least some differences within a universal and rationally motivated consensus. Second, it tries to separate this sort of normative consensus from evaluative and interpretive dichotomies that arise from gender differences or differences in race, class, and ethnicity. But, if feminism can not transcend gender difference nor emphasize it without losing both the subject of its theory and the motor of its practice, the question we raise with regard to a discourse ethics is whether it takes difference seriously enough. Can evaluative and interpretive differences be separated from normative ones and, if not, how can we think of a normative theory, that, as feminism does, tries to acknowledge difference without undermining the possibility of political and ethical theory itself? I shall first sketch those aspects of Habermas's discourse ethics that are relevant to my concerns and then consider the extent to which the problems it raises might suggest a solution to feminist dilemmas of difference.

Habermas's Discourse Ethics

Habermas's discourse ethics is meant to follow from an analysis of the communicative interactions in which "participants coordinate their plans of action consensually."[9] Habermas argues that competent speakers can themselves tell the difference between their strategic attempts to influence a hearer's actions causally and their communicative attempts to come to an understanding with him or her over a course of action, normative principle, or empirical fact.[10] In the first case, the speaker tries to influence the hearer's behavior by whatever means possible, including deceit, fear, manipulation and force. In the second case, a speaker seeks to motivate the behavior of a hearer rationally and therefore must be prepared to justify or give reasons for the claims involved in the speech act offer if challenged. "That a speaker can rationally motivate a hearer to accept such an offer is due not to the validity of what he says but by the speaker's guarantee that he will, if necessary, make efforts to redeem the claim that the hearer has accepted"[11]

Habermas specifies three dimensions in which hearers might challenge validity claims. A hearer can challenge a speaker to show the sincerity of a claim or, in other words, that the speaker is accurately representing his or her intentions. In this case, the speaker can redeem the claim only through actions that are consistent with the intentions he or she has expressed. But hearers can also challenge speakers to demonstrate either the truth of the existential judgments contained in their speech act offers, or the rightness of the actions or norms of action they propose. In both these instances, the redemption of the validity claims is discursively achieved insofar as speakers must offer reasons for the truth of existential judgments, or the rightness of actions and norms of action that hearers can accept.

What are the conditions of this acceptance? To the extent that rationally motivated assent is distinguished from its strategic counterpart, the discursive redemption of validity claims involves certain ideal conditions that Habermas sometimes refers to as an "ideal speech situation." The idea here is that in engaging in communication oriented to understanding, participants must make certain presuppositions about the structure of their communication. They must suppose that it excludes all constraints that would produce a forced agreement: constraints such as the threat of sanctions or unequal power relations among the parties to the agreement. Moreover, they must suppose that all participants in the discourse are equally situated with regard to it, that they are free from constraints of fear and force, that they have equal opportunities to contribute to it, that they are motivated only by the concern to come to an agreement over the disputed claims, and that they are open only to the force of the better argument. As Habermas writes, they must assume that "in principle, all those affected participate as free and equal members in a cooperative search for truth in which only the force of the better argument may hold sway."[12]

To be sure, actual agreements over claims to truth or to the rightness of actions or norms of action at best approximate these ideal conditions and reflect some of the constraints the ideal speech situation excludes. Still, Habermas insists that the structure of communication oriented to understanding contains or anticipates an ideal of reason insofar as speakers cannot engage in communicative understanding without assuming the possibility of unforced agreement to their validity claims. Indeed, following Karl-Otto Apel, Habermas argues that if one were to deny that argumentation has this pragmatic structure—if one were to claim that a rational consensus does not depend upon the exclusion of force, the constraint only of reason or the freedom and equality of participants—one would still have to rely precisely upon this structure in order to argue for one's denial. One would have to suppose that the denial was itself one that could motivate agreement within a communication community of free and equal participants engaged in a cooperative search for truth and motivated only by the force of the better argument.

As the principle of a discourse ethics, this analysis means that "only those norms may claim to be valid which could meet with the assent of all concerned in their role as participants in a practical discourse,"[13] or, in other words, in their role as participants in an ideal speech situation. On this basis,

Habermas introduces a principle of universalization or "U" as a procedure of moral-practical justification: "For a norm to be valid, the consequences and side effects of its general observance for the satisfaction of each person's particular interests must be acceptable to all."[14] This procedure is not a mechanism for generating norms or principles of action but is meant to adjudicate the validity of norms that are under dispute. The point is that where disputed norms could not be agreed upon in a practical discourse involving all concerned, then we have to acknowledge what Habermas calls the suppression of generalizable interests.

But what norms could be justified as the possible product of agreement in practical discourse? Does the ideal of universal consensus not ignore the importance of differences in the way different groups within a society or among societies might foresee consequences, understand their interests or, indeed, interpret the meaning of the norms under dispute? In other words, does the ideal of universal consensus not represent precisely the sort of false universalism feminism attacks in both others and itself? Must we assume that there are interests that are generalizable or that only one sort of attention to consequences or one way of understanding our interests or our norms can be rationally justified?

Suppose we explore the current controversy in the United States over the morality of surrogate motherhood or contract pregnancy. If we argue against the enforceability of surrogacy contracts on the grounds that they allow for the sale of babies, we understand the norm at issue to be one that involves the inviolability and dignity of human beings, the sanctity of the infant-mother bond, and so on. Surrogacy contracts, on this view, violate both the interests of the babies and the interests of those who might be pressured to sell their babies because of poverty, welfare policies, or the like. But we might also argue for the enforceability of surrogacy contracts on the grounds that human beings are free to do what they want with their bodies and that surrogacy contracts promote the equality of women. Prohibiting contract pregnancies, on this view, violates the interests of both childless couples and the surrogate mothers who would like to help them for whatever monetary or altruistic reasons they might have. Is there a generalizable interest here that would tell us whether surrogacy contracts are legitimate or not? And if there is a generalizable interest, with which group does it originate?

On a Habermasian view, this example misidentifies the range of disputes over which a discourse ethics can have dominion in a modern pluralistic society. "As interests and value orientations become more differentiated in modern societies," Habermas argues, "the morally justified norms that control the individual's scope of action in the interest of the whole become ever more general and abstract."[15] The norms under consideration in practical discourse, then, are not specific norms governing legitimate reproductive practices, for example. Rather, they are more general and abstract principles such as those of human rights or the freedom and equality of persons. On the one hand, these are less specific than the idea of contract pregnancy. On the other hand, however, Habermas insists that they are embodied in the legal systems at least of Western societies. For this reason, he argues, they cannot be deemed "irrelevant for the ethics (*Sittlichkeit*) of modern life"[16] even if the sort of discursive consensus under ideal conditions that justifies them is not also applicable to more specific disputes.

But what are the general and abstract norms to which Habermas refers? If we focus on the principles of freedom and equality, it seems obvious that different groups can interpret these principles differently depending on their concerns and interests as well as on their cultural traditions, values, upbringing, and the like. For those who support the legitimacy and enforceability of surrogacy contracts, for instance, the meaning of liberty seems to include the right of women to enter into such contracts, while the meaning of equality includes their full social and economic equality with men. Since the right of men to enter into reproductive contracts for the sale of sperm is not questioned, questioning the right of women to enter into similar and enforceable contracts not only denies their freedom and equality, but assumes that they are less rational than men, more likely to change their minds about the terms of the contract, and less capable of either calculating their own interests in an autonomous manner or pursuing them.[17] For those who oppose the enforceability of surrogacy contracts, however, the meaning of liberty includes a woman's right to change her mind about as momentous a decision as giving up her child, while the meaning of equality includes the rights of poor women not to be exploited by childless middle-class couples.

Such differences in the way in which we understand the norms of liberty and equality do not seem to be differences that can be transcended through argumentation in practical discourse. Rather, they seem to involve differences in sensibility and concern, differences in the aspects of contract pregnancy on which we focus, for example, differences in our understanding of both the value of motherhood or parenting and the characteristics in which we take it to consist, differences in our visions of a good society and differences in the context within which we understand the interests at stake. These, in turn, seem to have more to do with our cultural heritage, experience, and orientation than with the force of reason. Surely we can give arguments for or against our understanding of the norms of liberty and equality that are involved in the issue of surrogacy, but the ability of our arguments to persuade others does not seem to be independent of their values, traditions, and conceptions of the good.

The Habermasian response to observations of this kind is to distinguish between the justification of norms and their application. The assent of all concerned under ideal conditions is meant to determine the legitimacy of norms; it is not meant to contain prescriptions for their application to concrete situations.[18] Thus, if the norms at issue in the debate over surrogacy contracts are those of liberty and equality, these norms are legitimate because all concerned could assent to them as participants in a practical discourse, not because all concerned could assent to the way in which they were applied to the surrogacy case. Moreover, Habermas insists that questions of application themselves must ultimately be resolved in terms of well-justified normative principles, "for instance, the principles that all relevant aspects of a case must be considered . . . and that means should be proportionate to ends."[19]

But it is not clear that issues of justification can be so neatly separated from those of application. In the first place, suppose we were to understand our different evaluations of surrogacy contracts as a problem limited to application, as a difference in the way we think abstract and general principles, on the validity of which we do agree, are to be used to settle the question of the legitimacy of a practice. Still, what Habermas means by a well-justified applicative principle remains unclear. While we might agree on a norm that stipulates that all relevant aspects of a case must be considered in its adjudication, this norm would itself seem to be meaningless unless we can give some content to the notion of relevance. But precisely here we might disagree. Those who support the enforceability of surrogacy contracts might think that male fears of female autonomy are relevant as well as the motivations behind old adultery laws that were meant to protect men's interests in establishing paternity. In contrast, those who reject the enforceability of surrogacy contracts might think that they should be understood in terms of the meaning and significance of motherhood and the social consequences of bringing it into the realm of contract and business interests.

Similar disagreements over the considerations and contexts that are thought to be important would seem to arise in our efforts to decide on the means proportionate to a given end. We can give arguments for why a certain means is proportionate to the end, but assent to such arguments presupposes shared values and a shared understanding of the issues. Habermas claims that the history of a norm's application moves in a relatively stable direction in which we gradually eliminate extraneous considerations and come to agree on the way the norm is to be applied. This agreement and directionality, in his view, indicate that "learning processes" are possible in the dimension of application as well as in the dimension of normative justification.[20] But if we now apply the norm of equality, for example, so that it no longer supports practices that exclude human beings on the basis of their race or gender, do we do so because we have all learned in the same direction or because, among the multidirectional ways in which we have learned, certain ways have dropped out for complex, value-laden, and cultural reasons?

It may be difficult to separate justification from application, because of considerations similar to those we have already considered. If we are to accept the principle of equality as binding on our actions, we must first understand it. But how can we understand it unless we know what sort of disputes it is supposed to adjudicate and how? In fact, present court decisions (as well as feminist discussions) on the enforceability of surrogacy contracts appear to be attempts at determining meaning. The issue is not simply how we are to apply the principles of equality, liberty, and parental responsibility to the case of surrogacy. It is also how we are to understand these principles themselves or, in other words, what principles of equality, liberty, and responsibility *are* justified. Are they those that center on freedom of contract, contractual responsibility and contractual relations between independent agents? Or alternatively, are they those that center on the protection and promotion of non-contractual relationships and responsibilities? If our understanding of a norm is not independent of our understanding of how to apply it and if our understanding of how to apply it is not independent of our values and conceptions of the good, then it is not clear that our understanding of the principles of freedom and equality can be easily separated from our interpretations and evaluations or from the differences we have about them.

For Habermas, the procedure of universalization in discourse ethics is meant to act "like a knife that makes razor-sharp cuts between evaluative statements and strictly normative ones, between the good and the just."[21] Evaluative statements refer to a person's or group's interpretations of its desires, feelings, and needs, and these, he insists, are tied to its identity, cultural heritage, and conception of the good. As opposed to normative statements, evaluative statements do not lend themselves to, nor can they be suspended by, the requirements of a consensus that is meant to be universally binding for we cannot simply be argued out of the traditions, forms of life, and personal histories that have made us who we are. In contrast, Habermas thinks that we can take up a hypothetical or distanced attitude towards our norms. But, if any discourse over norms must specify what they are or mean, we seem to be already involved in questions of application that, in turn, engage our evaluative sensibilities.

At times Habermas himself undercuts the razor-sharp distinction he establishes by suggesting that our values must themselves be submitted to the universalization procedure of practical discourse. Thus, he argues that idiosyncratic evaluative claims, claims that fail to meet wider community standards, can be simply irrational.[22] And he writes that "even the interpretations in which the individual identifies the needs that are most peculiarly his own are open to a revision process in which *all* participate."[23] As he explains in another context, "Needs are interpreted in the light of cultural values and since these are always components of an intersubjectively shared tradition, the revision of need-interpreting values cannot be a matter over which the individual monologically disposes."[24]

But if the revision of our need-interpreting values cannot be a matter over which the individual *monologically* disposes, why should it be open to a "revision process in which *all* participate?" Why should all those affected by a proposed norm also participate in the process by which I might learn to understand my own need-interpreting values differently and how can this be matter for rational argumentation? Why not simply admit that normative questions cannot be settled independently of evaluative ones and that normative justification must include an exploration and articulation of our possibly differing values?

If our values are bound up with our cultural heritage and personal life history and if we cannot be simply argued out of this heritage and history and, moreover, if we cannot debate the legitimacy of our norms without engaging the questions of our values, how can we settle questions of the legitimacy of norms? Is the question of whether enforcing surrogacy contracts can be justified a matter of our particular evaluations of the meaning of liberty, equality, and parental responsibility and is any decision on the matter therefore destined to violate the interest and values of some group? It seems to me that if we take our interpretive and evaluative differences seriously and if we reject the idea that the only way of dealing with them is to transcend them through the force of argumentation, then we might allow for a kind of difference that will also help us make sense of what I call a critical and pluralistic feminism.

Aesthetic Change

Suppose we take our interpretive and evaluative differences seriously with regard to the question of the normative legitimacy of contract pregnancy or surrogate motherhood. Might we look, then, for a resolution of the issue not by relying on the force of the better argument but rather by looking towards the sorts of discussions in which we consider and explore our interpretive and evaluative differences? In particular, might we not look to the domain of art and literature in which interpretive and evaluative differences seem to be at home? The first important point to be made about these differences in aesthetic discussions is that we expect them. We expect that different interpreters will understand and evaluate the same text or work of art in different ways and even that the same interpreter will understand and evaluate the same text or art work in different ways at different times and in different contexts. Indeed, such differences are a large part of the vitality of literary and artistic criticism. We dismiss certain interpretations of a text or work of art as unworkable because they ignore significant parts of the text, fail to translate its language correctly, or make a shambles of its plot lines or characterizations. Yet, even if certain interpretations of a text or work of art can be wrong, we do not assume that only one interpretation of a text can be right.

A second point to be made about our interpretive differences in the realm of art and literature is that they are not ones that we simply tolerate. We take them seriously, though not as differences we must necessarily resolve. We read alternative interpretations of the texts and works in which we are interested as a way of checking and expanding our own interpretations, as a way of discovering whether we have overlooked important aspects of the texts or works or whether looking at them in a different way, with a different set of concerns and interests or within a different context, might reveal new dimensions of them. In discussing a text or work of art we can be convinced of the general adequacy and intelligence of our own interpretation, yet open both to the adequacy and intelligence of different interpretations and to the way we might use them to develop and enrich our own. This sort of openness to the interpretations and evaluations of others is less interested in their faults than in what they may see in the text or work that we have not and how we might integrate into our own interpretation the insights we find in it.

How are these two features of interpretive discussion relevant to the moral domain with which discourse ethics is concerned? In my view, they suggest the possibility of a similar sort of openness. If our normative differences are not always ones that can be resolved through the force of the better argument and if even what counts for us as the better argument involves our values, sensibilities, cultural traditions, and conceptions of the good, then we acknowledge that our moral and political differences are not always differences over right and wrong. Rather, they are simply differences in the way we understand our norms and integrate them with one another, differences, moreover, from which we can learn. Habermas admits the "one-to-one relationship" that he establishes between "the prescriptive validity of a norm" and the normative validity claim raised by a speech act offer is "not a proper model for the relation between the potential for truth of works of art and the transformed relations between self and world stimulated by aesthetic experience." Instead, an aesthetic experience can reach into and transform "the totality in which these moments are related to each other."[25] Habermas does not draw all the possible consequences from this situation. If we assume that our normative differences are connected to evaluative and interpretive ones, then, only by discussing and comparing our different interpretations can we provide a balance to our possible moral and political insensitivities or blindnesses. Moreover, we can check, expand, and improve our own conceptions of the principles we share. As in the aesthetic domain, the fruitfulness of our discussions are less dependent on the force of the better argument than on the insights into meaning we gain from one another.

Nor do our discussions lead necessarily to consensus. Because our normative assessments remain linked to our evaluative and interpretive ones, more than one set of such assessments can be "right." As in the domain of art and literature, we dismiss certain normative interpretations as simply unsustainable. Racist evaluations based on untenable empirical assumptions serve as an example. Still, the point of discussion remains that of examining, enriching, and developing our own evaluative and interpretive views, and not necessarily learning to agree with one another.

The idea of this sort of interpretive pluralism, a pluralism not only with regard to our differing values and conceptions of the good, but a pluralism with regard to the way we understand moral and political norms of action and principles of justice is suggested by some recent developments in political philosophy.[26] These developments reject the notion that moral or political philosophy begins from neutral premises in such conditions as those of ideal speech. Rather, they claim that it must begin with an ongoing form of life and its pre-existing moral and ethical content. The task of moral and political philosophy cannot be to take a god's-eye view of this content and evaluate it according to standards independent of it because as moral and political philosophers we are already immersed in it. But this circumstance means that political philosophy must make an interpretive turn. We cannot simply suspend or reformulate the ethical content of an ongoing form of life because it already forms the substance of the history of which we are a part and the context of the norms through which we suspend or reformulate it. The norms of our moral and political life are ones we must interpret rather than create. If we can interpret them differently given different hermeneutic perspectives, we are involved in a pluralistic logic in the moral and political domain similar to that which we expect in the domain of art and literature.

This conception of normative pluralism presupposes the non-exclusive and non-discriminatory character of our moral and political discussions. If we are to develop our own interpretations by engaging those that differ, we need to assure universal participation in our discussions without obstacles deriving from power, wealth, race, or gender. To this extent, the parameters of our discussions remain those of ideal speech. If we are to learn from our interpretive and evaluative differences, then we must encourage those differences. We must question any interpretation or evaluation that restricts in advance, whether through racist or sexist ideologies, or direct intimidation, the voices that can be part of our discussions. Still, such discussions no longer depend on the separation of norms and values nor do they necessarily end in rational consensus. Having excluded direct or implicit force, the effects of relations of power, fear, or the threat of sanctions, we might still have as many interpretations of the meaning of our norms of action and principles of justice as we have of our art and literature.

But how, then, does this notion of a critical pluralism allow for either a feminist perspective on social and political issues or for a feminist political practice? The discussion of surrogacy in feminist circles highlights differences among different groups of women who may understand the norms of equality and liberty differently and have different ideas of the meaning of motherhood and parental responsibility. As such, these differences support feminist worries about the false universalism implied by the attempt to specify a common feminist program or political orientation. At the same time, however, they emphasize the dilemmas of difference with which we began. If we emphasize our normative-evaluative differences as women, must we not give up on a coherent and unified feminist theory and practice? Conversely, if we give up on a specifically feminist normative perspective, do we not give up one of the vantage points from which difference becomes visible? The dilemma is that if we allow for a critical pluralism, for a pluralism that allows for different interpretations of our norms and principles, we acknowledge possible differences in our understanding of feminist norms and principles, and we must reject any undifferentiated feminist theory. But, if we allow for differences within feminism, we undermine the possibility of feminism itself as a coherent standpoint from which insight into difference is available. Is there a way out of this impasse?

In my view, normative and evaluative differences between different groups of women lead to the self-destruction of feminism only if they are assessed in terms of a practical discourse in which consensus is the goal and the point of articulating differences is to overcome or transcend them. But it remains one of the major contributions of feminism to have allowed us to recognize new and different normative perspectives, first those of women in opposition to those of men and subsequently those of different groups of women. If we attend to and allow for these differences within the limits set by the attention to pluralism itself, then we also require a new political ideal to that of consensus: namely that of differentiation in which we recognize the legitimacy of many different voices. This sort of pluralistic feminism relies on Habermasian standards to the extent that it precludes those differences that themselves preclude difference. If we are to recognize the legitimacy of different voices, then we cannot allow any to retain a monopoly on the discussion or to exclude the possibility of listening to others. These standards arise out of a critical pluralism itself, for if we are to learn from interpretations and evaluations other than our own, we must provide the conditions under which they can flourish in the communities to which we belong. This project also requires that as feminists we look for programs, policies, and solutions to our controversies that embody differentiation without cutting off possibilities for change.

Suppose we look again at the issues raised by contract pregnancy and try to allow for the plausibility of, at minimum, two different interpretations of the meaning of the principles of freedom and equality. According to one of those interpretations, freedom and equality mean the freedom of women to enter into contracts on an equal basis with men, with the same supposition of their rationality as contracting parties, of their understanding of their own interests and of their responsibilities under contract. According to the other interpretation, freedom and equality are the freedom and equality of different groups of women and children who must be assured of the social and economic conditions under which the possibilities of their exploitation can be eliminated.

As we have seen, each of these interpretations of the principles at issue is entwined with evaluative assessments of the importance of contract, the significance of motherhood, and even the good of social association. Hence, neither interpretation can be dismissed under the constraints of consensus without elevating one set of values or conceptions of the good above others. We allow for the validity of each interpretation as a plausible and illuminating understanding of principles we share, and look for solutions to our controversy over the enforceability of surrogacy contracts that are differentiated in the sense that they attempt to accommodate both or all the non-exclusionary interpretations of the principles we think are involved. Hence, we allow for the enforceability of surrogacy contracts under certain conditions. We work for the social and economic conditions that ensure that surrogate mothers and contractual parents enter into contracts on equal footing; we also try to establish grounds upon which the sanctity of the infant-mother bond can be recognized—and therefore develop new and more flexible forms of adoption and family relations. Whatever specific solutions we decide most adequately reflect the diversity of our legitimate normative difference, we can work for those solutions in a united and consensual way.

What allows for the unity of a feminist perspective under this conception is that we simply compromise our real views for the lowest common denominator in our diverse opinions. We agree to disagree on certain interpretations of the meaning of our norms and principles and focus on those concrete policies on which we can agree. Still, if we adopt this view of what a pluralist feminism is, we need to acknowledge that our compromises are a result neither of giving in to one another nor of trading off various interests for the sake of those to which we are more committed. Rather, our common work arises out of a recognition of the legitimacy of our differences. We acknowledge the adequacy of each others' interpretations and work together to develop a differentiated solution in which the diversity of our interpretive concerns can, as far as possible, be represented. The areas on which we do agree, then, issue from our recognition of our differences which in turn changes the goals towards which we work together.

Moreover, where the legitimate, non-exclusionary views of some groups cannot be represented, we at least work together to keep the discussion, reevaluations, and development of our perspectives open. In this way, we can follow through on both sides of the dilemmas of feminism; we can remain committed to criticizing the false universalism of traditional political and moral theories while insisting on the legitimacy of a unified feminist practice, the fundamental assumption of which is the possible legitimacy of a diversity of interpretive and evaluative-normative perspectives within the limits Habermas specifies with the notion of an ideal speech situation.

NOTES

1. See Christine Di Stefano, "Dilemmas of Difference: Feminism, Modernity, and Postmodernism" in *Feminism/Postmodernism*, Linda J. Nicholson, ed. (New York: Routledge, 1990), pp. 63–82.

2. Deborah L. Rhode, *Justice and Gender* (Cambridge, MA: Harvard University Press, 1989), p. 1.

3. See Carol Gilligan, *In a Different Voice* (Cambridge, MA: Harvard University Press, 1982).

4. See Nancy Fraser, "What's Critical about Critical Theory: The Case of Habermas and Gender" in *Unruly Practices: Power, Discourse and Gender in Contemporary Social Theory* (Minneapolis, MN: University of Minnesota Press, 1989).

5. See Sara Ruddick, *Maternal Thinking: Towards a Politics of Peace* (Boston: Beacon Press, 1989).

6. See, for example, Rhode, *Justice and Gender*, op. cit. pp. 310–11.

7. See, for example, Nancy Fraser and Linda J. Nicholson, "Social Criticism without Philosophy: An Encounter between Feminism and Postmodernism" in *Feminism/Postmodernism*, pp. 19–38

8. Fraser and Nicholson, "Social Criticism without Philosophy," p. 32.

9. Jürgen Habermas, "Discourse Ethics: Notes on a Program of Philosophical Justification" in *Moral Consciousness and Communicative Action*, trans. Christian Lenhardt and Shierry Weber Nicholsen (Cambridge, MA: MIT Press) p. 58.

10. Habermas, *The Theory of Communicative Action*, Vol. 1, (Boston: Beacon Press, 1981), p. 286.

11. Habermas, "Discourse Ethics," p. 58.

12. Habermas, *The Theory of Communicative Action*, p. 24.

13. Habermas, "Morality and Ethical Life" in *Moral Consciousness and Communicative Action*, p. 197.

14. Habermas, "Morality and Ethical Life," p. 197.

15. Habermas, "Morality and Ethical Life," p. 205.

16. Habermas, "Morality and Ethical Life," p. 205.

17. For my understanding of the position in favor of contract pregnancy, I am indebted to Carmen Shalev's illuminating study, *Birth Power: The Case for Surrogacy* (New Haven: Yale University Press, 1989).

18. Shalev, *Birth Power*, p. 206.

19. Shalev, *Birth Power*, p. 207.

20. Habermas, "Discourse Ethics, p. 105.

21. Habermas, "Discourse Ethics, p. 104.

22. Habermas, *The Theory of Communicative Action*, p. 17.

23. Habermas, "Justice and Solidarity: On the Discussion Concerning Stage 6'" in *The Moral Domain: Essays on the Ongoing Discussion between Philosophy and the Social Sciences*, Thomas E. Wren, ed., (Cambridge, MA: MIT Press), p. 247.

24. Habermas, "Discourse Ethics," p. 67–68.

25. Habermas, "Questions and Counterquestions," James Bohman trans., in *Habermas and Modernity*, Richard Bernstein, ed. (Cambridge, MA: MIT Press, 1985), pp. 202–203.

26. See, for example, Michael Walzer, *Spheres of Justice*, (New York: Basic Books, 1983).

11

Toward a Model of Self-Identity: Habermas and Kristeva

Allison Weir

One of the most important tasks facing contemporary feminist theorists is the task of reformulating and reconstructing our concepts of the self. We need new models of identity, of individuation, of agency and autonomy which will take account of the important critiques of these concepts generated by feminist theorists. In this paper I will work toward a model of self-identity which can address some of the concerns of both *relational feminism*, which argues that the ideal of self-identity too often conceals a defense against connection with others, and *postmodern* and *poststructuralist feminism*, which argues that the concept of self-identity can be understood only in terms of the system of meaning which produces it: a system predicated on a logic of exclusion of nonidentity or difference. My attempt to clarify a normative ideal of self-identity comes out of a conviction that we need to uphold a commitment to women's struggles for identity and autonomy in the context of feminist critiques of defensive atomistic individualism and critiques of the concept of the disembedded subject as the free and unfettered author of his destiny. We need to make a space for an understanding of self-identity and autonomy which will not clash with our conviction that individuals must be understood as embedded, embodied, localized, constituted, and fragmented, as well as subject to forces beyond our control. We need to understand ourselves clearly as actors capable of learning, of changing, of making the world and ourselves, better.

So it is important that I begin by saying what a defensible ideal of self-identity is *not*. It is *not* some sort of essentialist ontology, not an idealist conception of an original pregiven authentic self. It is not an alienated individualism severed from connections and solidarities, severed from collective struggles, immune to systems of power and oppression. It is not an attempt to repress or deny the embodiment, fragmentation, dividedness, and multiplicity of human selves, or the constitution of subjects in and through language and power.

The concept of self-identity I defend can be defined as the capacity to experience oneself as an active and relatively coherent *participant* in a social world. Essential to self-identity, then, is "the ability of a person to relate to him or herself and to be able to relate to others in a meaningful way, to act and react self-consciously."[1] This emphasis on a capacity for *meaningful* interaction with self and others takes us in two directions, for it introduces both reflexivity and intersubjectivity as essential components of self-identity. Reflexivity, for the meanings of my relationships to myself and to others come down to me: I am the one faced with the question of who I am and who I want to be. I am the one who must invest my existence with meaning for me; this meaning can be generated only through my participation in social meanings, which are intersubjectively constituted. The very concept of a self, of an I, of a me, is something which is constructed only through intersubjective interactions, which take place always in contexts of shared meanings. Similarly, my identity as this specific individual is constructed through my participation in communities, institutions, and systems of meaning, which organize my interactions with, and through which I interpret my interactions with, the world, my self, and others. My identity is produced through a complex process through which I am identified, and identify myself, in terms of intersubjective contexts of meaning.

The capacity, and the responsibility, to problematize and define one's own meaning (one's own identity) is both the burden and the privilege of modern subjects. As a subject who is no longer defined by a fixed position in a social system, I am (relatively) free (or, at the least, I aspire to a normative ideal of freedom) to determine, through my practices, who I am and who I am going to be. The flip side of this freedom is the burden of self-definition: every action, every decision becomes self-defining; every action, every position is open to question.[2] This freedom and this responsibility are absolutely inescapable in our daily lives. At the same time, along with the increasing need for self-definition goes an increasing production and differentiation of identity-attributes: of possible roles, attachments and affiliations, values, beliefs and commitments, needs and desires, styles and modes of expression. We are exposed to more and more frameworks for reflection on and demystification of the constitutive influences which shape our identities (such as family and relationship dynamics, unconscious processes, collective identities, economic, social, and linguistic systems, systems of power and oppression. . .).

Central to self-identity, then, is the capacity to sustain and in some sense reconcile multiple and often conflicting identities and to understand, criticize, and reconcile multiple and often conflicting interpretations of those identities, not to mention the capacity to live with and somehow reconcile all of the ambiguity and complexity of our lives that does *not* (and never will) readily lend itself to this identity-work. Ideally, these reconciliations are achieved not through the imposition of an identity which excludes or represses difference and nonidentity (the concern of post-modernists), but through a capacity to reflexively and practically accept, live with, and make sense of differences and complexity. This capacity is based not on a denial of connections with others (the concern of relational theorists), but on a cognitive and affective acceptance of intersubjectivity and autonomy and of the dependence on and independence from others, which underlies a capacity to recognize when my meaning differs from the meaning of others, and when my identity is bound up with the identity of a partial or general "we."

This is, of course, an enormously demanding project, the difficulty of which is increased as various identities are recognized as bound to systems of oppression, and with communities and institutions that define themselves through exclusions. This is acutely expressed by Gloria Anzaldúa who writes of her ongoing attempts to make some sense out of the conflicts among her various identities as a Catholic-raised, lesbian Chicana (Mexican, Anglo-American): "I have so internalized the borderland conflict that sometimes I feel like one cancels out the other and we are zero, nothing, no one."[3]

The experience of lack of self is the familiar dark side of a culture characterized by a growing pressure for self-identity under conditions of increasing fragmentation. But the other side of this pressure and this fragmentation is a freedom of conscious self-determination and a capacity for analysis: Anzaldúa describes her conscious choice to live her life as a lesbian and describes her struggle for self-analysis and self-making as a "path of knowledge" which opens up a process of analysis and critique of social and cultural institutions governing race, class, gender, and sexuality.

Essential to an individual's capacity to problematize and define her own identity are cognitive and practical capacities for self-knowledge, self-realization, and self-direction,[4] which involve cognitive capacities for learning, for critique, and for organization, and practical capacities for expression, engagement, commitment, and flexibility. The development of self-identity requires the learning of social and linguistic norms, through which the expression or realization of one's specificity, and the development of a capacity for the critique of norms, becomes possible. (I also want to say that it is through these practices of expression and critique that social and linguistic norms change and are kept open and diverse.) The development of self-identity requires the cognitive capacity to reflect on who I am and what matters to me, and to organize diverse identities and identity-attributes, into some sort of meaning-ful narrative or constellation. It also requires the practical, existential capac-ity to discover and define and *commit* to what matters to me, to my meaning, while remaining flexible and open to change. To some extent, all of this depends on an ability to resolve particular differences and conflicts into more general meanings.

This notion of self-identity as a capacity to *resolve* differences and conflicts has not been popular among feminist theorists. Iris Young, for example, argues that "any individual subject is a play of differences that cannot be comprehended" and that the struggle for self-identity (and the struggle for reciprocal recognition with others) is necessarily based on a logic of identity which *necessarily* denies differences.[5] For Young, identity and difference are mutually exclusive; thus, she argues for an ideal of "unassimilated other-ness."[6] Similarly, Luce Irigaray, Diana Fuss, and Jessica Benjamin all argue that the attempt to resolve contradictions is an act of domination, and it is better to leave contradictions and paradoxes unresolved.[7] All of these theo-rists make these arguments in the name of a model of the self as an open process of constant change.

But the struggle to resolve conflicts through an openness to difference is essential to the practice of change and the generation of new meaning. It is impossible to understand the developments in the self-understanding of femi-nists, and the feminist movement, without acknowledging the role played by individual and collective struggles to understand differences and make sense of and resolve conflicts. To take just one example, the "Sex Wars" debates were provoked by some women's struggles to explore sexuality, pleasure, violence, and desire past the boundaries set by anti-porn feminism. At the individual level, the struggle of a particular woman to analyze, articulate, and make sense of the relationships between her sexual desires, fantasies, and practices and her feminist values requires a struggle to reconceptualize the relationship between her feminist values and her experiences of pleasure and desire. In the process, both the understanding of feminism and the under-standing of desire—and, in turn, her own self-understanding—undergo change, a change that could not have happened if she had simply accepted paradox and had made no attempt to resolve it; if, that is, she had not taken either her desires or her commitment to feminist values seriously enough to attempt to resolve the apparent conflict between them. It is such individual and collective struggles to resolve conflicts which fueled the opening up of feminist discourses about pleasure and desire and radically changed the land-scape of feminist theory and practice.

The struggle to make meaning through attempting to resolve apparent contradictions is essential to the ongoing constitution of self-identity. Since it is impossible to make meaning in abstraction from the practical activity of making meaning for and with other people, the development of self-identity is possible only through the development of a capacity for mutual understanding, within intersubjective relationships. But this means that we have to be able to conceptually abstract from the relationships themselves to the intersubjective *meanings* which mediate relationships.

To put this another way, the problem of the *identity of the self* is bound up with the problem of the identity of meaning, and with the problem of the identification with, or the relationship to, others. It seems to me that attempts by feminist theorists to formulate a positive conception of self-identity often founder because one or the other of these elements is left out. *Relational theories* like Nancy Chodorow's focus on the relationship between self-identity and identification with others, but leave out any consideration of identity of meaning. Because they lack any concept of mediation through identity of meaning in language, they see the identity of the self and identification with others as locked in eternal opposition or merged into one. On the other hand, post-structuralist theories tend to focus on the structural homology between the identity of the self and the identity of meaning in language, but leave out any conception of mediation through social relations with others. Thus, they see the identity of the self and the identity of meaning in language as united in a logic or structure of totalizing repressive identity. The effect is that each is unable to *abstract*, either from concrete relationships or from the system of language, to a concept of the individual as a *participant* in the intersubjective constitution of *meaning*.

It is crucially important that feminist theorists reconsider a common tendency to see abstraction as the enemy. For example, Judith Butler argues that we need to reject any conception of agency as a capacity for reflexive mediation, because such a conception falsely "separates [the] subject from its cultural predicates," abstracts from the subject's color, sexuality, ethnicity, class, and the "illimitable et cetera," and abstracts from the process of signification or the linguistic constitution of the subject. Furthermore, the postulation of a capacity for reflection upholds a false "epistemological" conception of a subject who is separated from and opposed to its object/other.[8] This argument is surprisingly similar to the arguments of relational theorists like Evelyn Fox Keller, Susan Bordo, and Sandra Harding, among others, who criticize a characteristically masculine emphasis on abstraction, which they associate with the separation of subject and object, the denial of connections to others, and the domination of the other/object.[9] What is common to these otherwise disparate arguments is an association of abstraction and separation with domination or repression.

While there is much to be learned from feminist critiques of the abstraction of the individual from the intersubjective relationships and the contexts of power, language, and meaning that constitute us, there is also a danger here of sliding into absurdity. Once we get to the point where we reject any abstraction of the individual from contexts and any postulation of the individual's capacity for reflection on contexts, we effectively deny any capacity of agents to participate in, criticize, and change those contexts. In rejecting abstraction, feminist theorists forget that the capacity to abstract from particular relationships, from linguistic systems and social norms, is essential to a capacity to *criticize* those relationships, systems, and norms. The challenge, then, is not to reject abstraction for embeddedness, but to theorize a capacity for abstraction for detachment, for critique, which is not opposed to but continuous with, and in fact constitutive of, participation.

Toward a Developmental Theory of Self-Identity

For the early Frankfurt School theorists, the capacity for critique was the essential achievement of individuation. But in the melancholy story of the "Dialectic of Enlightenment," the development of the individual's capacity for critique entails the internalization of authority which, paradoxically, obliterates all motives for critique, and inhibits any capacity for genuinely independent thought.[10] Jessica Benjamin argues that Adorno's problem was that he was unable to shake his liberal bourgeois faith in reason and the autonomous individual, abstracted from contexts and relationships, and thus was unable to imagine any process of self-development besides the internalization of dominating reason.[11] Benjamin argues that the way to get out of the circle of internalizing domination for the development of reason is to reject both internalization and reason—to reject both internalization of social norms as the means, and autonomous rationality as the goal, of self-development. Benjamin's solution is to shift to a different model of self-development, focusing on spontaneous self-assertion and affective identification with particular others. But Benjamin's model of a spontaneous and embedded self provides the self with no capacity for abstraction from or critique of given contexts, and thus no capacity for participation in a social world. As a result, she is left advocating that we accept the paradox between spontaneous practices of self-assertion, on the one hand, and experiences of attunement with others, on the other.[12] This is a variation on the old opposition between the individual and society, the paradox of social identity and self identity, identity with and difference from others, which is a false paradox.[13] Like Adorno, Benjamin is unable to *mediate* the paradox of the self, because like Adorno, she equates the development of independent and critical reason with the development of domination.

In what follows, I propose that Jürgen Habermas's model of the development of self-identity as the development of a capacity for critique will serve feminism better than models of the self which reject resolution and abstraction, and hence, participation and critique. I shall supplement Habermas's model with Julia Kristeva's model of the development of self-identity through practices of affective identification and expression. Both Habermas and Kristeva, I shall argue, theorize the identity of the self in relation to both the identity of meaning in language and the identification with, or relationship to, others. But where Habermas focuses on the interaction of identity of meaning in language with intersubjective recognition, which underlies the development of moral identity through an orientation to normative validity, Kristeva focuses on the interaction of identity of meaning in language with affective relations with others, which underlies the realization of a self through a capacity for expression.

Both Habermas and Kristeva propose models of individuation as a capacity for participation in a social world, and both presuppose that this capacity depends on a capacity for mutual understanding through the internalization of linguistic and social norms. Both develop theories of internalization which are very different from Adorno's, and from Benjamin's. For Habermas, what is internalized is not simply authority but an experience of mutuality and a capacity for critique. For Kristeva, internalization is not simply a response to threat (as it is, still, for Habermas), but a source of pleasure.

Habermas

At the center of Jürgen Habermas's account of the development of self-identity is the capacity to question and criticize conventions. This requires a capacity to conceptually abstract from given contexts through an appeal to principles. And this capacity is learned through the internalization of social and linguistic norms. For Habermas, the development of self-identity is predicated on the development of moral identity.

Habermas draws on the work of George Herbert Mead to articulate a theory of the development of self-identity through linguistically mediated interaction. For Mead, "The fact that all selves are constituted by the social process . . . is not in the least incompatible with, or destructive of, the fact that every individual self has its own peculiar individuality."[14] In fact, it is only through "the social process" that a "peculiar individuality" can be realized. From Mead, Habermas draws a description of how socialization, the learning and internalizing of linguistic and social norms, produces not simple conformity to those norms, but true individuation. I shall take up this description at the ontogenetic level—at the level of individual development.

The crux of the interpretation Habermas draws from Mead, and what takes it beyond Freud, and beyond the thesis of the Dialectic of Enlightenment, is the concept of the perspective of the "generalized other": the idea that through linguistic interactions a human child develops an understanding of social norms not simply as expressions of arbitrary choice or self-interest, but as subject to demands for and tests of validity.[15]

For Mead, the child's self-identity, in both its epistemic and its practical dimensions, develops through the mechanism of taking the perspective of another, who, in an interactive relationship, takes up a performative attitude toward the self.

In the first stages of taking the attitude of the other, the child understands its interaction with its parents as a reciprocal satisfaction of interests expressed as imperatives. Once the child comes to recognize that the parents' expression of imperatives is connected with the parent's provision of care, the child responds to the threat of withdrawal of care by internalizing the parents' attitude toward herself.[16] At first the internalized attitudes are still tied to the concrete roles of a particular self and other. The attitudes or roles become detached from specific persons, and the transition to the perspective of the generalized other begins, with the introduction of a third-person or objective perspective. Thus far, the description of development applies as much to Freud as to Mead.

> Freud and Mead realized that these patterns of behavior become detached from the context-bound intentions and speech acts of individual persons, and take on the external shape of social norms insofar as the sanctions connected with them are internalized through taking the attitude of the other, that is to say, to the degree that they are taken into the personality and thereby rendered independent of the sanctioning power of concrete reference persons.[17]

At first, the objective or generalized norm of action is understood only in terms of an imperative which rests on choice—in this case, on the generalized choice, or arbitrary will, of the group. It is only with the transition to what Mead calls the perspective of the generalized other—and here we move beyond Freud—that the child comes to understand group norms not in terms of arbitrary will or choice and self-interest, but in terms of claims to validity: in terms of mutual obligations and expectations. The mechanism of internalization is essential to the development of this understanding.

> The authority of the "generalized other" differs from authority based only on disposition over means of sanction, in that it rests on assent. When A regards the group sanctions as his own, as sanctions he directs at himself, he has to presuppose his assent to the norm whose violation he punishes in this way. Unlike socially generalized imperatives, institutions claim a validity that rests on intersubjective recognition, on the consent of those affected by it: "Over against the protection of our lives or property, we assume the attitude of assent of all members in the community. We take the role of what may be called 'the generalized other.'"[18]

In other words, through internalizing the attitude of the generalized other, the child comes to recognize "objective" social norms as her own. Thus, I come to recognize or constitute myself as a member or participant in the "we." This connection between the self and the "we" is internalized, both in the sense of the development of understanding, and in the sense of the setting up of a motivational structure. In learning to orient her behavior to norms and take part in normatively regulated interactions, the child understands her self as a participant in a "we," and comprehend the meaning of a valid norm—i.e., that it rests, ideally, on the assent of each and all and as such is subject to criticism on the grounds that there are good reasons for my not assenting. The child makes a transition from a motivational structure based on interests and imperatives to a motivational structure based on an orientation to validity claims—on a recognition of shared expectations and obligations. Thus, internalization is the mechanism of both a comprehension of the meaning of social norms as, in principle, valid norms and an anchoring of those norms in a motivational structure.

It must be stressed that this account of the development of self-identity only works if we stipulate that the generalized other represents not an actual community consensus, but an ideal, a standard against which any norm must be measured. Contrary to what Habermas, and Mead, often seem to suggest, there is in modern societies no given social world of conventional norms that the child simply takes over and internalize. Rather, a child internalizes many different and conflicting normative positions. In order to participate effectively in interactions with primary others, and with institutions, a child may take the attitude of her mother's appeal to an "ethic of care," her father's appeal to an ethic of rights, her grandfather's appeal to an ethic of particular traditional conventions, and the ethic of strategic rationality in the pursuit of self-interest upheld by her favorite TV show. (More likely, each of her reference persons will represent a mixture of these attitudes and others.) She will have to deal with the differences between her mother who thinks homosexuality is sick and her aunt who's a lesbian and a gay rights activist, a black teacher who teaches the principles of universal equality and black pride and white friends who are racists. There is no actual given perspective of a unified conventional "we" which is the generalized other. What is internalized is a capacity to appeal to principles, to standards of normative validity. The child is forced to individuate through taking positions with respect to given conflicts. Ideally, she learns to do so through abstracting from her particular loyalties to each of her different reference persons, to appeal to principles.[19]

The crucial point here is that for Habermas, Mead's concept of taking the attitude of the other, which Mead understands as calling forth a response in oneself that one also calls out in the other, cannot be understood on the model of a simple response to a stimulus, but must be understood through a model of linguistic interaction. The response, can be understood "in the full dialogical sense as an 'answer'"; hence, what is internalized is not simply assent, taking the attitude of the other demands "internalizing yes/no responses to statements or imperatives."[20] Habermas takes this idea from Tugendhat, who notes that "consent only has significance against the background of the possibility of refusal."[21] What is internalized is a capacity for critique.

For Habermas, the capacity for critique grounded in linguistic communication underlies the development of both moral identity and more general personal identity. In analyzing the structure of role perspectives inherent in linguistic communication, Habermas follows Mead, who systematically connects "the role-taking effective in socialization with the speech situations in which speakers and hearers enter into interpersonal situations as members of a social group."[22] One takes over a reflected sense of self or "me" by adopting the other's perspective or expectations toward oneself. But the structure of linguistic interaction is such that the other, in recognizing you as a participant in interaction, expects you to take a position in response to her speech act. Thus, as a participant in the interaction, one must accept the freedom and responsibility of taking a position in response to the other's speech act. It is this freedom—and this responsibility—demanded of participants in linguistically mediated social interaction, which is the source of individuation.

> The performative attitude that ego and alter adopt when they act communicatively with one another is bound up with the presupposition that the other can take a "yes" or "no" position on the offer contained in one's own speech act. Ego cannot relinquish this scope for freedom even when he is, so to speak, obeying social roles; for the linguistic structure of a relation between responsible actors is built into the internalized pattern of behavior itself.[23]

The demand that one "take a position" is not restricted to questions of moral principle and the justification of norms; this is a demand found in any communicative interaction. In my response to another's speech act I am necessarily taking a position. Thus, individuation is an ongoing process: the development of a sense of self-identity (of a "me") takes place through a continual process of reflection on and assimilation of the actual positions taken, in practice, in my responses to other's speech acts. The element of spontaneity and unpredictability is introduced by the "I" which acts, in response to the acts of others.

> Thus in the socialization process an "I" emerges equiprimordially with the "me," and the individuating effect of socialization processes results from this double structure. The model for the relation between the two agencies is the "answer" of a participant in communication who takes a "yes" or "no" position. Which answer ego will give in any instance, what position he will take, cannot be known in advance—either by him or by anyone else.[24]

For Habermas the development of self-identity is a response to the demands inherent in the structure of linguistic communication.

> The individuation effected by the linguistically mediated process of socialization is explained by the linguistic medium itself. It belongs to the logic of the use of the personal pronouns, and especially to the perspective of a speaker who orients himself to a second person, that this speaker cannot *in actu* rid himself of his irreplaceability, cannot take refuge in the anonymity of a third person, but must lay claim to recognition as an individuated being. . . .
>
> Among the universal and unavoidable presuppositions of action oriented to reaching understanding is the presupposition that the speaker qua actor lays claim to recognition both as an autonomous will and as an individuated being.[25]

In linguistic communication, the speaker is required to recognize and take responsibility for herself as a "me," and to take positions in response to others as an "I." The demand made of participants in linguistically mediated interaction, that they accept the freedom and responsibility of taking an affirmative or negative position in response to an other's speech act, is what underlies the development of moral identity as a critical relation to social norms, and of personal identity as a critical relation to oneself.

Moral identity is based on the recognition "that a norm deserves to be valid only insofar as . . . it takes into account the interests of everyone involved, and only insofar as it embodies the will that all could form in common, each in his own interest, as the will of the generalized other."[26] It is this orientation to the validity of a norm that provides the individual with the basis for critique: if anyone's interests are being excluded, then the norm is not valid. If anyone presents reasons for not consenting, then the validity of the norm is called into question. And this is what makes it possible for the individual to abstract from particular norms to universal principles, to move from simple conformity to or deviance from given norms to a capacity to relativize and criticize given norms in the name of universal principles, but to do so as a participant in a social world.

For Habermas, this capacity for critique which is built into linguistic interaction, and built into the internalization of norms, is essential to not only moral but more general personal identity.

> The identity of the ego can . . . be stabilized only through the abstract ability to satisfy the requirements of consistency, and thereby the conditions of recognition, in the face of incompatible role expectations and in passing through a succession of contradictory role systems. The ego-identity of the adult proves its worth in the ability to build up new identities from

shattered or superseded identities, and to integrate them with old identities in such a way that the fabric of one's interactions is organized into the unity of a life history that is both unmistakable and accountable.[27]

The self-identity of the adult depends on the ability to "take over and be responsible" for integrating all of the different, often conflicting, positions one takes, into a narrative that is meaningful to others and to oneself. This requires a cognitive ability to resolve conflicts among particular positions by abstracting to more complex meanings, and by reflecting on practices in a process of self-critique: by asking the questions, what kind of person am I, and is this the person I want to be? For Habermas, this cognitive process of self-evaluation calls for an "appropriative form of understanding."[28]

But if the capacity for critique is essential, it is not a sufficient condition of the development of a meaningful and recognizable self-identity. There also has to be an existential commitment to the meanings you produce through your practices, and through which you critically judge and guide your practices.

What Habermas's developmental model doesn't answer is how we come to be able to make that commitment to a recognizable, integrated, and meaningful self-identity and keep it relatively open, flexible, and nondefensive. It is unable to account for varying levels of identity-competence; to account for why many—probably most—of us fail to successfully develop coherent and meaningful self-identities and typically err either on the side of rigidity and defensiveness—a failure to question and criticize—or on the side of mushy indistinctness—a failure to abstract from particulars and resolve contradictions. Nor can it account for why this failure often takes the form of a spirited resistance to identity, abstraction, resolution, and integration. To fill in this gap, I draw on the work of Julia Kristeva.

Kristeva

Kristeva's work is characterized by a profound ambivalence with regard to the nature of society, and hence of language and individuation. There are two different models in Kristeva's work of the development of identity through the internalization of linguistic and social norms. On one hand, Kristeva could be described as a Derridean poststructuralist with a stoic individualist twist. In this guise, Kristeva sees the "sociosymbolic order" as a closed structure that is essentially repressive and essentially patriarchal. To this extent she agrees with Derrideans, but she differs from them insofar as she insists that the structures of language and individuation are essential for human social interaction and participation. Thus, the only solution is to stoically accept the closed, repressive, patriarchal order of language as the only means of participation in social interaction, while at the same time constantly subverting it. Self-identity is a constant oscillation between stoic acceptance and subversion of the Law:

> A constant alternation between time and its 'truth', identity and its loss, history and that which produces it: that which remains extra-phenomenal, outside the sign, beyond time. An impossible dialectic of two terms, a permanent alternation: never the one without the other.[29]

But there is another track in Kristeva's work: in many of her writings, Kristeva understands individuation in terms of a not-impossible dialectic between system and practice, as a constant process of investment in and internalization of a language system that is constantly transformed through individual and social practices. Kristeva's "subject-in-process" is a subject who develops and changes through taking up positions, or identities, through an investment in a sociosymbolic order and thereby realizing and expressing her own heterogeneity (and in turn transforming language and society).

Against Derrida's invocation of a constant negativity in resistance to any identity, Kristeva argues that the refusal of identity renders negativity merely positive, leaving us in a space in which difference no longer exists. In its relentless subversion of Identity, Derrida's "trace" "marks anteriority to every entity and thus to every position: . . . the trace dissolves every thesis—material, natural, social, substantial, and logical—in order to free itself from any dependence on the *Logos*."[30] The effect of this resistance position, to any thesis, or identity is a theory which "gives up on the subject, and must remain ignorant [of the subject's] functioning as social practice . . . ."[31] For Kristeva, the subject constitutes itself only through positing, through taking positions or identities within a social world and a symbolic order—only by engaging in a world of shared or identical meanings, through which one can realize one's own meaning.

Like Habermas, Kristeva focuses on the need to take positions in everyday social interactions as central to the constitution of self-identity. Both Habermas and Kristeva argue that the capacity to take positions requires the development of a capacity to identify oneself with a social "we," in a shared symbolic meaning-system. But whereas for Habermas the need to take a position means the need to relate to norms in a critical and questioning manner, for Kristeva taking a position tends to mean taking a position of identity within the symbolic order, which will allow "nonidentity" or difference to emerge—to be realized or expressed—thereby producing a new position. Whereas for Habermas the pressure to individuate inheres in the freedom and responsibility to take an affirmative or negative position in response to others' speech acts, Kristeva analyzes the pressure to individuate in terms of the tension between unconscious drives and socio-linguistic systems, and analyzes the positing of identity as a condition for the expression or articulation of desires—and hence, the realization of a self and its meaning—in language. Kristeva provides no mechanism for moving from a conventional to a post-conventional, critical, moral identity, because she does not recognize a connection between identity of meaning and intersubjective validity. What she does offer is an analysis of the constitution of identity in terms of the expression or articulation of a self, through the expression of bodily heterogeneity and of affects, in language which is meaningful to oneself and to others. She provides an account of the development of a practical self-identity—of an identity which is postconventional insofar as it is an ability to relate meaningfully to differences within oneself and between self and others. At her best, Kristeva understands the tension between drives and language—both, forces beyond the individual's control—not as barriers to, but, as Axel Honneth has put it, as "enabling conditions" of the development of self-identity.[32] For the development of individual identity, or individual meaning, is only possible through the expression or realization of one's specificity in language—in a system of shared meanings, through interaction with others.

Kristeva's psychoanalytic analysis of the development of identity in terms of expression, rather than repression, produces some surprising results: against Lacan and Freud, who tend to argue that learning symbolic and social systems entails the repression of aggressive and pleasure-seeking drives, Kristeva argues that the development of a capacity for signification, or linguistic competence, emerges out of a deployment or expression of those drives. In the Freudian-Lacanian scenario:

> The symbolic function is . . . dissociated from all pleasure, made to oppose it, and is set up as the paternal place, the place of the superego. According to this view, the only way to react against the consequences of repression imposed by the compulsion of the pleasure principle is to renounce pleasure through symbolization by setting up the sign through the absence of the object, which is expelled and forever lost.
>
> What this interpretation seems to rule out is the pleasure underlying the symbolic function. . . .[33]

For Kristeva, the move into language and a social world—into linguistically mediated interaction—is not a fall, not a renunciation of pleasure. Rather it is "a separation which is not a lack but a discharge and which . . . arouses pleasure."[34] The pleasure Kristeva describes here is associated with what she calls abjection: an aggressive drive (corresponding to Freud's anal drive) for expulsion, destruction, separation, which underlies the rejection of dependence on the power of others, the separation of self and other, and the distinction between subject and predicate in language. Abjection interacts with the (oral) drive for incorporation: a drive toward both having and being, possession of and identification with others, and investment in language.

Kristeva describes the development of a capacity for signification—for linguistic competence and an orientation to meaning—in terms of the pleasures of abjection and incorporation.[35] And it is these experiences of pleasure which, for Kristeva, motivate the internalization of symbolic and social norms.

Thus, whereas Habermas argues that norms are initially internalized only in response to a threat and initially represent only the arbitrary dictates of authority, Kristeva argues that the development of linguistic competence and the development of self-identity through the internalization of sociosymbolic norms is a pleasurable process.[36] Moreover, she argues that these processes represent *for the child* a deliverance from utter dependence, from helplessness in the face of authority, to a means of signification—a means of participation in a social world through an orientation to meaning.

While Kristeva often advocates the "constant alternation" between identity and nonidentity as the "impossible dialectic" of the self, in many of her writings Kristeva upholds a normative ideal of an integrated self—a complex self-identity based on a reflexive and affective recognition and acceptance of the difference and nonidentity within the self. It is only through the cognitive recognition and affective acceptance of the complexity or internal differentiation of the other that the child comes to recognize and accept both the separateness of her self from others with whom she interacts, and the internal differentiation of her own self.

The developmental condition for this recognition and acceptance is the transition from prelinguistic or drive-based, to linguistically mediated interaction with others, and hence, the opening up of a social world. Central to this process is the internalization of social and linguistic norms. This internalization is mediated by experiences of pleasure, by affective relations, and by cognitive development.

According to Kristeva, the child moves from a relation to the primary caretaker based on satisfaction of needs to a relation based on a shared orientation to meaning. Too often, Kristeva describes this path of development in the terms of Lacanian psychoanalysis, as a transition from a relationship of immediacy or merging with the mother to an acceptance of the paternal Law of the symbolic order. Kristeva's twist to this story is that the investment in the phallic symbolic order is mediated by an identification with an idealized father and that the motivation for investment in the symbolic order is the recovery of the mother (the primary object) in language, and meaning.[37]

But Kristeva also tells the story in another way. In this other version, the child moves from a need-based relationship with the first caretaker (who is, typically, the mother) to a recognition that the mother's needs are not wholly satisfied by the child, that she has an other meaning in her life beyond the child. The child has to recognize, in some rudimentary way, that the mother is complex and internally differentiated. And the child is forced to recognize this through the mother's failure to satisfy all of her demands. In the process she learns that there is a realm of meaning that can satisfy desires, and she is able to identify with the mother's desire for and investment in that meaning. It is this identification with the mother's desire—with the mother's means of participation in a social world, with her investment in a shared social meaning—which mediates, ideally, the child's internalization of linguistic and social norms.[38]

The motivation for this internalization is not simply the threat of punishment but the promise of the gift of meaning—of a means for mediating relationships with primary others and for participating in a larger social world where desires can be satisfied.

It is this affective investment in social meaning which underlies the capacity to affectively accept one's own differentiation from others and the differentiation within oneself. It also underlies the capacity to develop an integrated sense of self, which will not dissolve into differences. One is able to realize one's self through expression of one's "nonidentity" in terms of shared meanings and this expression is mediated through affective investment in discourse with others.

Kristeva argues that the transference relationship—i.e., the relationship of identification with a loved other—

> is a true process of self-organization. This means that once the accidents, aggressions, and errors of my discourse (of my life), have been inserted into the transference dynamic, they are no longer those failures of a finalistic linear process that anguished me before. To the contrary, in transference love, "errors" are overcompensated; they produce the libidinal self-organization that has the effect of making me more complex and autonomous. Why? Because, as they are introduced by *means of discourse* into transference (into love. . .), the death drive, or the "negative" in Freud's sense of the term, enters the service of symbolic apprenticeship, autonomization, and greater complexity of the individual.[39]

The failure to develop an integrated sense of self-identity, is characterized by Kristeva as the development of linguistic competence through the learning of linguistic norms in the relative absence of any affective investment in those norms. One is able to address oneself to a universal other, but not to a particular other. Or, as Kristeva puts it, you get the "kit of representation but without the caboodle of drive. The caboodle remained in the emptiness of maternal fusion and/or maternal absence."[40] This happens when social and linguistic norms are experienced as primarily repressive and are only adopted in response to threat. And this happens in a social world in which too many given norms are oppressive—where, in particular, mothers, or primary caregivers, too often do not fully experience themselves as participants.

In this case, meaning comes to be understood only on the level of the universal and is nonparticularized. To affectively invest in general or universal meanings one needs to be able to make meaning for another—for, in particular, a loved other. The use of language without an addressee of discourse—without someone who is spoken to—leaves it empty of signification for the speaker.[41]

The strength of Kristeva's account, for feminism, is her insistence that the affective relationship cannot serve as an end in itself, as a means of producing individual or particular meanings. Rather, it serves as a means of investing in a world of shared meanings, of constituting and experiencing oneself as a participant in that world and of making those meanings constantly open to diversity and change.

The account of the development of self-identity that I presented here is, of course, far from complete. I show only that any understanding of the development of self-identity must take both of these constitutive elements into account: both the capacity to relate to norms in a critical way and the capacity to express or realize one's own meaning through affective investment in discourse with others. Both of these capacities entail the internalization of social and linguistic norms, an internalization of shared or identical meanings through relationships of identification with others. Both provide a way to unlock the paradoxes of the self: of individual identity versus social identity, of drives versus language, autonomy versus relationship to others.

In closing, I call attention to some unresolved problems in Habermas's and Kristeva's theories, which I have been unable to deal with adequately here. Both Habermas and Kristeva tend to conflate the learning of social norms with the learning of linguistic norms: for Kristeva, the two are conceptually conflated in the concept of a sociosymbolic order; Habermas differentiates conceptually between them, but the differentiation is not always evident in his analysis. Perhaps that's why neither provides much of an understanding of the ways in which particular, as opposed to general or universal collective identities and affiliations, influence and interact with the development of self-identity. I tried to redress the latter omission to some extent in this paper; the former problem proves more resistant.

NOTES

1. Rainer Forst, "How (Not) to Speak about Identity: The Concept of the Person in a Theory of Justice," in *Philosophy and Social Criticism*, forthcoming.

2. Here I want to point out that the line which Habermas draws between crucial existential choices and trivial preferences, dispositions and inclinations is in practice increasingly blurred. Even "preferences in automobiles and sweaters" (Habermas) are more and more subject to what Charles Taylor calls "strong evaluations." See Habermas, "On the Pragmatic, the Ethical, and the Moral Employments of Practical Reason," in *Justification and Application: Remarks on Discourse Ethics*, trans. Ciaran Cronin, (Cambridge, MA: MIT Press, 1993), p. 4; and Taylor, "What is Human Agency?" in *Human Agency and Language* (Cambridge, England: Cambridge University Press, 1985), p. 15 ff.

3. Gloria Anzaldúa, *Borderlands/La Frontera* (San Francisco: Spinsters/Aunt Lute, 1987), p. 63.

4. This is a variation on Diana Meyers's categories of self-discovery, self-definition, and self-direction. See Meyers, *Self, Society, and Personal Choice* (New York: Columbia University Press, 1989).

5. Iris Young, "The Ideal of Community and the Politics of Difference," in Linda Nicholson, ed. *Feminism/Postmodernism* (New York: Routledge, 1990), pp. 310–11.

6. Young, "The Ideal of Community and the Politics of Difference," p. 301.

7. See my discussions of these arguments in *Sacrificial Logics: Feminist Theory and the Critique of Identity* (New York: Routledge, 1995).

8. Judith Butler, *Gender Trouble* (New York: Routledge, 1990), pp. 143–44.

9. See Susan Bordo, *The Flight to Objectivity: Essays on Cartesianism and Culture* (Albany: SUNY Press, 1987); Evelyn Fox Keller, *Reflections on Gender and Science* (New Haven: Yale University Press, 1985); Sandra Harding, "Is Gender a Variable in Conceptions of Rationality? A Survey of the Issues," *Dialectica* 36, 2:3 (1982).

10. Max Horkheimer and Theodor Adorno, *Dialectic of Enlightenment*, John Cumming, trans. (New York: Continuum, 1972).

11. Jessica Benjamin, "The End of Internalization: Adorno's Social Psychology," *Telos*, 32, (Summer 1977).

12. See Jessica Benjamin, *The Bonds of Love: Psychoanalysis, Feminism, and the Problem of Domination* (New York: Pantheon, 1988) and my article "The Paradox of the Self: Jessica Benjamin's Intersubjective Theory," in *Thesis Eleven* 32, (1992).

13. In fact, I tend to side with Ernst Tugendhat: there are no paradoxical phenomena, only inappropriate premises and inadequate categories. See Tugendhat, *Self-Consciousness and Self-Determination*, trans. Paul Stern, (Cambridge, MA: MIT Press, 1986), p. 3. (Habermas invokes this same paradox in his early paper, "Moral Development and Ego Identity," in *Communication and the Evolution of Society*, trans. Thomas McCarthy (Boston: Beacon Press, 1979), p. 90.

14. Mead, *Mind, Self and Society*, ed. C. Morris (Chicago: University of Chicago Press, 1962), p. 201; quoted by Habermas, "Individuation through Socialization: On George Herbert Mead's Theory of Subjectivity," in *Postmetaphysical Thinking*, trans. William Mark Hohengarten (Cambridge, MA: MIT Press, 1992), p. 185.

15. Habermas differentiates among three types of validity claims: claims to truth, normative validity, and sincerity, which correspond respectively to objective, intersubjective, and subjective domains. (There is also a fourth claim to linguistic intelligibility.) Here we are focusing on the claim to normative validity or rightness. See Habermas, "What is Universal Pragmatics?" in *Communication and the Evolution of Society*, trans. Thomas McCarthy (Boston: Beacon Press, 1979).

16. Habermas, *The Theory of Communicative Action*, Vol. 2, trans. Thomas McCarthy (Boston: Beacon Press, 1987), p. 34. Habermas's claim, following Freud, that the internalization of social roles and norms is a response to anticipated threat is challenged by Kristeva.

17. Habermas, *The Theory of Communicative Action*, p. 34.

18. Habermas, *The Theory of Communicative Action*, Vol. 2, pp. 38–39; quoting Mead, *Selected Writings*, ed. A. Reck (Chicago: University of Chicago Press, 1964), p. 284.

19. Habermas argues that she appeals to an ideal "unlimited communication community" characterized by symmetrical relations of unforced reciprocal recognition. (See Habermas, "Individuation through Socialization: On George Herbert Mead's Theory of Subjectivity," pp. 186–88).

It can also be said, however, that in one sense there is a substantive, empirical agreement among all members of modern societies, which is implied by Habermas's procedural model for the discursive determination of normative validity: at some level, all individuals socialized in modern societies share the ideal of the rights of all individuals to freedom and equal respect, and the concomitant obligation of all to uphold those rights for others. This universal ideal will be held, at some level, by each individual, coexisting with, and logically contradicting, homophobic, racist, traditionalist, and pure self-interest positions.

20. Habermas, *The Theory of Communicative Action*, Vol. 2.

21. Tugendhat, *Self-Consciousness and Self-Determination*, p. 229. Habermas draws on Wittgenstein's analysis of the concept of a rule to argue that the connection between identical meanings and intersubjective validity is based on the capacity for critique. *The Theory of Communicative Action*, p. 15 ff.

22. Habermas, *The Theory of Communicative Action*, Vol. 2, p. 58.

23. Habermas, *The Theory of Communicative Action*, Vol. 2, p. 59.

24. Habermas, *The Theory of Communicative Action*, Vol. 2, p. 59.

25. "Individuation through Socialization: On George Herbert Mead's Theory of Subjectivity," pp. 190–91.

26. Habermas, *The Theory of Communicative Action*, Vol. 2, p. 39.

27. Habermas, *The Theory of Communicative Action*, Vol 2, p. 98.

28. Habermas, "On the Pragmatic, the Ethical, and the Moral Employments of Practical Reason," p. 5.

29. Julia Kristeva, *About Chinese Women*, trans. Anita Barrows (New York: Marion Boyars, 1977), p. 8.

30. Kristeva, *Revolution in Poetic Language*, trans. Margaret Waller (New York: Columbia University Press, 1984), p. 143.

31. Kristeva, *Revolution of Poetic Language*, p. 142.

32. Axel Honneth, "Decentred Autonomy: The Subject After the Fall," paper presented to the Society for Phenomenology and Existential Philosophy, Boston, October 1992.

33. Kristeva, *Revolution in Poetic Language*, p. 149.

34. Kristeva, *Revolution in Poetic Language*, p. 151.

35. See Kristeva, *The Powers of Horror: An Essay on Abjection*, trans. Leon Roudiez (New York: Columbia University Press, 1982); and *Tales of Love*, trans. Leon Roudiez (New York: Columbia University Press, 1987).

36. Kristeva's model is therefore more useful than Jessica Benjamin's, which relies on the substitution of identification with particular others for the internalization of social and linguistic norms and leaves us with no capacity for shared meaning. Kristeva argues that affective identification mediates and often subverts, but cannot replace internalization of norms.

37. See, for example, Kristeva, "Life and Death of Speech," in *Black Sun: Depression and Melancholia*, trans. Leon Roudiez (New York: Columbia University Press, 1989), p. 43.

38. I develop this interpretation in my "Identification with the Divided Mother: Kristeva's Ambivalence," in Kelly Oliver, ed. *Ethics, Politics and Difference in Julia Kristeva's Writing* (New York: Routledge, 1993) and in my *Feminist Theories of Identity* (New York: Routledge, 1994).

39. Kristeva, *Tales of Love*, p. 14.

40. Toril Moi, ed. "Freud and Love: Treatment and Its Discontents," *The Kristeva Reader*, (New York: Columbia University Press, 1986), p. 266.

41. Moi, ed. "Freud and Love," *The Kristeva Reader*, p. 264.

Index

Contributors

Seyla Benhabib is Professor of Political Theory in the Department of Government at Harvard University and a Senior Fellow at the Center for European Studies. Her previous publications include: *Critique, Norm and Utopia: A Study of the Foundations of Critical Theory* (Columbia University Press, 1986); *Feminism as Critique*, ed. with Drucilla Cornell (Polity Press, 1987); *The Communicative Ethics Controversy*, ed. with Fred Dallmayr (MIT Press, 1991); *Situating the Self: Gender, Community and Postmodernism in Contemporary Ethics* (Routledge and Polity, 1992); *On Max Horkheimer: New Perspectives*, ed. with John McCole and Wolfgang Bonss (MIT Press, 1993); and *Feminist Contentions*, with Judith Butler, Drucilla Cornell, and Nancy Fraser (Routledge, 1994).

She is currently working on a book on Hannah Arendt, *The Reluctant Modernism of Hannah Arendt* (Sage Publications, expected publication 1996).

Jane Braaten received her Ph.D. from the University of Minnesota in 1987. She published *Habermas's Critical Theory of Society* (SUNY Press, 1991). Currently, she teaches at the College of Charleston and is doing research in the feminist critique of reason and the history of approaches to reason and intellectual virtue.

Simone Chambers is Assistant Professor of Political Science at the University of Colorado at Boulder. Her main interests lie in the study of ethics and social and political philosophy. She is the author of *Discourse and Procedural Ethics,* published in 1994.

Jean L. Cohen is Associate Professor of Political Theory at Columbia University. She is the co-author with Andrew Arato of *Civil Society and Political Theory* (MIT Press, 1992), and the author of *Class and Civil Society: The Limits of Marxian Critical Theory* (University of Massachusetts Press, 1982). She has published widely in the fields of social theory, political theory, gender, and law. Her most recent article in the field of gender and legal theory is "Redescribing Privacy: Identity, Difference, and the Abortion Controversy," published in *Columbia Journal of Gender and Law*, Vol. 3, 1992, Number 1, pp. 43-177.

Jodi Dean is Assistant Professor of Political Science at Hobart and William Smith Colleges. She has written on civil society, solidarity, and topics in feminist moral and legal theory. Currently, she is completing a book, *Spaces for Difference: Feminism, Discourse, and Solidarity.*

Marie Fleming is Director of the Centre for Women's Studies and Feminist Research at the University of Western Ontario. She has a forthcoming book on gender and rationality in Habermas's theory of communicative action.

Nancy Fraser is Professor of Philosophy, Fellow of the Center for Urban Affairs and Policy Research, and an affiliate of the Women's Studies Program at Northwestern University. She is the author of *Unruly Practices: Power, Discourse, and Gender in Contemporary Social Theory* (University of Minnesota Press, 1989); the co-editor of *Revaluing French Feminism: Critical Essays on Difference, Agency, and Culture* (Indiana University Press, 1992); and the co-editor of *Feminist Contentions,* with Seyla Benhabib, Judith Butler, and Drucilla Cornell (Routledge, 1994).

Joan B. Landes is Professor of Politics and Women's Studies at Hampshire College in Amherst, Massachusetts. She is the author of *Women and the Public Sphere in the Age of the French Revolution* (Cornell University Press, 1988). Her publications have focused on questions of gender and family relations in Western political and critical theory, the contours of public and private life, and the relationship of feminism to democratic theory and institutions. She is currently completing a book of essays on the representation of freedom in political philosophy, and a study entitled "Graphic Politics: Image as Argument in the Political Culture of

Eighteenth-Century France" which explores the co-presence of sexual and political body metaphors in the visual and political vocabulary of the French Republic.

Johanna Meehan is Assistant Professor of Philosophy at Grinnell College and writes on Habermas, feminist theory, and psychological development issues. She is currently working on a book on the significance of the normative notion of autonomy for ethics and feminist theory.

Georgia Warnke is Professor of Philosophy at the University of California, Riverside. She is author of *Gadamer: Hermeneutics, Tradition and Reason* and *Justice and Interpretation*.

Allison Weir is Assistant Professor of Philosophy at Concordia University, Montreal. Her book, *Sacrificial Logics: Feminist Theory and the Critique of Identity* is currently being published by Routledge.